DICTIONARY OF PUPPETRY

DICTIONARY OF PUPPETRY

A. R. Philpott

Publishers   PLAYS, INC.   *Boston*

COPYRIGHT © A. R. PHILPOTT 1969

FIRST AMERICAN EDITION PUBLISHED BY
PLAYS, INC., 1969

LIBRARY OF CONGRESS CATALOG CARD NUMBER: 69–18110

MADE AND PRINTED IN GREAT BRITAIN BY
TONBRIDGE PRINTERS LTD., TONBRIDGE, KENT

ILLUSTRATIONS

Unless otherwise stated, all the photographs are by Violet Philpott

INTRODUCTION

The importance of this Dictionary, especially to the newcomer to puppetry, is that it not only fulfils the normal function of a reference book giving meanings of technical terms and related data but also provides an introduction to the whole world of puppetry: the puppeteers, the puppets, the puppetry organizations, the literature on the subject, technical information, ideas and theories. It can in fact *be read straight through from A–Z,* or the pages can be opened at random with a fair chance of discovering something interesting.

Puppetry is a branch of Theatre Art which has had a remarkable world-wide expansion since World War II, a fact which is reflected (a) in the regular holding of national and international festivals, exhibitions, congresses and conferences, and (b) in an ever increasing output of literature on the subject, both historical and technical. Part of the function of this Dictionary is to introduce this literature so that those who wish can extend their reading. Book lists, bibliographies, rarely give enough indication of the contents of the items listed; titles are sometimes misleading. Unless the bookseller is a specialist and unless the public library already has a good selection of puppet books, advice as to choice is difficult to obtain. The Dictionary has both a fairly extensive bibliography, as an appendix, and annotated entries related to each title.

In those countries which have national societies, these are obviously the most likely source of information both as to literature on the subject and on current activities. There is also an international body, UNIMA (union internationale de la marionnette) which has members in over fifty countries and a number of national branches.

Many exciting experiments have been made in the realm of puppet entertainment and there have been tremendous technical advances. Puppets have firmly established a place for themselves on television, having moved into that sphere in its earliest days. Puppet films have become a highly developed offshoot in some countries and have earned international awards.

The possibilities of puppets in advertising are fairly obvious but they have also shown surprising versatility in the fields of education and therapy, aspects which have featured in discussions at international conferences.

As the hundreds of books on different aspects of the subject, and various puppetry publications have not managed to exhaust the subject, a relatively modest size Dictionary could not be expected to do so. It can give leads, even whet the appetite, may even provide some entertaining reading.

The compiler of the Dictionary has had around forty years as a professional puppeteer, some twenty years as an instructor and nearly as long as editor of a puppetry magazine; he appreciates that there are always those to whom the most elementary things are quite new, and has therefore catered for the beginner. He has also provided a good deal of 'background' material to the existing literature, the outcome of personal research.

Cross-references have been provided and are indicated either by words printed in SMALL CAPITALS or by the formal 'q.v.' or 'see'. However, in some of the longer entries, to ensure the minimum of interruption during reading, it seemed worth while to risk a little duplication of material. The intelligent reader will look for related entries even if not indicated – and in most cases will not be disappointed.

The reader who wishes to become involved in puppetry in its practical aspects will gravitate towards one or other of the organizations and can be sure of a welcome from the enthusiasts. Participation, even as an onlooker, at one of the international events can be particularly rewarding. In 1969 Czechoslovakia holds its second international amateur festival and it has national events every year. Many European countries have annual festivals as does the United States. Britain has had two international festivals and, in 1968, one of its leading professional puppeteers was elected President of the international organization.

Abduction from the Seraglio (Die Entführung aus dem Serail). Comic opera in three acts; music by Wolfgang Amadeus Mozart, libretto by Gottlieb Stephanie. Theme: hero in sixteenth-century-Turkey follows lover kidnapped by pirates and sold to Pasha; they are caught while escaping, but forgiven. Various puppet theatre productions including that of the Salzburg Marionette Theatre and the Marionettenbühne in Munich.

Aberdeen Puppet Players. Student group at College of Education, Aberdeen, Scotland. Director, Barry Symes. Large scale puppet productions include *The Snow Queen, Treasure Island* and *Peter Pan.* Colour film, 16 mm. *No Strings Attached,* records whole process of producing a puppet play, as seen from the puppeteers' angle: hire terms on application to the College.

Abrafile. Versatile woodwork tool; can be used as ordinary round file for clearing or enlarging drilled holes or bent (cold) to form riffler for work on curved surfaces. Several sizes available from tool suppliers, ironmongers, some craft shops.

Abraham and Isaac. One of many plays of biblical origin featured in medieval puppet shows and reflecting the Mystery q.v. and Morality q.v. plays of the live actors. In early repertoire of the Roel Puppets directed by Olive Blackham, q.v. and produced by contemporary English touring company 'Polka' (presenting Mime and Puppets) q.v. directed by Richard Gill.

Abu Hassan. Comic opera by Carl Maria von Weber (1786–1826) q.v. and still popular as live production; among others, puppet adaptation by the Zurich Marionette Theatre, illustrated in Gauchat *Marionettes,* q.v. (Rentsch, 1954). Theme: Abu and wife Fatimah pretend to die in order to collect funeral expenses (which will be contributed by the Caliph and his wife) and then be able to pay debts; chief creditor offers to cancel debt in return for kiss from Fatimah; Caliph and wife disagree as to which spouse is supposedly dead and offer a reward for evidence as to which died first; Abu immediately recovers, there is a happy ending and the wicked creditor is punished.

Acetate sheet. Acetic acid product; used by some shadow puppet creators, shape being cut over cardboard template. Available in clear and coloured varieties; clear can be tinted with thin oil paint, coloured inks with added gum; coloured tissue paper, mesh materials, cake doileys, fern fronds, etc., can be sandwiched between two pieces and bonded with clear plastic adhesive. London supplier: BX Plastics Ltd.

Acetone. One of the Ketone family of solvents, main ingredient in many commercial paint-removers, resins, acrylics; highly inflammable. Used as solvent with Celastic, q.v. which some puppeteers (particularly in the United States) use for making heads and stage props.

Acoustics. Science of sound. Sound-waves are absorbed or reflected depending on nature of construction materials of theatre auditorium or hall, room or other performance area: brick, wood, plaster, fibre board, polystyrene tiles, and décor materials such as cloth, velvet curtains, carpet; presence and size of audience also influences quality of sound.

Ideally every member of audience should hear clearly all speech, music, sound effects. Puppet stage design and construction and performing positions of puppeteers influence audibility which must be checked by Producer. Recordings and amplification also need testing for quality and volume. Outdoor performances have special acoustic problems varying with site, wind conditions and other factors such as traffic noise and rival entertainments.

Acrobats and Mountebanks, by Hugues le Roux and Jules Garnier, translated by A. P. Morton (Chapman Hall, 1890). Interesting chapter on puppets. 'Although an open secret is now called Punch's secret, it is certain that the marionette theatre and the puppet dance are great mysteries in their way.' The author was very proud of being one of the few to get behind the scenes 'better defended than the opera' (at the Bermont Theatre in the Versailles Fair). The item was a one-act 'grand drama' *The Spanish Brigands*. The audience consisted of about a hundred urchins, grand-mothers and nurses. The first items were (1) two Polish soldiers in a military dance, (2) two Spanish dancers who executed some 'wonderful pirouettes and pigeons' flights.' (3) An india-rubber man who 'stretched and stretched' and, having touched his heels with his nose, sneezed, (4) more turns before the main item. Drawing shows fairly large puppets with head rod and hand wires – and a harp-player out front. The show-man said he had written the play himself and had a bookful of others – 'very old and never been printed' – but some of the titles are familiar, e.g. *The Passion, The Temptation of St Anthony, Hel, Genevieve de Brabant*. About one piece, in fact, the 'author's rights' found a pretext for coming to see the show, but did not recognise the play: 'I had changed it all.' There is also a mention of La Grille, who opened in the Fair of Saint-Germaine with an 'Opera de bamboche' in which the sole actor was a huge marionette that gesticulated to the melodies of a musician concealed in the prompter's box.

Acrylic. Thermoplastic resin used in some modern paints and adhesives.

Acting areas. Stage directions for actors' positions or moves are given as Stage Right, Stage Left, Centre 'upstage' or 'downstage' (furthest from and nearest to audience) – 'up' and 'down' dating from period when stage floor literally sloped towards auditorium whereas modern theatre has floor of auditorium sloped ('raked'). Puppet stages, whether manipu-lators above or below, involve consideration of *two* acting areas for each character: that where the puppet functions and the related area where the puppeteer functions. In modern puppet stages there may be two or more 'ACTING LEVELS' for the puppets and equivalent operating areas. In Poland there still exists a primitive form of stage known as SZOPKA and having a three-tier construction sometimes representing heaven, earth, hell. Contemporary CABARET or FLOOR SHOW performances some-times have puppeteer and marionette sharing same floor area, both in view of audience. In the traditional Japanese 'three-man puppet' theatre (BUNRAKU) the figure is held at chest level by main operator, two assistants sharing floor area.

Acting levels. In the live theatre dramatic use may be made of a rostrum, stairway, balcony – and even a sunken section for gravedigger's scene. Puppet stages have own scope relative to type of puppet and stage dimensions: HAND PUPPET stage can have second and even third PLAY-BOARD behind and above normal level (top front edge of booth) with space between for manipulators and adjusted floor levels. If stage equipped with BACKSCREEN of plywood or hardboard, window spaces at various levels can be used. If stage of open front type, without proscenium, roof top action is possible at top of backscreen. Characters can descend imaginary stairway below front playboard. With ROD type the ceiling is the limit. 'Space' itself can be explored as acting level in the MARIONETTE stage and also represent underwater level with fish swimming or mermaid ballet. SHADOW PUPPETS can make use of lower and higher levels of screen.

Acting (with puppets). Some actors prefer performing *without* puppets: this indicates a special approach on the part of puppeteers. The human-stage actor in a sense uses his own body as a kind of puppet when presenting a character; it takes on new mannerisms, new habits. The puppeteer is required to accept *the puppet itself* as the all-important element of the performance: for it is useless to 'act' – out of sight of the audience, e.g. on the BRIDGE of a marionette stage – to enter into the part personally, unless this acting is transferred to the puppet. Remarkable evidence of the ability to identify with the physical puppet character is seen in the performances of the Japanese 'BUNRAKU' three-man puppets, the three manipulators becoming as one in operation and at the same time co-ordinating with the voice of the narrator, q.v. who sits in full view at the *side* of the stage. The two men controlling the feet and left arm respectively are visible but completely clad in black (with gauze over face); the chief operator's face is visible, quite blank of expression, everything being concentrated in the puppet. In the case where a puppeteer also speaks for his characters the voices must seem to come from the puppets and this necessitates concentration on the physical puppet as well as on its character. Thus the actor-with-puppet has problems distinct from those of the stage actor: he has technical pre-occupations involving his own bodily movements related to those of the puppets. The co-ordination achieved by the Japanese puppeteers is a matter of long years of training. Performing with puppets is more than just 'manipulating' them: it is a matter of inward acting transferred (via hand, rod, string) to the puppet with which the actor is identifying as the character.

Actors' Remonstrance, or Complaint. A pamphlet published 24th January, 1643, written by an actor or actors of the 'private houses' and protesting that they had been prohibited although the 'motions' q.v. (puppets) were allowed to continue 'in force and vigour.' There were also some disparaging remarks about the puppetry.

Adam and Eve. Biblical characters were often transplanted from the medieval Mystery q.v. and Morality q.v. plays to the puppet stage, often too with Punch intruding and even dominating the performance. An advertisement for Hartley's puppets in the early days of Bartholomew Fair q.v. mentioned performance of *The Creation of the World* and a Hogarth q.v. engraving of *Southwark Fair* (1735) q.v. shows a painted cloth advertising the 'Fall.' Chambers' *Book of Days* q.v. mentions Powel's puppet show (1709) with Adam and Eve. The theory that Milton's *Paradise Lost* may in part have been inspired by a puppet version including these characters (e.g. as mentioned in Bramall *Puppet Plays and Playwriting*, q.v.) has not been substantiated. In Rome, at the Teatro dei Nottambuli (1951) a programme included an 'existentialist duet' using bare-hand puppets with sophisticated heads in *Adamo et Eva* by Eliane Gujonne. Moscow Central State Puppet Theatre repertoire includes

Isidor Stok's *Divine Comedy* q.v. a satirical version of *Genesis* (God and the Archangels played by human actors, Adam and Eve, Cherubim, Seraphim and animals by flexible puppets).

Addison, Joseph (1672–1719). English poet, essayist, critic; friend of Swift and Steele, contributor to *The Tatler* q.v. and *The Spectator* q.v.; author of poems in Latin including *Machinae gesticulantes: anglice a Puppet Show* q.v. which gives an idea of puppet shows of the period, with references to 'shimmering wires' and 'creaking inhabitants' and the conclusion that whatever mankind has done has also been replayed in the small puppet theatre. English translation of the poem (*The Puppet Show*) in *Works of Joseph Addison* by G. Sewell (Bell, 1912). The original is reproduced in Craig *The Marionette* (August, 1918) q.v. In *The Spectator* No. 500 commented on 'the motherly airs of my little daughters when they are playing with their puppets.'

Adhesive tape. Various types: gummed brown paper, decorator's masking tape, transparent sellotape (one or both sides coated); useful to puppet-makers for reinforcing, binding ends of wire, etc. Tony Sarg, q.v. one of the puppet pioneers in the United States, outstanding creator, used tape as one of main construction materials.

Additive lighting. The addition of one colour of light to another colour, producing the required colour.

Ad lib. (Latin, *ad libitum*, 'as one likes'.) To use dialogue not in the script or to introduce stage 'business'; improvisation. In music: follow your own feeling for a particular passage.

Adventures of a Russian Puppet Theatre, by Nina Efimova, q.v. (Puppetry Imprints, USA, 1935). Translated from the Russian by Elena Mitcoff, illustrated by Ivan and Nina. How Nina the painter and sculptor husband weathered the Russian revolution of 1917, travelling with a puppet theatre – and how they continued to work afterwards; how they produced shows, devised plays, made hand puppets and rod puppets, and their own development of techniques; also shadow figures. Pictures of their puppets and stage, from drawings and photographs.

Advertisement puppets. Window displays using puppets have been known to cause traffic disturbances. Bil Baird, q.v. American puppeteer, produced a show for the Chrysler Corporation at the New York World's Fair with glowing framework of the car assembling itself in the air. In England the Stavordale Marionettes toured a show advertising Sharpe's Toffee, mainly for children. *Use of actual products* – packets, tins, bottles, fresh fruit, vegetables, *these becoming puppets* – has been exploited in puppet film and TV commercials.

Aeroplane (airplane) control. Horizontal type of marionette control, preferred by some American performers, specially suitable for four-leg creatures with control approximately same length as marionette, strings attached to parts of spine, head, ears, tail. Name reflects construction, handle with cross-pieces.

Aesop (*c.* 620–520 B.C.). Greek storyteller, fabulist; themes of some FABLES original, others from probable Egyptian, Babylonian, Indian sources; early English edition by William Caxton (*c.* 1422–1491) printer, q.v.; contemporary collection of 40 fables retold by Louis Untermeyer (Paul Hamlyn, 1965) has inspirational illustrations of animal characters by A. & M. Provensen; many other editions. Source material for puppet-plays.

Africa. Little published material available about tribal puppets. *Africa: the Art of the Negro Peoples*, by Elsy Lenzinger (Art of World series: Methuen, 1960) has a few interesting references to puppets of the Pangwe, dancing marionettes representing spirits of the dead, and the puppet comedies of the Ibo, Ibibio and Bambara. *World Theatre*, Vol. XIV, No. 5, published by the International Theatre Institute, has illustrated article by Jacques Chesnais, French puppeteer and historian; he confirms that puppets undoubtedly exist in Africa but are neither numerous nor easy to locate. Also some material in Chesnais *Histoire Générale des Marionnettes* (Bordas, 1947). *World Theatre* also has article on contemporary puppet theatre in Cairo. Shadow shows of the same type as Turkish Karagöz are well known in Arabic-speaking areas.

Aicher, Professor Anton (1859–1930). Founder of the famous SALZBURG MARIONETTE THEATRE, Austria (1913); founder-member of UNIMA q.v. the international puppetry organisation; sculptor at the Salzburg Technical College; studied puppet performances at 'Papa' Schmid's theatre in Munich.

Aicher, Hermann. Son and successor of Anton Aicher, and present Director of the Salzburg Marionette Theatre, q.v., assisted by wife and daughters. Responsible for various developments on the technical side. In an article in *Puppet Theatre Around the World* (1960) expressed his feeling for the marionette, which he sees as 'an abstraction of the living actor', and this governs the style of the theatre. Important, too, is the observation that 'the leg, arm and hand movements are the essential elements of expression' (rather than the face, since the puppet face does not have the mobility of the actor's); therefore specially designed limbs with numerous joints and the relative strings are used. Head-joints are individual to each character to ensure maximum expressiveness. The figures used today are much larger than those of his father's period and are up to 3-ft. tall.

Alabastine Method. 'Alabastine' is a trade name for a type of plaster 'filler' q.v. and was the most widely known at the time when this method of making hollow heads for puppets was evolved; other makes are equally suitable although individual makers may prefer the texture of a particular brand. The actual head is built up over a plasticine model on a stand (see modelling) and consists of three layers of muslin (book-muslin preferably) impregnated with the filler; the latter is mixed with cold water to a thick creamy consistency and is ready to use immediately, staying workable up to an hour (extra water can be added if working in high temperature); the model is first covered with pieces of damp tissue paper (each overlapping): this protects the plasticine and ensures easy removal. Pieces of muslin about an inch to inch and a half square are next applied, plastering each and overlapping the edges; the mix must fill the mesh of the muslin; when the head is completely covered a second layer can be applied – or this can be done at any later time; it is advisable to add a little powder or poster colour to the mix for the second later; the cast is then left to dry hard. A craft-knife with a rigid blade is used to cut the cast open for removal, with the edge of the base of stand and the side of the head resting on the table; the halves are then joined, using same process, left to dry before painting. For a very smooth finish a little plaster only can be applied; small details such as nostrils, eyeballs, cheek-bones can be built up with cotton-wool (teased loose) and saturated with the mix. If necessary, surfaces can be lightly sandpapered. Result: lightweight and reasonably durable heads. Detailed instructions and diagrams in leaflet published by the Educational Supply Association.

Aladdin and his Wonderful (Magic) Lamp. Hero-tale from the *Arabian Nights* q.v.; has inspired operas, operettas, plays, ballets, pantomimes and puppet shows; in 'top ten' as puppet production; outstanding version at Moscow Central Puppet Theatre, puppet film by George Pal (1939), colour film by Hungarian State Puppet Theatre for West German television (1967).

Aldeburgh Festival of Music and the Arts. 1968 event included programme by the Hungarian State Puppet Theatre q.v. from Budapest with programme including Stravinsky *Petrushka* q.v. and Bartok *The Wooden Prince* q.v. ballets. The English Opera Group presented a new opera by Biristle, *Punch and Judy*, libretto by Stephen Pruslin, its premiere performance. The Hungarians later performed at the Bath Festival.

Aleš, Mikoláš (1852–1913). Czechoslovak painter, designer; popularised traditional puppetry and created national cult of Matej Kopecky (1775–1847) who introduced hero-puppet Kašparek; puppets made from wood and other materials to Aleš designs could be bought in various sizes; designs for puppets and scenery also printed for cutting out by children.

Alice in Wonderland. Lewis Carroll's masterpiece (1865) on the fantasy adventures of a little girl has often been adapted for the puppet stage, the puppets sometimes being based on the original illustrations by Sir John Tenniel. In France the Compagnie du Castelet used 70 puppet characters; in the United States Tony Sarg employed a live actress as Alice. Lou Bunin made a puppet film of the story (France, 1948).

Alienation. The concept of audience 'detachment' from characters and action on stage as opposed to 'involvement' – and an intellectual attitude towards the characters on the part of the actors presenting them. Theory stems from the work of the avant-garde German dramatist Bertolt Brecht q.v. (1898–1956) and is known as the 'A' Effect (Verfremdungseffekt: 'frend' = 'strange'). Gordon Craig q.v. (1872–1967), English theatre designer and theorist, hinted at same principle when discussing his concept of the 'übermarionette' q.v. (super-marionette) concerned with elimination of wrong approach by actors swayed by emotions. Alienation made theme for discussion at the international level in Prague, 1969, on occasion of puppet festival and congress. Contemporary developments in puppet theatre presentation methods may induce loss of illusion, e.g. when human actors appear on same stage as the puppets, or *as* puppets, or when a visible narrator addresses the audience; also when manipulators suddenly appear at end of performance. Young children readily believe in the 'reality' of puppets and spontaneously 'participate' from auditorium or in front of open-air Punch and Judy show. See AUDIENCE PARTICIPATION.

Aluminium. Sometimes used in sheet form for producing thunder effect by shaking. Also used for making strong figures for shadow show, cut with tin-snips.

Amateur. Dictionary meaning: 'One who cultivates an art or pursues a study from love or attachment and without reference to gain or emolument.' (Webster.) The term has acquired a secondary and somewhat derogatory meaning: 'inferior.' In practice the amateur may well produce work superior to that of the professional – the latter being preoccupied with earning a living. The inherent differences of talent and approach between one individual and another are the main factors in the production of quality either in puppet making or performing, or in playwriting. A critic may say of the work of a professional that it is 'amateurish.' The professional believes he must be good if he manages to make a living by his art. Ballyhoo by a live-wire agent may ensure engagements and box-office takings, but not necessarily repeat bookings. The professional also, in alluding to the 'semi-pro' – the individual with some other main source of income and who may therefore be able to offer cut-price terms –may forget that most professionals begin as amateurs. At the first international festival for amateurs, held in Karlovy-Vary, Czechoslovakia, in 1964, some of the performances were of a higher standard than much so-called professional work.

American Indian puppets. Articulated figures used in ceremonial rites and 'sympathetic' magic by Medicine Man (Shaman). Inverarity, puppeteer, anthropologist, author of *Manual of Puppetry* (Binfords and Mort, 1936) did some research among the Haida of the Queen Charlotte Islands off northern Pacific coast of Canada and reported in *Puppetry: Yearbook* (Puppeteers of America, 1933), condensed in the *Manual;* mentions Great Plumed Snake figure in Hopi ceremony. Illustrations in Inverarity *Moveable Masks and Figures of the North Pacific Coast Indians* (Cranbrook Institute, 1941). Chapter in McPharlin *Puppet Theatre in America* (Harper, N.Y., 1949) on puppets of American 'aborigines' with illustrations from Inverarity and museum sources. Coloured illustrations in Baird *Art of the Puppet* (Collier-Macmillan, 1965): marionette with doors in chest, opening to reveal soul or spirit, and Tsimshian fur-clad puppets. Museums with specimens include United States National Museum, Washington, D.C., Royal Ontario Museum of Archaeology, Museum of the American Indian, Heye Foundation, New York.

Amfiparnasso. See *L'Amfiparnasso.*

Andersen, Hans Christian (1805–75). Danish poet, writer of fairy tales, many adapted for puppet stage: *Emperor's New Clothes, Emperor's Nightingale,* the *Magic Tinderbox, Little Mermaid, the Storks, Marsh King's Daughter,* and others; Hungarian State Puppet Theatre performed the *Tinderbox* in Esperanto, q.v. Lotte Reiniger, q.v., creator of silhouette films, made shadow figures for *The Beetle* for the Hogarth Puppets. Trnka, q.v., Czechoslovak puppet film maker (using stop-motion figures), produced the *Emperor's Nightingale.* Theme of Polish film: *What the Moon Saw.*

Andhra Shadow Plays. Traditional folk-art in Andhra province in India. Shadow shows q.v. performed in the open (free) lasting all night; screen constructed from saris stretched between upright poles, lower edge knee-high, space below filled in with cloth. Figures cut from hide, up to two-thirds life size, in silhouette or translucent-coloured style; jointed at shoulders, elbows, wrists, knees, pelvis; figure held in cleft of long split cane and thin cane controls to hands. Second operator may be needed for complex dance movements. Plays (Tholubommalatta) are based on religious epics *Mahabharata* q.v. and *Ramayana* q.v. in serial form.

Angel. As in the live theatre, someone who is prepared to invest money in a production; a backer.

Aniline dye. Coal-tar by-product supplied in powder form, mixed with water; brilliant theatrical colours but not opaque; can be used on costume fabrics, puppet 'hair' (wool, hemp, string, etc.) or on foamed plastic for decor and as a stainer on plywood. Dyeing being a chemical process, materials should be tested beforehand; flame-proofed materials may need washing out (re-proofing after dyeing); cottons and muslins may take dye better if small quantity of vinegar or acetic acid added; a little salt increases absorption. Advisable protect hands with rubber gloves. Mixing proportions: 1-oz. powder first mixed to paste consistency with water: add 1 gallon water and bring to boil: 1 teaspoon salt. For speed can be mixed with hot size-water. Dilute or add powder as required. Also used as colorant in manufacture of 'gels' for stage lighting filters. Available from theatrical suppliers such as Brodie and Middleton, 79 Long Acre, London, W.C.2.

Animal characters. Live animals such as Dog Toby q.v. in the Punch and Judy show, or the Dancing Pig q.v. in Powel's show at Covent Garden as recorded in the *Spectator* and elsewhere, or the Cats q.v. as introduced by the French into the Polichinelle plays, go through their routines but are not 'actors'. Puppet animals can be of the domesticated type or jungle characters, using only their natural voices, or, as in many tales, speak with human voices (see ANIMAL PLAYS). There are also the 'personality' characters such as 'Muffin the Mule' q.v. (Hogarth Puppets) and 'Sooty' (Harry Corbett's teddy bear) – who use a kind of sign-language and talk only through their human colleagues. 'That Italian Mouse', Maria Perego's 'Topo Gigio' appears in short television programmes and requires four operators (and 'black theatre' q.v. technique). Violet Philpott's 'Freddy Fox' has a strong American accent and an eye for the ladies in the audience. Puppet Circus animals have their own range of possibilities, some of which no live animals could match. Each type of puppet has its technical scope and limits. Some of the large creatures in the Moscow Central State Puppet Theatre production of *Mowgli* (based on Kipling jungle stories) required two and three operators (rod type). On the shadow screen a kangaroo could leap over the highest tree or stand on its head, a hippopotamus emerge from the river. There is also the amusing Tiger Taming act as demonstrated by Soviet puppet-master Obraztsov q.v. in which the Tamer is swallowed whole (another version of which he discovered in China). From the performer's point of view it is often easier to 'identify' oneself with an animal character than with another human. From the audience point of view many things are acceptable from animal characters that would evoke a different reaction if the characters were human.
See *Animal Marionettes* and *Animal Puppetry*.

Animal Marionettes, by Paul McPharlin (Puppetry Imprints Handbook No. 10: Birmingham, Michigan, 1936); illustrated by drawings. Characters: Ant, Bear, Beaver, Bee, Blue Jay, Borzoi, Burro, Camel, Cat, Caterpillar, Centaur, Cock, Crow, Crab, Crocodile, Deer, Dog, Dragon, Dromedary, Duck, Eagle, Elephant, Fish, Fox, Frog, Giraffe, Goat, Goose, Grasshopper, Griffin, Hen, Horse, Kangaroo, Kid, Lamb, Lion, Lobster, Macaw, Monkey, Mouse, Mosquito, Mule, Octopus, Owl, Parrot, Pekingese, Pig, Rabbit, Ram, Reindeer, Robin, Satyr, Sheep, Snake, Spider, Squirrel, Swan, Tiger, Turkey, Turtle, Unicorn, Warbler, Wolf, Wren.

Animal plays. Perhaps because animals do not talk in human fashion in normal life, adaptations from popular stories usually make good puppet items: Beatrix Potter *Peter Rabbit* (Warne), Kenneth Grahame *Wind in the Willows* (Methuen), Kipling *Just So Stories* and *Jungle Books* (Macmillan paperbacks), A. A. Milne *Winnie the Pooh* (Methuen), Joel Chandler Harris *Uncle Remus* (*Brer Rabbit*) stories (Appleton Century), de la Mare *Animal Stories* (Faber) and tales from India in the *Panchatantra* (Phoenix Books), Aesop and La Fontaine Fables (many editions of both) and the jungle character stories in Lucia Turnbull *When Animals Talked* (Longmans). Original stories such as Violet Philpott *The Egg* (in *Eight Plays for Hand Puppets*, Garnet Miller) with jungle characters conceived with puppets in mind, can prove very popular. The type of puppet depends on range of movement desired: for sheer speed the hand puppet is best; for four-leg creatures usually the marionette is effective, but rod type has possibilities; the shadow show, q.v. also has fine possibilities.

Animal Puppetry, by H. W. Whanslaw (Wells, Gardner and Darton. ND). Includes marionettes and hand puppets; deals with oriental animals, horse, dog and other quadrupeds; large animals; apes and monkeys; marionette circus and menagerie; burlesque characters; birds, reptiles, fish and under-water creatures; insects, spiders and mollusca; mythological animals.

Animated Films. Whether a cine-camera is used, taking pictures of moving people or objects, or the 'stop motion' camera as used for making cartoon films from a series of drawings, the result is a length of film divided into 'frames' each of which shows *one phase* of a movement. To approximate to natural movement the cartoon artist must make 24 drawings for one second of screen time, of which the camera makes 24 'frames'. The same technique is used in making silhouette (shadow) films, but here the cut-out figures with movable limbs are rearranged (on a flat glass-topped table lit from below) and many thousands of adjustments are made even for the shortest film. With three-dimensional puppets the movements are also 'phased' – the figures somewhat resembling those of the artist's lay-figure, the position, the posture, even the expression of the face changed *between* single camera 'shots' – an arduous and exacting process. The results can only be judged when the finished film is projected. See *Animation in the Cinema, Design in Motion, Techniques of Film Animation, Industrial and Business Films.*

Animation in the Cinema, by Ralph Stephenson (Zwemmer, 1967). In International Film Guide series. Not a textbook, but has chapter on nature of animation and techniques. Survey of developments in America, Britain, Canada, France, Poland, Czechoslovakia, Yugoslavia, Italy, Germany, Japan, Soviet Union. Bibliography and filmography. A number of puppet film references.

Anti-climax. Properly, a point following immediately after the climax and underlining it; in a bad production it is something following the climax and weakening it, so that the build-up to the high point has been wasted.

Apology for Puppets, by Arthur Symons, in an essay in the *Saturday Review* (17th July, 1897), reprinted in *Plays, Acting and Music* (Constable, London, 1903, Dutton, N.Y., 1909). 'Having seen a ballet, a farce, and a fragment of an opera performed by puppets at the Costanzi Theatre in Rome . . .' was inclined to ask himself why there should be the intervention of any less perfect medium between playwright and audience.

Appliqué. Applied ornament or ornaments forming a design or pattern on the basic material, e.g. coloured felt shapes stuck or sewn to costume material.

Apuleius, Lucius (*c.* A.D.125 – not known). Roman satirical writer best known for *The Golden Ass, or Metamorphoses;* scholars have seen influences of his work on that of Boccaccio, Cervantes and Fielding. In *De Mundo*

B

(On the Universe), which is a free translation of an earlier Greek treatise 'Peri Kosmon' – at one time attributed to Aristotle – there is a reference to wooden figures with moving head, eyes, limbs, and some form of string control. This was first cited by Father Mariantonio Lupi (1695–1737) in *Storia Litteraria della Sicilia*, with various other classical references, and quoted by Magnin in his *Histoire des marionnettes en Europe* (1852). There is an English translation in Inverarity *Manual of Puppetry* (1936). Figures with moving parts and with string-control are not necessarily puppets – without some evidence as to *performance*. Speaight, *History of the English Puppet Theatre*, sees the use of the term 'machinists' as a possible indication of automata rather than puppets.

Arab Theatre and Cinema, Studies in, by Jacob M. Landau (University of Pennsylvania Press, 1958). Chapter 3 makes important contribution to history of the Shadow Play with an interesting discussion on the philosophy of puppetry. Sections on the Turkish contribution, Arabic performances in Medieval Egypt and further developments in Egypt, Syria, North Africa; the characteristics and importance of the shadow theatre. Author regards the Arabic shadow theatre as even more important than the Turkish 'Karagöz' q.v. (? derived from Egyptian 'qaraqush'). Another book by this author (not seen) is *Shadow Plays in the Near East* (Palestine Institute of Folklore and Ethnology, Jerusalem, 1948; in English and Hebrew).

Arabian Nights. The 'Book of a Thousand and One Nights', being the fabulous tales told by Scheherazade to save her life, her husband having killed each previous wife the morning after their marriage. The tales were originally of Persian, Indian and Arabic origins and were mentioned by Masude in 943 (as 'A Thousand Nights and a Night') and the present form is thought to date from 1450; the first European edition was that of Antoine Gallard (1704). Sir Richard Burton published a ten-volume edition (Benares, 1885–86) for 'subscribers only' – and Lady Burton's expurgated edition appeared in 1886–88 in six volumes. A number of the stories are among the top favourites with puppet theatres, such as *Ali Baba and the Forty Thieves, Aladdin and his Wonderful Lamp, Sinbad the Sailor*, with versions in Russian, French, Polish, etc. Some of the stories have also become hardy annuals on the Christmas pantomime stage. Tchaikowsky was inspired to write the orchestral suite *Scheherazade*. A new translation of *Aladdin* (and other tales) by N. J. Dawood is available in the Penguin Classics.

Aragoz. Name for small mobile puppet theatre of the Punch and Judy type in Egypt. Name possibly related to Karagöz, main character in traditional Turkish shadow plays.

Arbuthnot, Dr. John (1667–1735). Physician to Queen Anne; acquaintance of Swift and Pope; his *History of John Bull* (1712), a collection of pamphlets advocating the termination of the war with France was the origin of 'John Bull' as the 'typical' Englishman; in it occurs the intriguing phrase 'You look like a puppet moved by clockwork.' Elsewhere: 'What he lost to sharpers and spent upon country dances and puppet plays . . .'

Arc-en-Ciel Theatre. Interesting puppet theatre in Paris, established 1925 by Geza Blattner, Hungarian artist. Stage design and proscenium allowed use of marionettes, hand puppets or a special type of rod puppet (supported by a harness and operated by pedals). Productions included *The Mystery of the Virgin Mary* and Grimm's *The Little Tailor*. Theatre had to be abandoned during the German occupation, but some puppetry was possible at Valencay (an account of which appeared in *Puppetry* (1946–47), the year-book of the Puppeteers of America. After the liberation the Arc-en-Ciel activity began anew, a number of the productions being inspired by war-time conditions. Several interesting photographs appear in Beaumont *Puppets and Puppetry* (Studio, 1958), including the figure of 'Misery' – which Beaumont likens to a work by Goya or El Greco – the surrealist figures for *Le Mariage de la Flûte* (in which the characters' bodies are musical instruments) and a close-up of the pedal-control. Also a chapter in Gervais *Marionnettes et marionnettistes de France* (Bordas, 1947).

Archangel Gabriel and Mistress Goose. Czech puppet film by Trnka q.v., based on a story from Boccaccio's *Decameron*, q.v. Scene: Renaissance Venice; Theme: romance of amorous Friar and Lady who thinks he is the Angel Gabriel.

Architect's tracing linen. Fine grade, translucent, durable, used by some puppeteers for shadow-show screen. Obtainable from drawing-office suppliers.

Ariosto, Lodovico (1473–1533). Italian poet whose *Orlando Furioso* q.v. source of Sicilian q.v. marionette plays dealing with the Crusades, related to the earlier French 'chansons de geste' q.v.; romance and chivalry.

Aristophanes (*c.* 450 – *c.* 385 B.C.). Greek playwright of whose comedies eleven have survived entire, including *The Clouds, The Wasps, The Frogs, The Birds, Lysistrata;* puppet productions of the last two mentioned, possibly others: see individual entries. (*The Eleven Comedies*, originally published by the Athenian Society, London, 1912; Tudor Publishing Co., 1936, 2 vols. in 1; no translator's name given.)

Arm Puppets. Elongated hand puppet, usually monster type with moving jaw operated by thumb and fingers, body of cloth, corrugated card, or other material such as sleeve of old jersey, extending full length of arm.

Art of Animation: Walt Disney, by Bob Thomas and the Disney Staff (Simon and Schuster, 1958). Story of Disney Studio contribution to the new art, profusely illustrated.

Art of the Puppet, by Bil Baird (Collier-Macmillan, 1965). Important addition to puppet literature, profusely illustrated. Book for 'everybody' rather than the puppet specialist. Not a 'history' but providing much data on past and contemporary developments; particularly valuable for superb colour reproductions and numerous black and white photographs. Chapters on Masks, the Eastern heritage, Angels, Devils and Everyman, the Turkish Karaghioz and Punch and Judy; the Sicilian Orlando Furioso plays and their armoured knights; the Oriental tradition; contemporary developments.

Articulated. Having movable joints; usually reference to marionette construction but also applies to any type with jointed parts, e.g. rod puppets and shadow figures.

Aside. Term for remark addressed to audience by actor and which the other characters pretend not to hear.

A.S.M. Assistant Stage Manager. General assistant to the Stage Manager and responsible for the checking of props, equipment, assembling the performers, seeing to the curtains, acting as prompt, etcetera. In small puppet companies the work may be shared. In the one-man-show there is no A.S.M.

Atmosphere. In the theatrical sense, the overall 'feel' of a production from the audience point of view and brought about by many contributory factors planned to fit the producer's concept of the play, opera, ballet, music hall variety items, burlesque, etc. Technically: the stage settings, the lighting, music if any, style of costume, general colour scheme, manner of performing, will be determined by the type of production and related to the internal mood of the play or other item, established by the writer. This involves co-operation between producer, stage designer, lighting designer, costume designer, various technicians, and the actors themselves. A 'straight' play, a melodrama, theatre of the absurd or of cruelty, burlesque, or an item in which the mood changes from scene to scene or during scenes, call for differences in treatment. The use of 'black lighting' U.V. lighting, phosphorescent paint, or of various gimmicks, influences atmosphere. Performances which involve the audience directly, which evoke participation (vocal or physical) create a special atmosphere. Experiments have been made in the introduction of perfume, from under the seats, to help establish mood at particular moments. Tobacco smoke may be an essential ingredient in music hall performances or at a Sicilian marionette show with an audience mainly made up of fishermen or peasants. A play could be given in total darkness or, as in a traditional Chinese comic interlude, in imagined darkness – the actors behaving as though in the dark yet fully visible to the audience. Buildings themselves have an integral atmosphere.

Atellanae Fabula. Type of popular improvised satirical farce in early Rome (*c.* 540) given in Greek, Oscan and Latin; *Fabula*, general term for a play. *Atellanae* probably from Atella, town in Campania (present day Aversa on same site); stock characters in the plays, Maccus, Bucco, Dossenus, Manducus, are seen by some scholars as possible origin of later characters in the Italian commedia dell' arte, q.v., e.g. Pulcinella (Punch) could combine characteristics of Maccus and Bucco. A bronze Maccus was unearthed in Rome in 1727 (now in the Capponi Museum) with similar humps back and front. See Duchartre *The Italian Comedy* (Dover Publications, 1966).

Aucassin et Nicolette. One of the early French 'chansons de geste' q.v. – a chant-fable in prose and verse by an anonymous French author, *c.* 1200. Theme: the love of a young man and a maid and their adventures in a world which is a mixture of reality and fantasy. There have been various French and Belgian puppet productions and it is listed with about 40 other chansons in the repertoire of a Liége puppet theatre mentioned in Gervais *Marionnettes et Marionnettistes de France* (Bordas, 1947). An English version has been presented by the Hogarth Puppets, q.v. An English translation by Andrew Lang is included in *Mediaeval Age* (Dent, 1965, Dell Publishing, USA, 1963).

Audience participation. Phenomenon usually observable at any Punch and Judy show with children as audience and consisting of spontaneous or prompted arguments with Punch, Policeman or other character: 'Oh, *no I didn't!* Oh, *yes you did!* and so on. Audience of very young children tend to call out to any character in *any* play, shriek warnings, scold, threaten, become completely involved in the action on the stage: 'What's your name? You're naughty! Put that back!' etc. Experienced showmen know how to make use of such interruptions and remain in control of the situation. Even adults may participate but usually with tongue in cheek, although old ladies sometimes get completely carried away. The use of recordings, q.v. cannot be effective, no matter how often 'edited', as audience reactions vary at different performances. Discussion of the opposite phenomenon, 'alienation' q.v. intellectual detachment from the stage events, theme for international conference at Prague (1969), result of contemporary developments in the puppet theatre: use of live actors among the puppets, of narrators in front of the stage, and other techniques which may dispel illusion. Experiments in Children's Theatre also involve (prompted) participation, children leaving their seats, running round the hall, appearing on the stage in crowd scenes, etc. Incidentally, 'planting' *performers* among the audience, as mentioned in Fraser *Introducing Puppetry* (Batsford, 1968), even with puppets, does not really constitute *audience* participation.

Audiences. Strictly speaking, these consist of *listeners:* the *place* for listeners is an 'auditorium'; 'audio' has to do with *sound*, with hearing. When there is emphasis on *vision* the onlookers are known as 'spectators' (as at a football match). 'Audio-visual aids' consist of apparatus that makes appeal to both senses of sight and hearing; theatrical performances other than Mime are audio-visual. The English language lacks a satisfactory visual equivalent of 'auditorium' ('spectatorium') and has no precise word for theatre-goers once they are in their seats. *Auditorium* is correct for concert hall; *audience* for listeners; but what is the term for those who expect to see *and* hear? Theatre-goers are an essential element in the performance because (quite apart from the box-office returns) it is only from the audience reactions that the actors know if their acting and the production as a whole is effective. An empty or half empty House is even different acoustically (q.v.) and actors and audience alike are aware of this. If what is said on the stage is inaudible then the audience will become restless (vocal comments of 'Speak up!' are not unknown). If what is happening on stage is out of sight for some of the audience this also will cause restlessness. Assuming they have come to the right theatre, the audience is always right: i.e. it comes to be entertained, is eager to applaud, but the applause must be earned. The phenomenon of 'audience participation' and its opposite, 'alienation' are aspects dealt with separately and depend largely on the type and method of production. The fundamentals of human nature do not change much but the interests and tastes of successive (and even contemporary) generations may do so. Ideally every member of an audience should see and hear equally well: few theatres ensure this by their design. There is a special problem when an audience consists of children *and* adults: the Universal Puppet Theatre, q.v. to be built in Prague, Czechoslovakia, and planned by architects in consultation with directors and producers, includes (among many interesting features) adjustable-height seats: consideration of the audience should be the first requirement of all theatre planning.

Audition. Puppeteers, groups, companies – as with other entertainers – may be required to give demonstration performance to obtain municipal or other engagements.

Auditorium. That part of the theatre or other building occupied by the audience (spectators); needs careful study by the Producer as regards its 'sight lines' q.v.; ideally everyone in the auditorium should be able to see and hear equally well. A mobile puppet theatre has sight-line problems which vary from hall to hall (or out of doors) and vary also with type of stage (i.e. for below-stage manipulation and above-stage). A hall with a non-raked floor (flat) and a low platform on which a marionette stage is erected may mean that only the front rows of the audience will see much of the puppets. If on the other hand the platform is already high and on it is erected a hand-puppet or rod-puppet stage, then the front rows may have the worst of the viewing.

Australia. With no puppet tradition as a starting point, there are signs that puppetry is becoming established, and in 1965 an organisation known as the Marionette Theatre of Australia was constituted with a permanent professional company available for touring both at home and abroad. The inaugural nation-wide tour was by Peter Scriven's famous 'Tintookies', a show taking its title from an aboriginal word meaning 'the little people who live in the sandhills.' This Theatre is associated with the Elizabethan Theatre Trust and the Arts Council of Australia, and the objectives include assistance in the development of puppet groups by providing technical and artistic advice and by encouraging its practice in the schools. A training school for puppeteers is also to be established; original Australian plays and music are being commissioned. In 1968 one of the attractions at the Adelaide Festival was the appearance of the famous Salzburg Marionette Theatre, q.v. There is the likelihood of the forming of a national branch of UNIMA q.v., the international puppetry organisation. Some of the interest now seen is undoubtedly due to the earlier tours of the English company The Hogarth Puppets. The UNESCO-sponsored 'Expedition Alexandre' q.v. included Australia in its world-survey of puppetry. A number of Australian Teacher-Training Colleges have become aware of the educational possibilities and have formed or joined with local societies, e.g. the Puppet Guild of Australia, based on the Melbourne Teacher's College, the Australian Educational Society of Puppetry in North Adelaide. The Children's Library and Crafts Club movement, developed by Mary Matheson in the Sydney area, has a dozen or more centres for creative leisure activities including puppetry. Among her other activities, Mrs. Edith Murray has run courses related to occupational therapy. Richard Bradshaw from Sydney brought his shadow-show to Europe and delighted English and German audiences. One of the major problems is the size of the country, the long distances that must be travelled; but on the other hand the people 'down under' have the necessary vitality to establish their own tradition.

Austria. Salzburg q.v., with its famous Marionette Theatre, is a Mecca for the puppet-minded – and the Mozart lover will find this theatre largely identified with the composer, although it has a very extensive repertoire; it has become known throughout the world by its company's tours. Since the death of Teschner, q.v., his unique studio-theatre, the *Figurenspiegel*, has alas become a museum piece. Of contemporary growth is the Fadenbuehne theatre, q.v. in Vienna, founded by the artists Picca and Professor Arminio Rothstein. The earlier traditional buffoon character, Hanswurst, was displaced by Kasperle (as also in Germany) and – as did Punch in previous centuries – appeared in a great many plays.

Authorities. (a) Those who, among other things, and by virtue of the office they hold, can give permission (or otherwise), e.g. Municipal, Local Educational: entertainers wishing to approach schools must usually obtain L.E.A. permission; summer 'seasons' at seaside resorts will be by arrangement with the Municipal authorities; (b) those (scholars) who are thoroughly acquainted with all the documentation relative to a given subject (e.g. the Bible, the Law, or puppets in some remote part of the world); (c) those who have mastered an art or craft and can therefore speak about it with first-hand knowledge.

Automata. Mechanically operated figures which continue independently once set in motion, as distinct from the puppet which remains (or should) under the control of its human operator throughout the performance. Statues with moving heads and limbs and mechanical toys have been found from the second and third centuries B.C. Early literary references are sometimes confusing for the historian and even the context does not always clarify the terms used: an example of this problem, although the terms are being used metaphorically, is seen in Gale, Theophilus (*The Court of the Gentiles*) q.v. There is a chapter on automata in von Boehn *Dolls and Puppets* (Harrap, 1932, Cooper Square, USA, 1965). See next entry for standard history.

Automata, by Alfred Chapuis and Edmond Droz, translated by Alec Reid (Editions du Griffon, Neuchatel, and Batsford, London, 1958). A historical and technological study of early automata, articulated masks, animated statues.

Awaji Island. Off Port Kobe, Japan; regarded as the 'cradle' or birth-place of Japanese puppet theatre and one of the traditional centres of puppet-making; at one time most of the islanders were connected with puppetry and all-day shows are still part of the annual village festival of the goddess Benten-Sama. In 1958 a number of Awaji puppeteers travelled to Moscow at the invitation of the Soviet Ministry of Culture. An interesting account of present-day developments is given in Scott *The Puppet Theatre of Japan*, q.v. There is also some reference in Malm *Japanese Music and Musical Instruments*, q.v.

B

Babes in the Wood. Originally a ballad popular about 500 years ago, *The Children in the Wood*, or *The Norfolk Gentleman's Last Will and Testament*, based on a real or supposed (legendary) tragedy, which has had live theatre and puppet versions up to the beginning of the twentieth century before taking the pantomime form. Possibly related to the *Hansel and Gretel* fairy tale. There is an amusing disc by Jupiter Recordings, *jep OC*35, subtitled 'A Family Entertainment' (by V. C. Clinton-Baddeley).

Babies. In the *New English Dictionary*, Thomas Dyche (London, 1768), the definition of 'puppet' is given as 'a representation of man or woman, boy or girl, by little babies, that are moved by wires, etc., in shows.' There were also the 'Bartholomew Babies' or jointed dolls sold at the Fair. See also DRYDEN.

Baby Spot. Small power spotlight: 100–400 watt lamp. Used at short range to give sharp illumination of a selected acting area or focussed on a performer.

Back drop, back cloth. Large background curtain with conventional sky, landscape or other painted scene. Usually replaced by cyclorama in modern productions.

Bacon, Francis, Baron Verulam of Verulam (1561–1626). English statesman, philosopher, author. In his *History of Henry VII* (1622) has this: 'To make the people see . . . that their Plantagenet was indeed but *a puppit* or a counterfeit.' Echo of Shakespeare, *Midsummer Night's Dream*, Act 3, Sc. 2, 'Fie, fie! Counterfeit, you puppet you!'

Backflap. Type of pin-hinge which can be turned back on itself.

Backscreen. Hardboard or plywood background on an 'open' type hand-puppet booth (i.e. type without traditional proscenium, q.v.) and in which exits can be cut away and curtained. It also acts as a soundboard when the performers are inside and in front of the screen. Usually painted matt black, grey or other neutral colour; can have practical (and/or interchangeable) doors, windows, and can support temporary scenery (roof, house-front, etc.). Attached to main framework by means of wooden struts and bolts (detachable).

Bag puppets. (a) Young children create simple puppets from paper bags stuffed with cotton wool, foamed plastic chips, etc., as the head, features stuck on, cloth 'body' covering the performer's hand. (b) Obraztsov, or his translator, in *Chinese Puppet Theatre* (Faber, 1961) gives 'bag' as Chinese term for hand puppet, adding that the English definition 'glove puppet' is more precise. Term also translated as 'sack puppet.'

Baird, Bil. American puppeteer 'since age of seven', later associate of pioneer Tony Sarg; own theatre in New York, six-storey building with workshops; co-performer wife Cora (died 1967) former actress and Martha Graham dancer. Tours for State Department in India, Russia, Afghanistan, Nepal; creator of over 2,000 puppets including characters for film and television. Many commercial productions, including large scale item for Chrysler at Chicago World's Fair, New York Times fashion show, Radio City Music Hall. Film *Party Lines* for American Telephone and Telegraph Company. Created puppets for Orson Welles stage production of *Dr. Faustus*, Cora providing all the voices; by contrast, co-operation in Ziegfield Follies show. Author of *The Art of the Puppet* (Collier-Macmillan, 1965) q.v., magnificently illustrated from world-wide collection of paintings and photographs.

Baird, John Logie (1888–1946). Scottish inventor whose early experiments in creation of television resulted in new form of entertainment in which puppets have regularly featured; first model used was 'Bill' a ventriloquial doll who appeared on primitive television screen in 1927–28; English puppeteers who co-operated in early days include Waldo Lanchester q.v. and H. W. Whanslaw q.v., the latter describing the screen as about the size of a matchbox.

Ballad opera. Musical entertainment developed in eighteenth century, an English form of independent origin but resembling French vaudeville; spoken dialogue and ballads sung to well-known airs; parody of opera-proper, adopting theatrical conventions of farce, sentimental comedy, satire, burlesque; form established by John Gay (1685–1732) with his

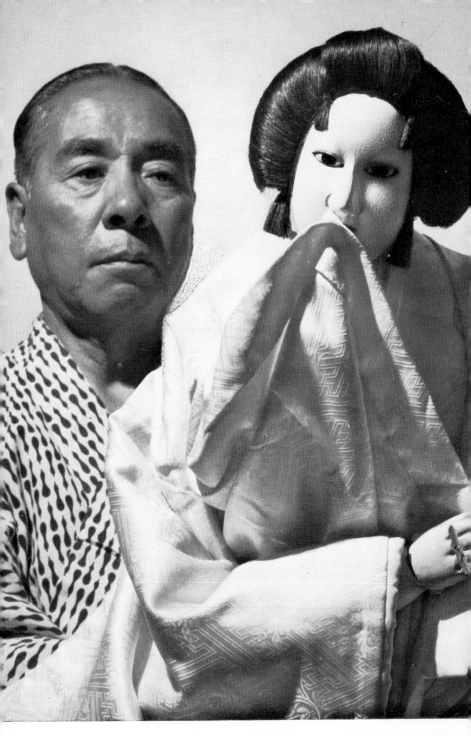

Japanese Bunraku Puppet Theatre: Monjuro, a leading puppeteer, with a female character

Above: Gnafron and Guignol, French hand puppets
Below: Achmed, from the silhouette film by Lotte Reiniger

Above left: Rajasthan marionette. Trick figure – reversible male/female character
Above right: Orlando, cross-eyed hero. Traditional Sicilian marionette
Below left: Burmese clown marionette
Below right: Princess. Shadow figure by Lucy Clause

Imp of Mischief: hand puppet by Pantopuck (A. R. Philpott)

Beggar's Opera (1728) q.v., which remained popular into early twentieth century and inspired modern version *The Threepenny Opera* (1928) q.v., libretto by Bertolt Brecht (1898–1956) and jazz music by Kurt Weill (1900–1950). This has had a number of puppet adaptations. Mozart's *Abduction from the Seraglio* q.v. in same form, in repertoire of the Salzburg Marionette Theatre.

Ballet (Italian 'ballera' to move, dance). Dramatic action in dance form with music, no dialogue. Various forms of puppet ballet have been developed, some related to the human original, e.g. Tchaikowsky *Nutcracker Suite* production at the Salzburg Marionette Theatre, and Saint-Saëns *The Swan* at the same theatre and in repertoire of famous Russian ballerina Pavlova. Experiments at the Bauhaus q.v. in Germany were made by Xanti Schawinsky (Switzerland) and Oscar Schlemmer (Stuttgart), who transformed live dancers into puppets and developed marionettes whose movements were those inherent in their construction: the *Ballet on Strings* by students at the College of Art, Kassel, West Germany was influenced by the Bauhaus pure-movement theory. Schawinsky also demonstrated the qualities of various materials – wood, metal, paper – and of colours as elements in theatrical movement. In England the Hogarth Puppets developed a series of marionette mime-ballets and Eric Bramall presented a *Ballet Mouchoir*, using simple handkerchief ballerinas (after an item by the Stavordale Marionettes). The Jacquard Puppets included a fantasy item *Moth Ballet* in their programme and the Lanchester Marionettes produced an *Underwater Ballet*. In France, Yves Joly included 'live hand' ballet in his sophisticated puppetry. The Hungarian State Puppet Theatre has won international acclaim with Stravinsky *Petrouchka* and Bartok *Wooden Prince*. Experiments with 'black theatre' lighting have given an apparent spatial freedom to puppets. Possibilities vary with each type of puppet. With marionettes the problem of 'flight' or 'elevation', a preoccupation with live dancers and balletomanes, hardly exists; this also makes burlesque an obvious possibility. A problem which does arise with puppet ballet is that of the *double* choreography which must be worked out: (a) the sequences of moves and actions of the puppet dancers at their own stage level and (b) the related moves of the puppeteers above, below or behind the puppets: (a) and (b) exert mutual influence. Complex dance movements with marionettes or rod puppets may require two operators to one figure, an additional problem for the choreographer. Marionettes may need special types of control and stringing. Hand puppet performers may each need to manipulate two figures simultaneously while themselves virtually dancing below them. Music is an integral part of ballet and future composers may write works essentially for puppet performance. Madge Anderson, in *Heroes of the Puppet Stage* (Harcourt Brace, 1923: Jonathan Cape, 1924) mentions a 'grand ballet' performed by puppets on the occasion of the marriage of Lucrezia Borgia to Don Alfonzo d'Este at Bologna.

Ballet on Strings. Marionette item by students of the College of Art, Kassel, Germany, influenced by experiments at the Bauhaus q.v., treating the puppets as a species of being acting according to their particular construction; no dialogue, no story-line, but figures producing own sounds due to design and materials used.

Balloon puppets. Various types: (a) Trick figures of the Fantoccini q.v. (Italian marionette), e.g. lady turns from crinolined creature into aeronautical balloon complete with basket and diminutive balloonist, or male variant with man in Turkish trousers; these require special stringing: constructional details in Inverarity *Manual of Puppetry* (Binfords & Mort, 1936), Nelson and Hayes *Trick Marionettes* (Puppetry Handbooks, USA, 1935); (b) balloons as heaving bosom of tubular head rod puppet as used in item satirizing speech-training class at Stanhope Evening Institute, London; (c) balloon as a character: e.g. in Lafaye striptease item (France) partnered by gloved hands (erotique); balloon as basic model over which paper-layer hollow heads are built up, balloon later deflated and removed (technique in Stuart Robinson *Exploring Puppetry*, Mills and Boon, 1967); (e) balloon *as* balloon stage-prop, e.g. in circus act with performing dogs or seals; (f) balloon *as* balloon, controlled by rod or string; (g) huge mobile balloons controlled from ground by ropes and paraded along New York's Broadway on Thanksgiving Day, organised by puppeteer Tony Sarg and sponsored by Macy's department store. Illustration in Baird *Art of the Puppet* (Collier-Macmillan, 1965) and mention of a carnival type dragon 125-feet long and filled with helium.

Balsa wood. (Ochroma lagopus.) Source: tropical America; also known as Corkwood. Extremely light weight, soft, difficult to split, yellowish-white. Used by model-makers and sometimes by makers of large marionettes where weight a consideration. Surface can be toughened by applications of plaster 'filler' or coats of model-makers' 'dope.'

Bamboccio. Early Italian term, interpretation of which not always clear in literary references; can refer to either (a) the Jumping Jack type, q.v., or (b) the marionnettes à la planchette, q.v. (on horizontal string).

Barrel organ. Cylinder ('barrel') with projecting pins (studs) moves tongue-shaped keys arranged in required order; keys control pipes similar to those of organ but with limited compass and tone colour; operated by handle. At one time used in small village churches for hymn tunes. Name often confused with 'hurdy gurdy' a different type of instrument.

Barry Smith. English puppeteer whose career began while still at school (1940) on the occasion of a talk on puppetry by the German puppeteer Paul Brann, illustrated by figures from his theatre in Munich, Barry Smith acting as his assistant. By age of 16, running a one-man show for children on a professional basis. Trained at the Central School of Speech and Drama and was immediately appointed as voice teacher at the Royal Academy of Dramatic Art; has also taught at the Royal Academy of Dancing, the Royal Shakespeare Theatre, the National Theatre and at a Teacher Training College. During this period was developing his style and enlarging his repertoire, using various kinds of glove and rod puppet, finally presenting his 'Theatre of Puppets' at the Edinburgh Festival (1965); since then has performed at the International Puppet Festival in Bucharest, the State Puppet Theatre in Budapest, the Hampstead Theatre Club, the Vanbrugh Theatre Club, the Little Angel Marionette Theatre, and at clubs and arts festivals throughout the country. Repertoire includes, besides original items, material adapted from Japanese legend, a thirteenth century Chinese play, English medieval drama, de Maupassant, Oscar Wilde and Grimm; work is mainly for audiences of adults and older children, but has programmes for young children also. Style of presentation simple and flexible, depending on the sight-lines, audience, and programme, sometimes working with an overhead play-board, sometimes behind a low one or with no play-board at all and in full view of the audience. As well as being teacher of voice and speech, has worked as actor and given verse recitals, so that it is natural that he should emphasise the 'acting' qualities of his puppets and the use of 'live' speech. Whenever possible, narration and dialogue is spoken by himself; when more complicated sound is needed, makes use of tape recording techniques to create evocative sound by means of music, real and abstract effects and even distorted voices. Believes that the justification of any technique is its success, as in all theatre, in making an immediate and direct contact with the audience – something which puppets can and should do supremely well.

Bartholomew Fair. Founded by Rahere, monk who had been Court fool and minstrel to Henry I and who built St. Bartholomew's Hospital (1123); held annually in London from 1133–1855 at West Smithfield ('smooth field') with puppet shows among the many attractions (mentioned by diarists Pepys q.v. and Evelyn q.v.). Morley (*Memoirs of Bartholomew Fair*, 1859) describes a 'knave in Fool's coat' persuading crowd to see puppet show. Early playbill (in the Harvard College Theatre Collection: reproduced in Speaight *History of the English Puppet Theatre* Harrap 1955 and Baird *Art of the Puppet*, Collier-Macmillan 1965) advertised John Harris's booth, with programme including 'the merry humours of Punchinello.' Alexander Stevens (1710–1784) described the fair in a poem mentioning 'Punch's whole play of the Gunpowder plot.' Ben Jonson's play *Bartholomew Fayre* (1631) q.v. includes an actual puppet show within the fairground scene and gives good idea of method of presentation. McKechnie *Popular Entertainments through the Ages* (Sampson Low, 1931) mentions a pamphlet about the fair and 'motions' (puppets).

Bartholomew Fayre. Jacobean comedy by Ben Jonson q.v., first printed 1631. No central plot, no outstanding hero; dominant theme the fair itself. Some satire on contemporaries. Act 5, scene 3 includes actual performance by puppets in a burlesque of Marlowe's *Hero and Leander* q.v. (or the Greek original?). The 'motion master' (puppeteer) Lanthorne Leatherhead 'interprets' q.v. for the puppets, standing in front of the booth. Contemporary productions: by the Old Vic in 1950, when George Speaight q.v. was responsible for the puppetry, puppets made by John Wright q.v.

Bartok, Bela (1881–1945). Hungarian composer; collector of folk music (Hungarian, Rumanian, Arabian). Wrote three works for the stage: *Bluebeard's Castle*, an opera, and two ballets: *The Miraculous Mandarin*, *The Wooden Prince*, q.v., the last being successfully produced by the Hungarian State Puppet Theatre q.v. and seen at the Aldeburgh and Bath Festivals, 1968.

Basketwork puppets. Polish designer Adam Kilian created large basketwork figures in style based on folk tradition for *The Spellbound Horse* produced at the 'Lalka' State Puppet Theatre, Warsaw (1960): illustration in *Puppet Theatre of the Modern World* q.v. Manipulators worked *inside* the puppets. This type of puppet also used by group at the Rishi Valley School at Andhra Pradesh in South India. Basketwork frames were used in construction of early English pageant figures (giants), some of which also had internal operators.

Bastien and Bastienne, by Wolfgang Amadeus Mozart (1756–1791), pastorale composed when 12 years of age, mostly singing and dialogue: story of lovers and wizard, happy ending. Private performance given in garden of Dr Mesmer the hypnotist. Favourite production with many puppet theatres, particularly at the Salzburg Marionette Theatre. Zurich Marionette Theatre version introduced black goat as 'symbol of diabolical power' in contrast to Bastienne's white sheep symbolic of purity and innocence, illustrations in Gauehat *Marionettes* (Rentsch, 1944).

Batchelder, Marjorie (Mrs. Paul McPharlin). American puppeteer, teacher, author; Vice-President of UNIMA, the international organisation. Developed special interest in rod puppets and educational aspects. First experiments with rod type in 1936, items produced including *St George and the Dragon;* produced Maeterlinck *Death of Tintagiles* in 1937 with specially designed stage. Author of *Puppet Theatre Handbook* (Harper, N.Y., 1947, Jenkins, 1948); co-author with Vivian Michael *Hand-and-Rod Puppets* (Ohio University, 1947); major work *Rod Puppets and the Human Theatre* q.v., historical and technical study of now widely adopted type of puppet. Has pointed out need for re-assessment of some material in puppet histories where authors failed to distinguish dolls, puppets, articulated toys, automata, movable images.

Bath Academy of Art. For many years a strong centre of puppet experiments by students under Helen Binyon, especially with shadow puppets; one item, a 'scissors ballet', outcome of experiment with everyday objects placed behind screen, given to music composed by students. (See *Puppetry Today*, Helen Binyon, Studio Vista, 1965.)

Bath Festival. The famous puppet-showman Martin Powell q.v. was first heard of in 1709 at Bath (mentioned in *The Tatler*), a fashionable spa; in 1968 the Bath Festival Society in association with the Arts Council of Great Britain and support from the Bath Corporation presented, in addition to Opera, Concerts, Ballet, Recitals, Chamber and Choral Music, Jazz, performances by the internationally famous Hungarian State Puppet Theatre, q.v. Bartok *The Wooden Prince*, Stravinsky *Petrushka*. (Also appeared at the Aldeburgh Festival.)

Batten. Term for length of rigid material, wood, iron pipe, etc., with many stages uses, e.g. top and bottom of backdrop, cross-piece joining two or more flats, support of flood or spotlights.

Bauhaus, the. Der Staatliche Bauhaus, Weimar, Germany; founded 1919 by Walter Gropius, as research and education centre with new concept of the function of man and the integration of the visual arts and crafts – art, architecture, industrial design. (Bau, haus; Der Bau, creative construction.) The idea of 'total' or 'organic' theatre was developed and carried over into the realm of puppets: there were experiments with actors as puppets, abstractions, light and colour, projection – and marionettes of a highly stylised design (the influence of which has been seen in the work of students at the College of Art in Kassel). Experimental stages used are now in the Munich Theatre Museum. Among others attracted to the Faculty were Paul Klee and Wassily Kandinsky, both interested in puppets. The centre moved to Dessau in 1925 and was closed by the National Socialist Movement in 1932. Laszlo Moholy-Nagy, Hungarian painter, photographer, art teacher, established a new Bauhaus in Chicago (1937), later to become the Institute of Design. The original Bauhaus published various works, and a Bibliography of its publications. Moholy-Nagy published *Vision in Motion* (1947) and *The New Vision* (4th edition, 1947). *Theatre of the Bauhaus*, by Oskar Schlemmer, Laszlo Moholy-Nagy, Farkas Molnar, with an introduction by Walter Gropius, was published in English translation by the Wesleyan University Press, USA, 1961.

Baum, Lyman Frank (1856–1919). American journalist, dramatist, writer of children's stories; best known for *The Wonderful Wizard of Oz*, q.v., which had 13 sequels, and which has had puppet adaptations as well as stage and film versions. Author of 60 books for children, including 24 for girls (under pseudonym 'Edith Van Dyne').

Beaumont, Cyril. Distinguished English ballet critic, historian, author, bookseller. For many years had small shop (now given over to pop and jazz records) in London's Charing Cross Road; shop for many years a Mecca for balletomanes and puppeteers. Author of *Ballet Design: past and present* (Studio publication), *Puppets and the Puppet Stage* (Studio, 1938), profusely illustrated; *Puppets and Puppetry* (Studio, 1958) with nearly 400 photo-reproductions, including some of earlier material, from world-wide sources; historical introduction.

Beauty and the Beast. Fairy tale with a number of variants. Similar story appeared in the *Piacevoli Notti* of Straparola q.v. in 1550; best known version that of the French 'contes' of Mme de Villeneuve (1744). One of the favourites for puppet production. Theme: Beauty is youngest daughter of a merchant who sets off to retrieve his fortune; the elder sisters ask for costly gifts to be brought: Beauty asks for a rose. On return journey merchant sees an apparently deserted garden, by a palace, picks rose, whereupon the Beast appears and demands youngest daughter in return for sparing merchant's life: Beauty dutifully goes to the Beast, pities him, agrees to marry him: whereupon a spell is broken and he is transformed into handsome Prince. Hence the need for creating a transformation puppet.

Beggar's Opera. Satirical ballad opera by John Gay (1685–1732), with English and Irish folk tunes collected and arranged by Dr Johann Cristoph Pepusch, and first performed London, 1728; continued in popularity into early 1920's (Lyric, Hammersmith) in new arrangement by Frederick Austin, and a further version by Benjamin Britten appeared in 1945. Brecht's *Threepenny Opera*, q.v. with German jazz music by Kurt Weill (1928) derived from Gay's work and has had a number of puppet productions, e.g. that of the 'Groteska' State Puppet Theatre, Cracow, Poland (illustration in *Puppet Theatre of the Modern World*, 1965).

Beheading of puppets. William Boulton, in *Amusements of Old London* (Nimmo, 1901) mentions the decapitation of a puppet by another puppet – 'after much formality.' Sidney, Raleigh, Charles I and Russell, died again in effigy for many years at May Fair. See also *Book of Days*.

Belgium. A country whose puppetry is mostly associated with traditional regional characters such as Tchantches q.v. of Liége, where some companies still perform episodes from *The Paladins of France* (similar in theme to those of the Sicilian Puppet Theatre) using somewhat primitive marionettes supported by a stiff head-wire (fil d'archal) and only one or two strings controlling limbs (technique also related to the Sicilian); a troupe took part in the second international festival in Britain (at Colwyn Bay) in 1968 – the stage becoming piled high with fallen warriors. The earliest puppets of this type had the head and torso in one piece, but present-day heads are joined at the neck. The repertoire includes plays of biblical origin (such as the Nativity) as well as the Charlemagne legends, and even the *Three Musketeers*. A noticeable feature is the relative heights of the characters (in order of importance). In Brussels, q.v. there is the Théâtre Toone whose dynasty began in 1812, and in the nineteenth century this city had 15 puppet theatres. Antwerp and Lille are other centres of puppetry. A Congress and international Festival of traditional puppetry was held in Liége in 1958 (see *Quand les marionnettes du monde* . . . .)

Bench Book of Puppetry, by H. W. Whanslaw (Wells, Gardner and Darton, 1957). Author was founder member of the British Puppet and Model Theatre Guild and produced many textbooks. The *Bench Book* is not strictly a textbook but is full of valuable information stemming from replies to questions over a long period. The alphabetical arrangement gives quick reference to a wide range of material. Appendices include recipes, details of puppetry societies, magazines and journals, puppets and films, puppets in London museums, and a bibliography. *Second Bench Book* is on similar lines, with appendices giving technical hints and suggestions, where to buy materials, contemporary British puppet troupes, puppet societies in Britain, list of the author's other books; bibliography.

Benzene. Distillation of coal tar and crude oil, colourless; used in manufacture of varnishes, lacquers, and as a cleaning agent. Highly inflammable.

Behind the White Screen, by Sotiris Spatharis (London Magazine edition, 1967), English translation by Mario Rinvolucri. Autobiography of Greek shadow-theatre player whose passion and creative genius have been largely responsible for revival of interest in the traditional Karagiosis which derived from the Turkish Karagöz, q.v.

Bethnal Green Museum, Cambridge Heath Road, London, E.2. A branch of the Victoria and Albert Museum. In 1963 on the occasion of the first UNIMA q.v. Praesidium meeting to be held in London, a joint Exhibition of Polish and British puppets, traditional and contemporary, was mounted, through collaboration between the Director, Mr Montague Weekley, the Polish Ministry of Culture, and the Joint International Committee of the British Puppet and Model Theatre Guild and the Educational Puppetry Association: (later known as British Section UNIMA). The Guild produced a special issue of its *Puppet Master* (Volume 7, No. 4) with photographs of some of the exhibits. In 1968 the Museum mounted a special display (permanent), including puppets from various parts of the world; also optical toys such as magic lanterns. The Venetian Marionette Theatre, formerly at the Victoria and Albert, was transferred to Bethnal Green.

Bib puppets. Alternative term for 'living marionettes' or 'humanettes' – operator's own head becomes puppet head, with puppet body and limbs of small scale, suspended from operator's neck, string or short rod controls for limbs, operator's body concealed by curtain or screen. Technique: Batchelder, *Puppet Theatre Handbook* (Jenkins, 1948).

Bible plays. Earliest recorded European puppet plays include *The Creation, Adam and Eve, The Fall, Noah and the Flood, The Nativity*, reflecting themes used in the medieval Mystery and Morality plays; there are many contemporary versions of these plays. Oliver Goldsmith (1728-74) mentions *Solomon's Temple (She Stoops to Conquer);* the *Referee* (1888) mentions *The Universal Deluge* presented at the Teatro Mercadante, Naples, and given at the Royal Italian Opera and Ballet Marionette performance in London (1888); there are several references in Ben Jonson's plays (1572–1637). Belgium, France, Germany had similar performances. McPharlin (1903–48) lists many items given in the United

States (*Puppet Theatre in America*). Contemporary English productions include *Creation* and *Noah*, Little Angel Marionette Theatre, London, and *Abraham and Isaac* by the 'Polka' Company (touring). Central State Puppet Theatre, Moscow, has produced Isidor Stok's *The Divine Comedy*, satirical version of *Genesis*, mixing live actors and puppets. H. W. Whanslaw wrote *Bible Puppetry* and *Twelve Puppet Plays* (Bible stories), published by the Religious Education Press; in Germany Aufban verlag published Baer *Biblische Puppenspiele*.

Bibliographies. Lists of books on given subject. Date of publication of bibliography determines limit of titles included. Von Boehn *Dolls and Puppets*, q.v., English edition of 1932, lists titles up to 1931. New printing 1966, list not revised although there has been far more literature on the subject since 1945. Encyclopaedias tend to have very limited and 'dated' bibliographies, because of the long preparation period. Minor works of more recent date may list important books not yet in major bibliographies. *World Bibliography of Bibliographies* (4th edition, 1965/6) has only three entries relative to puppetry, including *Puppets and Shadows: a bibliography*, 1931, comprehensive as far as it goes, but useless for post-1931 publications. Annotated references, as in Batchelder *Rod Puppets and the Human Theatre* (1947) q.v. are the most useful, giving clearer idea of contents, book titles often being inadequate. Present *Dictionary* has annotated entries (up to year of publication) with separate list giving publisher and date. UNIMA, the international puppetry organisation, began to issue a *Bulletin* (No. 6, series 4) which will eventually form basis of an international bibliography for the benefit of puppeteers everywhere. Many countries now have National Sections of UNIMA, which should simplify an international compilation.

Bibliotheques en musées des arts du spectacle dans le monde: international list of libraries and museums with theatre collections (some with puppet material): see *Performing Arts Collections*.

Billboard. The oldest and most widely circulated Entertainment trade-paper in the world, founded 1893. Published by the Billboard Publishing Co., 1564 Broadway, New York City; available from international newsagents.

Billy the Kid. Large scale puppet production based on music of Aaron Copland's American folk ballet, libretto Lincoln Kirstein, with co-operation between the Detroit Institute Puppet Theatre and the Detroit Symphony Orchestra, production design and direction by George Latshaw, who visited the actual jail from which 'The Kid' had made his dramatic escape (Lincoln County, New Mexico); production based on Sheriff Pat Garrett's account of Billy's life and times. Large puppets were essential for the presentation in the Ford auditorium and the technique was based on that of the Japanese Bunraku q.v. 'three man' type, but figures 8–9-ft. tall and requiring only two operators each, these being clad in black from head to foot; a wide range of action developed.

Bird control. Unusual carved and painted control in form of flying bird, used with some Burmese marionettes.

Bird puppets. Construction and action depends on type: hand, rod, string, shadow figure, and on materials used in making – carved wood, stuffed, painted, feathered. Natural sounds or human speech optional, depending on whether creatures just 'local colour' in pastoral or forest scene or appearing in fables with dialogue. Aristophanes' *The Birds* q.v., with its 'Cloud Cuckoo Land' has had a number of puppet adaptations.

Techniques: Whanslaw *Second Bench Book* (Wells, Gardner, Darton, 1957) and many textbooks.

Birds, the (Ornithes). Comedy by Greek playwright Aristophanes (*c.* 450 – ? *c.* 385 B.C.) on the Utopia theme. First scene is A Wilderness: second is Cloudcuckooland. Two old men seek a new and quiet life, being tired of paying taxes; one has a crow and the other a jay: they hope these will find Epops the Hoopoe (formerly a man); the old men acquire wings and a plan is hatched to create a sanctuary between heaven and earth. The play has had a number of puppet adaptations; was seen by Anatole France at Signoret's 'Petit théâtre' in Paris, q.v. (1888–92), where an unusual type of 'pedal' puppet was used; marionette production by Marjorie Batchelder (McPharlin) for M.A. degree at Ohio State University (1934).

Birthday of the Infanta, by Oscar Wilde, q.v. Story of Spanish Princess whose 12th birthday celebrations include a mock bull fight with boys on hobby horses and wickerwork bull, gypsies with apes, dancing dwarf and Italian puppets 'made out of wood and coloured wax.' Dwarf vain and comes up against a monster – himself in distorting mirror – and dies of broken heart. Perry Dilley, American puppeteer, among those who have made puppet adaptations.

Blackboard paint. Waterproof paint which dries matt ('flat') without gloss or shine; usually black but modern blackboards sometimes green; used on rod controls against dark background, rods become almost invisible.

Black-out. Quick cut-out of stage illumination – intentional – for dramatic purposes such as a transformation. Term also used in World War II when street illumination prohibited and windows screened as precautionary measure in air raids.

Black theatre. Type of production using selective-lighting technique long known in live theatres especially in 'magic'; adopted by many contemporary puppet theatres. Puppet operators wear black leotards and hoods or face masks, move invisibly on darkened stage, operating puppets lit from the stage wings or from above and below: objects appear to float in space: a chair or a sewing machine can dance. Sometimes fluorescent light used with glowing fabric or colours. French puppeteer Georges Lafaye responsible for the vogue; works with group behind a 'curtain' of light into which the puppets are thrust, sometimes using symbolic objects. Baird *Art of the Puppet* (Collier-Macmillan, 1965) q.v. has photo of a performance and diagram illustrating technique. Lafaye's work influenced development of the Black Theatre in Prague, Czechoslovakia.

Blackham, Olive. English puppeteer, Hon. Member UNIMA. Director of the Roel Puppets; began with small experimental marionette theatre *The Ark*, established in a loft in King's Heath, Birmingham, Warwickshire (1927–32). First marionettes used were 1-ft. high. Theatre moved to Cotswolds in 1932 and set up in granary of Roel Farm. Roel Puppets operated 1932–61 with many tours. Size of figures increased (20 ins. – 3-ft.) according to the play: particular study of characterising through appearance and movement. Repertoire of plays old and new, including two Japanese Noh plays, the miracle play of *Abraham and Isaac*, scenes from Shakespeare's *The Tempest*, contemporary English and American verse plays interspersed with farces such as Chekhov's *The Proposal*, the *Unwilling Martyr*, and original burlesques and satires. Performances given in many small theatres including 'The Curtain,' Rochdale, the 'Garrick',

Liverpool Playgoer's Clubs, the 'Crescent', Birmingham, 'Unity' and 'Players', London. Chosen to represent British puppetry at the 1937 Paris Exhibition; toured for the Arts Council and performed during the Music Festival in Cheltenham. In World War II a simpler form of staging developed: shadows, glove, glove-and-rod types used in addition to marionettes, and toured extensively, continuing after the war, and particularly useful at Training Colleges. Held Summer Schools 1936–58 in Village Hall at Guiting Power, near Cheltenham; new hall, after demolition of old, proved 'too grand' for carpentry. Author of *Puppets into Actors* (Rockliff, 1948) and *Shadow Puppets* (Barrie and Rockliff, 1960).

Blattner, Geza. Hungarian painter, puppeteer, domiciled in France; avant-garde, experimented especially with rod type, 'pedal' or 'key' type, multi-purpose stage accommodating several types of puppet, and 'back projection'; director of famous theatre *l'Arc-en-Ciel* opened 1925; first theatre *Le Prisme* in Montparnasse, Paris. Good chapter on his work in *Marionnettes et Marionnettistes de France* (Bordas, 1947); mimeographed paper on his theatre published by Columbus University, Ohio, 1941. Productions diverse, e.g. *The Mystery of the Virgin Mary* and Grimm *The Little Tailor*, and others on modern sophisticated themes.

Blue Beard. Included in Perrault (1628–1703) fairy tales (*Barbe Bleue*) *c.* 1657, but similar theme found in *Arabian Nights* and used by Offenbach and others. Name is nickname of imaginary possibly historical character notorious for cruelty and according to Perrault version actually having blue beard. Theme: forbidden room which wife enters during his absence and in which she discovers bodies of several previous wives. About to be killed herself when her curiosity discovered, is saved by two brothers who kill wicked husband; she inherits his wealth and marries a pleasanter man. There have been numerous puppet versions by those with taste for the macabre. Included in Penguin Classics (paperback).

Blue Bird, The (L'Oiseau blue); fairy-tale play by Maurice Maeterlinck (1862–1949), written 1905, first produced by Stanislavsky, Moscow, 1908; theme: fantastic journey of Tyltyl and Mytil in search of Blue Bird of Happiness. Many puppet theatre productions.

Blundall, John M. English puppeteer, Designer, Director. Clown Marionette speciality act in Music Hall. Designer: Revue, Pantomime, Ballet and Plays. Designed and made puppets for Television series *Fireball XL5, Stingray, Thunderbirds*. Designer-co-director, Caricature Theatre, Cardiff; designed and made puppets for *Culhwch and Olwen* for the Commonwealth Arts Festival; *Peter and the Wolf, Lady of the Lake*, for B.B.C. Wales. Resident Designer and Puppet Master to the Midlands Arts Theatre Company in the Midlands Art Centre for Young People, Birmingham. Developing new techniques in training actors (15s to 25s) and designers for the Puppet Theatre, and encouraging younger children (3–15) to express themselves through the craft and dramatic elements, using puppets. Puppets and designs in collections in France, Germany, Poland, Czechoslovkia, Russia, Japan and Ceylon.

Bobbin, Tim. Nineteenth century marionette clown who had the knack of appearing in all kinds of plays, in the true folk puppet tradition. Origin of name uncertain. Whanslaw, in his *Second Bench Book*, suggests possibility of derivation from famous 18th century Lancastrian schoolmaster John Collier (died 1786), who wrote dialect stories under the pseudonym 'Tim Bobbin.' Speaight in *History of the English Puppet Theatre* accepts the derivation and suggests the character might well be revived:

he might well become a hand puppet or a large rod puppet effectively, retaining his rural costume and accent.

Boccaccio, Giovanni (1313–75). Italian novelist and poet; chief work the *Decameron* (*Decamerone*, 1352) q.v., a collection of 100 tales, lively, humorous and sometimes licentious, of which some have been adapted for puppet production.

Bodleian Library, Oxford University. The original library was established in 1445, destroyed during the reign of Edward VI, re-established in the early seventeenth century by Sir Thomas Bodley; new library opened 1946; receives copy of every book published in the British Empire. Among its important collection of illuminated manuscripts (over 40,000) is the anonymous fourteenth century *Romans du bon roi Alexandre* q.v., containing two illustrations of hand-puppet shows (reproduced in a number of books; particularly good enlargement in colour in Baird *Art of the Puppet*); the British Museum has postcard colour reproduction of one.

Boîte à joujoux by Claude Debussy (1862–1918) q.v., a children's ballet on scenario by André Hellé, originally piano score (1913); a love triangle among puppets, a battle between toy soldiers and punchinellos, some light-hearted burlesquing of *Carmen* and *Faust* music. Puppet production by the Little Angel Theatre at the Queen Elizabeth Hall, London (August, 1968), with the British Chamber Orchestra, musical director Daniel Barenboim, Narrator Michael Flanders.

Boiardo, Matteomaria (? 1441–94). Italian poet whose source-material was the legend of Charlemagne and main work *Orlando Innamorato* (unfinished) and the hero reappearing in Ariosto's q.v. *Orlando Furioso* – the two works providing much of the repertoire of the Sicilian q.v. marionette theatres.

Bonding. Process of joining component materials or parts, e.g. surfacing of plywood with contact types of fabric; plywood itself is sometimes resin-bonded, especially where moisture-resistance important.

Book of Days. A Miscellany of Popular Antiquities in connection with the Calendar; Anecdotes, Biography, History: edited by R. Chambers, 2 volumes (W. & R. Chambers, 1881, Lippincott, Phila., USA). Vol. 2 has account of Powell's puppet show (gives Christian name Robert: showman was Martin), essay on respective merits of Punch and the 'Fantoccini' – described as 'the simulative theatricals of the streets' – technical details given: Fantoccini jointed and worked by 'a string.' 'Turks, sailors, clowns, etc., dangled and danced through the scene with great propriety . . .'. Illustration of booth is of Punch type. Reproduction of seventeenth century handbill mentions Punch's Theatre 'for the entertainment of four Indian kings' (at St Martin's Lane and Litchfield Street, London). Mentions Egyptian and Etrurian tomb figures, Indian and Chinese shows, 'ombres chinoises' performing *The Broken Bridge*, 'a not over-delicate drama.' There is also a reference to a 'beheading of puppets' in Mayfair, continued for some years, following the execution of Scottish lords and others after the 1745 rebellion. See also Beheading.

Book of Marionettes, A, by Helen Haiman Joseph (Viking Press, N.Y., 1929). A popular history partly based on Magnin *Histoire des marionnettes en Europe* (Levy Fréres, 1852) q.v., with illustrations of all periods treated. Marjorie Batchelder has pointed out need for more critical examination of some of Magnin's conclusions.

Booksellers. (1) K. R. Drummond, 30 Hart Grove, Ealing Common, London, W.5. Specialist in books on the crafts and puppetry (separate catalogues on each); stocks all puppet books in print, can search for out-of-print items. (2) Foyle's, Charing Cross Road, London, W.C.2. Drama Department: comprehensive range on all branches of theatre, including puppets. (3) Ifan Kyrle Fletcher, 22 Buckingham Gate, London, S.W.1: Special catalogues on theatre material; collectors' items. (4) Oscar Oswald, 7a Duke Street Hill, London, S.E.1: second-hand books on Punch, puppets, magic, ventriloquism; also monthly periodical, *Magical Digest*, which includes puppet material.

Booth. A portable stage which can be set up indoors or out; also known as a fit-up.

Boswell, James (1740–95). Scottish biographer, diarist; author of *Life of Samuel Johnson* (1791) recorded Oliver Goldsmith's q.v. contempt for puppets seen at a London performance and then breaking a shin trying to emulate puppet actions.

Bottler. Showman's term for the 'front man' whose function is to attract a crowd for the Punch and Judy show by playing drum and panpipes. During the performance may talk to Punch. Most important function: to collect coins from audience before it can escape. Some showmen have used the Dog Toby, q.v. to take the collection, using a tin mug.

Bouchet, Guillaume (1526–c. 1606). French author of *Les Sérées*, which Magnin cites in *Histoire des marionnettes en Europe* (1852) – with the description 'historiettes facétieuses' – imaginary discussions on 'all sorts of pleasantries' – and, according to Magnin, the first use of the word 'marionnettes' and evidence of a puppet theatre between 1590 and 1600. The word by itself does not indicate the *type* of puppet. See MARIONNETTE.

Bouchor, Maurice (1855–1929). French poet, playwright; *Les poèmes de l'amour et de la mer* (1876), *Le Faust moderne* (1878); closely connected with Signoret's 'Petit Théâtre' q.v. in the Galerie Vivienne, Paris, for which he translated Shakespeare's *The Tempest* (1889) and wrote several plays including *Tobie, Noël*, Le mystère de la Trinité (1889–90), performances of which were seen by Anatole France, q.v. and mentioned in his *Life and Letters*.

Boxers, The. Modernistic puppet ballet by Jacques Chesnais q.v. (France) with rod puppets designed by Fernand Leger. Illustration in Beaumont *Puppets and Puppetry* (Studio, 1958).

Boxing match. Usually an interlude introduced into Punch and Judy or other hand puppet show, sometimes in 'slow motion.' See also *The Boxers*, puppet ballet by French performer Chesnais.

Boy who wanted to know what Fear was: Nazi propaganda puppet film for children (Gebruder Diehl, 1935).

Bramall, Eric, F.R.S.A., H.R.C.A. English puppeteer; director of the Harlequin Puppet Theatre, Rhos-on-Sea, Colwyn Bay, North Wales; marionette specialist. First television appearances on BBC in 1946 and has since appeared on all major networks in Britain and in Europe; has three regular series on BBC Wales TV, *Lili Lou, Tedi Twt* and *Wili a Tili*, and on Yorkshire Television, *Jimmy Green and His Time Machine, Sugarball, Boy of the Jungle* and *The Magic Book*. Director of 1st international Puppetry Festival to be held in Britain (1951); organiser of Exhibitions at 2nd international event. Tours of Britain and the Continent since 1947. Author of *Making a Start with Marionettes* (Bell, 1960),

Puppet Plays and Playwriting (Bell, 1961) and, jointly with Chris C. Somerville, *Expert Puppet Technique* (Faber, 1964).

Brann, Paul (1873–1955). German puppeteer, founder of celebrated Art Puppet Theatre in Munich (Marionettentheater München Kunstler, 1905), which flourished to early 1930's. Inspired by work of 'Papa' Schmid q.v. and traditional South German woodcarvers. World-wide tours and domiciled in England during Nazi regime. Repertoire included plays and operas. Artists Klee q.v. and Kandinsky q.v. among his admirers. About 200 of his marionettes now in the Munich City Theatre Museum collection.

Bread and Puppet Theatre. A fugitive troupe (New York Street Theatre) presenting plays, usually short parables which underline Christian symbolism with contemporary political and social comment, combining action of live actors and giant puppets. Company are required to be actors, craftsmen, musicians, acrobats as well as puppeteers. Some figures used in the streets are 30-ft. tall, operators inside, controlled by poles. There is also a pamphlet printing B. & P. Press.

Brecht, Bertolt (1898–1956). Avant-garde German dramatist, poet, producer, theatre-theorist and influenced by Expressionist techniques. Marxist interest shown in production of *The Threepenny Opera* (*Die Dreigroschenoper* (1928)), libretto by Brecht, German jazz music by Kurt Weill, and inspired by the English *Beggars' Opera* q.v. by John Gay (1685–1732) itself a satire on 'bourgeois society' of his time and on opera style as such. *The Threepenny Opera* q.v. has had a number of puppet theatre productions. Brecht's main contribution to theatre-theory was the concept of 'alienation' q.v. (known as the 'A-effect'), which opposed the idea of 'involvement' both on the part of the actor and the audience: this due to the didactic content of many of his productions. The didactic content of medieval 'Morality' q.v. plays, on the contrary, had the purpose of stimulating religious emotion although the characters were abstract representaions of virtues and vices. Bamber Gascoyne (*Twentieth Century Drama:* Hutchinson, 1962) refers to 'Brechtian demonstrators or mere puppet figures.'

Brer Rabbit. Chief character in the Uncle Remus stories (Joe Chandler Harris, 1848–1908); always outwits Brer Fox the villain in most episodes. Given these two as stock character puppets, the addition of one other gives fresh possibilities, not necessarily Terrapin or Tar Baby. Rabbit character plays similar role in some African folk-tales.

Brer Rabbit Plays, by Barbara Lancaster (Macmillan, 1953). In the 'Puppet Plays for Schools' series for hand puppets. (1) *Brer Rabbit goes to Town*, (2) *Brer Rabbit and the Tarbaby*, (3) *Brer Fox plays 'Possum,'* (4) *Brer Fox Loses his Tail*. Average playing-time 10 minutes each. No fees for non-professional performances.

Bridge (French 'pont'). Backstage gallery erected for use of marionette manipulators, height related to proscenium opening, with steps or ladder at either end. Area below bridge concealed by backdrop. A 'leaning rail' q.v. is fixed at waist level along front of bridge and a 'hanging rail' q.v. provided at convenient position for storing off-stage characters. Second bridge may be erected immediately behind top of proscenium and providing increased action possibilities. Construction may be of timber or duralumin or other metal. Construction methods vary between permanent theatre and mobile stage. Individual needs may result in

variations of design, e.g. use of 'tree-top walkways' giving depth of action
in television production by Bil Baird (USA), manipulators stepping
across gaps between trees while moving characters through forest scene.
Construction techniques: John Wright *Your Puppetry* (Sylvan Press, 1951),
Jan Bussell *The Puppet Theatre* (Faber, 1946), John Mulholland *Practical
Puppetry* (Jenkins, 1961), Peter Fraser *Introducing Puppetry* (Batsford, 1968)
and most technical manuals.

British Children's Theatre Association (B.C.T.A.) formed in 1959 at
Leicester: President, Michel Saint-Denis, C.B.E. Aims include fostering
of first-class standards, study of problems of child audiences, methods of
production and presentation best suited to various ages, to hold discussion
meetings, to encourage discrimination on part of children in choice of
productions seen; to encourage playwrights to contribute material and
publishers to consider issuing, and to maintain a bibliography of recommended plays, produce a directory of children's theatres; to hold an
annual B.C.T.A. Conference. The association issues bulletins and news-
letters to its members. Membership: professional group, amateur group,
individual, associate. There is a Puppetry Secretary: Violet M. Philpott
(c/o Educational Puppetry Association, q.v.).

British Council, 65 Davies Street, London, W.1. Drama and Music
Section. Principal activities of the Council (established 1934) are overseas
where it maintains staff in 70 countries, the encouragement of English
language teaching and British studies and, in Britain, assistance to
overseas visitors in the professional, scientific, educational and cultural
spheres. The Council organises tours overseas by British theatre, ballet,
and opera companies, individual recitalists, and by orchestras and
individual musicians. From time to time visitors from overseas are put
in touch with the British puppetry organisations.

British Drama League, 9–10 Fitzroy Square, London, W.1. Founded
1919. Aim: to assist the development of the art of the theatre and to
promote a right relation between drama and the life of the community.
Since its foundation it has affiliated over 6,000 independent organisations;
has unique information and advice bureau and a library of over 150,000
volumes. Members receive the illustrated journal *Drama*, which has
occasional puppet material. Experts available to advise on dramatic
activity, professional or amateur.

British Equity. Recognised Trade Union for actors, actresses, singers,
dancers, producers, stage managers, in straight plays, musicals, revues,
mime, opera, ballet, films, radio and television. Address: British Actors
Equity Association, 8 Harley Street, London, W.1.

British Film Institute. Films for hire include silhouette (shadow puppet)
films by Lotte Reiniger. Address: B.F.I., 81 Dean Street, London, W.C.1.

British Museum. Founded 1753, opened 1759; situated in Great Russell
Street, London, W.C.1. Theatre material in various departments,
including Chinese shadow figures and Raffles Collection of Javanese
shadows in Ethnographical Section; Department of Drawings and Prints
has nine volumes of West's Toy Theatre; rare and diverse items, including
liturgical dramas, religious plays (Chester and York Cycles) in MSS
Department. Reader's Ticket necessary for use of General Library and
Special Departments; comprehensive holdings of English and foreign

puppet books, plays in all languages. Sales section has postcards of
oriental puppets.

British Puppet and Model Theatre Guild. Originally known as the
British Model Theatre Guild (founded 29th April, 1925). Initiative for
formation of the organisation came from H. W. Whanslaw q.v. and
Gerald Morice q.v. and was the outcome of correspondence following
the publication of Whanslaw's book *Everybody's Theatre*, previously a
series of articles on the model theatre, in 'Chatterbox.' About 15 people
attended the founders' meeting held in a small dancing school in Rupert
Street, London, W. Morice became Press Officer and Seymour Marks
the Hon. Secretary. In first five years membership grew to 800. An
exhibition was held in August, 1925, opened by G. K. Chesterton,
mainly of model theatres and a few marionettes; material also loaned to
exhibitions at Oxford and Wembley; in the autumn a room at Harold
Monro's Poetry Bookshop q.v. was loaned for the first monthly meeting.
In January, 1926, what was probably the first public performance with
flat cardboard figures, in *Ali Baba and the Forty Thieves*, was given on a
stage constructed by Waldo Lanchester q.v., 5 in. figures by Whanslaw,
scenes by various members. An exhibition of members' work held that
April was opened by Sir Barry Jackson, and another featuring the
Juvenile Drama of H. J. Webb, opened by Nigel Playfair (who also gave
a broadcast talk on the subject). In 1926 *Notes and News* was published,
occasionally changing its format. Various trophies were presented to the
Guild by generous members. Continental tours arranged by Gerald
Morice were always successful and led to many important contacts with
puppeteers abroad. Finances and headquarters were a problem, the
latter shifting to various parts of the metropolis, including Great Russell
Street, Pimlico Road, the famous George Inn at Southwark, Red Lion
Street (over a dairy) – and Great Ormond Street until the bombing in
1939. A further series of moves have taken place since the end of World
War II. Both before and after the War, exhibitions have been a regular
feature of Guild activities. The first President was Sir Barry Jackson,
followed by Edward Gordon Craig q.v. (who opened an exhibition at
the Players' Theatre in 1930), succeeded by H. W. Whanslaw (until his
death in 1966) and then by Cecil Madden, M.B.E., q.v., who, during a
notable career in B.B.C. Television, had had considerable contact with
Guild puppeteers. The Guild aims are: To encourage the Art and
Practice of Puppetry in all its forms and to foster interest in the Model
Theatre; to improve standards of Production and Performance; to act as
a channel of communication between enthusiasts everywhere, both
Professional and Amateur; membership is open to all who are in sym-
pathy with the objects of the Guild. Facilities include use of the Guild
Library, receipt of Newsletters and the official journal *The Puppet Master;*
frequent meetings, discussion, demonstrations, lectures. Enquiries: Hon.
Secretary, B.P.M.T.G., 90 The Minories, London, E.C.3.

British Puppet Centre. Established 1967 as Department of the Colwyn
Bay (North Wales) Borough Council and housed in an old monastery,
Rhos Fynach; holdings include British and foreign, antique and contemporary puppets, theatres, working models, dioramas. Facilities
include Information Room with up-to-the-minute data on exhibitions,
festivals, conferences, educational courses, etc.; also a puppet shop;
reference library, film library and occasional presentation of puppet
films; lecture-demonstration hall for use of visiting puppeteers; arrange-

ments made for Loan Collections from various sources, beginning with material from Germany. Activities include technical research and practical Courses; first course 'An Expert Approach to Puppetry' (1967), directed by Eric Bramall (Harlequin Puppet Theatre).

British Theatre Museum. Established 1962 at Perrin Gallery, Leighton House, Kensington, London, W. Purpose: centralisation of many scattered collections of theatrical exhibits. Chairman: Viscount Norwich. Meeting called by the Arts Council of Great Britain, at request of the Theatre Research Society, attended by representatives of all branches of theatre – including opera, ballet, circus 'and even puppets' (28th October, 1955). Museum has Trustees and a Constitution; is legally empowered to receive bequests. Formally opened by Vanessa Redgrave, British actress, 18th June, 1963. New acquisitions arrive continually. *Open Tuesdays, Thursdays, Saturdays.* Larger premises will be necessary and a National Museum is envisaged.

Brodie and Middleton, 79 Long Acre, London, W.C.2 (close to Drury Lane): theatrical suppliers. Canvas, scenic colours, sundries; art materials, paints of all types, brushes, plaster fillers, plasticine, aniline dyes, metallic powders. Catalogue available.

Broken Bridge, The. A favourite song of the eighteenth century, 'Sung with applause ... at the Ombres Chinoise' or shadow show. Theme: Old gentleman wishes to cross river via broken bridge; yokel on other side offers only abuse; old gentleman obtains boat, crosses, belabours yokel. Each showman has own variation of the verses. Version discovered by McPharlin appeared in *Puppetry* (Year Book, 1939), reproduced in Blackham *Shadow Puppets* (Barrie and Rockliff, 1960); interesting playbill from Harvard College Library Theatre Collection reproduced in McPharlin *Puppet Theatre in America* (1949).

Browning, Robert (1812–89). English poet, novelist. In *Pippa Passes*, part 4, the much-quoted lines: 'All service ranks the same with God, With God whose puppets best and worst are we.' A Browning *Concordance* gives 15 metaphorical references to puppets in his works; references to actual puppets in *The Ring and the Book*, including the Devil 'armed and accoutred, horns, hoofs and tail.'

Bruin Furryball in the Puppet Theatre, by Trnka-Menzel (Dakers: Artia, 1957). Delightful children's book with coloured illustrations by internationally famous Czech puppet-film maker and book illustrator; the adventures of a little Bear. There are other titles, *Bruin Furryball in his Forest Home, In the Circus, In the Zoo* (same publisher).

Brushes (paint). These are of many types, each designed for a particular class of work, a main distinction being between those intended for use with water-colours and those for oil colours. Provided brushes are used properly and cared for between use, it is usually an economy to buy the more expensive type; relays of cheap brushes which lose their bristle and shape and become unusable, in the long run, cost more. There are flat types, square-ended or filbert, round and pointed, with different lengths of bristle. Those for water-colour, so-called 'camel hair' (squirrel) are useless for oil colours; for oils the sables (more expensive) and white hog hair should be used. The larger the area to be covered the larger the brush; for spots, lines, fine detail in general, brushes which can be given a point. On no account should any brushes be stood on their bristles: once out of shape they are useless. Both water-colour and oil brushes can be cleaned with soap and water (and then thoroughly rinsed), making sure that no paint remains in between the bristles. Oil brushes can be swilled in turps or turps substitute, particularly if being used again with a change of colour. Bristles should be protected when not in use, e.g. wrapped in waxed paper. For scene painting, if large areas to be covered, decorators' brushes can be used.

Brussels (Bruxelles). At one time this Belgian city had many puppet theatres presenting the traditional plays. Théâtre Toone, established 1812, still functions, but at a new address: 21 Petite rue de Bouchers (Impasse Schuddenveld) close to the Grande Place. Present director, 'Toone VII' is well-known puppeteer Joseph Geal, who also presents his own hand puppet show. The traditional marionettes are unusual in that control is from the wings of the stage. During Lent a Passion play is performed, and a Nativity at Christmas. Normally the theatre has performances every evening except Sunday. It has a bar in authentic nineteenth century style.

Buckram. Coarse linen cloth with glue dressing; when wetted can be moulded over a modelled surface (clay, plasticine, etc.) stiff when set. Useful for hat shapes, masks, costume stiffening. Available from craft material suppliers or large drapery departments.

Bufano, Remo (1894–1948). American puppeteer of Italian parentage; producer, publicist, author; Hon. Member of UNIMA (in memoriam); originally performed *Orlando Furioso* in Italian in Sicilian tradition with armoured marionettes; extensive repertoire included folk tales such as *Hansel and Gretel, Rumpelstiltskin, Red Riding Hood*, and Andersen's *Tinder Box*, later adding Molière *Doctor in spite of himself*, de Falla *El retablo de Maese Pedro* (including two life-size figures), Shakespeare *Midsummer Night's Dream*. Built 35-ft. Clown, main figure in Billy Rose production of *Jumbo*. Created 10-ft. figures to design of Robert Edmund Jones and operated from platform 40-ft. up and by ground-level assistants, for production of opera-oratorio *Oedipus Rex* (Stravinsky) sponsored by League of Composers and conducted by Stokowski with Philadelphia Orchestra; made larger than life figures of Walrus and Carpenter for Eve le Gallienne production of *Alice in Wonderland*. *Oedipus Rex* figures now in Brander Matthews Theatre Collection, Columbia University. Author of *Magic Strings* (Macmillan, N.Y., 1929) and *Be a Puppet Showman* (Century Co., 1933).

Buffer. Showman's term for the live Dog Toby q.v. in the Punch and Judy show.

Bührmann, Dr Max. German authority on the Chinese shadow plays, Director of the San Mei Pan Ying Hsi, having studied the Chinese traditional style at first hand, performing with authentic figures. Repertoire includes *The Fight in the Mountains, The Forced Marriage, The Borrowed Umbrella, The White Snake*, and the *White Fox Demon*. Performances given in England on the occasion of the York Festival (1960) and in London at the Unity Theatre. Author of *Das Farbige Schattenspiel*, German text, photo illustrations.

Build Your Own Model Theatre, by Anthony Parker (Stanley Paul, 1959), illustrated by Diana Tull. Although author makes distinction between the 'Toy Theatre' of Pollock's and the design, making and working of *model* theatres, more the concern of the live theatre producer, scenic designer and technicians, it is interesting to note the title of the puppetry

society: British Puppet and Model Theatre Guild (originally British
Model Theatre Guild: 1925), whose concern is with performances.
Technically the book is of interest to both Toy and/or Model Theatre
enthusiasts.

Bulldog clip. Strong metal spring-clip as used in offices for holding
batches of papers; useful addition to puppet stage equipment for temporary fixing of lightweight scenery or props.

Bungoro Yoshida (1870–1962). See **Yoshida Bungoro.**

Bunraku: Japanese Puppet Play. Japan Photo Service Picture Book (Tokyo,
1939). 72 magnificent Leica photos by Yoshio Watanabe. Although a
number of other books on the Bunraku 'three man' puppets have appeared
this is a patricularly valuable item not only for the superb illustrations
but also for the text. Historical introduction is followed by chapters on
training and techniques, writers including two supreme contemporary
performers, Yoshida Eiza q.v. and Yoshida Bungoro, q.v.

Bunraku: the Art of Japanese Puppet Theatre, English text by Donald Keene,
photographs by Kaneko Hiroshi, introduction by Tanazaki Junichiro
(Kodansha International, Japan, in conjunction with Ward Lock,
London, 1950). 360 photographs. Chapters on the Pleasure of the
Bunraku, Art of Bunraku, Texts and Chanters, Samisen and Players,
Puppets and Operators, Gestures of Bunraku; list of plays, chronology
and short bibliography; actual recordings and music score. Important
account of the theatre with unique 'three man' puppets.

Bunraku-za. A Japanese puppet theatre in Osaka, with a unique performing technique, the main characters each requiring three manipulators, a fourth performer at one side of the stage narrating the story and
providing all the dialogue, while a fifth provides dramatic music from a
three-string instrument, the samisen, q.v. The name Bunraku is derived
from that of a theatre proprietor in Osaka, Uemura-Bunrakuken, who
made a puppet 'come back' in 1789 after the Kabuki (live theatre) had
borrowed both repertoire and techniques from the puppet theatre and
taken away its audiences. 'Bunraku' has become colloquial for 'puppet'
– but this is technically incorrect, the three-man style with narration and
music being known as 'ningyo-joruri' (ningyo: doll; puppet; joruri: an
earlier folk-art form of narration with music). Japan today has, in fact,
puppet companies which use hand puppets, rod puppets, string puppets
(marionettes). The joruri, q.v. narrator-singer is also known as 'Gidayu',
after the name of the most famous performer of his period, Takemoto
Gidayu (1651–1714). The original success of ningyo-joruri came about
through a remarkable coincidence: the appearance of a playwright who
came to be known as 'the Japanese Shakespeare' – Chikamatsu Monzaemon q.v. (1653–1724), who wrote over a hundred pieces for the puppet
theatre, many of which are still played and which were also borrowed
by the live-actor theatres – the refinement of the joruri by Gidayu, and
the development of the three-man puppet over a period of about 30 years.
A new 'convention' came into being, of having the performers in view
of the audience, with a stage front of knee height. The chief manipulator
wears ceremonial costume with wing-like shoulder pieces, the two
assistants are clad in black from head to foot, with a gauze mask over the
eyes. The chief operator holds the puppet in front of his chest by his left
hand, which enters the back of the figure and controls head movements
(also eyes, eyebrows, mouth) by a short rod and strings; the first assistant
controls the left arm; the second assistant, kneeling, is in charge of the

feet, or, in the case of female characters (legless) of the skirt movements which simulate walking, etc. The leading manipulator wears high footwear (hollow, silent) so that No. 3 does not have to lie flat while operating. The three must work as one, which involves years of training. The puppets are from three to five feet in height, weigh up to 30 lb., have highly stylised heads (mask-like) which are small in relation to the overall size – and are works of art in their own right. The head pivots in a shoulder-piece which supports the costume and from which tapes hang and are attached to a hoop at the waist-line. Operators graduate over many years, from the feet of the puppet, to the left arm, and eventually to the master role. Some performers specialise in the playing of female roles, as did Yoshida Bungoro, q.v., who died at the age of 92, almost blind, after performing for 77 years. Shutaro Miyake, in an article on the training of the Bunraku puppeteer (*World Theatre*, October, 1965) expressed the hope that some 'genius' would evolve a method of training whereby manipulation can be mastered 'scientifically' in a relatively short term. With American and European tours in recent years there are already signs of influence among Western puppet companies, variations on the Bunraku technique being developed, and it will be interesting to see if the West can produce the 'genius' which 300 years or so of Japanese experience has not succeeded in doing. See *Bunraku: Japanese Puppet Play; Bunraku: the Art of the Japanese Puppet Theatre; Puppet Theater of Japan.*

Bunyan, John (1628–88). English author whose *Pilgrim's Progress* q.v. has had various puppet productions, including version in Welsh by the Caricature Theatre, Cardiff.

Burlesque. An item (play, sketch) which parodies another – or any light satirical item. Puppets can be very successful in this genre, as the figures themselves can have a satirical quality, e.g. an ostrich which burlesques a prima donna who is past her prime. There can be a danger of unintentional burlesque, e.g. if a badly handled marionette is supposed to be Pavlova or some other great ballerina.

Burattino. Italian: hand puppet (plural: burattini). Etymology uncertain; some Italian-English dictionaries give translation as 'puppet *or* marionette.' P. C. Ferrigni gives his history the title *Storia dei Burattini* (History of Puppets, in the generic sense), but in the text stresses the difference between 'burattino' as the hand type and 'FANTOCCINO' as the marionette (string puppet); he sees the origin of the word in a type of cheap coarse cloth used for sifting flour, relating this to the cloth body or costume of the hand puppet. Ferrigni also states that the term was in use *before* the character of the same name appeared in the commedia dell' arte, q.v. performances. Duchartre, in *The Italian Comedy* (originally Harrap, 1929, now available in Dover Publications edition, 1966) maintains that Burattino was first one of the commedia 'masks' and later became the leading character in the *marionette* theatre and that by the end of the sixteenth century all marionettes operated by strings and a wire were called burattini 'instead of bagatelli or fantoccini' as previously. The contemporary Italian puppeteer Maria Signorelli, in an article in *Puppet Theatre Around the World* (New Delhi, 1960), states that her burattini are 'without strings and without complicated accessories, to which only the hand of the puppet player could give movement or life.' The 'Italian Fantoccini' – specifically marionettes – had a run of popularity in London in the nineteenth century.

Burmese puppets. Marionette type requiring up to 60 strings; high standard of production influenced human dance-drama. Developed in late eighteenth century with possible Indian or Chinese influences, by U Thaw, Minister of Royal Entertainments at the Court of King Siegu. Treated as a serious art, chief source of plays being the 550 'jatakas' or birth-stories of Buddha. Traditional show has 28 characters: votaresses, elephants (black and white), monkey, horse, parrot, tiger, various ogres, a yogi, king, prince, ministers, astrologer, hermit and clowns. Shows given on bamboo platform, operators behind a curtain. Stage set with court scene one side and other as forest, reminiscent of the type seen in Ceylon.

Business. Term for the incidental actions of stage characters, such as arranging flowers in a vase, playing with a monocle, lighting a pipe; may be straightforward or comic. In a hand puppet show the stage 'business' is largely a matter of handling props – a watering-can, fishing rod – or, in the Punch show, the game with the row of bodies which change places while Punch is resting. Like so many of the showmen's terms, it is impossible to pin-point the origin, or, rather the new use of an existing word which may have several other meanings.

Buskins. Special footwear for increasing height of actors. Small terra-cotta figures and a famous ivory statuette from Rieti, now in Paris, show actors raised six to seven inches. Chief operator of the three-man puppet in Japanese Bunraku q.v. theatre uses similar device to increase height so that operator of the feet can kneel conveniently; contemporary European performers, e.g. in Moscow Central Puppet Theatre, use a variation of this, made of cork, when actors using hand or rod puppets are of mixed heights. Term 'clog' or 'patten' also used.

Bussell, Jan. English puppeteer, co-director (with wife Ann Hogarth) of The Hogarth Puppets, established 1932; Praesidium member of UNIMA q.v. and elected its President in 1968. B.B.C. Television producer 1937–48. Author of *The Puppet Theatre* (Faber, 1947), constructional; *The Puppets and I* (Faber, 1950), autobiographical; *Plays for Puppets* (Faber, 1951), Editor; *Puppets Progress* (Faber, 1953), autobiographical and travel; *Through Wooden Eyes* (Faber, 1956), autobiographical and travel; *The Art of Television* (Faber, 1952), theory; *Twelve Plays* (Pelham Puppets, 1963), original puppet plays; *The Pegasus Book of Puppets* (Dobson, 1968), constructional.

C

Cabaret puppets. Usually solo marionette items without formal stage or scenery, performer and puppet sharing same floor space, spotlight on puppet, artiste in evening dress or all black costume. Probable originator of this genre American puppeteer Frank Paris, who toured night clubs with his *Stars on Strings;* Bob Bromley, also from the United States, appeared with floor show in English and German theatres; Eric Bramall, director of the *Harlequin* Puppet Theatre in North Wales, is well known to British audiences; Heather and Martin Granger, an English man-and-wife team have played in Paris and elsewhere; in Germany Albrecht Roser successful performer in this style. Polished, slick presentation is vital ingredient of such acts. Cabaret shows using shadow figures were a feature of the *Chat Noir* q.v. in Paris in nineteenth century.

Calendar. Special issues of the UNIMA Bulletin (issued by the Union Internationale de la Marionnette, q.v., Prague) consisting of a list of names of puppet notables past and present, arranged by date of birth; includes puppeteers, dramatists, music composers, authors; issued in English and French (No. 1, 1962).

Calico, unbleached. Ideal material for cloth bodies for hand puppets, protective bags, etc. Available in variety of widths.

Caliph Stork, by Wilhelm Hauff, adapted for marionette play by Ursula am Bühl. Theme: magician changes Caliph and his Grand Vizier into storks as punishment for over-curiosity; Indian princess (turned into Owl) obliges Caliph to marry her in payment for secret word to remove spell. Productions by Zurich Marionette Theatre and Salzburg Marionette Theatre, and others.

Cambodia (S.Asia). Shadow puppet performances similar to those of the *Nang* q.v. in Thailand; perforated hide with fine filigree effect, character or characters in framework of scenery (no individual action), light from fire or candles, operators dancing during performance, figures controlled by rods; traditional instrumental music and narration; performances mostly limited to special occasions such as cremation ceremony of important person or birthday of high official.

Cane. Thin round or flat varieties as used in basketry can be used for lightweight framework constructions for rod-puppet torso and small stage-props such as bird-cage, shopping basket, carpet-beater. Thin round or split garden canes useful, with stiff wire extensions, as controls for rod or shadow puppets.

Čapek, Dr Karel (1890–1939). Czech dramatist, poet, essayist, and brother **Josef Čapek** (1887–1927), painter, illustrator, collaborated on *The Insect Play: or the World we Live in,* satirical comedy in which characters are a Man, Ants, Beetles and Butterflies, with a satirical theme. Ideal for and frequently adapted for puppet production. Earlier satire: *R.U.R.* (Rossom's Universal Robots) on the machine age.

Caran d'Ache (Emmanuel Poire: 1858–1909). French book illustrator and caricaturist born in Moscow, contributor to various periodicals and early exponent of the strip-cartoon (name is French version of 'karandash': pencil, crayon). Collaborated with other artists in presenting shadow-figure shows at the famous Chat Noir, q.v., including 1808! on themes related to Napoleon's campaigns (described in Blackham *Shadow Puppets*, q.v.).

Cardano, Girolamo (1501–76). Italian physician, mathematician, philosopher, author; credited with the discovery of 'the formula for the resolution of cubic equations' and a 'system of suspension in a double concentric circle' – yet was unable to comprehend the range of action produced by a single horizontal string running from the knee of a puppeteer and through the chest of a small puppet (or puppets) to a short post at the end of a plank (marionettes à la planchette) q.v. described in his *De Vanitate Rerum* (1557). In *De Subtilate Rerum* (1551) he mentions marionettes that fought, danced, played dice and could blow trumpets – but apparently was more impressed by the effects achieved with a single string. (Cited in Magnin *Histoire des marionnettes en Europe*, 1852.)

Cardboard. Versatile material in a variety of forms: flat sheet of various thicknesses, boxes, tubular shapes of many diameters, cheese boxes, etc. Construction possibilities both for simple forms of head-making (school or stylised professional) and for décor. Two-piece tubular heads with one section sliding up and down over the other, giving a moving mouth effect (section cut away), with hand and rod controls (internal) and second operator with live hands or rod-controlled plastic foam, wood, or stuffed hands, used in large hand or rod stage. Corrugated card can be bent into curved shapes for scenic effects or for making fantastic monsters. Thin stiff card used for cut-out figures for shadow puppets. Cereal carton can be used for toy theatre figures (as mounting for printed figures). Yves Joly in France has used Bristol board quality in his *Paper Tragedy* item, new figures being required for every performance: one having been cut in half by villain with large pair of scissors, the other gone up in smoke and leaving only ashes.

Caricature Theatre Company (Theatr bypedau caerdydd). Formed 1966 as non-profit distributing company registered as a Charity. Director: Jane Phillips (Wales). Company includes professional actors, artists, teachers: average age 25. Company plays in Welsh and English; some teachers of Art, Speech, Drama, Dancing, some from Children's Theatres, Welsh B.B.C., Welsh National Theatre. Team work involves performing, script-writing, voice-recording, ballet choreography, lighting schemes, wardrobe maintenance, clerical work. Company has had four designers, including John Blundall (stage, television, puppet theatre designer), Jane Phillips (puppeteer), Marion Davies (art teacher) and Graeme Galvin (graphic artist, with puppet background). Productions include: *Culhwch and Olwen*, *Peter and the Wolf*, and T.V. version of *The Lady of the Lake* (part of Teaching Welsh series); a ballet based on *Goldilocks and the Three Bears*; *The Pilgrim's Progress*; *The Tinder Box*. *Caricatures*, a collection of dances and mimes by Jane Phillips.

Caricature Theatre Ltd. A registered non-profit distributing company (1966), assisted by financial aid from Welsh Committee of the Arts Council and Arthur Phillips; originally touring company with six actors, designer, director. Repertoire includes *Culhwch and Olwen* (Welsh legend), *Peter and the Wolf* (Prokofiev) and *Caricatures* (Jane Phillips); *Goldilocks and the Three Bears* (as a ballet), *L'Enfant et les Sortileges* (Ravel-Colette), *Pilgrim's Progress* (Bunyan) and *The Tinder Box* (Andersen). Productions planned: *The Rose and the Ring* (Thackeray), *The Happy Hypocrite* (Beerbohm) and a Welsh programme based on Welsh nursery rhymes (commissioned by National Eisteddfod in Barry). Company tours for Cardiff, Glamorgan and Monmouthshire Education authorities, schools and colleges. Performances at the Midlands Arts Centre, Liverpool; Bluecoat Arts Forum, Durham, and Caerphilly Festivals, and at two international puppet festivals (Brunswick and Munich, Germany). *Pilgrim's Progress* commissioned by Welsh National Theatre Company for the Royal National Eisteddfod in Bala. Tour of Welsh Music Clubs, for Arts

Council; Christmas season at Belgrade Theatre, Coventry (for children). Participation in 2nd international puppet festival at Colwyn Bay (1968). Ambition: to establish permanent puppet theatre in Cardiff.

Carnival of Animals (Carnaval des Animaux), by Camille Saint-Saëns (1835–1921); orchestral suite for unusual combination of instruments and written as a 'musical joke', some items humorous but including the well-known *Dying Swan*, made famous by Russian ballerina Pavlova, in whose memory the Salzburg Marionette Theatre created a special item for their repertoire. Some items make ideal material for shadow figures. Columbia and other recordings available.

Carr, John, O.B.E. Director of Jacquard Puppets (Great Britain), Vice-President of British Puppet and Model Theatre Guild; took part in first Guild television appearance at Alexandra Palace (1937). Repertoire includes *St George and the Dragon* (hand puppets), *Moth Ballet* (marionettes), *Peter and the Wolf*, Prokofiev musical fairy tale (marionettes).

Carroll, Lewis (1832–1898). Pen-name of Charles Lutwidge Dodgson, author of *Alice in Wonderland*, q.v., which has inspired many puppet productions.

Carving. To shape by cutting away material from block larger than shape envisaged: in contrast with modelling, building up shape. One of oldest crafts known to man. Traditionally wood was the medium, where readily available, as with the great toy-making industry in parts of Germany in the Middle Ages; craft carried over into puppet making. Most carvers will not use other methods. One form of carving, done mostly with the knife, is known as whittling: the Swiss surrealist puppeteer Schneckenburger made all his first puppets with a pocket knife. Craft skills can only be learned by experiment with tools and materials even if an apprenticeship can be served with a professional carver. First requirement is to obtain a knowledge of tools and how to keep them in good cutting condition; woods have their different cutting qualities, traditionally being local varieties. Puppet makers have individual approaches to the work: some will design on paper, transfer outlines to the block of wood, others will make a plasticine model first and keep this alongside as the cutting proceeds, and others work straight on the wood with no preliminaries except a mental visualising of 'the shape concealed in the wood.' There are many books on woodcarving but, as with puppet manipulation, no book can show movements. Contemporary carving includes use of polystyrene (styrofoam) using heat-gun, craft knife and various unconventional tools such as bread knife or old files hotted up in a gas-jet. Foamed plastic is available in block form and is cut with scissors, razor blade, craft knife. Carver to the Salzburg Marionette Theatre, Joseph Magnus, working with wood, outlines *groups* of heads on single blocks, to ensure correct relation of size. Book on carving by a puppeteer: John Wright, *Your Puppetry* (Sylvan Press, 1951), q.v.

Casein. Skimmed milk product used as binding medium in decorator's water paints and in various proprietary adhesives.

Caspar and his Friends, by Hans Baumann (Dent, 1967; Ensslin and Laiblin Verlag, 1965). English translation by Joyce Emerson, Foreword by George Speaight, Illustrations by Wanda Zacharias. Ten puppet plays for professional or amateur; brief episodes in which the traditional German cousin of Punch takes the leading role (Kaspar, Kasperl). Traditionally, too, the audience always becomes involved, and such a character has many classroom possibilities for the teacher. In these lively little plays the hero's friends are birds and animals and even inanimate objects such as brooms and signposts. There are some hints on performing. There are no performing fees.

Castelet, castelette. French variants of Italian CASTELLO.

Castello. Italian term for hand-puppet booth; illustration in Flemish medieval ms. *Li Romans du bon Roi Alexandre* q.v., by Jehan de Grise, shows the type that probably gave the name, having castellated towers at sides of stage. Fine full-page colour reproduction of the illustration in Baird *Art of the Puppet* (Collier-Macmillan, 1965). French variant: castelet, castelette.

Castlemayne, Lady (1641–1704). Barbara Villiers, Duchess of Cleveland, mistress of Charles II of England, married Roger Palmer, who became Earl of Castlemayne. The entry for 30th August, 1667, in Pepy's *Diary* noted her attendance at a puppet play *Patient Grizill*, q.v., at Bartholomew Fair, and a crowd waiting to see her come out.

Casting. (1) In the theatrical sense: selecting actors or actresses for particular roles; (2) making a mould (casing) of Plaster of Paris or other material, from a clay or plasticine model, removing the model, then building up the finished head (or other object) inside the mould, removing when set. The mould can be used many times if necessary, giving replicas of the original model.

Catalan puppet. Type of hand puppet peculiar to Catalonia, N.E. Spain, using a five-finger technique, three in the wooden shoulder-piece (carved in one piece with head) and thumb and fifth finger in the arms (which have thin metal tube extensions with fitted carved hands). Hands sometimes interchangeable: for instance if a sword fight is to take place. Stout cloth underbody connects shoulders and arms; costumes interchangeable between scenes. The main character is known as Putxinellis, Catalan variant of Pulcinello, which is also the source of the English Punch. Other traditional characters include Titella, Cristofel, Cristeta and la Cascarria, and a Devil (el dimoni): Cristeta is the heroine. Because of the method of construction the figures are larger which gives good viewing to a big audience.

Catalyst. Subject which changes physical state of another substance without itself undergoing change. Used with polyester resin.

Cats. The play of *Richard Whittington* was a favourite with early English puppet-showmen; no details as to cat, live or puppet. Cats (live) favourites with French showmen in eighteenth and nineteenth centuries: Baird *Art of the Puppet* (Collier-Macmillan, 1965) has colour reproduction showing Polichinelle in Punch-type booth with 'dog' on the playboard: anatomically it is a cat. Puppet cats have appeared in all types: hand, rod, marionette, shadow figure. A magician is turned into a cat in *The Magic Gloves*, hand puppet play by Violet Philpott, the slim glossy black cat being already on the hand inside the Magician, for quick transformation. Cat is one of the four animals in Grimm's *Musicians of Bremen Town*. Domestic scenes such as Cinderella's kitchen are natural habitats for cats. Cats have appeared in puppet films: *Puss in Boots*, a Lotte Reiniger silhouette film, and a German puppet film for young children (*c.* 1938).

Celastic. Trade term for cotton flannel impregnated with long-life plastic (fire-retardant); softened by saturation with solvent (acetone) becoming plastic for shaping, setting hard in half an hour. Industrial use: foundry pattern repairs; widely used in United States for puppet-making, usually in mould made from plasticine model, but can be used direct over model (necessary to use 'parting agent' to prevent Celastic sticking to model or inside of mould). Result: light, strong, practically unbreakable. Sandpapers well and can be painted. Essential to work in well-ventilated room. Can be used over plastic wood or polystyrene (styrofoam) as a toughener, without adding weight. A special solvent has been developed for use with polystyrene. Technique described in detail in: Creegan, *St George's Book of Hand Puppetry* (Follett, Chicago, 1966); chapter in Merten *The Hand Puppets* (Nelson, 1957). USA suppliers: Creegan Distribution Co., 273 Belleview Boulevard, Steubenville. UK suppliers: Adrian Marchant Ltd., Surbiton Studios, Brittania Road, Surbiton Surrey.

Celastoid. Trade term for non-flam cellulose acetate substitute for celluloid.

Cellulose acetate. Plastic product made by treatment of cellulose with acetic acid and other ingredients. Available in wide range of colours and non-flammable variety. Widely used as packaging material and as photographic film. Possibilities in shadow puppetry.

Cement. Originally term for builder's mortar but used widely for adhesives or bonding agents for joining wood and other materials. Supplied in tubes and tins.

Cervantes Saavedra, Miguel de (1547–1616). Foremost Spanish author. *Don Quixote* (*El ingenioso hidalgo Don Quijote de la Mancha:* 1605–12) tells of a knight-errant's fantasy world, a satire on romances of chivalry. Episode in which knight sees a puppet-show and draws his own sword to go into the attack inspired de Falla's music for *El retablo de Maese Pedro* (*Master Peter's Puppet Show*), which has had many puppet productions. Baird *Art of the Puppet* (Collier-Macmillan, 1965) has an interesting reproduction of a sketch by artist Gustave Doré, giving an impression of the scene, showing the hands of the performers manipulating marionettes by means of short strings with wire loops over fingers, Don Quixote and other spectators, the fighting figures and a number of decapitated heads. A hand puppet version was produced by Dr Jan Malik, Czech puppeteer and Director of the Central Puppet Theatre in Prague. Various English editions for those wishing to make original playscripts.

Ceylon. Traditional marionettes probably derived from Indian sources, some being technically related to those of Rajasthan. Tilakasiri *Puppetry in Ceylon* gives the term *rukada* (from Sanskrit 'rupa' and 'khanda') which originally meant 'miniature figure' or 'replica' or 'doll' – but now used exclusively for *puppet*. As in many other countries, references in early literature are sometimes confusing and may mean mechanically operated statues. Characters in plays, as in India, come from Hindu mythology with familiar gods and goddesses. Traditional puppets are of carved wood (local variety known as *kaduru*, which is light-weight and easy to carve). Performers were divided into two groups: operators, speakers, calling for skill in co-ordinating and synchronising speech and action. Stage usually improvised from portable screens and curtains and divided into three acting areas, main scenes occupying the centre, minor scenes at two sides. Manipulation is from a bridge which is 'masked' by black screens.

Traditional marionettes averaged 4-ft. in height. Some official support is now given to developments, including the introduction of hand puppets for school use. Jayadeva Tilakasiri, lecturer in Sanskrit at the Peradeniya University, in co-operation with the Arts Council of Ceylon and the Cultural Ministry has provided main stimulus to contemporary developments. His book was published by the Department of Cultural Affairs, in the Art of Ceylon series, No. 1, 1961.

Chair of Puppetry. Theatre Faculty of Academy of Arts, Prague, Czechoslovakia, has established a Chair of Puppetry and a School (opened 1959) for training of young professional actors, directors, set-designers, lighting technicians and writers; four-year course; students receive educational grants. Director: Dr Erik Kolar.

Chambers, Robert (1802–71). English author, co-founder with brother William of publishing house; established *Chamber's Journal* (1832); compiled *Book of Days*, an antiquarian miscellany (1862–64) which has puppet references.

Chansons de geste. Old French epics, Songs of Deeds', of which the earliest and most famous is the *Song of Roland* q.v., written about the end of the eleventh century and concerning a military disaster of the year 778 (Charlemagne, q.v.). This has been the source of various puppet episodes in the traditional theatres of the North of France and Belgium: the repertoire of one company in Liége (listed in Gervais *Marionnettes et Marionnettistes de France*, Bordas, 1947) has 40 chansons, including *Aucassin and Nicolette*, q.v. (which has been produced by the Hogarth Puppets, q.v.). In Italy Roland became Orlando, e.g. *Orlando Furioso (Orlando Mad)* by Lodovico Ariosto, q.v. (1473–1533), which is still source of serial plays in the Sicilian puppet theatres. There is a relationship between the types of puppets, all using a rod control from above (in some cases from the side)

Chap Book. Small books containing fairy tales, ballads, etc., sold by 'chapmen' – itinerant traders. An enquiry in *Notes and Queries* (15th November, 1862) asked where a chap book 'containing the patter of the peripatetic Punch' could be obtained. Reply (13th December, 1862) publishers W. J. Reid of Charing Cross, 3rd edition, illustrations by Cruikshank: 'the volume is scarce' – evidently an edition of the Payne Collier *Punch and Judy* q.v. A modern example, the series issued by the Poetry Bookshop, of which No. 20 was by Gordon Craig, q.v. *Puppets and Poets*.

Chapman, J. Vincent, F.C.P., Secretary of the College of Preceptors, Bloomsbury Square, London, W.C.1; President and one-time General Secretary of the Educational Puppetry Association, which has its headquarters in the basement of the College. One of the leading spirits in the early developments of puppetry in education and the various activities of the Association. In 1963 made it possible for the first Praesidium meeting of UNIMA (the international puppetry organisation) to be held in London, at the College, which is centrally situated. College also the venue for many years of the E.P.A. Schools Puppetry Festivals.

Characterisation. Art of conveying to an audience the personality of character portrayed, a total effect of physique, make-up, costume, speech, manner of moving, reactions to other characters. With puppets many of these elements are built into the puppet, but it still requires sensitive manipulation and an identification with the character by the performer.

D

Charing Cross. Best known today as London's terminus for the Southern Railway, but at one time a site for puppet shows, as recorded by Pepys in his *Diary* entry for 20th March, 1667 (when he took his wife to see 'Polichinelli' – which was 'prettier and prettier' and 'extraordinary good entertainment') and in an entry in the Overseers Books, St Martin's in the Fields, 29th March, 1666, 'Rec. of Punchinello, ye Italian popet-player for his booth at Charing Crosse £2.12.6.' On the occasion of some London festival there should be a celebration performance, as there was at the famous site in Covent Garden for the Punch Tercentenary q.v. – but not during the rush hour.

Charivari Puppets. Director Violet Philpott (London) q.v. Experiments with hand puppets, large scale rod and shadow types. Performances in Arts Theatre, Toynbee Theatre, Stanhope Evening Institute. Note: 'Charivari' is French term for burlesque serenade in which music is produced from domestic pots and pans. *Punch* the English periodical, had 'The London Charivari' as sub-title on its first issue (1841), deriving this from satirical Parisian periodical by Charles Philipon and suppressed by Napoleon. An illustration 'Costume de Polichinelle' from *Charivari* (1833) is reproduced in Maindron *Marionettes et guignols* (1900).

Charlemagne (*c.* 742–814). Emperor (King) of the Pranks devoted life to defence and expansion of Christianity; led expedition against Arabs in Spain (778) and disaster due to treachery recorded in various chronicles. The French epic *Song of Roland*, one of the 'chansons de geste' or 'songs of deeds', describes death of Roland, a Duke from Brittany, in the incident. Story has provided basis for folk-puppet plays in France, Belgium and Sicily (where Roland becomes Orlando). English translaton of the *Song* available in Penguin Classics.

Chat Noir, Le. A cafe-club in the rue Victor Masse in Paris with an artistic clientele (writers, artists, artisans of Montmartre) which became famous for its shadow-theatre in the period 1887–97, and had many imitators. The club was run by Rodolphe Salis, with informal entertainment sessions by poets and authors; a Guignol (hand puppet) theatre was introduced, and the painter Henri Riviere converted this into a shadow show by fixing a serviette across the proscenium and displaying a cut-out silhouette against this. A great deal of experiment followed. Large figures were cut from zinc instead of card, but with little individual animation. Elaborate lighting effects were contrived. Other artists, such as Caran d'Ache, became involved, perspective and 'depth' effects were evolved – and even 'white shadows' (ombres blanches) obtained by cutting figures out of black grounds. Programmes were a mixture of poetical, satirical and humorous items. Some 40 productions were devised in the ten years of the club's existence.

Chaucer, Geoffrey (*c.* 1340–1400). English poet, author of the *Canterbury Tales;* in *Prologue to Sir Thopas* and *The Miller's Tale* the words 'popelote' and 'popet' occur, former from Old French 'poupelet': pet, doll, darling; 'popet' from 'poupée, = puppet, dainty little person, related to twentieth century usage 'my poppet.' No clear documentary proof of actual puppets brought over by French minstrels in thirteenth century. Term 'puppet' (and variants) often had meaning of *doll* rather than *puppet:* context does not always clarify. The term 'baby' often had similar meaning.

Chekhov, Anton Pavlovich (1860–1904). Russian dramatist and short-story writer; closely associated with the Moscow Arts Theatre. Some of his farces, such as *The Bear, The Wedding,* have had a number of puppet productions; English puppeteer Olive Blackham q.v. produced *The Proposal;* the Central Puppet Theatre, Prague, adapted *A Complicated Story;* the Chinese Art Puppet Theatre produced *The Chameleon.* Trnka q.v., the famous Czech puppet-film maker, based *The Story of the Double Bass* on one of the stories.

Chesnais, Jacques. French puppeteer who has toured extensively with his 'Comédiens de Bois'; author of *Histoire Générale des Marionnettes* (1947); contributor of important article on African Puppets to *World Theatre* (October, 1965). Has notable item using modernist rod puppets *The Boxers* (ballet) q.v.

Chesterton, Gilbert Keith (1874–1936). English journalist ('G.K.') and short story writer (*Father Brown* series); Toy Theatre enthusiast. 'My toy theatre is as philosophical as the dream of Athens' (*Tremendous Trifles* 1909), adding that very big ideas could be represented in very small spaces. Early association with the British Puppet and Model Theatre Guild.

Chignolo. Small town in Lombardy from which the French national puppet 'Guignol' q.v. may have derived name.

Chikamatsu Monzaemon (1653–1724). Japanese playwright (pseudonym of Sugimori Nobumori) usually known as the 'Shakespeare' of Japan; wrote over a hundred plays for the puppet theatre, tragedies and domestic dramas inspired by feudal conditions; many of the plays were taken over by the live-theatre (Kabuki) and have remained in the repertoire of both forms. Takemoto Gidayu (1650–1714) outstanding performer of joruri (ballad narration with samisen q.v. accompaniment) produced a number of the plays, and new technical developments of the puppets began in the same period, leading to a 'golden age' of puppetry. Gidayu's name became synonymous with joruri. There is an interesting chapter on the puppet theatre and on Chikamatsu's understanding of the requirements of the successful puppet play in Keene *Japanese Literature* (Murray, 1953) – an introduction for Western readers – 'the texts must be live and full of action.' Synopses of four of the plays (and some by other playwrights) are contained in A. C. Scott *The Puppet Theatre of Japan* (Tuttle, 1963). Keene translated *Four Major Plays of Chikamatsu,* published by Columbia University Press, 1960.

Children's libraries. Public libraries today are more than places for borrowing books or using the reference sections; ideally they are cultural centres. Many children's libraries now introduce puppetry into the autumn and winter evening programmes of talks and demonstrations; some of the modern libraries have their own theatres. Usually there is co-operation with local schools; an entertainment with a demonstration of puppet-making and some impromptu performing by the children not only helps to stimulate an active interest in puppetry at school and in the home but also leads to research in books on techniques, costume, design, etc. One London library gave its children facilities during the summer vacation to prepare their own show, with a professional puppeteer available for discussion on technical problems, culminating in a well-attended performance. In Australia the Children's Library and Crafts Movement is well established, with a policy of encouraging constructive play and artistic creation – including painting, clay modelling, woodwork and puppetry.

Children's Theatre. *The Oxford Companion to the Theatre* (OUP 3rd edition, 1967) includes 'and puppeteers' in its definition; *Children's Theatre*, by Davis, Watkins and Busfield (Harper, N.Y., 1960) addressed to 'serious workers and students of the modern children's theatre' does not concern itself with what is especially a branch of *children's* theatre (as well as, many now think, of the adult theatre also). In Czechoslovakia the 'live' and the puppet theatres are on an equal footing, by Law. Children's theatre is concerned with plays (or other material) produced and presented to child audiences; there are professional and amateur companies, some with their own theatre buildings, nearly all mobile and performing in schools. 'Child Drama' concerns acting *by* children, for its own sake and not for audiences. There are more and more conferences at which children's theatre is discussed and demonstrated. There is a British Children's Theatre Association and an international association. In the formulating of the Constitution of the latter there was consultation with UNIMA, the international puppetry organisation. Some children's theatres have begun to include puppet items in their repertoire; the Unicorn Theatre Club, operating at the Arts Theatre in London, has had guest performers. From the children's viewpoint, the puppet show is undoubtedly a branch of theatre to be accepted as readily as that of the live actors; there is no real rivalry, but there are good and bad productions in both realms.

China. There is a tradition that Chinese puppetry originated in the Han Dynasty (206 B.C. – 220 A.D.). Marionettes were already flourishing by the middle of the eighth century A.D. – but exact origins are as obscure as elsewhere. An article in *China Features*, by Lin Shih, mentions three branches of puppetry known in ancient times but of which almost nothing specific is now known: 'chemical puppets' – of which only the name has survived – 'water puppets', probably related to those of Vietnam (on which an article appeared in *Puppet Theatre Around the World* (Bharatiya Natya Sangh New Delhi, 1960) – and 'living puppets', which were possibly children acting as puppets, supported on adult shoulders. A Chinese painting on silk, of the sixteenth – seventeenth century, *The Hundred Children*, shows small children performing with marionettes on a low table or platform, using the paddle shape control (British Museum has postcard reproduction), the style being that of the modern 'open stage' (without proscenium). This is also reproduced in Baird *Art of the Puppet* (Collier-Macmillan, 1965), together with fine whole-page colour reproductions of the better known shadow figures. Obraztsov the Russian puppetmaster visited China, wrote a book on its theatre, of which the section on puppets has been translated into English (*Chinese Puppet Theatre*, Faber, 1961) and has 37 photo-illustrations: he was impressed by the skill of the performers with various types of puppet. A one-man street puppet theatre consisting of a curtain reaching to the ground (or, in some illustrations, tied in around the performer's ankles, has a decorative roof and backcloth with exits; this is partially supported by the pole on which it is carried from site to site, and partly by wall or fence. Like the USSR, the New China has its cultural developments, including puppets of all kinds. The Chuanchow Marionette Theatre, known throughout China for its performances, has a repertoire of both traditional and contemporary plays. Training of the puppeteers begins at about 13 years of age and lasts six years. The marionettes can take up a brush and write, drink from a cup, use a fan, draw a sword from its sheath and return it, mount and dismount a horse, practice fencing and, in the modern items, jump on to bicycles, shoot, carry out bayonet practice, perform folk dances – the heroes being workers, peasants, soldiers. Each marionette has 20 or more strings; a juggling elephant has 32 and can balance a basket of peaches on its trunk, toss and catch it, toss it on to its head. The marionette control requires use of all fingers. The Chuanchow company (formed in 1952) has over 800 traditional items in its repertoire. In Fukien there are rod and hand puppets as well as marionettes. National festivals of puppetry were held in 1955 and 1960, including the highly developed shadow shows. It is only this type which has any real technical information in English: *Chinese Shadow-figure Plays and their making*, by Benjamin March (Puppetry Imprints, Detroit, 1938). The Field Museum of Natural History, Chicago, has a collection of some 1000 shadow figures acquired in 1901; there is some material in *Oriental Theatricals*, by Dr Laufer, who made the collection which includes scripts and sound recordings. There is a case of shadow-figures in the Ethographic Department of the British Museum.

Chinese Puppet Theatre, by Sergei Obraztsov (Faber, 1961), translation from Russian by J. T. McDermot; part of larger work on Chinese Theatre and first hand study by Soviet puppetmaster; 37 illustrations from photographs. Interesting notes on 'powder puppets', 'floating puppets' and use of the 'U-dyu-dyu' or Chinese equivalent of the English 'swazzle' used for the Punch voice; mentions marionettes with 20 to 40 strings, moving eyes, moving eyebrows, jaws and fingers. Important contribution to literature on subject.

Chinese Shades. The Victorian English showman's term for the French 'ombres chinoises' or shadow show. This had little in common with the original Chinese show with its delicately designed and coloured figures, and followed the style of the French silhouettes. A detailed account of a performance given in the street at night with a white cloth screen stretched across the proscenium of a Punch and Judy stage, was contained in Mayhew's *London Labour and London Poor* (1852). He was told by the showman that the proper name was 'Lez hombres' – having been so told by a Baron Rothschild, for whom he had performed – but that the showmen called it the 'Chinese galantee show.' The light was provided by candles. This particular showman stood in front of the stage and did the speaking; he also played music on the 'pandean pipes.' The dialogue required four different voices. Shows were also given at private parties, lasted about an hour and a quarter, for which the payment was a pound. On the 'effect' of fire: 'It's a dangerous concern the fire is, for it's done with a little bit of the snuff off a candle, and if you don't mind you go alight.' Spring Books have reprinted selections from Mayhew, edited by Peter Quennell, this interview being included in *Mayhew's Characters*. The text of a Punch show is given in *Mayhew's London* (1949). For an account of the French 'ombres' see Blackham *Shadow Puppets* (Barrie and Rockliff, 1960), which also contains a copy of 'A Favorite Song' which is 'sung with applause' in the *Broken Bridge*, one of the favourite items of the Ombres Chinoises.

Chinese Shadow-figure Plays and their Making, by Benjamin March (Puppetry Handbooks No. 11, Puppetry Imprints, 1938); with three plays from the Chinese, notes by Paul McPharlin, photo-illustrations; author one-time Curator of the Detroit Institute of Arts; authoritative on technical details, construction, manipulation, scenery, music.

Chinese Shadow Figures. Although the larger figures of the Javanese Wayang and the even larger ones of the Andhra (India) have a remarkable degree of incised design, that of the Chinese (average height 12 ins.) is even more impressive when placed alongside these: design, cutting and colouring are of an extreme delicacy. Traditionally animal skin was the material used (donkey, sheep, goat, water-buffalo), giving tough, durable, non-warping figures, treated to give translucence before colouring; those of the contemporary Communist era are of plastic, showing the same skill in cutting but harder in their colouring. The problem which is inherent when creating translucent figures with overlapping joints is that the double thickness gives darker areas: this the Chinese artists overcame by devising a system giving only a wheel-like outline around the pivot point where the parts are joined by knotted thread. Faces, always in profile, are stylised, those of heroes and women being incredibly incised to leave only a thin outline plus an eye and eyebrow. Costume design shows an exact balance between solid and cut-away areas. Usually the limbs of both humans and animals are in two pieces, the heads are detachable (so that various characters of the same category can share the same bodies: an economy which is important when a large number of characters are involved). The controls consist of three thin bamboo rods terminating in lengths of stiff wire, looped at the end to take thread attached to the movable part and to the front of the neck (point of support). Although there are no leg controls a skilled operator can make a figure walk, sit, kneel, bend from the waist: the supporting rod being held in one hand, the others chop-stick fashion in the other. The screen size is fairly standard and related to the size of the figures, about 5-ft. wide and 3-ft. high, usually of translucent cloth (in early times mulberry paper was used); bright embroidered drapes mask the surrounding areas; the light source is centralised on a rear frame. In the same way that the Javanese figures when stationary have the end of the rod stuck into soft banana stem along the base of the screen, the Chinese use a shelf covered with rough sacking or felt. As in their live theatre, simple symbolic scenery is used to indicate different locales: a chair or a table indicates a room. The repertoire of traditional plays included some hundreds of items – and on the occasion of a private engagement the host could make his own choice. Unlike the Javanese, the Turkish, the Greek shows, which usually involve a solo performer, the Chinese companies vary from three to eight, some of whom are also musicians as and when required during performance. The source for the plays, traditionally, was the Chinese history, largely militaristic, its folk tales and romantic legends, and domestic comedy; religion and magic also provided material – the shadow screen being ideal for rapid transformations, flights, and other spectacular happenings. Whether the new plays with their propagandist ingredients are as entertaining as the old is for the people of New China to decide. Full-page colour reproduction in Baird *Art of the Puppet;* detailed technical illustrations in Blackham *Shadow Puppets.* Technique: March *Chinese Shadow-figure Plays and their making,* q.v.

Cinderella, or the Little Glass Slipper. Perrault's fairy tale, among the top ten as theme for pantomime and puppet theatre; productions with all types of puppets. Theme: beautiful girl imposed on by ugly step-sisters and step-mother; fairy godmother transforms mice and pumpkin into coach and horses, and rags into beautiful costume so that heroine can attend a ball. Condition: must be home by midnight. Meets handsome prince; loses slipper while hurrying home. Prince discovers mysterious owner by trying the slipper on feet of all the ladies in the kingdom. Delightful silhouette-film version by Lotte Reiniger (apply British Film Institute).

Cinemoid. Trade term for plastic colour-filter, non-flammable cellulose-acetate sheeting, used with stage lighting projectors; available in over 40 colours and clear. Latter sometimes used for shadow puppets. Suppliers: Strand Electrical Co., 29 King Street, London, W.C.2. Branches in Melbourne, Australia, Toronto, Canada.

CIPEMAT (Centre International pour les Etudes des Marionettes traditionelles). International centre set up in Liége, Belgium, 1958, concerned with traditional forms of puppetry. First meeting Paris, 1959. Headquarters: the Musée de la Marionnette at Lyon; Hon. Secretary, M. Roger Pinon, 64 avenue Blonden, Liége, France.

Claque. Audience members who applaud because they have been paid to do so; or who do the opposite, being paid by a rival company.

Coat hanger. Wooden household variety with hook for hanging up. Can be adapted as marionette control particularly for horizontal characters. Metal screw-eyes can be positioned at ends or underneath or along sides to suit stringing requirements, or holes can be drilled to take short lengths of dowel (curtain rod) extending each side, with holes pierced or screw-eyes to take strings. Interesting actions possible from experiment in handling. Hook used for storage on hanging-rail. Illustrated in Philpott *Modern Puppetry* (Michael Joseph, 1966).

Codmans, The. Outstanding family of Punchmen now in the fourth generation. The original 'professor' toured the country in a caravan and had been in the circus; he came from Llandudno where one of the present Codman's operates. A site for the outdoor Punch theatre was established in Liverpool, at Lime Street, and became a landmark, in use for over 100 years (a new booth, however, was presented by the Sandon Studios Society in 1923). An article about this notable family appeared in the special issue of the BPMTG *Puppet Master* following the Punch Tercentenary celebrations in 1962 and includes a reproduction of an old print showing the booth in Lime Street. One of the present Codman's was among the guests at a reception held during the International Puppet Festival at Colwyn Bay (1963), with his Dog Toby.

Coleridge, Samuel Taylor (1772–1834). English poet: *Ancient Mariner*, *Kubla Khan*, etc. In *Biographia Literaria* (autobiography and philosophy) wrote: 'She very much reminds us of those puppet-heroines, for whom the showman contrives to dialogue without any skill in ventriloquism.' In *Tombless Epitaph* a reference to 'The hollow puppet of a hollow age.'

Colette, Sidonie Gabrielle (1873–1954). French novelist. Wrote libretto for *L'Enfant et les Sortilèges* q.v., a divertissement, a 'ballet pour ma fille', for which Ravel wrote the music. It has had various puppet productions, including that of the Caricature Theatre, Cardiff, Director Jane Phillips.

Collodium paper. Chemically treated paper used in the theatre for flashes. (From theatrical suppliers.)

Cologne, Germany. In addition to the famous Haenneschen Puppet Theatre, with the Rhineland rod-type of figures, there is an important collection of puppets and documents in the Theatre Museum of Köln University (Institut für theaterwissenschaft).

Colour. Physiologically: an optical effect, a sensation caused by light falling on the retina of the eye and being translated by the brain.

Theatrically: one of the contributory factors in the creation of mood and dramatic effect. In a completely dark room there are no colours. The impact of black and white and of colour films or television are different: puppets lose a great deal on the screen when the colours are missing. Technically, the choosing of colours is inseparable from the power and quality of light in which the colours will be seen: the same colour seen by daylight, by moonlight, by modern street-lighting, or under various coloured lights on a stage, becomes a different colour. The stage designer is concerned not only with the colours used for costumes but also their relationship with the colours of the décor; on a small puppet stage it is easy to cause the puppets almost to disappear against an over-colourful background. The *relationships* of colours should be considered from the start of preparations – and everything tested under stage lighting conditions. A knowledge of colour values can only be acquired by experiment. The *names* for colours vary between manufacturer and manufacturer, as to costume materials, as to paints, and even to colour filters for lighting. There are books on 'colour theory' – but even these are not fool-proof, simply because of the nature of printers' inks and the different natures of fabric colours (dyes) and paints; in any case the size of the samples is usually inadequate. Even experiments with model theatres can be deceptive, a fact only appreciated when everything is 'blown up' to full scale. The designer with a long experience of working with colours will be able to visualise the whole stage, the setting, the costumes, and the effect of lighting – and of changes of lighting – upon these. It is possible to stage a whole production in a range of greys (it has been done in the live theatre); nobody has yet staged a play in which *everything* – the stage itself, floor and walls, and costume and make-up – was of the identical shade of red. The impact-value changes if an all-black costume has one red heart added. The *balance* of colours is important; apart from patterns *on* materials, there is the overall pattern formed by all the colours used to create the stage picture. On the smaller puppets, small patterns tend to blur at a distance: plain colours, clear spotted or striped materials can be effective; whereas the same designs blown-up to life size might be over-dominant. Contrasts are usually needed – if only to distinguish one character from another: a dozen actors of the same physique all in identical Harlequin costumes would be indistinguishable. The terms 'cool' – for the blues and greens – and 'warm' for the reds, oranges, yellows – are relative: *actual* effects depend on the balance (or imbalance) of colours used. The reflective power of shiny or matt materials needs to be studied. In creating puppets it is wise to have costume materials alongside when painting faces; if the hair is chosen first this will influence the face colour, and *vice versa*. The actual effect of eye colours at a distance needs checking: black, dark blue, dark brown, at a distance are hardly distinguishable. The beginner tends to work at close quarters and then to be surprised to discover how different everything looks on the stage. Preliminary experiments can result in eventual economy of time and materials.

Colour filter. Translucent medium – glass, gelatine, plastic – used with stage lighting equipment.

Commedia dell' arte. Form of improvised comedy with masks, flourished in Italy in sixteenth – seventeenth centuries, originating in Tuscany *c.* 1550, which spread throughout Europe. Alternative term: commedia all' improviso; influences perceptible in works of Shakespeare, Molière,

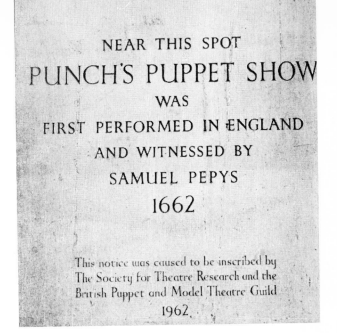

NEAR THIS SPOT
PUNCH'S PUPPET SHOW
WAS
FIRST PERFORMED IN ENGLAND
AND WITNESSED BY
SAMUEL PEPYS
1662

This notice was caused to be inscribed by
The Society for Theatre Research and the
British Puppet and Model Theatre Guild
1962.

Above: St Paul's Church, Covent Garden, London – inscription unveiled during
'Punch Tercentenary' celebrations, 1962
Below: George Speaight with Pollock Toy Theatre. Final scene of *The Miller and His Men*

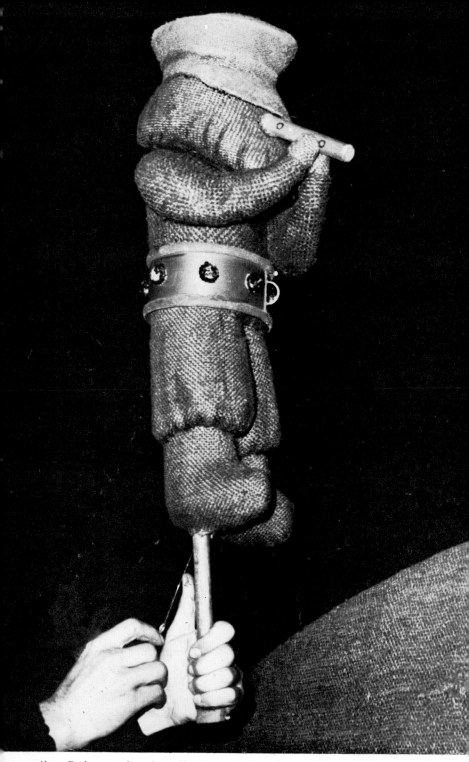

Above: Rod puppet from *Petrouchka*. Hungarian State Puppet Theatre, Budapest
Opposite: Javanese shadow figure

Chinese shadow figures

Goldoni and other playwrights, although in the original form full scripts
were not used, the actors working from an outline plot (scenario) giving
cues for entries and general action, with a large amount of 'stage business'
which might or might not be related to the main line of development.
The actors were professionals (as distinct from the 'commedia erudita'
employed by the Courts) and each had a 'stock character' reappearing in
many episodes, with a fixed type of role, some of these characters still
existing in pantomime, such as Harlequin, Colombine and Pierrot. The
puppet Punch is a derivative of the commedia Pulcinella. In France the
character Arlequin also transferred to the puppet stage, and numerous
play-titles (as also in England) included his name, such as *Harlequin
Dick Whittington, Harlequin Puss in Boots, Arlequin roi de Serendib*. Performances were often in the street on a platform with simple background and
places for entry or exit. Kay Dick (*Pierrot*, Hutchinson, 1960) mentions
an old Dutch scenario for an item *The Marvellous Malady of Harlequin*,
which has illustrations showing Harlequin as a mother, with the suggestion that Colombine was the father. In Broadbent *A History of Pantomime* (Citadel Press, N.Y., 1965) there are references to 'platts', related
to the Italian scenario, giving minimum of cues, and possibly earliest
form of written instructions for performers in Pantomimes. The use of
'stock characters' can have some advantage for the puppeteer in the
economy of producing new material: it is a policy in fact adopted where
shows take a serial form, as with the traditional Sicilian marionettes, q.v.
in which the main characters reappear in various episodes over a period
of months; the various traditional characters such as Punch (although
in only a repeated play), Guignol in France (in hundreds of plays),
Kasper/Kasperle in Germany (hero in a wide range of plays) may be
regarded as 'stock' types, as may any of the 'personality' characters of
television, Muffin the Mule, Sooty the Teddy Bear, Topo Gigio the
Italian Mouse, or any new creatures given regular series of appearances.
In Czechoslovakia the famous characters Hurvinek and Spejbl, q.v.
have a theatre named after themselves and are certainly 'stock' types.
Standard work on the Commedia: Duchartre, *The Italian Comedy* (Dover
Publications, 1965).

Commedia dell' arte, by Winifred Smith (Blom, N.Y., 1964). Study of the
Italian improvised comedy: definition, origin, travel through other countries, in Elizabethan and Jacobean England; advent of musical and
spectacular entertainments, popular theatre and marionette shows,
playwrights Goldoni and Gozzi, the French Fairs. Appendix of illustrations 'An Invitation to the Commedia by way of illustrations from private
and public collections.'

Comment construire et animer nos marionnettes, by Marcel Temporal, noted
French puppeteer (Editions Bourrelier, 1942, 4th enlarged edition,
1955); brief general introduction, but mainly on technical aspects,
including manipulation, of hand and string puppets, illustrated by drawings; 15 variations of marionette-controls shown; important chapter on
modern developments of the 'marotte' q.v.

Commonwealth Arts Festival: Cardiff, 1965. An event remarkable for
its scope, various forms of dance, opera, choirs, symphony orchestras,
a poetry conference, pop and variety, various sports, a film festival and
performances by the Caricature Puppet Theatre, a Welsh company
directed by Jane Phillips, presenting *Culhwch and Olwen* q.v. taken from
the Tales of the Mabinogion, the source of all Welsh legends.

Commonwealth Institute, Kensington High Street, London, W.8. Institute replaced the former Imperial Institute, South Kensington. Among its exhibits are shadow puppets from Malaysia (Wayang Kulit) representing Rama and Ravana, characters in a play based on the Hindu *Ramayana.* A set of modern silver tea-spoons with designs of handle based on shadow-figures also on view. The Institute has a cinema where there have been occasional presentations of *Wayang Kulit,* 16 mm. colour film by the Malayan Film Unit, 1956. This film can be hired.

Complete Puppet Book, edited L. V. Wall and G. A. White (Faber, 1956). The second of three editions of *The Puppet Book,* third edition returning to original title and heavily revised, compiled by members of the Educational Puppetry Association; chapters on educational aspects and techniques for all types of puppets, stages, lighting, play production, puppetry in youth clubs, libraries, and in therapeutic work. Note: 3rd edition, edited A. R. Philpott, has additional material.

Concordance. Dictionary of words, phrases, passages, from works of a major author, e.g. Shakespeare, or a composite work such as the *Bible,* giving precise location by chapter, verse, line, for each entry. Valuable for research purposes. Literary references to puppets occur in the works of many writers; any Concordance in the public library reference room is worth consulting. Arranged alphabetically, a search takes little time. Words to look for: *puppet, marionette, shadow, motion, Punch, raree, galantee.* Having traced the source, then the original work can be consulted for full context. The majority of references will be in metaphoric form and may show little technical knowledge of puppets. The number of entries varies widely between author and author. *Concordance to the Poems of John Keats* (Carnegie Institute, Washington, 1917) has only one item: 'Puppet . . . Erminia's last new puppet (from *Otho the Great,* tragedy in five acts). Robert Browning is more fruitful, 15 entries, including the frequently quoted 'God's puppets best and worst are we . . .' (from *Pippa Passes).* *Shakespeare Word-Book* (Routledge, 1908) is a simplified title and there are 20 examples of *different* meanings of 'motions'. *Complete Concordance to Shakespeare* (Bickers, revised 1889) gives 89 examples of 'motion.' Another variation of title: *Lexical Concordance of the Poetical Works of . . .* Others worth exploring are Shelley, Herrick, Tennyson, Dickens, Chaucer. Some earnest scholar may some day produce a Concordance of puppet words to be found in all the concordances.

Constructions. As with modern sculpture, puppets can be built up from various objects or raw materials instead of being carved or modelled.

Contemporary. Existing or occurring at the same time. Loosely used as synonymous with 'modern', whereas traditional forms of puppetry exist alongside the modern, *both* being contemporary.

Control (controller, crutch, perch). Handling device to which strings of marionette are attached to simplify control of movements. Design and construction varies, some countries have traditional forms which have been found best for particular purposes; individual performers often have personal preferences. Strictly speaking, it is the particular needs of each marionette that should determine type of control and it is probably impossible to develop an 'all purpose' type. The human hand itself is the basic control; in India some marionettes have only a single string attached to the head and the waist (spine) of the figure, the string being looped over the manipulator's hand. An unusual variation, also in India, is the use of a wooden or metal ring around the performer's head (like a crown), to which are attached the supporting strings, the puppet arms being controlled by rods (downwards). The simplest form may consist of a single stick to which all the strings are attached. The next development is the addition of a second stick to which either the hand or the leg strings are attached. The second stick can then become a cross-piece attached to the first, fixed or removable. This leads to the evolution of the so-called 'AEROPLANE' control, which may have a rocking leg-bar at the 'propeller' end. The 'VERTICAL' type gives a different hand grip and may have certain refinements technically: it may have a rocking bar set in a slot at the top end, or this can be on a hook or held by a clip in order to be removable: again this can be for leg or hand strings. The vertical type may have a 'tail' projecting at an angle at the rear and base, taking the spine string. Wire projections to take run-through hand strings are another feature. Some traditional marionettes in Europe had 'TURNIP' controls – more pear shape – with leather tabs on the surface, to which strings attached and manipulated by other hand. TRICK figures usually need specially designed controls and may need to take a double set of strings. There are also MULTIPLE CONTROLS taking several dancers, either in line or in circle. The size of the control can be a limiting factor if characters need to be closely positioned – and the Salzburg marionnettes q.v. have small controls which are used in operatic and ballet items. The traditional Chinese control may have to accommodate 20–40 strings. Although the term has come to be associated with marionettes, in fact each type of puppet has its control, the live hand or rods, or a combination of these. Teschner q.v. the famous Austrian puppeteer, developed a technique with internal rods and strings operated from below stage. Temporal *Comment construire et animer nos marionnettes* illustrates 15 marionette controls.

Convention. In the theatrical sense: a particular style of a production or of elements in the production. These may be traditional or reflect contemporary trend. For full appreciation by the spectators the significance of the method of production and of performance must be understood, these constituting a kind of 'language.' A performance in a language foreign to the spectator must lose much of its value. Mime (action without dialogue) and ballet (mime with music) are conventional forms. The complex range of movements of the Kathakali dancers (India) involve years of training and would be pointless unless the audiences also educated in translating meanings from action. One manual lists nearly 500 hand gestures alone ('mudras') and these will be used simultaneously with head, neck, feet, eye movements. The deaf and dumb people have their own sign language. There are traditional gestures and postures in stage melodramas: the pointing finger, the hand on heart, head on chest, hand over eyes, fingers against forehead, hands in prayer, eyes to heaven, hands saying 'keep away' – many of these being adopted by the actors in the early silent films. There can be conventions in scene-shifting, which may be done in full view of the audience. There is the convention of the Japanese BUNRAKU puppet theatre, each puppet having three visible manipulators, one in ceremonial costume, two completely in black: it is the tremendous quality of the puppet action that takes the attention away from the performers so that they become virtually invisible. Bertolt Brecht, q.v., the avant-garde German dramatist-producer, introduced a convention by having stage mechanisms visible and by using title-boards; Marcel Marceau the French mime, in addition to his highly developed technique for conveying meaning by movement and gesture, uses an assistant to introduce each item with a placard held in a 'frozen' posture. A Chinese item has an amusing convention: the stage is fully lit, but the actors perform as though in darkness, while being in full view of the audience. Conventions may derive from actions and gestures in everyday use or may be entirely artificial. To have significance the movements of puppets must have some relationship with human movements, animal movements, but modified according to their construction.

Cool. Relative to colours of costume, scenery, lighting: the less intense shades of blue and blue tints. Effects are relative, as can be discovered by trying a whole production with only blues, and then using contrasting warm colours (reds, oranges, orange-yellows) and then going to the other extreme using all warm colours.

Coping (or Scroll) saw. Metal frame of the fret-saw variety but shorter, with strong blade which can be set at any desired angle for cutting shapes in wood including curves.

Copydex. Trade term for white adhesive useful for sticking cloth to cloth, paper to paper, or other materials which may be required to remain fleixble during use. Surplus adhesive rubs off easily and rolls off fingers. Supplied in tubes and jars from most craft suppliers.

Copyright. In essence: the Law is concerned with preventing unauthorised copying of physical material and not with the reproduction of ideas, and protects the rights of authors, composers, record-makers and publishers, the ownership of literary and musical property. All performers, promoters, producers, adaptors, should be familiar with the regulations laid down in the Act of 1956 and there may be amendments from time to time. The United States adopted the Universal Copyright Convention for international protection (in 1955). The advent of radio and television raised new problems such as private recording from broadcast material. In addition to various legal publications there is a useful section in the *Writers' and Artists' Year Book* (A. & C. Black: latest edition), which can be seen at most public library reference rooms. Useful book for the layman: Margaret Nicholson *Manual of Copyright Practice* (Oxford University Press, 1956) and for writers, publishers, agents. R. R. Hardy Ivamy *Show Business and the Law* (Stevens, 1955) has as main concern all in any branch of entertainment. The Advertising Association, 1 Bell Yard, London, W.C.2, has *Questions and Answers on Copyright and Performing Rights*. Consult *re* specific performances (e.g. in theatre or hall) Phonographic Performances Ltd., 62 Oxford Street, London, W.1 and Performing Right Society, 29 Berners Street, London, W.1. Note *re* photographs: the negative belongs to the photographer even if work is commissioned; negative must be paid for separately. The earliest known grant of copyright was for books, Venice, 1469.

Corbett, Harry. English puppeteer famous for characters 'Sooty' (teddy bear) and 'Sweep' and, after some controversy about introducing a note of sex into children's programmes, a girl friend 'Sue.' Fifteen years with B.B.C. Television. Number of 'Sooty' films available on hire from Gaumont British Film Library, Perivale, Middlesex.

Cork. Outer layer of the bark of the cork tree, a species of oak. Corks (bottle-stoppers) sometimes used as noses on improvised puppet heads (e.g. cheese-box). Thick varieties of virgin cork or composition type sometimes used by short puppet operators, either attached to normal footwear or made up into special 'clogs' to add height.

Cortés, Hernando (1485–1547). Spanish adventurer and gold-seeker; had his own retinue of entertainers including one who was puppeteer and conjuror. This was recorded in the diary of the expedition, in Mexico, kept by Bernal Diaz del Castillo, and was, according to Paul McPharlin (*The Puppet Theatre in America*) 'in conformity with the practice of the period' – but there are no details as to the type of performance.

Costume. Theatrical clothing designed to suit particular character and type of puppet, technical considerations influencing choice of material and method of assembly. Scale of figure affects suitability of certain materials: for small figures felt may be too stiff, brocades may be too heavy. Study of a wide range of materials from both the theatrical angle and the purely technical is essential; effectiveness at a distance and under stage lighting must be checked. Textures and colours have inherent dramatic qualities. Effectiveness may depend on contrast between character and character. Some colours have traditional associations: black, white, red, green, purple, but values may be relative. Coloured stage lighting will affect the dye or pigment colours. A brilliant costume placed in front of a brilliant piece of scenery may vanish; most colours gain in front of black. A burlesque production could reverse the normal colour values and associations. Usually it is the plain colours, materials with simple design of spots or stripes, rather than those with complicated floral designs that prove most effective, but there are no rules other than that of testing under performance conditions. In the case of marionettes it is important to use materials that will not impede free movement of joints and it may be necessary to pass knee strings *through* a long costume. The 'costume' of flat figure type may be painted, that of coloured shadows incorporated in the overall design. In oriental shadow figures every detail of costume design may be significant, traditional, obligatory, part of the characterisation of king, princess, demon, wizard. In all cases the costume is part of any given character, obvious examples being Red Riding Hood, Father Christmas and other traditional types. The 'STOCK CHARACTERS' of the Italian commedia dell' arte (improvised comedy) – Harlequin, Punchinello, Pierrot, and others – had garments as essential part of the characterisation. Aesthetically, there should be relationship between colours of hair, skin, costume, décor, lighting. Young children making puppets in school or at home will choose if there is any choice possible or they may use anything available for immediate results. In the case of hand puppets it is advisable to have an inner garment of fairly strong but supple material (a 'body') which will reduce wear and tear on costume material during performance as well as conceal the shape of the hand. The cloth body is attached to the puppet neck, the costume is removable for pressing or cleaning.

Counterbalance. Construction principle in making of marionette to ensure correct return movements of parts lifted by strings, also counter action to tendency for body to sway when legs or arms moved. Stabilisation of the whole figure begins with the lower part of torso where weight may need to be added, amount depending on scale of figure and basic material used in construction (wood, stuffed cloth, etc.). Usual weighting material is lead in form of snippets from sheet lead, covering from electric flex, fisherman's weights, costume weights, solder, ball bearings. This may need to be set into drilled holes or, in case of feet, fixed with small nails.

The precise quantity for any part is a matter of trial and error and adjustment. One character may *need* heavy, clumsy foot movements; another may need floating arm movements. Authority on subject: W. A. Dwiggins *Marionette in Motion* (Puppetry Imprints, Birmingham, Mich., USA, 1939); general principle discussed in Whanslaw *Second Bench Book* (Wells Gardner Darton, 1957).

Countersink. To drill a hollow in the surface of wood or metal to take head of screw or bolt so that this sinks flush with surface; also the name for special 'bit' for such drilling. A useful variety of the 'bit' has been marketed, set in an unbreakable handle, avoiding need to insert in drill.

Counterweight system. Method of raising and lowering stage scenery mechanically from floor level, by means of ropes, blocks, weights, storage area being situated above stage ('the flies': scenery 'flown') invisible to audience. Some modern productions deliberately leave the flown scenery in view of the audience, there being no proscenium arch to hide it. The raising and lowering can provide a kind of continuity compared with the break caused by lowering or drawing stage curtains.

Covent Garden. Famous for its market (fruit, vegetables, flowers) and its Opera House, in the heart of London; the area has numerous historical associations with puppets, beginning with those seen by Pepys in 1662, a fact recorded in an inscription on the external wall of St Paul's Church (Inigo Jones: the 'actors' church'), where the 1962 'Punch Tercentenary' celebrations q.v. were held; the 'Little Piazza' was also the site for Martin Powell's shows (1711–1713), as mentioned in *The Spectator*. The famous Bow Street Police Station is nearby.

Cowper, William (1731–1800). English poet and letter writer; *John Gilpin*. In *Retirement* wrote: 'With limbs of British oak and nerves of wire, And wit that puppet-prompters might inspire.'

'Crackers.' Professional name of Punchman Glyn Edwards, q.v.

Craig, Edward Gordon (1872–1967). English actor, designer, theorist, author; son of famous actress Ellen Terry and eminent architect William Godwin. Worked for some time with Henry Irving's Company, but developed somewhat revolutionary theories about theatre and experimented with scenery and lighting schemes. His ideas as to true function of theatre and on acting were better received abroad than in England, and in 1907 he settled in Florence where he established a theatre school, the Arena Goldoni, in 1913, closing at onset of World War I. Made a deep study of puppets and included a number of articles on these in his publication *The Mask* (1908–15, 1918, 1923–29) and published *The Marionnette* (1918–19), 12 issues, including five plays ('motions') for puppets, and the results of his research (mainly Italian, but including Japanese Bunraku and other material). His concept of the 'übermarionette' – supermarionette – disturbed the acting profession for many years in spite of his attempts to clarify this: he was not concerned to replace the live actor by the puppet, although he was against bad acting as well as intensely interested in puppets. *The Actor and the Übermarionette* appeared in 1908 in Vols. 1 and 2 of *The Mask* and incorporated into *On the Art of the Theatre* (1911: paperback edition, Mercury Books, 1962). His *Puppets and Poets* appeared in *The Monthly Chapbook* (February, 1921). Further references to the übermarionette occurred in *The Theatre Advancing* (Constable, 1921), in which he said that the marionette theatre was the 'true' theatre; the übermarionette was really 'the actor plus fire, minus egoism' (qualities also to be desired in the actor with puppets). Some critics feel that his greatest influence, often unacknowledged, was on the 'live' theatre, but he certainly had considerable influence on the renaissance of puppetry and was for some years President of the British Puppet and Model Theatre Guild; made Hon. Member of UNIMA. One of his puppet plays was reprinted in McPharlin *Repertory of Marionette Plays* (USA, 1924). An exhibition of designs for marionettes held in London in 1920. 'King Penguin' book, with introduction by Janet Leeper, *Designs for the Theatre: Edward Gordon Craig* (1948). *Scene: E. Gordon Craig*, with foreword and introductory poem by John Masefield was published by Humphrey Milford and Oxford University Press in 1923 following an exhibition of designs and models. A commemorative exhibition was held in 1967 at the Victoria and Albert Museum, London, including models showing his scheme for stage screens, his designs, books, three small puppet heads and a jumping-jack used as a model for an illustration. The Society for Theatre Research has published a bibliography by Jean Kyrle Fletcher and Arnold Rood. A definitive biography can be anticipated.

Cravat Circus. Sophisticated item by French puppeteer Georges Tournaire with figures created entirely from men's ties (neckwear); central rod for general movement. Illustration in *Puppet Theatre of the Modern World* (Harrap, 1965).

Creation of a Marionette, The. 16 mm. colour film, Kodachrome, silent, produced and directed by Douglas Fisher; made in workshops of Lanchester Marionettes, demonstrating making, manipulation and presentation, concluding with a performance. Suitable for showing to schools, colleges, youth groups, women's institutes, educational and drama courses. Enquiries: The Puppet Centre, 39 Henley Street, Stratford-upon-Avon, Warwickshire.

Credulity, Superstition, Fanaticism. Satirical engraving by William Hogarth (1697–1764) showing a preacher in a pulpit holding puppets by short thick single cord: witch on broomstick in one hand, devil in the other; other figures adorn the sides of the pulpit. Similar method of control is seen in another engraving *A Just View of the British Stage.*

Cremorne. Famous Victorian pleasure garden founded 1832 on site now occupied by four chimneys of the Chelsea Power Station. The opening proceedings included a performance by Bean's Band, on the lawn, a show by Cremorne's Punch and Judy, and a Pyramidal and Tumbling act.

Crêpe hair. Used in theatrical wig-making and available from theatrical suppliers, some craft shops. Coarse wool or hair of long fibre, scoured, combed, dyed in range of colours, spun, plaited on two strands of thin string (which crimps it). Also used for certain styles of puppet hair, but puppet makers use wide range of other materials – not necessarily more or not so expensive as crêpe – to contribute to differences of characterisation.

Cromwell, Oliver (1599–1658). English soldier-puritan who became Lord Protector of the Commonwealth of England, Scotland, Ireland; suppressed the live Morality Plays q.v. by two bills – (1) suspension, 1642, (2) abolition, 1645 – but allowed the 'motion men' (puppeteers) to continue.

Cruikshank, George (1792–1878). English etcher, painter, caricaturist; illustrator of *Punch and Judy* text by J. Payne Collier (Prowett, 1828, and many later editions); preliminary sketches made during actual performance by old Italian showman named Piccini. Blanchard Jerrold *Life of George Cruikshank* (Chatto, 1883) mentions a puppet with extending neck and another that could remove its hat and which the showman defied all other performers to do.

Crutch. Term sometimes used for the MARIONETTE CONTROL, the device to which the strings are attached to facilitate handling.

Cucurucu. Name given to Pulcinella (commedia dell' arte q.v. character) by Jacques (Jacomo) Callot, famous engraver (1592–1635). Reproduction of engraving in Duchartre *The Italian Comedy* (Dover, 1966). Good name for a puppet, incidentally, but not for Punch.

Cue. Verbal or visual signal from one actor to another.

Cue sheet. Instructions to theatre technicians *re* lighting changes to be made during performance.

Cunard puppets. Hand puppet caricatures of officers and men of famous Q.E.2 liner; marketed by Lucytoys, Egham, Surrey.

Cure. The process of hardening, usually in reference to plastics materials; the changing of physical properties of material through chemical reaction.

Cybernetic Grandma. Stop-motion puppet film (1963) by famous Czech puppeteer Jiri Trnka; science-fiction satire against abuse of technology, by young writer Ivan Klima. Child has two grandmothers, one normal, one a fantastic child-minding machine. (Trnka q.v. was given title of National Artist in 1963.)

Cylindrical (tubular) puppets. Variation of the rod type. Cardboard heads, usually fairly large, simple cylinder shape, painted features, optional modelled details and applied hair. Variation: double cylinder, one sliding over other and producing mouth movements (one section cut away) synchronised with speech. Large figures usually require two operators, one controlling the head by internal hand and/or rod, optional mechanism for moving eyes made from table tennis balls, second operator providing live arms and hands: this needs considerable rehearsal to ensure synchronisation. Another variation: cylinder in two hinged sections giving jaw movement. Highly stylised productions given by Stuttgart Youth Club, director Anni Weigand (item with male choir characters *in Parodies from a Top Hat*); Sofia Central Theatre, Bulgaria (*The Clockmaker*); Stanhope Evening Institute group, London, satire on speech training class.

Cynthia's Revels, satirical Comedy by Ben Jonson, q.v. (published 1601), an attack on Court behaviour; the Palinode contains these lines: 'From making love by attorney, courting of puppets, and paying for new acquaintance, *Chorus:* Good Mercury defend us.'

Czechoslovak Puppeteer (Československy Loutkař). Puppetry periodical for professionals and amateurs published by Orbis, Prague, 2. Illustrated articles on current puppet productions, festivals, etc.

Czechoslovakia. Traditionally one of the 'homes' of puppetry, in heart of Europe, its capital Prague is official centre for UNIMA, the international puppetry organisation. In 1948 a Law passed gave equal status with live theatre, with puppeteers on State Theatre Council. In sixteenth century, English, Dutch and German puppet troupes introduced various types; Mikolaš Aleš (1852–1913), painter and designer, helped to popularise puppetry and created national cult of Matè Kopečky (1775–1847), who introduced hero-puppet Kašparek, puppets made from wood and other materials to Aleš designs were sold in various sizes. Kopečky memorial at Kolodeje and Lužnici unveiled 6th July, 1947; sculptor Jan Jiřikovsky, created larger-than-life figure of Kašparek sitting beside a cracked comedian's drum. The original Kašparek now in National Museum, Prague. Versatile propagandist Dr Vesely (1885–1939) brought about formation of some 3,000 puppet groups, mostly amateur. Ludmila Tesarova (1857–1936), kindergarten teacher, inspired educational developments. More 'literary' items produced in 1920–30's. Two characters introduced by Professor Skupa (1892–1957), Hurvinek and Spejbl, son and father, became national and international 'stars'. A Chair of Puppetry was established concerned with training of professional performers, producers, craftsmen, offering a 4-year Course. There are now many professional theatres and mobile groups. A literature exists of over 1,300 Czech and other items; a puppetry magazine (*The Puppeteer*) is available from bookstalls and newsagents. At the international level, Dr Jan Malik, Secretary-General of UNIMA, Director of the Central Puppet Theatre, Prague, playwright, author of *Puppetry in Czechoslovakia* (Orbis 1948 and available in English) is responsible to a large extent for world-wide relationships. Amateur festivals are held every year in Chrudim and a first international amateur event was held at Karlovy-Vary (Karlsbad) in 1964. Major event, probably 1970, will be opening of a Universal Puppet Theatre for presentation of every kind of production, performances for children and adults, with museum and library facilities, workshops, beautifully situated. In the field of puppet films Jiři Trnka is outstanding with an impressive number of national and international awards and an established position as children's book illustrator.

Culhwch and Olwen. One of four Welsh tales on the Arthurian legend included in the *Mabinogion;* bird and beast characters as important as man; episodes of fighting, hunting, magic. Theme: Culhwch refuses to marry step-mother's daughter and, to win Olwen, daughter of monstrous giant Yshaddaden Pencawr, has to perform forty tasks or 'problems'. Puppet production by Caricature Theatre Company, q.v., Cardiff, Wales, directed by Jane Phillips, designs by John Blundall, presented at Commonwealth Arts Festival, 1965.

D

Dance. Wide range of possibilities with puppets of different types: (a) rather limited movements of FINGER PUPPETS with operator's index and middle fingers forming the legs; (b) loosely controlled figure or figures with horizontal string running through the chest and tied to a short post at the end of a plank on the ground, the other end looped around per-

E

former's knee (with music) (see MARIONNETTES A LA PLANCHETTE);
(c) waltz and figure-dances with HAND PUPPETS, the operators dancing
below stage; (d) folk dances and 'abstract' movements in space by large
ROD PUPPETS (overhead); (e) FLOOR SHOW or CABARET MARIONETTES,
operator sharing floor space with dancer; (f) solo marionette ballerina
dancing *The Dying Swan* (Saint-Saëns) at the SALZBURG MARIONETTE
THEATRE, in homage to Pavlova, or the same theatre's *Nutcracker Suite*
(Tchaikowsky); (g) 'BLACK THEATRE' ballet with illuminated figures
moving in dark space. The important factor in all cases is the particular
anatomy of the puppet and its method of control. In his famous essay
comparing live dancers and marionettes, Kleist q.v. was only concerned
with the string-controlled type, which can overcome the force of gravity
in a way beyond the power of the human dancer: which can lead to
humorous developments too, as there is no limit to the puppet's 'elevation'. On the other hand, a badly manipulated marionette becomes a
burlesque of itself. Some Oriental forms of dance have been based on
the movements of marionettes.

Dancing Dolls. A term which the fond mother with no knowledge of
puppets will apply (beforehand) to *any* type of show. The showman
interviewed by Mayhew (*London Labour and London Poor*, 1852) said that
the 'proper title of the Exhibition of dancing dolls' was *Fantoccini*, the
Italian term for the marionettes of the period.

DaSilva Marionettes, The. English company, formed 1957, Director
Ray DaSilva Palmer, partnered by wife Joan (former dancer). Earlier
toured Canada with *Punch and Judy* and participated in Puppeteers of
America Festival (1957), which inspired experiments with marionettes
and other types. Returned to England in 1962 having performed at the
Canadian National Exhibition, Houston, 'Music Hall', Texas (audience
of 3,000 crippled children) and elsewhere. In addition to tours throughout
Britain have twice toured in Germany. Performances in 'stately homes',
theatres, night clubs, schools and institutions, churches. Summer season
at Morecambe (1967) utilised the only self-contained portable puppet
theatre in the country, tubular scaffolding and canvas structure seating
200. Repertoire includes *Punch and Judy*, *The Haunted Belfry* (hand
puppets), *Summoning of Everyman* (hand and rod), *Marionette Cabaret*,
Aladdin (marionettes), *How the Jellyfish lost its Bones* (marionettes and
hand puppets), *Circus Caprice* (marionettes), *Jack and the Beanstalk* (hand
and rod), *The Small One* (marionettes and shadows), *Rumpelstiltskin* (hand
and rod) and 'Great Britain's first Puppet Spectacular,' *Snowwhite and
the Seven 'Musical' Dwarfs*, a two-hour show involving simultaneous
operation of marionettes and hand puppets on a 20-ft. high stage.
Another development is 'Puppet Theatre in the Round' with audience
on all sides as in a circus.

Davenant (D'Avenant) Sir William (1606–68). English dramatist,
producer, manager, poet Laureate 1638; possibly Shakespeare's godson;
presented first English opera *The Siege of Rhodes* (1656) and introduced
scenery and actresses. In *The Long Vacation* (pre-1642) mentions showman
with puppets acting 'our old queen Bess ' – and *Sodom and Gomorrah*. In
Playhouse to be Let a satire on French comedies, mentions 'new motion
men of Norwich, op'ra puppets' (Act 1).

Davenport's. The Magic Shop (at the sign of the Rabbit out of the Hat)
facing the British Museum in Great Russell Street, London, W.C.1.

Suppliers of everything for conjuring and magic, jokes, Punch and Judy figures, Ventriloquial Dolls, Punchmen's 'swazzles', etc.

Death of Tintagiles, by Maurice Maeterlinck (1862–1949), one of the 'three little dramas for puppets' – naively fatalistic play which was the playwright's own favourite – the tremendous love of sister for younger brother whom Death finally claims. Although critics have doubted if these plays were in fact intended for puppet production there have been a number, including that of Marjorie Batchelder, who built a special 'architectural' stage (illustration and technical drawing in her *Rod Puppets and the Human Theatre*) (Ohio University Press, 1947). There have been various editions in English, including a pocket edition, *Death of Tintagiles and Other Plays,* Duckworth and Allen and Unwin, 1924.

Debussy, Claude (1862–1918). French composer whose style influenced contemporary musical developments; used puppet themes for some works, e.g. *Fantoches,* No. 2 in *Fêtes Galantes,* set 1; *La Mer,* popular as background music for underwater puppet scenes and used for a ballet-pantomime by the Kay-Heddle marionettes, Toronto, Canada. *Boîte à joujoux,* q.v. as puppet production with the British Chamber Orchestra (Queen Elizabeth Hall, 1968) by the Little Angel Theatre, q.v.

Decameron, The, by Giovanni Boccaccio (1313–75). Famous collection of 100 stories (1471) told in ten days by seven ladies and three young men during the plague of 1348 in Florence. Scholars see source of material for various later writers. The legend of *Patient Griselda,* q.v. found its way to the puppet stage and was seen by Lady Castlemaine, q.v. as recorded by Pepys (*Diary,* 30th August, 1667). TRNKA, famous Czech puppet-film maker, used the story of the lecherous monk who pretends to be Archangel Gabriel (*Archangel Gabriel and Mother Goose*). Various English translations, including one by J. M. Rigg, in the *Everyman Library* (1903), 2 vols.

Dekker, Thomas (1570 ?–1632). English playwright; *Shoemaker's Holiday* (1600). In his *Satiromastix* (1602) – his response to ridicule in Ben Jonson's *Poetaster* – wrote: 'Hold silence, the puppet teacher speakes.' In *Jests to make you merry* (1607) mentions the 'interpreter' of the puppet show, in a comparison with performances of old plays. In *The Wonderful Year* (1603, with a description of the plague in London, there is a reference to the 'quaile-pipe' voice of a motion-man (puppet player) in a performance of *Julius Caesar,* when mentioning the safety-first device of holding the nose between thumb and finger when meeting strangers with risk of contagion. Dekker collaborated with Chettle and Haughton on a play *Patient Grissil,* q.v. (original in Boccaccio's *Decameron,* q.v., also used by Chaucer in his *Clerk's Tale*) – a puppet version recorded by Pepys, q.v. The Dekker version contains the song 'Art thou poor, yet hast thou golden slumbers'.

De Falla, Manuel (1876–1946). Spanish composer. His puppet-opera *El retablo de Maese Pedro* (*Master Peter's Puppet Show*), based on incident in Cervantes' *Don Quixote* q.v. and a favourite item with puppet theatre producers. Score from J. W. Chester, London (published 1923).

Defoe, Daniel (c. 1660–1731). English essayist, novelist, fiction writer; son of James Foe, a butcher. Visited Punch's Theatre in Covent Garden, where Punch appeared in pantomime *The History of Sir Richard Whittington.* His story of *Robinson Crusoe,* based on real life adventures of Alexander Selkirk, often produced with puppets.

Delaney, Mrs (1700–88). In *Life and Correspondence* (1861): 'The Little Poppets are very well cut but you must take more pains about the trees and shrubs, for no white paper must be left.'

Demmeni, Yevgeni Sergeivitch. USSR actor, film-director, director of State Puppet Theatre, Leningrad; author of important manual on puppet technique (in German) *Puppen auf der Bühne* (Henschel, 1951).

Dental plaster. Finely-ground plaster of Paris: very quick setting. Mixed with water, used for making moulds from clay or plasticine models for casting of heads. Mixed with thin glue (size) makes tough surfacing material, e.g. over a cardboard Easter Egg.

Desarthis, Robert. French puppeteer, founder-director of the famous Théâtre de Marionnettes du Jardin du Luxemburg, Paris; Praesidium member of UNIMA since 1962. Interesting account of his early career in Gervais *Marionnettes et Marionnettistes de France* (Bordas, 1947). Gave first performance at age 7 (1916); received Gold Medal at the Exposition Internationale (1937); documentary film *Les Comediens à la tête de bois* (1944); repertoire has ranged from *Ali Baba, Robinson Crusoe, Puss in Boots, Aladdin,* to *Don Quixote.* Illustrations of Russian Dancers from *Michel Strogoff* and scene from *Don Qhichotte* in Beaumont *Puppets and Puppetry* (Studio, 1958).

Design in Motion, by Halas and Manvell (Studio, 1962). Important book on film animation techniques; includes McLaren abstracts hand-drawn on film. Also see *Technique of Film Animation,* by same authors (Focal Press, 1959).

Detroit Institute of Arts (USA). In 1954 received first annual grant from the *Detroit News* for the purpose of activating puppetry and founding a permanent puppet theatre in Detroit. A Department of Theatre Arts was established and a permanent exhibition mounted including the Paul McPharlin collection of nearly 300 puppets – marionettes, hand, rod, shadow, toy puppets – eighteenth to twentieth century material, later acquisitions bringing total to nearly 700. Proceeds of McPharlin Memorial Fund used for acquisitions such as Victorian puppet theatre (*c.* 1870) with puppets, scenery, scripts; puppets of pioneer performers; those of Remo Bufano (1894–1948) and some of the gigantic figures he created to Robert Edmond Jones designs for League of Composers production of Stravinsky's *Oedipus Rex,* q.v. There is also a 1,000 volume library which includes titles on theatre, ballet and opera as well as puppets. The Institute acts as a clearing house on all aspects of puppetry and has files of correspondence and photographs. Activities include programmes presented by leading puppeteers and commissioning of local performers to visit hospitals and centres for handicapped children; workshop facilities and training courses. Illustrated booklet *Puppets: Past and Present* (1960) related to the exhibits, has foreword by Gil Oden, Curator of Theatre Arts.

Deutsches Institut für puppenspiel, Bochum, Germany. Established by Fritz Wortelmann, founder of thr Deutscher Bund für Puppenspiel and founder-editor of puppet review *Der Puppenspieler.* Publishes well-illustrated series of monographs on work of individuals, companies, theatres in various countries (*Meister des puppenspiel*), also the review *Figurentheater.* Institute organises annual puppet festivals and competitions with German and invited guest performers from other countries.

Dextrine (Dextrin). Strong adhesive (starch product) in powder form, mixed with water to syrup consistency; can be mixed with plaster 'fillers' as hardener ('Alabastine' q.v. technique of puppet head-making).

Diaghilev, Sergei Pavlovich (1872–1929). Founder-director of the famous *Ballets Russes* which influenced modern developments; commissioned Stravinsky, de Falla, Ravel and other composers to write ballet music, and Bakst, Benois and Picasso as designers; dancers included legendary names Pavlova and Nijinsky, Massine, Fokine, Karsarvina. Stravinsky's *Petrouchka* has had international award for puppet production by the State Puppet Theatre, Budapest, Hungary (seen at the Aldeburgh and Bath arts festivals, 1968).

Dibdin, Charles (1745–1814). English composer, singing-actor, eccentric, employed as residential composer by Garrick at Drury Lane Theatre. Built own puppet theatre on Exeter 'Change (1775) productions satirising contemporaries of the live theatre. Famous for nautical songs such as *Tom Bowling*. Wrote 70 operas and musical dramas; his *Waterman* (first performed 1774) adapted by The Hogarth Puppets. An interesting letter appeared in *Notes and Queries* (21st April, 1888) about a performance at the Patagonian Theatre, Exeter 'Change, from an account given in Pyne's *Wine and Walnuts*, vol. ix, from which it appeared that the actors were not 'living giants' but 10 in. marionettes, presented on a stage six feet wide, planned and conducted by Dibdin and a Hubert or Herbert Stoppelaer, 'painter, actor, dramatic writer, singer and a great humourist'. After a few seasons the theatre fell into other hands and became 'a mere puppet show', was sold up and made way for De Loutherbourg's Eidophusikon, 'which in turn made way for the menagerie of wild beasts'.

Dickens, Charles (1812–70). English novelist. In *Household Words* mentions Italian marionettes 'capable of anything . . . they know what the soul of wit is and are brief. Their tragedy . . . is terrible; their farce irresistible. They are brilliant in opera, overwhelming in ballet'. Chapter 16 of *The Old Curiosity Shop* has a description of two itinerant puppet showmen sitting among tombstones in a churchyard and making 'needful repairs', one binding together a small gallows and the other fixing a black wig to a puppet head. Little Nell and her grandfather see them and are told it would destroy all the illusion if the general public were allowed to see the puppets off-stage; the little girl mends Judy's dress. The showmen's names were Codlin and Short, and it is possible that the one is derived from the famous Codman family, now in the third or fourth generation of Punch performers. In chapter 18 Jerry, a showman with dancing dogs, produces one which had formerly been a Toby in the Punch show. In *Hard Times* Mr E. W. B. Childers says: 'When Sissy got into the school here, her father was as pleased as Punch.' In *Pictures from Italy* there is a description of 'The Theatre of Puppets, or Marionetti' – a famous company from Milan – 'the drollest exhibition I ever beheld in my life'. He said they *looked* between four and five feet high, but were in fact much smaller, and that a musician's hat put on the stage became alarmingly gigantic. Among the characters was a comic hotel-waiter, with extra leg joints and an eye that could wink at the audience. Besides the comedy he also saw a Ballet – a burlesque in which the dancers do fantastic pirouettes and leaps – and adds 'I shall never see a real ballet with a composed countenance again'. On another occasion he saw a play called *St Helena, or the Death of Napoleon*, which was immensely amusing although it had no real plot. He obviously witnessed some real puppetry, for Napoleon's boots did marvellous things of their own accord, 'doubling themselves up and getting under tables, and dangling in the air, and sometimes skating away with him, out of all human knowledge, when he was in full speech . . .' Gordon Craig obviously enjoyed this passage, reproducing it in full in *The Marionnette* (No. 8, February, 1918), and it is also given in Inverarity *Manual of Puppetry* (Binfords and Mort, 1936). McPharlin, in *The Puppet Theatre in America* (Harper, N.Y., 1949), says that observers of the American scene such as Dickens and Mrs Trollope managed to miss seeing puppet shows there – because they had not arrived in the right season or looked in the right places. In *Our Mutual Friend* there is a mention of a peepshow which had originally started with scenes of the Battle of Waterloo 'and had since made it every other battle of later date'. There have been a number of adaptations for the puppet stage of *Oliver Twist, Christmas Carol*, and *David Copperfield*.

Dido and Aeneas, opera in 3 acts: Music by Henry Purcell (1659–95), libretto by Nahum Tate (1652–1715: Poet Laureate, 1692): theme based on Greek myth, the tragic love of Queen Dido of Carthage for Trojan hero. Notable puppet production by German group directed by Harro Siegel (now domiciled in Florence).

Diluant. Thinning substance, e.g. turpentine, added to paint to give desired brushing consistency.

Dimmers. Equipment for reducing *or* increasing flow of electric current to theatre lighting apparatus, varying the intensity as required. Various types available suitable for puppet stages. Advisable to consult theatre lighting specialists such as Strand Electric, 29 King Street, Covent Garden, London, W.C.2 (branches in Toronto, Canada, and Melbourne, Australia).

Dissecting skeleton. Marionette with head and limbs that fly apart and re-assemble, usually with macabre setting such as graveyard at midnight with appropriate music – firm favourite with audiences. Two sets of strings are used for temporary dismemberment and reassembly. Technique: Whanslaw *Specialised Puppetry* (Wells, Gardner, Darton).

Distemper. Scene painting medium consisting of paint pigments combined with glue-size.

Disraeli, Benjamin (Earl of Beaconsfield, 1804–81). British statesman and novelist. In *Vivian Grey* (4 vols., 1826–27, V. IV) a young man's adventures in love and politics, wrote 'A long grinning, wooden figure, with great staring eyes, and the parrot nose of a punchinello.'

Dividers. Also known as 'shims' q.v.

Divine Comedy, The, by Isidor Stok (USSR); play parodying *Genesis* from the *Bible*. Masked human actors as God and Archangels; puppet Adam, Eve, Serpent, Seraphim and Cherubim, Animals. Scenes of God creating light and darkness, firmament and stars, earth and living creatures. Helped by Archangels, assembles man and woman, not without some preliminary muddle with the limbs. Adam complains about the woman; a new one, Eve, is made from a spare rib after an amusing surgical operation. After 'the Fall' due to the Serpent, forgiveness and decision to remain earth-bound.

Doctor Dolittle. There are 12 'Dolittle' books for children, written by Hugh Lofting (1886–1947) all about the adventures of a remarkable gentleman who understands the language of animals. Some of these have been adapted for puppets – as far afield as the Soviet Union – and one inspired

a Lotte Reiniger silhouette film. Three are available in Puffin paperbacks. The titles of some immediately suggest puppet possibilities: The
Story of Doctor Dolittle; *The Voyages of Doctor Dolittle*; *Doctor Dolittle's*
(a) *Post Office, Circus, Zoo, Caravan, Garden*; *Doctor Dolittle in the Moon*;
Doctor Dolittle's Return; *Doctor Dolittle and* (a) *the Secret Lake*, (b) *the Green
Canary*, (c) *Puddleby Adventures*. The first stories were originally in the form
of illustrated letters to his own children.

Doctor Faustus (Puppet Play). See Faustus, Doctor.

Dolls and Puppets, by Max von Boehn (Harrap, 1932; Cooper Square, USA.
1965: translated from the German *Puppen* and *Puppenspiel*, 2 vols., Bruck-
mann, 1929). English translation by Josephine Nicoll; 30 plates in
colour and 464 other illustrations; with a note on puppets by George
Bernard Shaw. *Part I: Dolls:* On prehistoric idols, ancestor images,
fetishes, amulets and talismans, image magic, votive images, funeral
images; waxworks, the mannequin. Toy dolls in ancient times; early toy
dolls in Europe; the Fashion doll; the toy doll in nineteenth century and
in the modern period; dolls of exotic peoples; dolls used for decorative
purposes; porcelain figures; utensils in doll form; the doll of the stage;
edible dolls; the doll in literature. *Part II: Puppets:* Automata and
movable images; the origin of the puppet show; table decorations and
the Christmas Crib; the tin soldier; the puppet show in antiquity;
marionettes in the sixteenth to eighteenth centuries; marionettes in the
nineteenth century; shadow theatre in the Orient; Occidental shadow
theatres; marionettes in the Far East; puppets of to-day; How our
marionette theatre started. The puppet play of Doctor Faust (text):
Bibliography. (Note: the 1965 edition has the original bibliography,
although many important additions to the literature on the subject have
been made since 1932.)

Dolls and Puppets of the Eighteenth Century, as delineated in 24 drawings by
Fritz Kredel. Preface by Joseph C. Graves (The Gravesend Press, Lexing-
ton, Kentucky, 1958: de luxe edition, limited). Delightfully produced
small book with 24 drawings hand-coloured through stencils by Schauer
and Silvar at Darmstadt. The illustrations of dolls are of items from the
famous collection of the Princess Augusta Dorothea, who, when widowed,
created in her castle a fabulous village of dolls, with over 400 characters
– calling this creation 'Mon Plaisir'. Monks, the court tailor, nuns, dress-
makers, a variety of craftsmen contributed perfect miniature reproductions of the pre-Goethe period. The illustrator Fritz Kredel is himself a
creator of dolls and puppets. The marionettes reproduced are from the
Italian Comedia dell' Arte (characters who reappeared later in the plays
of Molière) – Arlecchino, Desdemona, Scapino and others. The strings
have been omitted in the illustrations, but there is an obvious sympathy
between the illustrator-puppeteer and the earlier craftsmen.

Don Quixote (el ingenioso Hidalgo de la Mancha), by Miguel de Cervantes
Saavedra (1547–1616), first published 1605–12, many later editions:
translation by P. A. Motteux (1712) available in *Everyman* series, 2 vols.
Chapters 25–26 of particular interest to puppeteers as giving a clear
picture of the puppetry of the period in which the eccentric knight errant
Don Quixote and his faithful squire Sancho Panza become incidentally
involved (seventeenth century). The marionettes are described: they had
glass eyes, eyelashes, delicately carved faces. The booth is set up in the
courtyard of an inn; in front stands a young assistant with a white wand
in his hand, who points at the characters and explains the action of the

play: 'The ears of all the spectators hung on the mouth of the interpreter.' This use of 'interpreter' was widespread, is found in Jonson
Bartholomew Fayre – with puppet booth set up in the fairground – and
in various references in Shakespeare. The showman says that the play
Melisandra's Deliverance is taken from the chronicles of France and the
Spanish ballads; Don Gayferos the hero rescues his wife from the Moors.
During the performance, Don Quixote, who confuses fantasy and reality,
draws his own sword and joins in the stage combat, slashing the puppets
and their strings. The show (in the translation at least) is referred to as
'a motion,' the popular name in England for the puppets of the period.
An illustration by Gustave Doré (reproduced in Baird *Art of the Puppet*)
is probably the result of 'artistic licence'; the audience stands close to the
stage, which is crowded with puppets and decapitated heads, with the
hands of two performers controlling five of the figures, two thin wires to
each (operators' fingers through wire loops); one operator manages two
marionettes with one hand. Incidentally, the showman also had a fortune-
telling Ape – and an Ape often featured in French shows of the period.
The work as a whole was a satire on the 'false and absurd' tales of chivalry.
The particular episode inspired the composer de Falla (1876–1946) to
write *El Retablo Maese Pedro* for the theatre of Princesse de Polignac,
which has had many puppet productions, English edition *Master Peter's
Puppet Show* (J. W. Chester).

Donne, John (1576–1631). English poet: love, religion, Court life; in
Satyre II has the intriguing line: 'As in some Organ, Puppits dance above.'

Downstage. The area of the stage nearest the audience. Term dates from
period when stage floor sloped, uphill from the front. Curiously, with the
hand puppet or rod puppet stage, the audience looking slightly upwards,
as the puppets leave the front and move towards the backscreen they
appear to go downhill unless this illusion is counteracted by a gradual
raising of the figures.

Dramas and Dramatic Dances of Non-European Races, by William Ridgeway
(Putnam, N.Y., 1915); has material on puppets in Java, Burma, Japan,
Hindustan, and expresses opinion that puppets had a longer history in
Europe – as opposed to view expressed by Pischel in *The Home of the
Puppet Play* (1902) that India was the true birthplace. See remarks in
entry on INDIA.

Dramatic Parody by Marionettes in Eighteenth Century Paris, by Frank W.
Lindsay (King's Crown Press, N.Y., 1946). A Columbia University
doctor's thesis dealing with the texts of 29 plays, 7 published and the rest
in manuscript, performed by puppets in parodies of live dramas in the
Paris Fairs of 1722–60.

Drapes. Theatrical abbreviation for 'draperies'; any soft curtaining used
as part of stage decor.

Draw-curtains. Stage curtains which divide in the middle and are pulled
to the sides.

Dresden, Germany. Important puppet-theatre collection in the City
Museum (Staatliche Puppentheatersammlung). Souvenir booklet com-
memorating first 50 years issued 1963 includes some puppet photos and
historical notes. Dresden Trikfilm Studio, directed by German puppeteer
Carl Schroeder, produces films of 'live' performances of hand puppets.

Droll. Term used in seventeenth and eighteenth centuries and, depending
on the context, means a farce, *or* a puppet show, *or* some other amusing
entertainment; also the clown or comedian himself.

Petrouchka: rod puppet

Above left: Sea horse, marionette by Waldo Lanchester
Above right: Prince and princess, rod puppets from *The Wooden Prince*
Below left: Mounted hand puppet by Lucy Clause
Below right: Mounted rod puppet from the Tandarica Theatre, Bucharest

Punch and crocodile in Glyn Edwards' Punch booth (figures attributed to Wal Kent)

Old English marionette: clown

Drop. Showmen's term for money dropped into collecting box, hat, etc. Making the collection is known as 'bottling'.

Dryad Handicrafts. Head Offices: Northgates, Leicester. London shop: 22 Bloomsbury Street, W.C.1 (close to British Museum). All craft materials and equipment; pamphlets on puppets to make from felt; Dutch dolls (for converting into simple marionettes).

Dryden, John (1631–1700). English poet, dramatist, critic; *Absalom and Achitophel* (1681), *Fables Ancient and Modern* (1699), etc. In *Sir Martin Marr-all, or the Feigned Innocence* (1608–1668): 'I know no way so proper for you as to turn poet to *Pogenello*' – an unusual version of 'Punchinello'. In *Persius* (1693) Notes: 'Those Baby-Toys were little Babies, or Poppets, as we call them.' Little jointed dolls were sold at Bartholomew Fair and known as 'Bartholomew Babies'. See BABIES.

Dual control. Specially designed control giving simultaneous action to two marionettes; precise construction depends on range of movement required.

Duke of Edinburgh Award Scheme. Puppetry syllabus provided for guidance only (a) for beginners, (b) for those with some knowledge and skill in the art (c) for the more advanced. Principle of assessment is the degree of interest, progress and genuine sustained effort shown by candidate during stipulated period, not the attainment of any fixed standard. Type of puppet to be made at each level not stipulated: candidates may choose several types, but not discouraged from specialisation. Each type of puppet considered in its own right and not as part of a progression. Further details from the Scheme Office: 2 Old Queen Street, London, S.W.1.

Dumas, Alexandre (Davy de la Pailleterie, 1802–70). French novelist and dramatist; *Count of Monte Cristo*, *The Three Musketeers*, *La Tour de Nesle*, in the repertoire of some of the French puppet companies (late nineteenth century) listed in Gervais *Marionnettes et Marionnettistes de France* (Bordas, 1947).

Dumb show. Acting with movement and gesture only, without dialogue.

Dummy. Rather derogatory term for Ventriloquist's puppet. Leading performers treat their characters as members of the family.

Duranty, Louis Emile. French author who wrote and performed puppet plays of literary quality with topical satire; opened theatre in the Tuileries Gardens in Paris (1861) in collaboration with sculptor Leboeuf; closed in two or three years for lack of public interest. Published book of 24 plays (1864), in which Polichinelle is the dominant character: *Theatre des Jardins des Tuileries* (Dubuisson, 2nd Ed., 1880, Charpentier). English translation of one item, *Le Tonneau* (*The Cask*) in Baird *Art of the Puppet* (Collier-Macmillan, 1965).

Dutch dolls. (? Deutsch: of German origin). Wooden figures with jointed limbs; head, neck and body usually in one piece, but can be converted to give head movement. Sometimes used as marionettes after loosening of joints and adding strings. They were much cheaper in the days when Whanslaw mentioned them in his *Everybody's Theatre* in the 1920's, but are still obtainable in various sizes, e.g. from DRYAD's and POLLOCK's.

Dvorak, Antonin (1841–1904). Famous Czech composer: *New World Symphony*, *Slavonic Dances*, etc. Used subject of traditional Czech puppet play for libretto of opera *The King and the Collier* (1874).

Dwiggins, W. A. American puppeteer and author of book on the Püterschein system of marionette construction and control *Marionette in Motion* (Puppetry Imprints, 1939). Privately published *Jeremy; Afterpiece for Marionettes* (G. G. and M. D. Taylor, Mass., 1944) from his own repertoire: theme of Friar who took advantage of women's charity.

E

Early Japanese Puppet Drama, by C. J. Dunn (Luzac, 1966). Author is Reader in Japanese at the School of Oriental and African Studies, London; widely travelled in Japan. Comprehensive well-documented study of the pre-Bunraku era, illustrated by 19 reproductions from early prints; considers methods of performing and plays before the evolution of the Bunraku, q.v. techniques.

Edinburgh International Festival of Music and Drama. First organised 1947 and held annually in Edinburgh, Scotland; has become one of the most significant of European festivals. In the early days Miles Lee's 'Mews Theatre' (puppets) was among the fringe activities, until he went abroad; in 1950 Ben Jonson's *Bartholomew Fayre* q.v. was performed by the Old Vic company, the puppet-scene being the responsibility of George Speaight (puppets by John Wright); in 1959 Barry Smith's 'Theatre of Puppets' appeared; in 1966 Sergei Obraztsov the Soviet puppet master, as solo artiste; and in 1697 Michael Meschke's Marionette Theatre from Stockholm presented Jarry's *Ubu Roi*, q.v. and the *Wizard of Oz*, q.v.

Educational puppetry. Term has two interpretations (1) performances of puppet productions having the purpose of developing social and cultural understanding on the part of audiences, (2) personal development through practice of puppetry in school, youth club, training college, further education centre. An extension of (2) is the application of puppetry in the therapy field, both physiological and psychological. It should not be assumed that the desired results will automatically follow from either approach, but it is of particular interest to educators that the possibilities have become themes for discussion at the international level at puppet conferences. An example of (1) is in the presentation of a special show for pre-school age children to show them that school is a happy place, a Bulgarian show in which the characters were mother and baby rabbits charmed even the adult puppeteers at an international festival. Another example is that of a doctor in Wales who used puppet plays in 'preventive medicine' to remove apprehension in young children due for inoculation. In the same category are road and home safety programmes. These examples tie in with modern audio-visual aid theory. Other programmes might be devised purely for social indoctrination

motives and plays can be used with religious content. The effectiveness
of any of these applications will depend on the quality of the content of
the plays and on the skill of the performers. Methods used in (2) vary
widely. In schools it is possible to link all the lessons to a puppetry project,
the resulting performance being a stimulus to work in individual subjects.
Teachers may have a specialised interest such as puppetry purely for
speech training; puppetry can also be used in speech therapy: a child who
stammers may lose this impediment when taking the part of a puppet
character in a play. In practice it is the putting of emphasis on the
dramatic aspect that usually has the maximum results. If the work stops
at the mere making of puppets, however enjoyable this occupation,
opportunities of further development will be missed. Methods of making
will be adapted to the age group, or even the mental age group, of the
pupils. Part of the educational value may be in creating original plays
or adapting from the literature of the age group. There have been
developments in the use of puppetry in the learning of primary school
French; the language problem for immigrant children is also being tackled
through puppet play. Puppets well used by a teacher in a stage can rivet
the attention of the young audience on what is happening and being
said by the characters. Study of children's drawings made following a
puppet show prove the vividness of such experiences. In schools and clubs
for children economy both of time and materials is usually a dominant
factor; the development of methods using scrap materials has other
advantages than economy: the handling of ready-made objects such as
discarded or new pulp flowerpots (inexpensive), egg boxes, cartons of
various shapes, liquid soap containers, sox, offcut materials from dressmaking sources, and a variety of useful things for hair (string, hemp,
wools, small pieces of fur or fur fabric, etc.) these may stimulate even the
mentally retarded, the slow learner, the educationally sub-normal
pupils as well as the higher grades. Puppetry has been applied very
successfully in literacy campaigns, e.g. in Mexico and India. In Britain
puppetry has a place in the syllabi of most Colleges of Education (teacher
training) and is studied in Occupational Therapy and Speech Therapy
training centres. There is an Educational Puppetry Association based in
London (formed 1943) which has offered courses to teachers, published
what has become the standard textbook for educationalists, inexpensive
instructional leaflets, etc., and held school puppet festivals and exhibitions.   In the United States a first-class item *Puppetry in the Curriculum*
was made available to teachers by the New York Board of Education;
it gives a careful analysis of the values at each grade. A major value of
puppetry – as compared with 'live' drama in schools or clubs – is the
anonymity of the performer hidden in a stage, the fact that physique is of
secondary importance, that an enormous range of parts is possible
(including animal characters impossible to play effectively on the human
stage) and that every child who wishes to can take part; there is no 'star'
system. The therapeutic aspect is treated elsewhere in this volume.

Educational Puppetry Association. Formed in 1942 as offshoot of the
British Puppet and Model Theatre Guild, q.v. and adopted the title
'E.P.A.' in 1943; membership is open to all interested in the educational
possibilities of puppetry. A National Committee was set up, with John
Cox, M.A., as the first President, followed by Dr E. Davies, M.C., M.A.,
D.PH., Director of Education for Willesden. Among the first Vice-
Presidents was H. W. Whanslaw, the 'father' of the Guild. Present
President: J. Vincent Chapman, F.C.P., Secretary of the College of

Preceptors, and for many years Hon. General Secretary of E.P.A. Originally intended as a 'temporary address', the Association has had its headquarters in the basement of the College of Preceptors (Bloomsbury Square, London, W.C.1) for over 20 years; it has broadened its aims during the period in which puppetry in education has gained acceptance (for instance, the therapeutic possibilities were not mentioned in the original aims); it has held exhibitions, schools' festivals (until London traffic problems became prohibitive), a succession of Courses of Instruction (evening and vacation); it issued first a monthly news letter to members, expanded this into a magazine (*Puppet Post*), which has had several formats and has settled into a twice-a-year 32 pp. issue containing a great variety of material: news (including international puppet events), technical articles, items on all the educational and therapeutic aspects, correspondence and book reviews. Interim news-letters ('Spotlight') also go out to members. The Association has made a major contribution to the literature on the subject in its *The Puppet Book* (Faber: 3 editions, 1956, 1960, 1965), which has had world-wide distribution; it has built up a wide range of Instructional Leaflets for the benefit of students and teachers, and has published a book of plays contributed by members: *Eight Plays for Hand Puppets*, edited A. R. Philpott (Garnet-Miller, 1968). The Association has co-operated with many other organisations, including provision of lecture-demonstrations. It has members today in some 20 countries; it has representation on the National Section of UNIMA, the international puppetry organisation. From the earliest days of its activities many professional puppeteers have co-operated with the Association; early issues of the magazine contain technical articles by H. W. Whanslaw, Jan Bussell, and others, and at every Festival puppeteers gave their services – including Percy Press and his famous Mister Punch. Students have attended from other countries, including a group from Hawaii University, individuals from Germany, France, Sweden, Italy, New Zealand, Thailand, India, Ceylon, various parts of Africa and the United States. The E.P.A. Headquarters is normally open to visitors Monday evenings during school term, from 6.30 p.m. (entrance via 23a Southampton Place, W.C.1); at other times by appointment only, most of its Council members being in the teaching profession. Details of membership, of forthcoming Courses, lists of literature available; s.a.e. to Hon. Secretary.

Edwards, Glyn. English puppeteer; professional name 'Crackers'; born into family with Variety Theatre connections and from 14 years of age helped parents at children's entertainments; at 17 bought a set of Punch and Judy figures from a retiring showman at Bournemouth and spent six months learning to use the swazzle, helped by Punchman Sydney de Hempsey (author of book on Punch); participated in the Punch Tercentenary celebrations organised by the Guild and the Society for Theatre Research in 1962 and appeared in television programme on the work of the Guild, demonstrating the Punch show of the younger generation of Punchmen. Resident Punchman at Sheerness-on-Sea, 1963. Joined the Charivari Puppet Company and appeared with them at the international puppet festival in Karlovy Vary, Czechoslovakia (1964). Regular performer as children's entertainer at private functions, fetes, galas, schools, and for local councils throughout England; guest artiste performances at the 'Little Angel' Marionette Theatre, London, also as member of their resident company. Played 'Noah' in John Wright's rod-puppet production of the mediaeval play at the British Puppet

Festival during the Hastings Celebrations (1966). Performer in the Lord Mayor's Show, London (1968), and with the Charivari Company at the Arts Theatre. B.B.C. Schools Television appearance demonstrating Punch and Judy. South Coast tour (1968) sponsored by publishing firm, promoting their juvenile publications and featuring one of their cartoon characters (Harold Hare) in the Punch show. Council Member of the British Puppet and Model Theatre Guild and of the Educational Puppetry Association; member of the Committee of the British Section of UNIMA.

Effects. (a) Theatrical illusion, visual and audio, such as wind, rain, thunder, lightning, running water, snow, smoke, fire, crashes, creakings, breaking glass, shot, gongs, bells, chimes, train or car or aeroplane noises, crowd noises. (b) Equipment for producing these effects. Techniques: Napier, *Noises Off*; Batchelder, *Puppet Theatre Handbook*; Inverarity, *Manual of Puppetry*; Green, *Stage Noises and Effects*; many others include chapters. Gramophone or magnetic tape recordings available for wide range of effects, public performance rights usually go with purchase. Large theatres may have Effects Director responsible for all stage illusions and off-stage noises.

Effects projector. Lighting equipment using discs and slides for projecting effect of clouds, rain, snow, lightning, etc.

Efimova (Yefimova) Nina Simonovich (1877–1948). Russian painter, co-founder (with husband) of rod-puppet theatre (influenced by Austrian artist-puppeteer Teschner, who had adapted from traditional Javanese type); Member of Honour of UNIMA (in Memoriam). Productions included *Banquet of Authors* with life-size rod-puppets representing Tolstoy, Gogol, Pushkin, Gorky, Chekhov and others: and a 10-ft. Shakespeare. Repertoire built from Russian folk-tales and Krylov fables, Andersen and others; excerpt from Macbeth. Author of *Memoirs of a Petrushka Player* (Zapiski Petrushechnika: Moscow, 1925), English edition. *Adventures of a Russian Puppet Theatre* (Puppetry Imprints, USA, 1935) includes description of development of hand-and-rod type.

Efimov (Yefimov) Ivan Semionovich (1878–1959). Russian sculptor, co-founder (with wife Nina) of puppet theatre using modern rod puppet technique. Hon. Member UNIMA (in Memoriam).

Egg heads. Cardboard Easter eggs make good basic shapes for hand puppet heads; add cardboard tube neck; use vertically, horizontally, tilted; polystyrene (styrofoam) q.v. eggs, lightweight, can also be used for hand or rod types, surface reinforced with layers of paper and glue or celastic, q.v.

Egg-trays. The type used by dairies and made of white or grey pulp, end-opening. Widely used in schools in craft work and as basic heads for puppet monsters, having a ready-made jaw movement. The half with the deep hollows converts into puppet owls by the addition of costume and bottle-top eyes (hand puppets). A tougher plastic variety is available in Woolworth's and elsewhere for more durable, professional work. The larger type of pulp tray sometimes adapted for decorative purposes.

Elastic. Flat, round, varieties, and in rubber band form; useful in the puppet workshop, e.g. for temporary attaching of sword to hand, chin-strap for helmet, or for applying pressure to wigs while adhesive is setting; sometimes used as part of complex mechanism for elaborate shadow figures.

Electric light bulbs. Some textbooks advocate use of as base for shaping paper-layer or other heads; risk of broken glass should be sufficient deterrent.

Electricity. Stage lighting equipment must be suitable for mains supply available; lamps, dimmers, etc., must be of correct voltage, which should be stated when being purchased (as also for household equipment). Wattage (number of watts) refers to consumption of power in an electrical circuit at any moment: 1,000 watts consumes ten times 100 watts.

Elizabethan Stage, The, by E. K. Chambers (Oxford, 1923), in 4 volumes; some puppet entries; Appendix D includes historical items from Documents of Control: July 14, 1573, a letter to the Lord Mayor of London seeking permission for 'certain Italian players' to show 'an instrument of strange motions' – and on July 19 a letter giving permission. 'Motions' q.v. was popular term for puppets in that period.

Elyot, Sir Thomas (? 1490–1546). Political writer, translator; author of *The Dictionary of Sir T. Elyot, Knyght* (1538): see Gesticulator.

Emperor Jones, by Eugene O'Neill, American playwright, q.v. Theme: murderer becomes self-imposed dictator of a West Indian island; predictable ending; dramatic incessant drum-beats during flight through forest. Productions in the United States by Ralph Chesse, San Francisco (marionettes) and Jero Magon, New York (marionettes and flat rod figures).

Emulsion paints. Oil-in-water or water-in-oil types, tiny drops of one suspended in other; can be used on wood, plaster, rubber, paper; relatively quick drying; available in intermixable colours.

Enamels. Paints made by grinding or mixing pigments with varnishes or lacquers, having high gloss, smooth durable finish.

Encylopedia of World Art (McGraw Hill, USA, 1966: translation from Italian edition, 1958). Volume XI has lengthy chapter on puppets and marionettes; photo-illustrations.

English Fairs and Markets, by William Addison (Batsford, 1953). Interesting account of St Bartholomew and other famous fairs, some references to raree q.v. shows and puppets and 'all the fun of the fair'; mentions Henry Fielding, author of famous novel *Tom Jones* (1749), who was thought to have had a booth in the fair, because of an advertisement in the *Daily Post,* 23rd August, 1729: 'Mr Fielding's Great theatrical booth in the George Inn yard, Smithfield' – the Mr Fielding later found to be a Timothy.

Entertainment agencies. These usually advertise in local newspapers and accept engagements for artistes on their books, deducting commission from fee paid; some specialise in children's parties. Re-engagements are usually through the agency. Major toy shops such as Hamleys of Regent Street, London, W., have their own department for bookings, as also Foyles bookshop in Charing Cross Road, London, W.C.2. Reputable agencies require artistes to arrange audition of actual performance before agreeing to accept engagements.

Epic. (a) Heroic; narrative poem of some heroic deed; (b) a type of drama, acting, stage setting: using an anti-naturalistic technique.

Eric Bramall Marionette Cabaret. The first British complete act 'floor show' q.v. to be presented (as far as is known). Eric Bramall, director of the Harlequin Puppet Theatre, q.v., is best known for his Cabaret. Began as teen-ager and toured extensively on the Music Halls and in many pantomimes. Notable acts: *Kasperl*, a little boy pretending he is an old man, *Figaro*, *Madam Olive*, the *Two Harlequins* (with a large marionette operating a smaller figure). Appearances in films and TV at home and abroad.

Esperanto. Artificially created international language begun by Dr Lazarus Ludovic Zamenhof (1859–1917), who published a small textbook in 1887, in Warsaw, under the name of 'Dr Esperanto' (Esperanto = one who hopes). Esperanto has now become synonym for 'international language'. Zamenhof renounced all rights, being only concerned with the overcoming of language barriers. A first World Congress of Esperantists was held in 1905 at Boulogne-sur-Mer, France, and Congresses are held every year in various parts of the world. Postage stamps have borne the portrait of the founder, and there are national associations. Puppet performances have been given in Esperanto in Poland, at a Congress in Brussels and another in Budapest (which has an Esperantist Group of players: *see* HOWARD, T.E.).

Etymology. Study of origin of words. Word usage always precedes written form; early spellings non-standardised (Shakespeare's name had several spellings); research can only pinpoint first known written usage, impossible to date original usage except of new contemporary words such as radio, television. Major dictionaries (e.g. *Webster International*, Bell, 1961, 3rd edition) incline to caution regarding puppet terms, derivations being 'assumed' or 'attributed to': 'popet (ME) from poupette, little doll, assumed im. of poupe, doll, whence F. poupee – doll, from (assumed) VL puppa, altern. of L.pupa, girl, doll, puppet'. It will be seen, from individual entries in present *Dictionary*, that scholars are divided in views as to origin of 'marionette', 'pantin', 'motion' and so on, 'motion' having many other meanings as well as being popular term for puppet or puppet show, many of the variants appearing in Shakespeare's plays.

Evelyn, John (1620–1706). English author (science, gardening, numismatics) best known for his *Diary* published 1818 and which contains a number of references to puppet shows: one item (1st March, 1644) was of particular interest to Gordon Craig, q.v., who devoted a good deal of space to a commentary on the *Diary* in his *Books and Theatres* (Dent, 1925) and remarked that neither of the puppet historians Magnin, q.v., and Maindron, q.v., seemed to have noted it; this was about a puppet theatre in a Palace in the rue de Seine, St Germain, at the bottom of a garden and equipped with scene changes, the characters being painted on light board and cut out, manipulated by someone underneath who also spoke the dialogue; Evelyn gave 15 lines to this (1st March, 1644), comparing well with the brief entries in Pepys' *Diary*. An entry for 3rd February, 1644, mentions puppet players, mountebanks and 'operators' on the front of the Isle de Palais; one for Christmas Eve the same year relates to a Nativity scene in the Church of Minerva in Rome. For 24th January, 1684, an entry regarding the Fair held on the frozen Thames, with shops and stalls and 'sliding with skates, bull baiting, horse and coach races and puppet plays'. The *Diary* was published in 1818 and there is an *Everyman Library* edition in two volumes edited by William Bray, 1901; 2nd edition, 1952: Dent.

Everybody's Theatre, by H. W. Whanslaw (Wells, Gardner, Darton, 1923). Book on the toy theatre and marionettes; landmark in publication of puppet literature, having considerable influence on revival of interest in

Great Britain and on individuals who, with the author, founded the British Puppet and Model Theatre Guild, q.v.

Every-Day Book, The, or Everlasting Calendar of Popular Amusements (in three volumes), by William Hone (Tegg, 1838). A number of interesting references to puppets. Flockton, 'the last eminent motion-master at Bartholomew Fair', had trained a Newfoundland dog to fight his puppet representing the devil, always finally winning and running off with the puppet. In literature there are many references to 'motion', from Shakespeare onwards, with obvious variations of meaning: Hone adds that, in common talk, a single puppet was called a motion. There is an account of the use of puppets by the priests of Witney in Oxfordshire in a presentation of The Resurrection, with Christ, Mary and others, including a Watchman who made 'a continual noise like the sound caused by the meeting of two sticks' and who therefore came to be known as Jack Snacker of Wytney. There is a mention of an early playbill (in the British Museum) which announces scriptural subjects (at Crawley's booth in Smithfield) during the time of Bartholomew Fair: 'the Old Creation of the World, yet newly revised, with the addition of Noah's Flood; also several fountains playing water'. There are references to puppet items in *The Tatler* q.v. and *Spectator* q.v. concerning Powell's show. Under 'the Season' there is a reference to Punch and Judy presented to 'successive crowds in every street', and there is a reproduction of a Cruikshank illustration of 'Candler's Fantoccini,' the 'front man' being equipped with drum and panpipes. Another item is on the BEHEADING OF PUPPETS, relating to the execution of Lord Lovat and others.

Everyman. Fifteenth century Morality Play by anonymous English author, possibly from Dutch original *Elckerlijk,* by Dorlandus. Early editions of *The Summoning of Everyman,* 1509–19, two each by Pynson and Skot. Theme: title character summoned to Divine Judgment, by Death; characters are abstractions: Good Deeds, Knowledge, Beauty, etc., from whom Everyman seeks support. *Jederman,* by Hofmannsthal, q.v., has same theme (1910). Play constantly revived with frequent new editions; included in the *Everyman* series by Dent. (There have been puppet adaptations.)

Expedition 'Alexandre'. UNESCO-sponsored world survey of puppetry, carried out by French puppeteers Philippe Genty and Serge George travelling in small car and making colour-film; for part of journey accompanied by Michike Tagawa from the Takeda Marionette Theatre in Tokyo. Star member of team was 'Alexandre' – 3-ft. tall marionette-cum-journalist. Enquiries as to availability of film should be made to UNESCO.

Expert Puppet Technique, by Eric Bramall and Christopher C. Somerville (Faber, 1963). A manual of Production for puppeteers. Introductory chapters on: What is puppetry? and Why puppetry? Also on writing the script, recording the script, the designing of the puppet and its manipulation, stage and settings, lighting, rehearsals and performances. Seven photo illustrations. A script of *The Damnation of Faust* adapted from Christopher Marlowe's *The Tragical History of Dr Faust* is taken as basis for study of production, and it is stated that playing Tragedy with marionettes is good discipline (it can accidentally turn into comedy). It is marionette technique in particular that is dealt with in this book.

Exploring. American television programme for children (NBC); over five million viewers, including many adults. Programmes concern science, social subjects, and 'The New Maths', Architecture, Music, Nature Study. Dr Albert Hibbs (physicist, space-satellite designer) uses puppets Albert Chipmunk, Calvin Crow, Sir Geoffrey Giraffe and Magnolia Ostrich to put over the programme, assisted by veteran puppeteers Paul and Mary Ritts.

Exploring Puppetry, by Stuart and Patricia Robinson (Mills and Boon, 1967). Practical book with 140 illustrations, some in colour, photographs and drawings, giving ideas and techniques for making and using Shadow, Hand, String, Push-on and Rod Puppets, Peepshows, Toy Theatres and Masks; particularly slanted for schools, colleges, clubs, the home. Range of up-to-date quick methods, step-by-step instruction. Covers lighting, stages, sound effects; lists materials and suppliers, books, films, museums, societies, publications of interest to puppeteers.

Extender. Inert material, white or colourless, for diluting colour pigments.

Eyes (for puppets). With all features, stylised or realistic, it is the effect at a distance which is important. Techniques include: painting, simple hollows, actual holes as in some sculptures – relying on play of light and shade for changes of expression – and light-reflecting materials such as glazed paper, coloured-head drawing or map pins, glass beads, chair nails, buttons, sequins, metal foil: coal and pieces of broken glass have also been tried. If eyes are painted, advisable *not* to paint highlights: these will be static, whereas a gloss paint will reflect light and give moving highlights. Complex moving eyeballs sometimes used, operated internally by a mechanism. Some of the Japanese Bunraku q.v. heads have movable eyebrows as well as moving eyes. Surrealist figures may have eyes on stalks. Techniques: Fedotow *Technik des puppentheaters*, Mulholland *Practical Puppetry*, Houlden *Ventriloquism for Boys and Girls*, and other textbooks. One television-film company, aiming at super-realism, experimented with photographs of living eyes added to pupils of puppet eyes.

F

Fables. Fictitious stories with purpose or stressing wisdom and moral virtues; traditionally take the form of animal tales satirising human behaviour. Originally circulated by word of mouth. Many versions found in different countries, continents. *The Panchatantra* ('The Five Books.') in India goes back 2,000 years and is possible source of some Aesop, La Fontaine and other written works. English translation from original Sanskrit *The Panchatantra*, by Arthur W. Ryder (University of Chicago Press, 1956), has the five classifications: loss of friends, winning of friends, crows and owls, loss of gains, ill-considered action. AESOP, Greek fabulist, flourished about 600 B.C. and added some original items to those extant from earlier sources. LA FONTAINE, French fabulist, and Russian KRYLOV also benefitted from existing material. Animal characters lend themselves to puppet treatment; items such as *Country Mouse and Town Mouse*, *Fox and Grapes*, *Chanticleer and Fox*, have had puppet versions and provided material for cartoon films. Contemporary illustrated editions of the various authors provide visual inspiration.

Facer-board. Showman's term for the facia, the proscenium arch of a Punch and Judy booth, which may be purely decorative or bear an inscription.

Fadenbühne, The. Modern puppet theatre in Vienna, founded by artists Picca and Professor Aminio Rothstein. First performance, 1957. Repertoire includes *Anita and the Iceberg*, a parody of film life; *Faust*; Gogol's *The Government Inspector*; a popular musical variety item, *Vienna on Strings*.

Fairy Tales. In 1964 an International Conference was held in Brussels, with the theme: *The Fairy Tale and/or Realism in the repertoire for children 6–12 years*. The patrons were the Province of Brabant and the National Ministry of Education and Culture. Among those taking part were representatives from Children's Theatres and Puppeteers from a number of countries. There is a difference between the tale told in narrative form and the tale brought to life by actors or actors with puppets: entertainers as well as educationalists and psychologists are interested in children's reactions. In a report by Dr Bender and Adolphe Woltmann in 1935, following experiments with puppets in their therapeutic work with children at the Bellevue Hospital in New York, it was stated that they had found it impossible to successfully replace genuine folktales by any artistic or psychological plays written by adults. The term 'folk tales' is the broader classification, and many so-called 'fairy' tales have no fairies in them: but there is always the element of fantasy and often of magic. It is not true that the fairy tale belongs 'to no particular time and place except perhaps childhood and the nursery', as stated by Geoffrey Brereton in the introduction to the Penguin edition of *Perrault's Fairy Tales*: it has always been the adults who have orally handed on the folk-lore beliefs, and in some parts the beliefs are by no means dead. Sceptics should read *Fairies at Work and at Play* as observed by Geoffrey Hodson (Theosophical Publishing House, 1925, 1930) and in which he describes the appearance and activities of Brownies and Elves, Gnomes, Mannikins, Undines and Sea Spirits, Fairies, Sylphs, Nature Spirits and Elementals. This involved occult vision of a high order, to which is related the 'second sight' of some country folk, particularly the Celtic, and perhaps of young children everywhere. The modern psychologist in talking of a collective spiritual memory is as much putting a label to what is not clearly understood as is the myth-maker of ancient times. One of the most brilliant of contemporary Polish designers for the puppet theatre, Adam Kilian, says 'Imagination and the themes of fairy tales make it possible for form and colour to flourish' (*The Puppet Master*, Spring, 1964), and Henryk Jurkowski, of the Polish Ministry of Culture, adds 'Poetic fairy tales are the main fare offered as far as Polish puppet plays are concerned' and that a characteristic thing about fairy stories is that they often serve to show the 'different peculiarities of the world of people' (*The Puppet Master*, December, 1962). One of the characteristics of being 'grown up' is the disowning of 'childish' beliefs. This does not put an end to fantasy, but this may be catered for in other ways, by novels, detective stories, science-fiction. Folk tales often have moral overtones, involve heroism and other virtues. The modern fairy-tale of *Peter Pan* by J. M. Barrie has become an annual theatrical event; it is the mothers and fathers and aunts and uncles who unanimously reply 'Yes!' when the audience is asked 'Do you believe in fairies?' The Hodder and Stoughton edition (*c.* 1910) has Arthur Rackham q.v. illustrations, which give a good idea of the modern arrtist's concept of the Little People. A great deal of the appeal of Shakespeare's *Midsummer Night's Dream* is in the introduction of fairy scenes: and it is difficult for the human actor to compete with puppets in this realm.

Fairy Tales, Myths and Legends, Index to, by Mary Huse Eastman (Faxon, Boston, 1926: 2nd revised enlarged edition). Lists of books analysed; lists for storytellers; directory of publishers; also a supplementary volume.

Falla, Manuel de. See DE FALLA.

Fantoccini. Italian term for marionettes or marionette show, usually associated with trick figures. 'Fantoccio' (puppet) from 'Fante': boy or child. 'Fantoccino': little puppet. French variant 'fantoches' sometimes used with reference to puppet films. English showmen adopted the term, eighteenth-nineteenth centuries mainly for trick items (clowns, dancing sailors, transformation types. Théophile Gautier in his *Constantinople* (1854) refers to the 'fantoccini' of the French *shadow* theatre Seraphin, q.v. in a comparison with the Turkish shadow show Karagöz, q.v. A Cruickshank illustration Puppets in 1825 (reproduced in McKechnie *Popular Entertainments* (1931) shows 'Candler's Fantoccini' 'patronised by royalty', with clown-like figure on stage, audience, drummer with pan-pipes tucked into top of shirt. Whanslaw *First Bench Book* lists showmen who used the term in their notices. There is little evidence of manner of control of the fantoccini: there are references here and there to 'strings' and to 'wires'. The street showman interviewed by Mayhew (*London Labour and London Poor,* 1852) refers to strings only, which would be technically right for trick-puppet control; wires may have been in use originally for straightforward plays. The fantoccini gave indoor as well as street performances, from 1770–80, at Hickford's large rooms in Panton Street, Haymarket, and at 'an elegant little theatre' called Variétés Amusantes, belonging to Lord Barrymore, in Savile Row, London.

Fantoche, fantoches. French variants of Italian 'FANTOCCINI'.

Fatal Puppet Show. Strictly speaking, 'Fatal fire at puppet show'. Hone's *Everyday Book* (Tegg, 1827) contains extract from Parish Register of Burwell in Cambridgeshire, dated 3rd September, 1727: 'seventy-six perished instantly in a barn' – members of audience watching puppet show. No details of actual show.

Faust, Georg. Historical person (1480–1538) possibly behind German legendary figure Dr Faustus, wandering 'conjuror' mentioned in documents 1488–1541; his 'pact with the Devil' always a popular theme; first printed version of the puppet-play which influenced Goethe appeared in 1587 at Frankfurt: *The History of that Everywhere Infamous and Black Artist and Conjuror Dr. Faustus' Compact with the Devil* (author unknown). Marlowe (1564–93) based his *Tragical History of Doctor Faustus* (1593) on a translation by 'P.F.' (1592). English translation of puppet-showman Guido Bonneschky (Hann, 1850) play 'an heroicomic drama in four acts' appears in von Boehn's *Dolls and Puppets* (Harrap, 1932: Cooper-Square, USA, 1966), q.v.

Faust (Dr. Faust, Dr. Faustus). Legendary character possibly based on historical person Georg Faust, q.v., mentioned in German documents of 1488–1541). German puppet shows introduced the dramatic play concerning the well-known theme of Faust's pact with the devil (anonymous printed version, Frankfurt, 1587). Goethe (1749–1832) saw a puppet performance as a boy and this remained in his mind until, 50 years later, he wrote his masterpiece *Faust*. In his autobiographical *Dichtung und Wahrheit* he mentions the 'weighty theme' of the Faust play. He was also acquainted with the German *Historia von D. Johann Fausten* (1587). In Goethe's version Faust bargains with Mephistopheles: soul against a single moment of absolute satisfaction. The German puppet versions added the comic character Hanswurst, q.v., who gradually from being an assistant to Faust's servant became the dominant character. Some versions had musical arias; there was a pantomime *Harlequin Dr Faustus* produced at Drury Lane in 1724, and POWELL's puppet theatre in Covent Garden added Faust to the normal programme of farce and pantomime. It has been said that one version or another has been in the repertoire of every contemporary puppet theatre. The text from the manuscript of a puppet showman, Guido Bonneschky (1850) is included in von Boehn *Dolls and Puppets*, q.v. An extract in French appears in Mignon *J'aime les Marionnettes* (Editions Rencontre, 1962). Eric Bramall, *Expert Puppet Technique* (Faber, 1963), uses play as a production study. Story inspired many musicians: Gounod wrote an opera *Faust*, Smetana an overture *Dr Faustus*; Berlioz *La Damnation de Faust*; Boito *Mefistofele*, and Busoni *Dr Faust*.

Faustov. Name of scientist in *I-Ho-Ho*, q.v., puppet production at the Moscow Central State Puppet Theatre (play by Evgeny Speransky): theme is the survival of the past in the minds and conduct of people. Main characters played by live actors; witches, devils, mermaids and fairies by puppets.

Faustus, Doctor, the Puppet Play of. An Heroi-Comic Drama in Four Acts, from the MS. of the puppet showman Guido Bonneschky; published for the first time faithfully in its original form by Wilhelm Hamm, 1850; text is reproduced in von Boehn *Dolls and Puppets*, q.v. (translated from the German); one of the most widely performed puppet plays in Europe, showmen usually making own versions. Characters include Kasperle, q.v., 'a travelling genius', Mephistopheles and various supernatural spirits and, among the apparitions, Samson and Delilah and David and Goliath.

Felt. Closely matted wool fibres, sold by yard or in handy size squares (Craft suppliers); wide range of colours; cuts without fraying. Thin variety used for heads of stuffed puppets or as collage on faces (can be shaped during gluing); also for decorative costume details; usually too stiff for small-scale costume; gives flexible hands, partly stuffed, for hand type. Also useful for stylised decor, foliage, etc. Difficult to wash or dry-clean.

Festivals. Since World War II there has been a significant number of national and international puppetry festivals. Puppeteers, performers and playwrights, producers and technicians, critics and theoreticians, educationalists and psychologists, have found attendance at major events the most economical and satisfying way of sampling the puppetry of many countries, of meeting people with similar interests; but professional performers now find it impossible to attend all the events, because of their work commitments. Usually a Conference is held at the same time of such events and periodically there occur the Congresses of UNIMA, q.v. the international organisation. Czechoslovakia has held its first international *amateur* event (Karlovy Vary, 1964) and a further is planned for 1969, with national events every year; Rumania has held three international events at Bucharest (1958, 1960, 1965); Italy, international festival and conference (1961); Great Britain, two international events, at Colwyn Bay (1963, 1968); Belgium held an international festival of traditional popular puppet-theatres, at Liege (1958); Germany has had events in various cities, at Brunswick (1963), Munich (1966), Bochum (annually); USSR, Soviet theatres, at Moscow and Leningrad (1964); Hungary, national, 1966. The United States has a national festival each year, organised by the Puppeteers of America, q.v., in a fresh location each time; 1967 the venue was in Canada at the time of 'EXPO 67'. The European events usually involve UNIMA collaboration, directly or indirectly. Details of forthcoming events can be obtained from any National Section of UNIMA or from the national organisation (*see* UNIMA).

Fibreglas (Glass Fibre). Generic term for woven or non-woven glass filaments used in re-inforced plastics; molten glass drawn into fine fibres. Strength-to-weight ratio higher than that of any other structural material. Can be mould-cast using polyester liquid resin, giving almost indestructible products. Used in construction of small boats, fishing rods, and available in household and car repair outfits as well as in bulk. Technique: matting is saturated with resin, shaped in mould or direct over plasticine model (for puppet head). Roof insulation variety can be directly modelled, using inert 'filler' and building up over paper core. Standard work by Thelma R. Newman, *Plastics as an Art Form* (Pitman, London, Chilton Co., Philadelphia; Ambassador Books, Toronto: 1964) gives basic terminology, processes, trade names and sources of supply, step-by-step techniques; profusely illustrated. *New Materials in Sculpture*, by H. M. Percy (Tiranti, 1962), also good on techniques.

Field Museum of Natural History, Chicago, USA. Holdings include 1,000 Chinese shadow-show figures acquired 1901 by Dr Laufer; also play scripts and sound recordings of Chinese music. Published *Oriental Theatricals* (Laufer, 1923) with section on puppets; illustrated.

Fielding, Henry (1707–54). English dramatist, novelist, pamphleteer. In his masterpiece *History of Tom Jones, A Foundling* (1749) – available in 'Everyman' edition – a character complains that 'the fine and serious part' of *The Provoked Husband* had been included in a Punch-show; and elsewhere a mention of the days when puppet shows were 'good scripture stories' – and the wicked carried off by the devil. In *The Author's Farce*, about an impoverished author who has the idea of doing satirical puppet shows, a further complaint: that a man could not 'thrive by his wit' when theatres were puppet shows and fools led the Town.

Figurenspiegel. Unique puppet theatre created by Professor Richard Teschner, q.v. and (since his death) now in the theatre collection of the Austrian National Library. Proscenium consists of large gold frame around a concave lens, surrounded by the astrological signs of the Zodiac. Illustrations in Beaumont *Puppets and Puppetry* (Studio, 1958) and Baird *The Art of the Puppet* (Collier-Macmillan, 1965).

Figuren-theater (Puppet Theatre). Periodical published by the Deutsches Institut für Puppenspiel, Bochum, Germany; particularly well illustrated by photographs. Articles on current performances, festivals; book reviews. Orders, enquiries: D.I.P., 463 Bochum, Bergstrasse 115.

Figurines (French, from Italian *figurina*, dim. of *figura*: figure). Small carved or modelled figures or statuettes, in terra cotta or other medium, sometimes painted; numerous examples have been found in ancient tombs and ruins (and now scattered in museums) some with movable limbs, some with head-rod similar in style to that of the large Sicilian marionettes still in use; no evidence as to whether used as toys or puppets. Illustrations in von Boehn *Dolls and Puppets*, q.v., Baird *Art of the Puppet*, q.v., and elsewhere.

Fil d'Archal. Old French term for *wire* 'string' for marionette.

Filler. (a) Plaster or other composition for filling cracks or holes in wall or ceiling; some specially bonded to give good grip, some with cellulose ingredient; available under various trade names (Alabastine, Polyfilla, Templaster, etc.) supplied in one to five pound packets; ready for immediate use when mixed with cold water, yet remains workable for up to an hour (depending on room temperature), unlike Plaster of Paris (which sets rapidly and shrinks). Hollow puppet heads can be made by combining filler and muslin (book muslin ideal) which mutually re-inforce; can be done by the direct method, i.e. by lamination over plasticine model (with a preliminary layer of damp tissue paper as parting-agent) or in a mould cast from model. (Leaflet on method, published by the Educational Supply Association, available from Educational Puppetry Association). Ideal painting surface; can be sand-papered; features such as lips, nostrils, eyelids, can be modelled in cottonwool saturated with filler. (b) Various solids in powder form (including the above) for mixing with polyester resins either for economy by providing bulk or for special effects, e.g. metallic finish, or for insula-tion or fire-proofing properties. Addition of filler is known as 'loading'. Techniques: H. M. Percy, *New Materials in Sculpture* (Tiranti, 1962). Also see ALABASTINE METHOD.

Film distributors. Consult telephone directory for current addresses (London) or Trades Directory (usually available in local public library). British Council, Educational Aids Department; British Film Institute; Chinese Arts Institute; Contemporary Films, Ltd.; Esso Petroleum Com-pany; Educational and TV Films, Ltd.; Central Film Library; Gaumont-British Film Library; High Commissioner for Malaysia; Information Service of India; Lanchester Puppet Centre (39 Henley Street, Stratford-upon-Avon); Vauxhall Film Hire Service. All these have puppet films, some from other countries. Hire charges vary. *List of Puppet Films*, q.v., prepared by T. E. Howard for the British Section of UNIMA, available in revised edition from BRITISH PUPPET AND MODEL THEATRE GUILD or the EDUCATIONAL PUPPETRY ASSOCIATION, q.v.

Film-strip. Short lengths of cine-film used for 'still' projection (equivalent of series of slides). Widely used in education: content can be from photo-graphs, diagrams or printed matter, with spoken commentary during viewing. Some instructional film-strips relative to puppetry, including Primary Puppetry Series *Glove Puppets* by G. H. Mallory and L. G. W. Sealey, distributed by the Educational Foundation for Visual Aids (on the 'Alabastine Method'); Craft Series *Puppets: Modelling and Casting* (colour), the Educational Productions Ltd. (on the paper-layer method of head-making and on costume).

Films (cinematic). Various types with puppet subjects: (a) Documentary, such as Waldo Lanchester's *Creation of a Marionette*, made in his workshops demonstrating processes and concluding with a performance (available with projector and projectionist; apply The Puppet Centre, 39 Henley Street, Stratford-upon-Avon); (b) Stop-motion, using static figures moved into new positions between camera shots (phased); popular with advertisers, e.g. Joop Geesink *Getting Warmer*, on the history of domestic heating from Garden of Eden onwards; also Alexander Ptushko (USSR) satirical item *The New Gulliver* (1935), in which live actor employed as Gulliver, the rest being puppets, some 3,000, including some diminutive figures dominated by a ring-master; TRNKA, Czech film-master, uses this technique: his *Midsummer Night's Dream* (Shakespeare) earned Grand Prix at a Cannes Film Festival (1959); (c) Fictional: techniques either as for documentary or animation (stop-motion), or combined, as in *Belle au bois Dormant* (*Sleeping Beauty*), with designs by Rochefoucauld and music by Poulenc (1934). Language-teaching films usually use hand puppets, e.g. short items in use with Nuffield Foundation language-teaching course (Leeds University); (d) Silhouette or shadow type: best known are those of Lotte Reiniger, e.g. *Papageno* with themes from Mozart *Magic Flute*. Reference works: *Industrial and Business Films*, q.v., *Technique of Film Animation*, q.v., *Animation in the Cinema*, q.v.

Finger puppets. Two main types (1) small creatures, such as birds, snails, fitting over the index finger; (b) group of baby chicks, etc., each fitting on one finger of a net glove, sheltering under the wing of the mother bird; (2) small figure with index and middle fingers in the legs *downwards*, knuckles forming knees, head and body stuffed, short string control for arms. Amusing for hospital patients, especially children. Construction details in Merten *The Hand Puppets*, q.v., and Batchelder *Puppet Theatre Handbook*, q.v.

Finnegan. Said to be a 'household word' in Eire; name of ventriloquial puppet who lives and works with Eugene Lambert q.v. and his family. See also WANDERLY WAGON.

Fiorillo, Silvio (*c.* 1632). One of family of actors performing in the Italian COMMEDIA DELL' ARTE style and possibly the first Pulcinella: but there are other theories as to origin of PUNCHINELLO and PUNCH.

Fire precautions. Regulations govern seating and exit facilities of public halls and theatres where performances given; includes provision of adequate equipment (extinguishers, etc.). Inflammable material must be fireproofed; local authorities or theatre fireman may test effectiveness of proofing by applying lighted match or blow-lamp: fabric may char but must not glow or flame. FIREPROOFING is not permanent: fresh treatment required at regular intervals. Mobile puppet stages should also be fireproofed. SEE NEXT ENTRY.

Fireproofing. Recipes vary according to materials to be proofed. Consult theatrical suppliers. One formula: 1-lb. each borax and salammoniac in 3 quarts water: brush or spray on fabrics, scenery, etc. *Results not permanent*: further treatment advisable at regular intervals. SEE PREVIOUS ENTRY.

Fireworks. (a) Actual fire-crackers are used in performance of Vietnamese 'Water puppets' q.v. given on platform in lake; (b) stage 'effects', e.g. in shadow show with coloured disc revolving behind screen in which patterns pricked out in blacked-out section (see Blackham *Shadow Puppets*, Barrie and Rockliff, 1960). 'Crackers' mentioned in Jonson *The Alchemist*, in a puppet play. See GUNPOWDER PLOT. See also FIRE PRECAUTIONS.

Fisherman and his Soul, story by Oscar Wilde (in manner of Hans Andersen).

Theme: tragic love of fisherman and mermaid. In order to live with Sea Folk, man barters soul with Witch; after three years of underwater life, man is reclaimed by Soul and cannot lose it twice; man found drowned with mermaid in his arms. Priest refuses to bless the Sea; Sea-folk go elsewhere. Puppet production by the Little Angel Theatre, London. Underwater scenes particularly effective with marionettes.

Fish-line. Used by some marionette performers for stringing; available in clear and water-green, grey and black, with various breaking-strains to suit different weights (nylon, rayon, silk).

Fist puppet. American term for the HAND or GLOVE type: e.g. Ficklen *Handbook of Fist Puppets*; Milligan *Fist Puppetry*. Obraztsov, Russian puppetmaster, commenting on Chinese 'BAG' puppet, felt the English 'GLOVE' to be the more appropriate term.

Fit-up. Showman's term for portable puppet stage or 'booth'; dates from Middle Ages when trestle-and-board stages used in streets.

Flash point. Lowest temperature at which a combustible liquid will give off inflammable vapour. Label on bottle should indicate this.

Flash powder. Highly inflammable chemical substance (lycopodium) ignited by electric current (fire torch) used for theatrical explosion and smoke effects; also used in manufacture of fireworks. Obtainable from theatrical suppliers.

Flat figures. Two-dimensional cut-out puppets, usually in profile (a) for Toy Theatre, (b) Shadow Theatre, (c) some contemporary rod puppets, (d) traditional Javanese shadow figures. Von Boehn *Dolls and Puppets* (Harrap, 1932, Cooper-Square, USA, 1965) mentions flat *marionettes* at Heidelberg, with head wire, strings to hands. Illustration of Blattner's 'silhouettes à fils' (flat marionettes) in Bordat and Boucrot *Théâtres d'Ombres*, q.v.

Flexible mould. Stretchable mould for casting, allowing a good degree of undercutting q.v. in the model. A range of materials made from vinyl resins are used, known as Vinamold. Technique: *New Materials in Sculpture*, by H. M. Percy (Tiranti, 1962), q.v.

Flies. Space above a stage and behind the proscenium arch, used for storage of scenery, this being 'flown' down and up as required.

Floating puppets. (a) Mentioned by Chinese historian Sun Kai-ti (in Obraztsov *Chinese Puppet Theatre*, Faber, 1961) and apparently Chinese equivalent of the Vietnamese 'water' puppets, figures waist-up only, mounted on wooden bases for floating on lakes. (b) Term for marionettes when feet fail to rest on stage floor.

Flocking. (a) Fibrous material used in upholstery. (b) Short-fibred, shredded or ground wool, cotton, rayon, etc., used for decorative surfacing in display work, available in various colours and sprayed or hand-applied on to adhesive. Can be used on puppet heads, scenery, etc., and also available in paper-sheet form (from Craft materials suppliers).

Floor show. Usually marionette items given without formal stage structure or scenery, on floor or low platform, sometimes neutral backscreen, operator walking on with puppet and sharing same acting area. Lighting usually from two spotlights focussed on puppet. Act without the usual stage particularly suitable when item is one in variety programme of mainly 'live' turns.

Fluorart. Trade name for fluorescent poster colour. Suppliers: Winsor and Newton.

Foamed plastic (plastic foam). Industrial product supplied in sheet form or blocks of various thicknesses, or granulated variety for cushion-filling; range of colours and can be painted or dyed. Easily cut with scissors, blocks for puppet heads or bodies, or granulated for stuffed cloth figures; noses or ears of this material can be used with simple junk-box puppets; also has scenic possibilities.

Folded-paper puppets. Traditional Japanese 'Origami' art adapted to puppet-making. Standard book on technique: Shari Lewis and Lillian Oppenheimer (founder of American Origami Centre) *Folding Paper Puppets* (Stein & Day, 1962; Muller, 1964).

Folk tales. Stories stemming from old beliefs, myths, legends, often with magical events. Published collections abound and are frequent source of themes for puppet plays. Apart from such items as *Folk Tales of the World*, with one volume per country, Hungary, China, England, etc. (Routledge and Chicago University), also worth while studying *Standard Dictionary of Folklore, Mythology and Legend* (Funk and Wagnall, N.Y., 1950). Research since the pioneer work of the brothers Grimm and others has shown common origin of many tales (ancient India), and these are classified in Stith-Thompson *Motif-Index of Folk Literature* (Rosenkilde and Bagger, Copenhagen: Indiana University Press, 1955; 5 vols. and index). In addition to the well-known fairy tales (Märchen) of Grimm, an English translation of Grimm *Teutonic Mythology*, by J. S. Stallybrass (Bell, 1900), is available in four volumes.

Folk Theatre of India, by Balwant Gargi (University of Washington Press, 1966). Some references to the Putliwalas of Rajasthan (marionette operators); mentions the frequently repeated idea that puppets preceded the live drama, since the leading character in Sanskrit plays is known as 'sutradhara' or 'holder of strings'. Also reference to the Tholu Bommalata shadow plays of Andhra, seeing similarity with the Wayang Kulit of Indonesia.

Fontaine, Jean de la. See LA FONTAINE.

Food names. Labels for Low Comedians and their puppet relatives: Dutch *Pickleherring*, Italian *Macaroni*, French *Jean Potage*, German *Hanswurst* (Jack Sausage) and old English *Jack Pudding*.

Football puppets. (a) Hero in play *Miček-Fliček* by Czechoslovak puppet-master Dr Jan Malik, is marionette whose head is a football with hair, eyes, nose, mouth, and arms and legs growing out of it; he is rather a naughty ball and is adopted by old couple as their 'son'; is carried off by a paper kite (with face) but eventually rescued. Play has been introduced into repertoire of other puppet companies (originally at the Central Puppet Theatre, Prague); included in an illustrated book for children by Kamil Bednar *Puppets and Fairy Tales* (Prague: English edition, 1958). (b) Hero in marionette play by Morris Cox, *Fudgefoot the Footballer*, produced by English amateur group; unusual feature is body consisting of football bladder (under costume) inflated by hand-pump from under stage. Synchronised with 'magic', hero becomes team-worthy and ends by *flying* away.

Fraccuradi. Italian term (obsolete) for rudimentary form of hand puppet made from pea-pods.

France. From the Middle Ages onwards it is only when some wandering
showman settles in one place, usually a major city where it will be possible
to earn a living, that any specific record is made. The fourteenth century
Flemish ms. in the Bodleian Library, *Li Romans du Bon Roi Alexandre*,
indicates the use of hand puppets and a simple portable booth. During
or before the sixteenth century the marionnettes à la planchette were in
evidence, probably arriving from Italy; but even the origin of the term
'marionnette' has been impossible to resolve by scholarship. Magnin in
Histoire des Marionnettes en Europe (1852) says the earlier terms were
'marmouzets', 'mariettes' and 'marioles'; but the word 'marionnette'
is used in France as the generic word (with added words to distinguish
different *types*) as is seen from Magnin's title. In the early or mid-1600's
Brioché (Briocci) set up his puppet theatre near the Pont Neuf in Paris;
he also practised dentistry and became famous for his performing monkey
(who came to a sad end at the hands of Cyrano de Bergerac). Magnin
quotes a book-keeping entry (1669) of a payment to Brioché for entertaining the Dauphin with 'marionnettes' (of what type?). In the seventeenth and eighteenth century there were puppet performances in the
Fairs (at Saint-Laurent and Saint-Germain) and some rivalry between
the live actors and the puppeteers. The French character Polichinelle
(like Punch) derived from the Italian Pulcinello, developing national
traits. A live cat seems to have been a feature of many of the hand puppet
shows. At the artistic as distinct from the folk-art level, French writers
and painters were attracted to the production of various forms of puppet
theatre. George Sand founded a private theatre at her chateau in Nohant
(1847), her son Maurice making the puppets and plays and performing
to the literary circle. In 1861 the author Duranty and the sculptor
Leboeuf co-operated, giving performances of literary plays in the
Tuileries Gardens, published in 1864 as *Théâtre des Marionnettes des
Jardins des Tuileries*. 'Ombres chinoises' – black silhouette shadow figures
having little in common with the traditional Chinese coloured figures
– became popular (appearing earlier in Italy and Germany) and in
addition to the fairground shows two notable theatres were established
by artists, that of Dominique Seraphin (1776) and of the 'Chat Noir' of
Rodolphe Salis (1887), of which there is a detailed account in Blackham
Shadow Puppets q.v. In 1862 the 'Theatron Erotikon de la Rue de la
Sante' was established by a group of poets, painters and musicians – the
auditorium seating about 20. Towards the end of the eighteenth century
– right away from Paris, in Lyon – Laurent Mourguet introduced the
character who was to supplant Polichinelle: Guignol – and to such an
extent that his name is now the general term for hand puppets: 'guignols'.
The original Guignol reflected the character of the Lyonnais silk weavers,
in character and costume, and the theatre continued after Mourguet's
death and up to the present. (There is also an important puppet museum
collection in Lyon.) The Parisian Guignol has his own characteristics and,
unlike Punch, has appeared in countless plays. *Marionnettes et marionnettistes de France* q.v. by Gervais (Bordas, 1947) contains biographical
material on a number of twentieth century companies and individuals,
with photographs, and an impressive list of their repertoires and French
publications. An unusual type of rod puppet was developed at Signoret's
'Petit Théâtre' where puppetry was of a high literary order, and Anatole
France one of its 'fans'. Contemporary France has a number of highly
individual, experimental, sophisticated puppeteers. Its national section
of UNIMA (the international organisation) publishes a fine periodical,

UNIMA France, available by subscription, and which promises to include material in English. (SEE SEPARATE ENTRY.)

France, Anatole (Jacques Anatole François Thibault: 1844–1924) French man-of-letters, critic, Nobel Prize-winner for Literature, 1921; believed in 'the immortal soul of marionettes and dolls' and had an 'infinite desire' to see marionettes replace human actors. Unlike Gordon Craig, English theatre theorist, whose concept of the 'ÜBERMARIONETTE' offended the acting profession – but was only aimed at the *bad* actors – France found the plays of the Comedie Française spoiled for him by the *good* actors. Records seeing M. Signoret's puppets at the 'Petit Theatre' q.v. in Paris – where an unusual type of puppet was used, the 'pedal' q.v. or 'clavier', operated from below by strings and levers. Productions were of the 'literary' variety, including items by Hrotswitha, q.v. Shakespeare and Cervantes. The original essays on these in *Le Temps* reprinted in *On Life and Letters* (John Lane, 1914–24). There is also a charming account of visit to a Guignol show with small girl companion (*My Friend's Book*, Bodley Head, 1913). There have been puppet adaptations of two stories *Our Lady's Juggler* and *The Man Who Married a Dumb Wife*.

Francis, Derek. English actor (stage, film, television). Before going on the stage in 1940 was at the Brighton School of Art. Did scenic and costume design in addition to acting; made the costumes and props designed. In 1960 mounted first marionette production *Beauty and the Beast*, for his daughter's fourth birthday treat and an audience of 60 friends (in a Barnes church hall). Second production in 1961 *A Christmas Legend*. Increasing interest in puppetry led to building a fully equipped puppet theatre seating 30 people, in his garden in Barnes (1962) – where many performances of the two productions were given. Plays re-written and puppets re-made for second editions. Audiences increased, work started on two new plays, an adaptation of Dickens' *Christmas Carol* and of a Macdonald fairy story. In 1966 the need to expand became urgent and a new home for family and puppets was found in Wimbledon; a new theatre in which puppetry can be developed on a larger scale is envisaged for 1969. Believes firmly that puppetry is a genuine theatre art form and that every puppet show should be total theatre: scenery, costumes, lighting, music, script and puppets combining as a whole to create this. Also believes that puppets should never do what other branches of the theatre can do better, such as opera or Shakespeare, but that they have their own material unique to their capabilities. Penny Francis, his wife, helps with the writing of scripts, selection of music, and performing. Puppet construction is of wood, with faces, hands and other features modelled in plastic wood.

Fringe. The silk, cotton, rayon, etc., varieties for lampshades or upholstery or from old shawls, useful for puppet hair or decor.

Frost Fair. River Thames froze over frequently in fifteenth–sixteenth centuries. EVELYN in his *Diary* recorded seeing puppet show and other attractions – on ice (entry for 24th January, 1684). (*Diary* available in Everyman edition, Dent.)

Funeral March of a Marionette. Orchestral music by Gounod (1818–93), originally intended to become one movement of a burlesque suite. Used with puppet productions for 'atmosphere', e.g. in televised version of *Robinson Crusoe*, introducing a ghost (by present author).

G

Galanty show. Also Gallantee, gallante, gallanti, gallanty. A form of shadow-figure show seen in London streets *c.* 1830 onwards, performed with a white sheet stretched across the proscenium of a Punch and Judy portable booth, illuminated from behind by candles or lantern, the figures on the screen being black silhouettes. Usually one operator inside the booth and a musician ('bottler': collector) standing in front with drum and/or panpipes to attract a crowd. Mayhew, in *London Labour and London Poor* (1851) recorded an interview with a street showman of a 'Chinese Galantee Show' – for which the 'proper' name was 'Lez Hombres' (i.e., the 'ombres chinoises'); light was by three candles, six per evening, and there was always the risk of fire. Rival attractions included the magic lantern (projectors) and these two types of entertainment are sometimes confused in literary references. Hone's *Everyday Book* (1824) has a description of a performance of the *Prodigal Son* and *Noah's Ark* and a scene from *Pull Devil, Pull Baker*. Attempts at etymology include 'gallantry' or a show for 'the gallants'; Italian 'galanti' (plural of 'galante', meaning 'fine' and often used of small shows (Barrere's *Dictionary of Slang, Jargon, Cant* (Bell, 1897); Johnson's *Dictionary of English Language* (2nd edition, 1827) does not include the term; Whanslaw includes an interesting chapter in *Shadow Play* (Wells Gardner Darton, 1950) and mentions Italian shadows seen in the early 1700's (reference in Morley *Memoirs of Bartholomew Fair*: 1857) with the interesting conclusion that 'motions', used by Shakespeare a number of times, could refer to shadow shows; in fact, Ben Jonson introduces a form of shadow show into *Tale of a Tub* (1596) and calls each scene a Motion. However, in *Bartholomew Fayre* (1614) the 'motion man' has a form of hand puppet. One of Whanslaw's drawings (Figure 25) with the caption 'Gallantee showman from an eighteenth century French print' is of a man with a box on his back, topped by a lantern. He provides the text for an old galanty play *Billy Waters*.

Gale, Theophilus (1628–78). Non-conformist tutor who left his library to Harvard College. In *The Court of the Gentiles* (1669) is this interesting and frustrating reference to puppets: 'They are but your Automata, those artificial machines or Images called Puppits.'

Gallows. (a) The hangman's equipment used in the traditional Punch and Judy show, which some showmen have abandoned since the 'No hanging' Bill; (b) Equipment for supporting marionettes when 'on stage' but temporarily out of action, e.g. standing or sitting, to free manipulator's hands for active characters; usually in form of wooden batten or metal bar (over the acting area) with hooks and/or chain links to take the hook of the control.

Gamelan. Name for the Javanese orchestra which accompanies the WAYANG puppet show, mainly percussion instruments such as gong and cymbals (gamel = hammer). Melodies not based on fixed keynote, akin to modern Western atonal theory. Orchestra is conducted by the 'DALANG' – the solo performer who manipulates all the puppets.

Gammer Gurton's Needle, by 'Mr S., Master of Arts': Farce Comedy in five acts, attributed both to John Still, M.A., and to William Stevenson; one of earliest extant English comedies, in rhymed doggerel. Contains famous drinking song 'I cannot Eat but Little Meat'. Action and dialogue relate to loss of a needle eventually found in the breeches which had been repaired. In 1958 a puppet version was presented by 'The Puppeteens' in the Detroit Puppet Theatre (Detroit Institute of Arts). Live version at the Midlands Art Centre, Birmingham, designs by puppeteer John Blundall.

Gautier, Theophile (1811–72). French poet, novelist, journalist; interesting description of Turkish Karagöz show (shadows) in *Constantinople* (Paris, 1856); English translation of puppet section in Craig *The Marionnette* (Nos. 7 & 8) and Inverarity *Manual of Puppetry* (Binfords & Mort, 1936).

Gauze curtain. Stage curtain which is invisible when lit from rear (without front lighting) and opaque when lit from front only; semi-opaque if lit from front and rear together. 'Effects' such as clouds may be projected on to curtain by lantern; used for transformation scenes, underwater effects. Materials: butter-muslin, mosquito-netting, scrim, 'theatrical gauze'.

Gay, John (1685–1732). English poet, playwright, originally a silk-mercer. Wrote libretto for ballad-opera *Beggars' Opera* q.v. (produced 1728), which was performed up to early twentieth century; lyrics set to English and Irish airs of the period, collected by a Dr John Christopher Pepusch (German composer). *The Threepenny Opera* q.v. with libretto by BERTOLT BRECHT and German jazz music by Kurt Weill had its origin in Gay's opera, and has had many puppet productions. In Gay's *The Shepherd's Week* there is a reference to 'raree' shows and Punch.

Gel coat. Term for first coat of resin applied to mould surface and forming the surface of a LAMINATED cast; is allowed to set before application of FIBRE GLASS in the laminating process. Can be pigmented with colours or loaded with plaster or metal 'FILLER'.

Gels (Gelatines). Colour medium (in frames) sliding over lighting reflector (e.g. footlights) to filter off unwanted colour. Affected by heat. Modern plastic variety made of non-flammable cellulose acetate sheet known as 'Cinemoid' available from Strand Electric and Engineering Company, Ltd., King Street, London, W.C.2, and conforms to fire regulations.

Gentlemen, the Marionnette, by Edward Gordon Craig q.v. (1872–1967); chapter in his *The Theatre Advancing* (Constable, 1921). 'There is only one actor . . . who has the soul of the dramatic poet and who has ever served as true and loyal interpreter of the poet, that is the marionnette.' Craig wrote a great deal about puppets, in his periodical *The Mask* (1908 with intervals to 1929) and *The Marionnette* (1918–19) and undoubtedly helped the twentieth century revival, but was criticised (a) by the actors of the live theatre, who thought he wanted to replace them by his 'ÜBERMARIONNETTE' (super-marionette), and (b) by puppeteers who felt he had contributed little to technical developments. Actually, his first love and main preoccupation was the human theatre.

Geometric marionettes. Type reflecting cubist art. In Baird *Art of the Puppet* (Collier-Macmillan, 1965) an illustration shows two figures 'after Buckminister Fuller' consisting of connected triangles of metal rod; umbrella ribs would be suitable. Art-teacher students from the Hochschule für Bildende Kunst, Berlin, performing at the Goldsmith College, London (1962), had an item *Spiel mit Glas*, in which the marionettes were a pink disc, a triangle of glass, and a box-like figure whose sections opened and closed; mirrors on the stage reflected these objects and lighting cast shadows (with music).

Germany. As elsewhere in Europe, the first puppet shows were those of the wandering showmen crossing the borders of the surrounding countries, in both directions. Today the country is one of the strongholds of puppetry. As elsewhere a traditional Punch-like character, HANSWURST (Jack Sausage) dominated the early plays. GOETHE saw a performance as a boy and the memory stayed with him and influenced the creation of his greatest work *Faust* (mentioned in his autobiographical *Dichtung und Wahrheit*). A few private theatres existed in the seventeenth–eighteenth centuries. In 1802 Christoph Winter established his famous HAENNES'CHEN Theatre in Cologne, using a form of rod puppet which has become associated with the Rhineland theatres. Around 1830 there was a development of the Toy Theatre, with sheets of characters to cut out, in Berlin, Mainz and Nuremberg. In 1858 Joseph Leonhard Schmid, known as 'Papa' Schmid, q.v. acquired the little Heideck theatre in MUNICH, this becoming the first permanent professional theatre and influencing many others. Count Franz Pocci, q.v., who was Director of the Court Musicians and later became Lord High Chamberlain, wrote 46 comedies, many of which are still played. The Munich artists Puppet Theatre was founded by Paul Brann in 1905 and another was established by Ivo Puhonny at Baden-Baden in 1911. Today the Munich City Theatre Collection has the largest collection of puppets and related material in the world, and has been the centre for international events. MAX JACOB, who became the President of the international puppetry organisation (UNIMA q.v.) and held that office until his death in 1967, founded the Hartenstein Puppets – later known as the HOHNSTEINER TROUPE – whose style and technique with hand puppets became the criterion for all German companies. A puppet periodical *Puppet Theatre* appeared in 1922 edited by Dr Alfred Lehmann. Puppet study groups were developed in many areas, and the Federal Republic established a training centre for puppeteers directed by HARRO SIEGEL, at the Brunswick School of Industrial Art. Today there is a privately circulated review, *Perlicko-Perlacko*, edited by Dr Hans R. Purschke of Frankfurt. There have been international festivals at Brunswick and Munich and annual events at Bochum in the Ruhr, organised by the DEUTSCHES INSTITUT FÜR PUPPENSPIEL, which also holds training courses and issues several publications (see *Meister des puppenspiels* and *Figurentheater*).

Geschichte des schattentheaters im Morgen und Abendland, by George Jacob (Hanover, 1925). Comprehensive study of the shadow theatre and its developments during migration from East to West; exhaustive bibliography of relative literature in all languages (pre-1925).

Gesticulator. In a Latin Dictionary compiled by Sir Thomas Elyot (1538) he gives the definition 'a posture-master or mime, or he that playeth with puppettes'.

Ghelderode, Michel de (1898–1962). Belgian playwright whose work shows strong influence by and affinity with Breughel's paintings, with demonism and Rabelaisianism as the dominant qualities in his plays. Some of his plays, such as *Don Juan* and *Le Mort du Doctor Faust*, are in semi-puppet style, with live actors reflecting puppet action. He also wrote specifically for puppets, e.g. *Le Mystère de la Passion de Notre Seigneur Jesus Christ, avec tous les personnages pour le theatre de marionnettes, reconstitue après spectacle* (Bruxelles, 1925) with a preface by the author, a Passion Play based on the narration by an old Belgian showman. An illustration from a production at the Toone Theatre, Brussels, is included in the UNIMA book *Puppet Theatre of the Modern World* (1967).

Gidayu. Term for narrator in the Japanese BUNRAKU Puppet Theatre, derived from name of celebrated performer Takemoto Gidayu (1650–1714), who opened own theatre in Osaka (1685) and was a close friend of CHIKAMATSU MONZAEMON (1653–1724), who became known as the 'Shakespeare' of Japan.

Gigogne. Popular French marionette, 'Mère Gigogne' (seventeenth–nineteenth centuries) with a startling knack of producing 170 or so 'children' from under her skirt. A drawing is reproduced in Baird *Art of the Puppet* (1965).

Gilbert, Sir William Schwenk (1836–1911). Co-author with Sir Arthur Sullivan (1842–1900) of a number of light operas, several of which have had puppet adaptations, e.g. *The Mikado, Pirates of Penzance, H.M.S. Pinafore.* Gilbert's *Bab Ballads* also used as source material for puppets.

Glass fibre (fiber). See FIBREGLAS.

Gloss. Light-reflecting, particularly with reference to paint finishes, as distinct from 'matt' or 'flat' (non-shine); also 'high gloss' quality. Too much light-reflection from painted puppet faces blurs details; except where used deliberately for effect, gloss best limited to eyes and mouth. 'High lights' should *not* be painted in eyes: natural reflected light moves as puppet moves and is more effective. Most paints shine while wet.

Glove puppet (American 'FIST' or 'HAND'). So-called because performer's hand is inside cloth body, fingers divided between puppet neck and arms, hand inserted through open bottom end of body which is attached to puppet neck. Head usually hollow or partly so, controlled by one or more fingers inserted in neck, thumb and others fingers in arms. Allocation of fingers usually a matter of personal preference, several variations (a) index finger in neck, thumb in one arm, middle finger in other; (b) index finger in neck, thumb in one arm, little finger in other, two fingers tucked into palm; (c) index and middle fingers in neck, thumb in one arm, ring and little fingers in other arm; (d) two-handed variety: both thumbs in neck, remaining fingers in arms. Legs are occasionally added, as with Punch and the German Kasper, which may be stuffed and used only when puppet sitting on playboard, or given occasional action by operator's other hand. Punch usually stays on same hand throughout the performance, all the other characters being 'left handed', due to the fact that three-finger technique results in high and low shoulders, non-interchangeable; handshape with two fingers in neck gives interchangeable puppets, an advantage when making exits or entries on right or left of stage. Variation of the hand type is the hand-and-rod. Many methods of making heads for this type and many textbooks giving techniques.

Gloy. Trade name for office and school paste. Leaflet No. 3 issued by Associated Adhesives Ltd. (8th Avenue, London, E.12) deals with paste-and-paper method of puppet making.

Glue. Term now generally synonymous with 'adhesive'; origin – animal (bone, hide) or vegetable, and modern synthetic-resin. Bonding (adhesive) properties vary with different types, nature of surfaces being joined, nature of materials.

Goethe, Johann Wolfgang von (1749–1832). German poet, novelist, dramatist, best known for his major work *Faust*, published in two parts in 1808 and 1832, which has been produced in every form (opera, ballet, pantomime, shadow play, marionette play). In his childhood his first dramatic efforts were with a miniature theatre, and in his autobiographical *Dichtung und Wahrheit (Poetry and Truth)* he says that a puppet performance seen as a student remained vividly in his memory. The stage-struck hero in *Wilhelm Meister* had a puppet stage. Goethe gave his own son a puppet theatre for Christmas in 1800 and made some of the scenery for it. (SEE GOETHE HAUS.)

Goethe Haus. The house where Goethe spent most of his life, in the Frauenplan, Weimar; collection includes small puppet theatre which may be the one given by him to his son August at Christmas (1800). In a Report by Walter Röehler in the Quarterly Review of the Goethe-Gesellschaft, No. 3, 1938, the possibility that the scenery was modelled on the real theatre scenery of Goethe's day is discussed. Included are Baroque style back-cloths and an Egyptian temple for the *Magic Flute*, an Empire Room, etc. The theatre was equipped for two types of puppets – string puppets (marionettes, of which none have survived) and a mechanically-operated type mounted on wheels. Cut-out figures were attached by wire to wooden bases, and movable limbs connected by fine wire to the chassis which moved across stage in grooves (by strings); the rotation of the wheels moved the limbs. Besides people and swans, gondolas and a cloud-machine were available. Originally there had been a super-section with pulleys and an understage is indicated by trap doors. The Goethe Haus at Frankfurt has the remains of the puppet theatre given to Wolfgang by his grandmother (stage floor and proscenium only).

Gogol, Nikolai Vasilyevich (1809–52). Russian novelist, dramatist, short-story writer: *Diary of a Madman, Dead Souls*, etc. His amusing story *The Nose*, q.v., has had puppet productions, e.g. by the Japanese theatre PUK. *The Night Before Christmas* was in the early repertoire of the Central State Puppet Theatre, Moscow. The Fadenbühne Marionette Theatre in Vienna produced *The Government Inspector*.

Goldoni, Carlo (1707–93). Italian dramatist, poet, librettist. When young found completely equipped puppet theatre in a palazzo and produced Mantelli's *The Sneeze of Hercules* and wrote other plays for himself. Wrote some 150 plays for the human theatre and became rival of Gozzi, many of whose plays have remained in repertoire of various European puppet theatres.

Goldsmith, Oliver (1728–74). Irish born English playwright, novelist, poet: *Vicar of Wakefield, She Stoops to Conquer*. In *Polite Learning* (xiii) mentions 'a youth, just landed at the Brille, resembles a clown at a puppet show'. Boswell (1740–95) in *Life of Johnson* (1791) tells of an occasion when Goldsmith expressed contempt for puppets, while watching a show in which one tossed a pike, and later broke his shin in attempting to show his superiority in jumping over a stick. However, McPharlin, in *Puppet Theatre in America* (1949), draws attention to Joseph Cradock's *Literary Memoirs* (1826), in which Goldsmith is vindicated of any stupidity about puppets.

Goldsmith's Toy Theatre. Included in the normal curriculum of the Gold smith College in London, S.E. (a Teacher Training centre) is the study and appreciation and making of Toy Theatre productions; an activity begun during the War years has become integral part of the illustration department, staff and students co-operating. The stage is a fixture, set in a hardboard partition; the proscenium is changed to suit a particular production; lighting system is elaborate. Plays are original or adaptations and have included *Alice in Wonderland*, Anderson's *Little Mermaid*, *Bluebeard*, *Pilgrim's Progress*, and 'a fable for artists' *The Emperor's New Pictures*. In 1962 the College was host to a group of German students from the Hochschule für Bildende Kunst, Berlin, who gave several demonstration performances of modern techniques with shadow figures, developed during their own Course.

Gounod, Charles François (1818–93). French composer; masterpiece, *Faust* (after Goethe, 1859); popular work, *Ave Maria* (adapted, set to 1st *Prelude* of Bach's 'Well-tempered Clavichord'). His *Marche funèbre d'une Marionnette* (1873) has been translated as *Funeral March of a Marionette*, q.v., although the French term only indicates 'puppet' – of no specific type.

Gozzi, Count Carlo (1720–1806). Italian dramatist; wrote satirical plays and fables, hoped to revive the Commedia dell' arte. Many of his plays have remained in repertoire of various European puppet theatres, the most notable being *Love of Three Oranges*, q.v., and *King Stag*, q.v. Prokofiev set the former to music for the Chicago Civic Opera.

Grand Turk. One of the traditional 'come-apart' trick marionettes inherited from the Italian 'FANTOCCINI'; figure turns into six smaller figures derived from the head, arms, legs, body. Seen in London from *c*. 1780 and still in repertoire of some companies. Technique: Whanslaw *Everybody's Theatre*; Whanslaw and Hotchkiss *Specialised Puppetry* (both Wells, Gardner, Darton).

Great Britain. The history of the English puppet shows is nearly an inch thick: Speaight's *History of the English Puppet Theatre* (Harrap, 1955), as well documented as is possible and listing the showmen who flourished between 1600 and 1914 and the plays performed from 1500–1914. It remains uncertain as to when puppets first arrived from the Continent or what type or types of puppet were seen in Shakespeare's day, when the popular term for puppet or puppet show was 'motion' q.v., but which also had many other meanings, not always clarified by the literary context. Ben Jonson's *Bartholomew Fayre* contained a play within a play, an actual puppet show in the fairground, undoubtedly authentic in style, from which the *type* of puppet can be fairly reliably deduced (but is not stated): the play given by the puppets is a burlesque of the classic *Hero and Leander* q.v. PEPYS recorded in his famous *Diary* various visits to puppet shows and mentions a play *Patient Grizill* q.v. derived in some roundabout fashion from Boccaccio's *Decameron* q.v. There are official accounts of payments made for the use of sites at CHARING CROSS and elsewhere and the mention of Italian puppet-players. Pepys also refers to 'Polichinelli' (several spellings) and shows given at Court. The earliest 'Punch' would seem to have been a marionette and could not have indulged in the kind of slapstick action associated with the later hand-puppet character. Play titles show biblical and folk-lore sources and legendary items such as *Whittington and his Cat*. The function of the 'INTERPRETER' who stood in front of the stage and explained the action

G

may also have been to take up a collection, as does the modern 'bottler' – but shows were sometimes inside a booth and payment made on entering. The Punch play as known today evolved, the earlier Punchinello appearing in all manner of plays (including the biblical) and becoming anglicised. The same process occurred all over Europe: Mr Punch's 'cousins' reflect the temperament of the countries of their adoption. In England by the eighteenth century puppet shows had become 'the talk of the town' and the repertoire included operas and pantomimes: the term 'fantoccini' was borrowed from the Italian showmen and gradually acquired the sense of 'trick marionettes'. In the nineteenth century there were travelling companies indulging in a great deal of publicity. The Toy Theatre, a form of puppet show suitable for the drawing rooms of Regency and Victorian England, attracted adults as well as 'Juveniles' and became the do-it-yourself hobby of the period, immortalised by Robert Louis Stevenson's essay on 'Penny Plain, Twopence Coloured' (the remarkable history of which George Speaight recorded in his *Juvenile Drama: the history of the English Toy Theatre*, Macdonald, 1947). Early in the twentieth century a revival of interest began; writers of the calibre of G. B. Shaw, q.v. Gordon Craig, q.v. and G. K. Chesterton, q.v. stimulated activity, and Harold Monro's Poetry Bookshop in London's Bloomsbury included puppet shows as well as poetry readings by Edith Sitwell and others. The first monthly meetings of the British Model Theatre Guild (as it was first known) were held there, following publication of H. W. Whanslaw's *Everybody's Theatre* (Wells Gardner Darton, 1923) and the enthusiasm this aroused. Gerald Morice, q.v., co-founder with Whanslaw, of the Guild, became an authority on the subject, organised tours in Europe to further stimulate interest and later established a column in the showmen's paper (*World's Fair*, q.v.) which still appears. Visits by the Italian 'Teatro dei Piccoli' directed by Vittorio Podrecca q.v. were a further stimulus (as in many countries). Another outstanding figure was Waldo Lanchester, q.v., who, after joining forces with Whanslaw in London, eventually established a theatre in Malvern, and later a Puppet Centre in Stratford-upon-Avon. Television from its earliest days attracted puppets and ensured a wider audience, creating at least one 'star' – MUFFIN THE MULE (The Hogarth Puppets). A further development was the use of puppets in education, leading to the formation of the Educational Puppetry Association, q.v. One of the symptoms of a steadily expanding interest in this branch of theatre art is in the constant flow of new books on the subject, as a glance at this *Dictionary's* bibliography will show. An annual feature, in addition to the 'seasons' at the seaside (Punch and other shows) are the 200 or so performances by puppets in the London Parks during the summer. There is a permanent puppet theatre at Colwyn Bay – twice the centre for international puppet festivals (the *Harlequin*, directed by Eric Bramall, q.v.) and London has its '*Little Angel*' directed by John Wright, q.v. A Welsh company (*The Caricature*, directed by Jane Phillips, q.v.) participated in a Commonwealth Arts Festival, and several companies have taken part in international events abroad. Some, like *The Hogarth Puppets*, q.v., are well known in Australia, South Africa, Canada – and the Director of that company, Jan Bussell, was elected President of the international organisation UNIMA, q.v., in 1968.

Grieg, Edward (1843–1907). Norwegian composer whose *Peer Gynt* was inspired by dramatic poem by Ibsen, q.v., and has had adaptations for various puppet productions including large-scale marionette version by the Tatterman Company in Detroit.

Grimm, the Brothers, Jacob (1785–1863) and Wilhelm (1786–1859). Born in Hanau, Germany. At first studied Law, but then became deeply interested in philology and mythology, becoming the founders of the scientific study of folklore, collectors of folk-tales (Märchen) from verbal sources, folk-books and manuscripts. The 1812 volume developed into a large collection which was translated into every major language and even into Esperanto. The first English translation *Household Tales* (1884) is popularly known as *Grimm's Fairy Tales*. Many of the tales have been adapted for puppet stage production, such as *Briar Rose, The Bremen Town Musicians, One-Eye, Two Eyes, Three-Eyes, The Frog Prince, Hansel and Gretel, Rumpel-stiltskin, Show-white and Rose-Red*. Some of the tales are also found in Perrault's collection *Histoires et contes du temps passé avec des moralités* (1697), e.g. *Little Red Riding Hood, Cinderella*. An attractively illustrated edition by Czech puppet-film maker Trnka has been published by Paul Hamlyn (1961 and 1964).

Gropius, Walter. German architect; organised and was director of the Bauhaus, q.v. until 1928; moved to the United States: Chairman of the Department of Architecture, Harvard (1938–53); wrote introduction to *Theatre of the Bauhaus* (1961), q.v.

Ground row. In theatre, on marionette stage or that of Toy theatre, a low horizontal 'FLAT' or piece of scenery UPSTAGE, sometimes used to conceal light source for CYCLORAMA.

Guignol. French hand puppet whose name has become the popular term for all hand puppets (marionnette à gaine). The original character was born in Lyon, *c.* 1815, creation credited to Laurent Mourguet, q.v. The French puppet historian Maindron, in *Marionnettes et Guignols* (1900) says there are no references to Guignol before end of eighteenth century and that his character is pure Lyonnais – but quotes M. Onofrio, a magistrate of Lyon, anonymous author of two volumes *Le Theatre lyonnais de Guignol* (1865–70), who saw a connection of the name with a small town in Lombardy, Chignolo, and – but 'only a conjecture', the name of the hero in an ancient Italian repertoire. Paul-Louis Mignon, in *J'aime les Marionnettes* (1962), says Laurent was given a *marionette*, a 'Girolamo' (the popular puppet of Milan), by an Italian workman from Chignolo; another puppet, named Gnafron, insisted on calling Girolamo 'Chignol' (in another version Gnafron was created *after* Guignol); Chignol became Guignol. Girolamo is said to have been a mixture of Arlequin and Pierrot from Italian tradition, but must have adopted the character as well as the costume of the Lyonnais silk weavers. Yet another theory has been given: that 'Guignol' is essentially a Lyonnais word, as seen in the phrase 'C'est guignolant!' i.e. 'Very amusing . . . '. However, Larousse *Grand National Encyclopedia* gives the derivation as from 'chignol: coming from China ' . . . Guignol did not stay in Lyon, although Mourguet's descendants continued to perform with him: he multiplied and, in Paris, acquired Parisian characteristics. Unlike Punch, his distant cousin, Guignol appears in dozens of plays, many of which have been published; his impressive repertoire is included in an appendix to Gervais *Marionnettes et marionnettistes de France* (1947). Ten of Mourguet's plays were published in 1815 *Theatre Lyonnais de Guignol*. There are Guignol theatres in Paris in the Champs-Elysées and the Jardin du Luxembourg. Anatole France, q.v., had a fondness not only for the literary puppet plays at the

Petit Théâtre of M. Signoret, as recorded in his *On Life and Letters*, but also for Guignol, and wrote charmingly of seeing a performance when accompanied by a little girl, Suzanne (*My Friend's Book*, 1913).

Gulliver's Travels into Several Remote Nations of the World. Swift's satirical masterpiece (1726) has had many puppet-theatre productions; Ptushko, Russian film director, made *The New Gulliver* (1935), using live actor for the hero and stop-motion puppets for the Lilliputians, feature-length and in form of boy's dream, introducing a workers' revolt against monarchy and a king with a speech impediment. (Ptushko later made another film using live actors and puppets: *The Golden Key*.)

Gunpowder Plot. Mentioned by Leatherhead the puppet-master in Ben Jonson's *Bartholomew Fayre*, q.v., as his best attraction: 'There was a get-penny!' He would give nine performances in an afternoon – to an audience of about 20 people. In Jonson *The Alchemist* (Act I) there is a mention of 'crackers in a puppet play' and it is likely that fireworks would be used in the Gunpowder Plot.

Gunungan. Symbolic 'mountain' or 'tree' which occupies centre of shadow screen at beginning of WAYANG KULIT performances, during intervals and (reversed) at the end. Javanese form is leaf-shape; Balinese is umbrella-like; both have stylised tree in middle.

Gypsum. Natural hydrated calcium sulphate, used in manufacture of PLASTER OF PARIS. When clear and transparent is known as Selenite; when massive and granular, known as Alabaster.

H

Habanera. Item from Bizet's *Carmen*, in repertoire of Soviet puppetmaster Sergei Obraztsov, q.v. (hand puppets), burlesquing the over-passionate singer; illustrations in Obraztsov *My Profession* (Moscow, 1950). Originally an African negro dance introduced into Cuba; Creole Country Dance.

Hadamowsky, Dr Franz. Director of the theatre collection of the Austrian National Library and author of important book on the life and work of Richard Teschner (*Richard Teschner und sein Figurenspiegel*, Vienna, 1956) internationally famous puppetmaster. The book reveals for the first time the unique technical developments which contributed to the magic of the performances in the 'Figurenspiegel' q.v., the theatre whose proscenium consisted of a large concave lens in a golden frame. Stage, puppets, documents, are now in the National Library, Vienna.

Haenneschen Theatre. Famous puppet theatre established in Cologne, Germany, in 1802 by Christoph Winters, using the rod-puppet technique of the Rhineland theatres and still functioning in the original style, with successive generations of 'regulars' making up the audiences. The farces include a number of stock characters, the hero being Hans (Haennes'-chen), with the perpetual joker Anton (known as Tuennes). The control consists of a long, thick wooden rod reaching to the ground, encasing an iron rod which supports the figure, the legs being free, one arm controlled by a wire. When Hans runs he has a most amusing leg movement which requires considerable skill on the part of the operator as he trots below stage. Scenery is three-dimensional, partly fixed, some interchangeable and 'flown'. Audience participation is the regular order of all perform-ances – even with the adults.

Hair. Theatrically effective materials for puppet hair include: string or rope (unravelled, natural or dyed), HEMP, jute, knitting or carpet wools, embroidery silks, ostrich plumes, fur, fur fabric, raffia (natural or plastic variety), felt strips, theatrical CRÊPE HAIR, sculpted paper, copper wire. Materials in strands usually made up into wigs on gauze base; fur fabric and self-backed materials can be glued direct to head. Styling best done after preliminary fixing. Removable wigs sometimes desirable: can be attached by strips of cloth or tape fitted with PRESS-STUDS (half inside wig, half on head) – particularly useful for elegantly styled heads when packing for transport or storage. Wooden heads sometimes have carved hair; paper-pulp heads sometimes modelled and painted. Materials which move give a feeling of life: in some scenes hair may need to come down or be pulled, or the hero may have to climb up the heroine's long tresses to reach the balcony.

Hand Ballet. Item in which the live hands are the puppets. Contemporary development brilliantly explored by French puppeteer Yves JOLY and assistants. Hands sometimes in white or coloured gloves, sometimes forming shapes as in hand-shadow play. Normal hand or rod puppet stage.

Hand puppet. Term mainly used in the United States, equivalent of English 'glove puppet', q.v. – the hand being inside the cloth body, fingers controlling head and arm movements. In Germany the term is 'handpuppen' – but Merten in Canada wrote two books, (a) *The Marionette*, (b) *The Hand Puppets*, the latter including the Rod, Finger and Shadow types, as well as the 'glove'. 'Fist puppet' is an American variation. There is also a 'talking hand' type used by some ventriloquists: the hand itself is disguised, given hair, eyes, moustache, thumb forming lower jaw; a variation of this is the 'talking mitten' made of stockinette or other stretch material, details of the face painted or stuck on one side, with slit for mouth. (*Ventriloquism for Beginners*, Douglas Houlden: Kaye & Ward, reprint 1968). Most textbooks, except the few concerned only with marionettes, give methods of making the hand or glove type. See also HAND-SHAPES.

Hand-and-rod puppet. Puppets operated from below stage with some variations of technique: (a) one hand internally controls head movements, other hand manipulating one or both puppet-hands by thin rod or rods; (b) head manipulated by short internal rod; (c) large figures may need two performers. Techniques: *Hand-and-Rod Puppets*, Batchelder and Michael (Ohio University, 1947); *Rod Puppets and the Human Theatre*, Batchelder (Ohio University, 1947).

Hand-and-Rod Puppets, by Marjorie Batchelder and Vivian Michael (College of Education, Ohio State University, Columbus, 1947). First of series in

Adventures in Education. Book based on experiments by authors and a Junior High School, presenting plan for group production and advocating use of STOCK CHARACTERS; detailed instructions and diagrams for making puppets and stages. 15 illustrations.

Hand Puppetry, Sir George's Book of. See SIR GEORGE.

Hand Puppets and String Puppets, by Waldo Lanchester (Dryad Press, 1st edition, 1937, constant repeats). Useful small textbook by noted English puppetmaster.

Hand-shapes. The basic anatomy of a HAND or 'GLOVE' puppet is the human hand itself. The limits of action and expression are determined by the hand (and arm), by what it can and cannot do. Obraztsov the Russian puppet-master, brilliant solo artiste with hand puppets, has called the hand 'the soul of the puppet' and has demonstrated the sensitivity of control possible (a) in an item in which the two characters have only a ball head each and no costume, (b) in another in which a wine-drinking character has a dish-cloth face which becomes more and more distorted after each successive emptying of the glass: in each case the hands have maximum freedom and remain fully flexible. Anything which cramps the hand or fingers reduces the range of action and sensitivity. The hand should therefore be the first concern of the puppeteer – especially of the beginner, as a habit once acquired is not easily discarded and may even involve the re-making of a puppet. It cannot be stressed too strongly that it is the *inside* of the hand puppet which governs the degree of control possible. If the neck of the puppet is too tight, too long, too short, or if the span across its chest and under its arms is too narrow, if the cloth body is too short, not only will the action be cramped, but the hand and arm will tire quickly. The internal structure of the hand, the action of the tendons controlling the fingers, the action of the wrist joint, the bones and muscles of the fore-arm, need to be understood – not theoretically but by through experiments. If the two fingers on the outer side of the hand are tucked down into the palm, the pull of the tendons will be seen in a movement of the middle finger. If the whole length of the index finger is inserted in a cardboard tube it will be seen that the only action is that of a goose-neck: it should be possible to use the small joints of the fingers – and the bottom edge of the neck should reach only to the middle joint of the finger, unless a gooseneck *is* required. The traditional hand-shape for the Punch and Judy operator is the 'three finger' arrangement: index finger in neck, thumb in one arm, middle finger in other arm, two fingers tucked into palm. This gives a high shoulder and a low shoulder (inside) and a one-sided paunch – although this may be disguised by the costume. Textbooks sometimes give the 'glove' pattern showing this high-and-low shape, whereas puppets made to this pattern will fit only *one* hand comfortably, will not be interchangeable. In the Punch show this is of no consequence: Punch is on one hand throughout the show: the other characters can all be made to fit the opposite hand. In other types of shows, particularly in group work where the entries and exits of characters may be at different points, it is often desirable to be able to change hands: this is easily demonstrated by bringing in a puppet at the right hand end *on the left hand*, the fore-arm, wrist, hand are all immediately affected. The range of possible handshapes has been illustrated in Fedotow *Technik des Puppentheaters*: the choice will depend on the range of action desired for a particular character. Creatures which move horizontally, e.g. tortoise, squirrel, will have the operator's hand angled at the wrist, the fore-arm being below stage. For the vertical puppet, two fingers in the neck, the thumb in one arm and the remaining two fingers in the other arm give maximum freedom, ability to handle stage props securely, a natural waist-line at the wrist – and a body shape which permits use on either hand. Such hand-shapes (included in Fedotow illustrations) as *two thumbs* in the neck, the other fingers as arms, have some individual possibilities, but limit the performer to one puppet at a time. Whichever shape is chosen, *size* is important, the need for the most comfortable fit: this is seen in the extreme where a small child tries a puppet meant for an adult hand, or *vice versa*. Again, the smaller and the weaker the hand the more it will be affected by an ill-fitting puppet. The CATALAN hand-puppet is unique in that it has a wooden shoulder piece in which *three* fingers are inserted; the arms are given extensions, and the whole figure is larger (and can be seen by larger audiences), but there is a sacrifice of head movements. The hand is the soul of the puppet only if it is left free and has a range of action from the subtle to the bold and vigorous.

Hand with Five Fingers. Puppet item produced at the Rumanian State Puppet Theatre 'Tandarica' in Bucharest. Satire on fights in film thrillers: nightclub brawl with broken bottles, glasses, plates, smashed chairs, entangled legs and bodies.

Handle puppets. Term used to describe the small figures used in the Polish szopka, q.v., operated by short wire or stick control and moving in slots in base of stage.

Handless puppets. Two-handed type seen in some seventeenth century Japanese illustrations; operators' arms inserted from below and as far as elbow, puppet sleeves empty. When puppet holds fan or sword, probably live fingers control these; rod or other internal mechanism possible. Reproductions in Dunn *Early Japanese Puppet Drama*, q.v.

Hands. There can be as much difference of character in puppet hands as in puppet heads. The hands are usually much more active than the heads, and the eye of the spectator is attracted by movement, will therefore notice hands particularly. This is even more likely with the (legless) HAND PUPPET, as it can carry, hold, or throw objects effectively. The MARIONETTE hands can be as full of character as the head and, provided they are properly jointed and strung, have an expressive range of gesture. Beautiful or strong hands which merely float or wave aimlessly lose their beauty or strength. Secure control of objects handled by the hand type depends on a careful designing and positioning of the hands so that the operator's fingertips can grip the object firmly. Semi-stuffed felt hands (on the hand type) are flexible and gain in expressiveness, e.g. in stroking the chin or putting an arm around another character. The French GUIGNOL and the CATALAN hand puppets have stiff fore-arms, giving an elbow angle and extra arm length – but less flexibility. Experiments can be made with the angle at which the hand joins the wrist, both with hand and marionette types; differences here lend to characterisation. The string to a marionette hand can pass through from the palm side – or be attached to a tiny screw eye in the palm – or it can be attached to the back of the hand, or to the upper edge, or attached to the wrist itself. The only rule is that it contributes to CHARACTERISATION and function. Hands will need special attention if a prop such as a sword or a wand are to be attached. The hands of shadow puppets can be very expressive, although always in profile; the Chinese variety sometimes have special wrist joints. Chinese marionettes may have hands with individual finger movements – and appropriate strings. A hand may also change shape simply by being reversed – the finger joints opening when the palm is turned upwards. The chief operator of the Japanese 'three man' puppets controls the head and right hand, both having the means of subtle expressiveness. For a puppet-maker to concentrate on the head at the expense of the hands is to miss a vital factor in characterisation.

Hansel and Gretel. Ancient tale of children lost in the woods and finding an edible house, falling into hands of witch and boy put in cage to fatten up – but witch tricked into uncomfortable end in the oven. Included in the Brothers GRIMM collection and a firm favourite with puppet theatres. Also opera by Humperdinck, q.v.

Hanswurst. 'Jack Sausage': originally a seventeenth-eighteenth century German stage buffoon, origin obscure; mixed characteristics, being hero in farce and clown in tragedy, boaster, coward, intriguer, gourmand, at times vulgar and even obscene. Reappeared on puppet stage but eventually gave place to Kasper or Kasperl, a universally popular character who appeared in every kind of play. These 'food name' characters appeared in many countries: English 'Jack Pudding', French 'Jean Saucisse', Dutch 'Pickelherring', and others.

Happy Prince, The, by Oscar Wilde (1856–1900); fairy tale theme: gilded statue asks swallow to remove ruby and take it to poor woman with sick son (bird puts ruby in woman's thimble, fans boy's head with wings); next it is asked to take sapphires and give these to a poor playwright and a poor little match girl; finally removes gold to give to the poor – only to die of cold itself. The municipal authorities decide to melt down the statue; angels take the swallow and the unmelted heart to heaven. Puppet production by (among others) The Hogarth Puppets.

Harlequin (Italian *Arlecchino,* French *Arlequin*); one of the comical servant characters (zanni) in the COMMEDIA DELL' ARTE improvised comedies in Italy (sixteenth–seventeenth centuries); character a mixture of stupidity and cunning, given to deceiving and self-deception; costume of typical colourful diamond-patch. Appeared on the puppet stage at the Paris fairs and in London (eighteenth–nineteenth centuries), name often included in play title, e.g. *Harlequin Bandit Chief, Harlequin Aladdin, Harlequin Ali Baba, Harlequin and Aesop, Harlequin Bluebeard, Harlequin Faust, Harlequin Don Quixote;* Allardyce Nicoll lists dozens of titles in *History of English Drama,* 1660–1900 (Cambridge, U.P., 1959); see also Speaight *History of the English Puppet Theatre* (Harrap, 1955). In the English 'Harlequinade ' – a derivative of the commedia, Harlequin and Columbine were the young lovers (eighteenth–nineteenth centuries), but eventually the clown character Pantaloon became the dominant figure. There are two Harlequin Puppet Theatres: that of ERIC BRAMALL, Rhos-on-Sea (Colwyn Bay) – twice the centre of international festivals – and the *Arlekin* at Lodz, Poland, director Henryk Ryl.

Harlequin Puppet Theatre, Rhos-on-Sea, Colwyn Bay, North Wales. Founded 1958; Director Eric Bramall, q.v. Theatre gained for its design the Civic Trust Award, 1959; first theatre ever to be built in Britain solely for puppet playing; seating capacity 118. Repertoire of over 60 productions: Opera, Ballet, Plays, Musicals, including *The Mikado, Ali Baba and the Forty Thieves, Casse Noisette, The Magic Toyshop, Danse Macabre, Le Ballet Mouchoir; The Damnation of Doctor Faustus, Harlequinade; Wayang Golek, The Golden Touch, Alice in Wonderland;* Revues and Variety

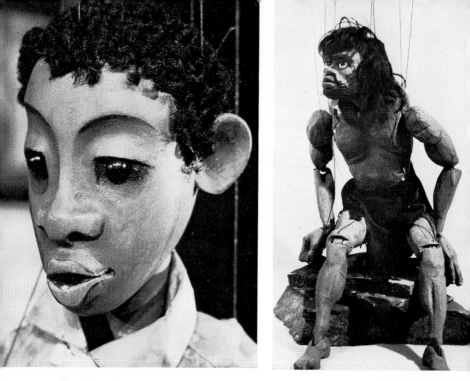

Above left: Nap, marionette from *A Trumpet for Nap*. Carved by John Wright
Above right: Caveman, marionette carved by Stanley Maile
Below left: The devil, rod puppet from *The Soldier's Tale*
Below right: Tim Bobbin, late-Victorian marionette

Opposite: Little Angel Theatre, Islington, London.
Above: 'Anonymous', rod puppet in Barry Smith's Theatre of Puppets

Punch and Judy: marottes designed and made by Violet Philpott

include *Puppet Circus, Gaiety Music Hall, The Village Concert, String Pie,* and *Divertissements.* Two major new productions are presented each year, mainly marionettes but occasionally glove, rod or shadow puppets. Principal season from Whitsuntide to late September; also Christmas, Easter seasons and occasional openings for weeks of experimental puppetry. Theatre also in use throughout the two International Puppetry Festivals at Colwyn Bay in 1963 and 1968.

Harlequinade. Privately circulated periodical, critical review and open forum for puppeteers, edited by C. C. Somerville, associate of Eric Bramall, director of the Harlequin Puppet Theatre, Rhos-on-Sea. First issue: June, 1966; no fixed publication date. Enquiries: C. C. Somerville, The Laurels, Woodlands Road, Colwyn Bay, North Wales.

Harness. Equipment worn by puppeteer working below stage to support large rod type puppet or prop such as boat in which hand puppet rides. Construction varies with problem: a waist belt with a socket to take bottom of main rod (similar to standard-bearer's outfit), or two curved wooden rails connected at base and sitting on operator's shoulders, supporting rod (with boat, etc.); a mobile 'PEDAL' puppet also developed on these lines. Related is ring control worn on head by operator of one type of puppet used in India, with strings supporting the puppet and leaving operator's hands free to control arm movement by rods (downwards).

Harris, Joe Chandler (1848–1908). American writer and journalist, best known as author of books on Negro folklore, including *Uncle Remus: his songs and sayings* (1880), *Nights with Uncle Remus* (1883), *Tar Baby and other Rhymes* (1904), *Told by Uncle Remus* (1905), *Uncle Remus and Brer Rabbit* (1907). Many fresh editions, often illustrated. Widely used for puppet-play source material in schools. Hand-puppet play versions of three stories, adapted by Barbara Lancaster, in the Macmillan Series of Puppet Plays for Schools.

Harvard University Library (U.S.A.). Holdings include fine collections of rare English and American playbills, e.g. John Harris item (puppet booth at Bartholomew Fair, *c.* 1700) reproduced in Speaight *History of the English Puppet Theatre* (Harrap, 1955).

Hawthorne, Nathaniel (1804–64). American short-story writer and novelist: *The Scarlet Letter, Tanglewood Tales;* in his *English Notebooks* (1870) mentions 'Tumblers, hand-organists, puppet showmen . . . and all such vagrant mirthmakers'.

Haydn, Franz Joseph (1732–1809). Austrian composer; wrote five puppet operettas for the private marionette theatre of Prince Esterhazy while resident musical director at his chateau in Eisenstadt; most of the scores lost, but *Philemon and Baucis* has been produced by modern marionette companies, e.g. the Lanchester Marionettes, q.v.

Haydon, Benjamin Robert (1786–1846). English historical painter; author of *Thoughts on the Relative Value of Fresco and Oil Painting* (1842); painting in the Tate Gallery 'Punch, or May-Day' (1828) q.v. shows street Punch and Judy show, q.v.

Hazlitt, William (1778–1830). English writer. In his *Table Talk, or Original Essays on Men and Manners* (1821–22), uses the less usual variant of 'puppet' or 'marionette' in 'Our hypocrites are not thinking of these little *fantoccini* being'.

Heel bar. Short, stiff wire projection at bottom and rear of vertical marionette control, operated by little finger when backward step has to be made by heel-string action.

Hemp. Leaf-fibre used in rope-making; also known as 'plumber's tow'. Useful for theatrical hair; natural colour pale straw, easily dyed. Can be plaited or made up into wig. Obtainable from rope and canvas suppliers, ironmongers, theatrical suppliers.

Hero and Leander. In Jonson *Bartholomew Fayre* (1631) the puppet play is a parody on the Greek legend of Hero, a virgin priestess of Aphrodite and Leander who swam the Hellespont at night to be with her, only to be drowned on a stormy night when the guiding light failed (and the priestess then drowning herself). The puppet-showman changed the venue to the Thames. The story occurs in Ovid *Heroides* (authorship doubted) and in a poem by Musaeus Grammaticus, q.v. Was also adapted by Christopher Marlowe (1564–93).

Heroes of the Puppet Stage, by Madge Anderson (Harcourt Brace, 1923; Jonathan Cape, 1924), illustrated by author. History of Mr Punch, ancestry of Punchinello, the Japanese Romeo and Juliet, Harlequin's company, Gozzi's *Love of Three Oranges*, q.v., Play that lasts a year, Casperl and the Faust Play. Somewhat romanticised items of history, suitable for children.

Heroic puppets. Term is reference to size rather than to character: outsize figures such as the 10-ft. rod puppet Shakespeare made by Russian puppeteers the EFIMOVS, or gigantic figures by REMO BUFANO (U.S.A.) for production of OEDIPUS REX (Stravinsky) and controlled by puppeteers on a platform 40-ft. up and by others on the ground. Perhaps related to the medieval pageant 'giants' are the figures created by the BREAD AND PUPPET THEATRE (U.S.A.) requiring internal operators.

Highland dancers. A complaint about the noise of Powell's puppet show by 'Ralph Belfry' in No. 372 of *The Spectator* (7th May, 1712) mentioned the performance of *The Destruction of Troy* 'adorned with Highland dancers'. The street showman interviewed by Mayhew (*London Labour and London Poor*, 1852) mentioned Scottish hornpipe dancing as one of the FANTOCCINI items.

Histoire des Marionnettes en Europe depuis l'antiquite jusqu'a nos jours, by Charles Magnin, q.v. (Levy Frères, 1852, 2nd edition, 1862). The puppet history which has formed basis of all later general histories; originally published in serial form in *La Revue des deux mondes* (1848); only part published in English translation, chapter 4, on English puppets (in *Sharpe's London Journal*, 1848–49, q.v.). Several commentators have advised reconsideration of Magnin's conclusions regarding classical Greek and Latin references to puppetry in antiquity (part 1). Part 2 briefly covers the Middle Ages; Part 3, the 'Modern' (as at time of writing): brief chapters on Italy, Spain and Portugal, more extensive on France, England and Germany. Maindron *Marionnettes et Guignols* (1900) borrowed heavily from Magnin, but added a good deal of new material and, of even more importance, many illustrations (Magnin has none). These two books should be read in conjunction. They are, of course, 'collectors' items'. Consult Public Library – or British Museum Reading Room (Reader's Ticket necessary).

Histoire du célèbre théâtre Liégeois de marionnettes, by Rodolphe de Warsage (Libraire Nationale d'Art et d'Histoire, Van Oest, Brussels, 1905). Full history, techniques, Flemish theatrical conventions, repertoire of the Liège puppets.

History. Latin *historia*: story or narrative of past events. Twentieth century usage has the further meaning of *the events themselves*. The earliest history-technique is that of simple narration, one generation to the next. By the time a form of writing has been evolved, the history has become legend. There is no authentic record as to who made the first puppet, when, where, why, out of what material and with what means of control: but there are legends. Two Chinese legends are mentioned by Obraztsov in *The Chinese Puppet Theatre* (Faber, 1961), q.v., one is about a puppet-master in the tenth century B.C. who saved his life by cutting open his puppets to prove they were not really capable of flirting with the Emperor's wives. The other legend attributes the saving of a city from its enemies by an ingenious effigy made to dance on the city wall, exciting the attacking chief's wife to jealousy so that she persuaded him to call off the attack. Ignoring the possibility of either legend being based on fact, there can be no doubt that the *concept* of puppetry already existed. Where traditional forms of puppet show are still extant, e.g. the shadow-plays of ANDHRA in India, the Javanese 'WAYANG', the SICILIAN armoured puppets, these can be studied at first hand: but origins remain obscure. Rarely does literary research produce any clear picture of the puppetry of the past: the existence of puppet shows at a particular period may have no more evidence than that found through local records of fees paid for use of sites, e.g. 'Punchinello, the Italian puppet player for his booth at Charing Cross' (quoted in L.C.C. *Survey of London*, 1935, from the Overseer's Books of St. Martin's-in-the-Fields, London, 1667). Somtimes play-titles will give clues as to content, e.g. those based on biblical themes (*The Creation of the World*, *Noah*, etc., frequently having puppet versions) or an item in the *Diary* of Samuel Pepys, that for 30th August, 1667, mentioning *Patient Grizzil*, q.v., whose origin can be traced through a number of versions by other authors back to Boccaccio's *Decameron*. Again, a term or a phrase for 'puppet' as used in a period in which only one *type* existed would be clear enough in that period but might be confusing at a later time when several types co-existed. The term 'MOTION' in Shakespeare's day meant both 'puppet' and 'puppet show' – but had at least a dozen other meanings, as evidenced in the Bard's own plays. The one clear reference to a puppet show is in the *Winter's Tale*, Act 4, sc. 3: 'He compassed a motion of the *Prodigal Son*.' There is no indication of type of puppet here, but in Ben Jonson's *Bartholomew Fayre* and his *Tale of a Tub*, two types are shown in action, hand puppets in the first (because of the type of booth and the fact that the puppets were carried in a basket) and some primitive form of shadow-show in the second and the *items* themselves being termed 'motions'. There are many instances of the use of (the equivalent of) 'puppet' in a metaphorical sense in various classical Greek and Roman writers. The showman who talked with Socrates at the real or imagined banquet described by XENOPHON in the *Symposium* used the term 'my puppets' and it could have been an allusion to his live actors (as seemingly no puppet show was given on that occasion): but the use of the term is evidence enough of the existence of puppets. Father Mariantonio LUPI (1695–1737) gathered together references in Aristotle, Apuleius, Horace, Herodotus, and others, including them in a learned *Dissertazioni* – and this became the starting point for Charles Magnin's *Histoire des marionnettes en Europe* (1852) – itself the starting point for all later histories. English translations of Lupi appeared in Gordon Craig's *The Marionnette* (June, 1918) and Inverarity's *Manual of Puppetry* (1936): Marjorie Batchelder (*Rod Puppets and the Human*

Theatre, 1947) and others have stressed the need for critical re-assessment of all such material to clear up technical confusion. The possible origin of puppets in moving statues, the overlapping with automata and movable toys in many references – these may never be resolved by re-assessment, only by new and clearer documents. The student in the twenty-first century will be better placed, as the twentieth century is providing documentary material in the form of films and sound recordings, slides, photographs, a wealth of literature (including vast quantities of press-cuttings as well as books). With the resources of the international organisation UNIMA and the co-operation of its National Sections it may yet be possible to achieve a clearer picture of earlier periods. One place where observation may find a clue to the origin of puppets is in the Nursery: young children have an inherent faculty for puppetising their playthings.

History of the English Puppet Theatre, by George Speaight (Harrap, 1955). The standard work on this aspect and the criterion for any other book on the puppetry of any other country. As authoritative as devoted research and full documentation can make, justifying the statement in the final chapter that decisive proof has been given of the puppet's 'ancient and honorable history as a medium of drama and of satire' – and that it has pleased artists and wits as well as peasants and nursemaids. The historian of the late twentieth century developments, continuing where Mr Speaight leaves off, will have a simpler task in that contemporary documentation is so highly organised, including that of active puppetry associations, these now including an international organisation UNIMA. The history begins with the Mediterranean Mimes, moves on to Puppets in Europe (Socrates to Louis XIV), the English Clown and Puppets in England from Chaucer to Cromwell; Punchinello arrives; eighteenth century English puppet theatres become 'the talk of the town'; Punch evolves in the eighteenth century; chapter VIII is devoted to a study of Punch and Judy, and IX to the marionettes of the nineteenth century, concluding with a chapter on the twentieth century revival. The book is profusely illustrated, has over 40 pages of Notes related to the main text, Appendices listing showmen from 1600 to 1914 and plays performed from 1500 to 1914. The latter include Folk Plays, Biblical; Folk Plays, Historical and Legendary; Comedies, Farces, Dramas (eighteenth century), Burlesques and Satires, Ballad Operas, Comic Operas and Operatic Burlesques; Pantomimes (eighteenth c.); Dramas, Comedies, Farces (nineteenth c.); Pantomines and Extravaganzas (nineteenth c.); Foreign plays and operas; Divertissements of the Ombres Chinoises (shadow plays).

Hofmannsthal, Hugo von (1874–1929). Austrian poet and dramatist. *Das spiel von Jedermann* ('Everyman') has had puppet adaptations. In *Forspiel für ein Puppenspiel*: 'From this drama I rise and step over into that other drama which is called human world and human life.' Bilingual edition of *Poems and Verse Plays* (Routledge, 1961).

Hogarth, Ann. English puppeteer, co-director (with husband Jan Bussell) of the Hogarth Puppets; one-time Secretary B.P.M.T.G. Wrote scripts and manipulated the puppets for the *Muffin the Mule* television series with Annette Mills. Dramatised and presented the *Little Grey Rabbit* series on T.V., 1949, *et seq.* (first glove puppet series on T.V. to use wide staging). Author of: *Look at Puppets* (Hamish Hamilton, 1960), illustrated book for children; the *Muffin Annuals* from 1951–54 (London University Press) and various *Muffin* stories published by the Brockhampton Press.

Hogarth Puppets, The. English company directed by Jan Bussell and
Ann Hogarth, established 1932. Tours include South Africa, Australia,
Canada, New Zealand, Germany, Belgium, etc. Specialise in performing
in (human) theatres: in London at the Cambridge, St Martin's, Vaudeville, Arts, Duke of York, Lyric Hammersmith. Regular summer seasons
in London Parks, 1947–67. Regular television appearances from 1937.
(See also *Muffin the Mule*.) International Festival award for performances
in Bucharest, 1958. *Master Peter's Puppet Show* (de Falla), produced for
the Ingestre Festivals, 1957 and 1958. *The Water Babies* (Kingsley),
produced for Lyric Theatre, Hammersmith, London, 1956. Productions
in repertoire include: *Macbeth* (Shakespeare), *Aucassin and Nicolette*
(traditional), *Two Slatterns and a King* (E. St Vincent Millais), *The Happy
Prince* (Oscar Wilde), *Blue Beard* (traditional), *The Waterman* (Dibdin),
The Luckless Lovers (K. S. McKay) and numerous specially devised ballet-
mimes for puppets.

Hogarth, William (1697–1764). English painter, engraver; satirical
subjects. Of particular interest to puppeteers is his *Southwark Fair* (also
known as *The Fair* and *The Humours of the Fair*), issued in 1735, reproduced
in *Wm Hogarth, His Original Engravings and Etchings*, Heinemann, 1913):
details in individual entry. There are also simple types of puppets, used
satirically, in *A Just View of the British Stage*, q.v., and *Credulity, Superstition, Fanaticism*, q.v., directed at the theatre and religion respectively.

Hohnsteiner, Die. Two famous hand-puppet companies in Germany,
founded by MAX JACOB (1888–1967), who became President of the international organisation UNIMA; shows the criterion for all German hand-
puppet players, Max Jacob himself being the supreme player of the
traditional character KASPER (Kasperle). Companies directed by (1)
Harold Schwarz, (2) Friedrich Arndt.

Hole saw. Tool similar to thin round file but with elongated teeth and a
gimlet end for drilling the initial hole in which to insert the tool, which
can then cut in any direction with normal up and down saw-like action.
Can be used with plywood, hardboard, solid wood boards; useful in
areas inaccessible for conventional tools.

Hone, William (1780–1842). English bookseller and author. *The Ancient
Mysteries Described* (1823) on the English Miracle plays; *The Every-Day
Book* (1826), q.v., a weekly miscellany, followed by *The Table Book*
(1827–28) and *Year Book* (1839); editor Strutt's *Sports and Pastimes of the
People of England* (1830), q.v., which has many puppet references.

Hone's Every-Day Book (Tegg, 1826). See *Every-Day Book*.

Horace, Quintus Horatius Flaccus (65 B.C. – 8 B.C.). Roman poet,
contemporary and friend of Virgil. As pointed out by the Jesuit scholar
Mariantonio LUPI, q.v., among a number of references to puppets in
Classical Literature, there is an item in the *Satires* (Book 2), 'Duceris ut
nervis alienis mobile lignum'. Speaight, in his *History of the English Puppet
Theatre*, q.v., says the sentence has also been seen as an allusion to a whip-
top rather than a wooden figure moved by wires, but provides no reference; in either case it is a comparison with the man who is controlled by
the will of another. Even if a case can be made for the puppet the lack
of technical detail is frustrating for the puppeteer even more than the
historian. There is a translation by Lord Dunsany and Michael Oakley
in the *Everyman Library* (Collected Works, 1961).

Hornpipe dancing. The street showman interviewed by Mayhew, as recorded in his *London Labour and London Poor* (1852), said that the 'exhibition' (performance) began with a sailor dancing a hornpipe and was followed by tight-rope dancing – and then a Scottish hornpipe; all items typical of the Fantoccini performances.

Horniman Museum. London Road, Forest Hill, London, S.E.23. Important ethnographic collections, arts and crafts in all parts of the world, including puppets – particularly Javanese – with a Polish 'SZOPKA' and a number of the small puppets used in this. Library has a few scarce puppet titles. Seasonal lectures on Eastern music, etc. Note: closed Mondays.

Hortus Deliciarum. Twelfth century encyclopaedia compiled by Herrad von Landsberg, Abbess of Hohenberg (1167–95), illustrated by miniatures. *Children at Play* frequently reproduced in puppet books (e.g. Baird *Art of the Puppet*, Collier-Macmillan, 1965) shows two puppet knights sword-fighting, controlled by two horizontal and crossed cords held by an operator at each end of a table (used as stage) and apparently related to the MARIONNETTES A LA PLANCHETTE type; latter have cord passed through chest, but illustration probably stylised and not technically correct. Text makes psycho-religious use of 'puppet'.

Houdini, Harry (1874–1926). American Magician and phenomenal Escapologist; son of the Rev. Dr Mayer Samuel (changed name legally); at one time employed as Punch and Judy operator at a circus (mentioned in Kellock *Houdini, His Life Story*: Harcourt Brace, N.Y., 1928); first successful aeronaut in Australia (1910); author of several books.

How to do Punch and Judy, by Sidney de Hempsey (Max Andrews, N.D.). Author professional showman and member of the International Brotherhood of Magicians. Introduction on the Romances of Punchman; the complete playscript; how to make Punch and Judy puppets, costume, portable stage with proscenium, properties, manipulation, novelty scenes, advice on performing; clear instructions for making the 'call' or 'swazzle' and on producing the Punch voice; list of things *not* to forget.

Howard, T. E. Archivist British Puppet and Model Theatre Guild, London; committee member of the British Section of UNIMA (the international organisation); organiser of Guild Summer Schools; lighting technician; compiler of two important lists: (a) *List of Puppet Films for hire in Great Britain*, q.v., (b) *International Directory of Puppet Theatres*, q.v. United Kingdom correspondent for International Esperanto-Society of Puppeteers (enquiries c/o British Unima).

Hrostwitha. Also: Hrotsvitha, Hrosvitha, Roswitha. Celebrated Benedictine nun (*c.* 930–1000) at Gandersheim convent, Saxony; poet-dramatist who wrote in Latin in style of Terence, preaching the Christian virtues and ultimate triumph of Chastity. Some of her six plays (*Abramo, Callimaco, Dulcizio, Gallicano, Punuzio* and *Sapienza*) have been performed by puppets and were mentioned by ANATOLE FRANCE after a visit to M. Signoret's 'Petit Théâtre' in Paris (*On Life and Letters*, third series, translated Bernard Miall: Bodley Head, 1924); he gives a charming account of her life. A French translation of the mss. in Munich was made by Charles Magnin) Paris, 1845), author of *Histoire des Marionnettes en Europe* (Levy Freres, 1852).

Hugo, Victor (1802–85). French poet, dramatist, novelist, leader of the Romantic school. *Les Miserables* has been source of puppet plays.

Humanettes. See LIVING MARIONETTES.

Humperdinck, Engelbert (1854–1921). German composer of fairy-opera *Hansel and Gretel*, text by his sister Adelheid Wette, which has been a favourite with many puppet theatres. Also wrote incidental music for Shakespeare's *Merchant of Venice, Romeo and Juliet, Twelfth Night* and *The Tempest*, for Maeterlinck's *Blue Bird* and Aristophanes' *Lysistrata*.

Hundred Children, The. Chinese painting on silk, sixteenth–seventeenth century, showing children playing with small marionettes on low platform, using the small 'paddle' type control. Postcard reproduction in colour available at British Museum.

Hungarian State Puppet Theatre. 'Allami Bábszinház' founded 1949 in Budapest; Director: Dr Deszo Szilagyi, q.v., formerly known as 'Mesebarlang' (Cave of Tales), founded 1947 under the auspices of the Hungarian Women's Democratic Federation. In 20 years presented over 90 productions in 17,000 performances to over four million spectators; company of 160 working in eight groups; annual programme of about 20 plays; performances not only in the capital but also in nearly 500 towns and villages. Participants in various international festivals, winning an award for productions of Bartok *The Wooden Prince* and Stravinsky *Petrushka* (using rod puppets) at the third Festival held at Bucharest, Rumania (1965), these items being given at the Aldeburgh and Bath Festivals (1968) and in London. The repertory is extensive, including such items as *Aladdin, Gulliver, The Emperor's New Clothes*; during the Shakespeare 400th anniversary celebrations presented *Midsummer Night's Dream* to adult audiences, hailed by the critics as more successful than 'live' performances. In a fresh direction there have been adaptations of modern one-act plays by Weyrauch, Mrožek and Beckett ('Puppets and Men'). There is a group performing in Esperanto, q.v.

Hungary. Apart from the usual itinerant showmen, with the traditional folk-puppet hero Vitez-Laszlo, cousin of Punch, and the eighteenth century private marionette theatre of Prince Esterhazy, for which Haydn, q.v., wrote little puppet operas, puppetry seems to have begun only after World War II – but has made tremendous strides in this period. Puppetry is regarded as a vital part of theatre and there is special emphasis on children's theatre. In the period 1945–50 over a thousand companies, large and small and all amateurs, operated throughout the country. The first professional company was formed in 1949, the 'Allami Babszinhaz' or State Puppet Theatre, q.v., taking over from one established in 1947 by the Women's Democratic Federation. Experiments were made with all types of puppet, and the visit of the Soviet puppetmaster Sergei Obraztsov in 1951 had the same stimulating effect as in most of the countries he visited; new techniques were developed; Hungarian folklore and fairy-tales were explored and found their rightful place in the theatre, and the State Theatre is at the international award level. The People's Educational Institute has published more than 130 puppet plays and professional textbooks.

Hurdy-Gurdy. Musical instrument; English name for French 'Vielle' and sometimes mentioned in connection with itinerant puppet shows (often wrongly applied to the 'barrel organ'); known in medieval times as 'organistrum' (Latin); origin unknown, English term dating from eighteenth century. Instrument has four to six strings set in vibration by turning of a hand-cranked wooden wheel (rosined) at the lower end;

one or two strings, with fingerboard, for the melody, the lower strings as drones.

Hurvinek. Like pepper and salt, this should be 'Hurvinek and Spejbl' – son and father marionettes created by noted Czechoslovak puppeteer Professor Skupa (1892–1957), Hurvinek being carved by Gustav Nosek (1926) and Spejbl by woodcarver Karel Nosek (1920). The puppets have their own theatre in Prague, the Hurvinek and Spejbl Theatre, have appeared in films, and Hurvinek even appeared on a postage stamp. They are internationally famous and beloved throughout Czechoslovakia.

I

Ibsen, Henrik (1828–1906). Norwegian poet, dramatist, whose *Peer Gynt*, dramatic poem with roots in folk-lore, inspired music by GRIEG and has been adapted for puppet stage by various companies.

I-Ho-Ho. Puppet play by Evgeny Speransky, U.S.S.R., produced at the Central State Puppet Theatre, Moscow, director Sergei OBRAZTSOV. Theme: hero, Faustov, a modern scientist, discovers that evil spirits really exist; he is conducting experiments at an Institute of Homo-Homuncular Formations (I-H-H) and his journalist girl-friend, sceptical, presses a button in the laboratory, releasing hordes of demons. Production involves new techniques: modern cybernetics, electronic units to detect and exterminate demons, spirits, syrens. Only the demon of love survives. Scientist and girl played by live actors; witches, devils, mermaids, fairies, all puppets.

India. The author of *Der Heimat des Puppenspiels*, Richard Pischel (Halle, 1900: translated as *The Home of the Puppet Play*, 1902), put forward the theory that the puppet theatre everywhere preceded the live drama, certainly in India. William Ridgeway, author of *The Dramas and Dramatic Dances of Non-European Races* (1915), disputed this and, according to Marjorie Batchelder (*Rod Puppets and the Human Theatre*, Ohio University, 1947), refuted it; puppets originated much earlier in Europe according to Ridgeway. George Speaight (*History of the English Puppet Theatre*, Harrap, 1955) sided with Ridgeway, too, in this 'fundamental dispute'. However, Devi Lal SAMAR, Director of the Lok Kala Mandal, Udaipur, an Institute concerned with research in all the theatre arts, and who has been responsible for organising Indian national puppet festivals (and also participated with a troupe at international festivals in Europe), says specifically 'In India the drama owes its origin to puppetry because in the initial stages of Indian life it was not considered good to imitate our ancestors and great personalities through human drama.' (In an article in *Natya*, Theatre Arts Journal, 1966). Thus puppetry is seen to be closely linked with the religious and social life of the people, as in Indonesia, long before it attains any purely entertainment value. Further evidence that the puppet form preceded the live drama has been seen in the use of the term 'suthradhara' (literally 'the holder of strings') for the principal actor in classical Sanskrit drama. Whether literary evidence can substantiate its use prior to (say) the tenth century is not so important as the significance of the term. More important than any debate about history and origins is the fact that in the last decade or so there has been a great revival of the traditional forms of puppetry, and some new developments, with the stimulus coming from the visits by Soviet Union and Czechoslovak companies. The traditional types include marionettes, shadow puppets, hand puppets and the rod type (and some interesting hybrids). Some types are more 'realistic' in their characterisation, but usually, as with the Indonesian puppets, there is a taboo against life-like representation; according to Devi Lal Samar the Rajasthani marionettes, which are small and stylised and usually have only a single string looped from the figure's waist to its head, passing over the hand of the operator, the characters represent creatures from the celestial world, presenting the world to itself. The figures are legless (long-skirted), but so constructed that slight variations of the string produce movements of head, shoulders and hands. The language is also non-human, produced with a form of reed-whistle not unlike that of the Punch SWAZZLE, but made of bamboo; this is interpreted by the puppeteer who gives the rhythm. Expression is largely through movement. Performances are usually informal with improvised stages and no scenery, many of the puppets being visible to the spectators even before coming on stage. 'Tolu Bommalata' is the popular shadow play ('the play of hide-fashioned toys') associated with the Andhra province, the screen for which is made from two saris, one above the other and joined with thorns, the bottom edge being knee high. Themes for plays – which continue until dawn, through the night – are derived from the two great epics, the *Mahabharata*, q.v., and the *Ramayana*, q.v., with gods and demons, animals and warriors. As with most of the professions, the puppeteers usually come from families of puppeteers. In Orissa there are still troupes of puppeteers using marionettes and shadow figures, performing on festive occasions, but often having to earn their living by agriculture, carpentry or other non-ancestral professions. The string puppets are of two types, one without legs. There are no special scripts but plays are based on episodes in the life of Krishna and Rama. A unique method of control of marionettes is found in Southern India, the figures being large and heavy, the weight being taken by strings attached to a cloth-covered ring on the puppeteer's head (and to the puppet's head and waist) with rods downwards to the puppet hands. The most detailed accounts of the various types of Indian puppets (with illustrations) are to be found in *Puppet Theatre Around the World* (New Delhi, 1960), which originally appeared in issues of *Natya*, a Theatre Arts journal. Good colour illustrations also in Baird *Art of the Puppet* (Collier-Macmillan, 1965). See also INDIAN PUPPET THEATRE.

India Rubber Man. One of several trick marionettes seen by author of *Acrobats and Mountebanks*, Hugues le Roux, at Versailles Fair (1890). Figure stretched in various ways, finally touching heels with nose. No technical details.

Indian Puppet Theatre. A registered Society and Public Trust, membership open to any citizen of INDIA; non-commercial. Aims: revival of the

Puppet Art; mass-education *re* National building plans, social reforms, medical therapy. Activities: exhibitions, festivals, conferences; organised third All-India Puppet Festival in Bombay (December, 1964 – January, 1965); formation of an All-India organisation. Address: Sitladevi Estate, Temple Road, Mahim, Bombay-16.

Indonesia. Puppets and shadow shows are traditionally a factor in spiritual education throughout Indonesia. The shadow play in particular was probably related to ancient ancestor-worship and initiation ceremonies: its exact origin is as obscure as it is in most countries, especially because it did not have a purely entertainment function. Indonesian myths and the *Mahabharata*, q.v., and *Ramayana*, q.v., epics from India provided material for the plays, Moslem stories being added with the coming of Islam. Some of these plays travelled to Bali and Malaya, Thailand, Cambodia, from Java. The puppeteers (dalangs) are required to undergo a long period of training, not only in the techniques of handling the puppets but also in the study of ancient lore and philosophy, and in the control of the gamelan orchestra which accompanies the performances. In the twentieth century the audio-visual-aid possibilities have been appreciated by the Government and exploited in community development schemes. There are still dalang schools where the art can be learned. A valuable chapter with fine colour plates in *Indonesia: The Art of an Island Group*, by Frits A. Wagner (Methuen, 1959), on the Javanese and Balinese *Wayang*; also a first-hand account by Beryl de Zoete in *Dance and Drama in Bali* (Faber, 1938).

Industrial and Business Films: A modern means of communication, by Leopold Stork (Phoenix House, 1962). Useful chapter on puppets and model animation; objects such as bottles, cartons can be 'puppetised' (e.g. Mackeson Stout puppets used in some TV commercials) and even Trade-marks (e.g. Egg Marketing Board symbol of Lion) become puppets.

Inert. White pigment (e.g. GYPSUM) with low obliterative power, almost transparent in oil, used in paint manufacture.

Insect Play, The. Best known play of the brothers Čapek (Josef, 1887–1927; Karel, 1890–1939); sub-title, 'Or the World We Live In.' Satire on human social vices and crimes, the only human in the play being the Vagabond, an 'Everyman' type. Czechoslovak and other puppet productions. English translation included in International Modern Plays, Everyman Library, No. 989.

Instant puppets. Journalistic term for quick-to-make types for school-children, mainly created from scrap materials – disguised tin cans, chocolate boxes, sox, handkerchiefs.

Interior (Interieur). One of Maurice Maeterlinck, q.v., *Trois drames pour les marionnettes*; doubts have been expressed (by puppeteers) as to whether these plays were really intended for puppets and would make good 'puppet theatre' – but they have nevertheless had a number of puppet productions. J. Fuller-Maitland, editor of Grove's *Dictionary of Music*, produced *Interior* in 1908, using artists' lay-figures as marionettes after obtaining some figures and instruction from an old folk-puppeteer. The play is mystical and symboliste in treatment: an Old Man and a Stranger have to bring news of a death to the family which can be observed through a window. An English translation by William Archer is available, included in *The Death of Tintagiles and Other Plays* (1st edition, 1899;

reprints, 1915 and 1923; pocket edition by Duckworth and Allen and Unwin, 1924).

Intermedia. A group in Vancouver concerned with Communication and which includes 'projected puppetry', q.v., in its programme of experiments. The local Puppetry Guild has space in the same premises, so there is a possibility of co-operation; anyone interested in computers, cybernetics, electronics, and puppets should contact the group at 575 Beatty Street, Vancouver 3, B.C. INTERMEDIA will assist in bringing together artists, scientists and technicians, who will collaborate on the use of techniques and materials such as polarised light, U.V., Infra red, strobe effects, complicated electrical circuitry, motors, exotic plastics. Part of the concept is to have a new type of museum whose contents will be stored on photographic emulsion and magnetic tape, and objects from anywhere in the world will be shown by means of stereoscopic projections in the original dimensions: final technical developments making three-dimensional projection a possibility. In the field of education it is hoped to set up workshops for teachers or *anyone* interested to experiment with the new techniques, to prepare audio-visual productions available to schools and universities in British Columbia. Experiments with cinematic film and animated film are also envisaged, including television screening. Interests embrace all the arts: architecture, dance, opera, drama, puppetry, poetry.

Italian Comedy, The, by Pierre Louis Duchartre (Dover Publications, N.Y., 1966; originally Harrap, 1929). Authorised translation from the French by Randolph T. Weaver. A 367-page study of the Commedia dell' Arte, the improvisation scenarios, lives, attributes, portraits and masks of the characters, with a new pictorial supplement; 259 illustrations. In a brief chapter on the marionettes the author admits that they are so ancient in origin that it is impossible to tell whether the puppeteers borrowed the stock characters from the ATELLANAE (predecessors of the commedia) or *vice versa.* Terminology should be compared with Ferrigni's in *Storia dei Burattini* – and there is confusion in some Italian/English dictionaries as to *types*: BURATTINI, FANTOCCINI. Ferrigni is definite that the commedia character Burattino was *puppet* first, *hand* puppet, giving the name to hand puppets in general (as in France, 'guignol' – the character – has become the generic term for hand puppets). Duchartre maintains that Burattino was first a commedia character and that the puppet burattini were controlled by a wire and strings. Certainly contemporary usage is: burattini, *hand* puppets, and marionetti, string type. (Signorelli, in *Puppet Theatre Around the World*), q.v. There are two illustrations of marionettes (from the Civic Museum, Venice). Chapter XVI is also of interest to puppeteers, dealing with the ancestry of Pulcinella (PUNCH) – with a gap in the period between 540 and the sixteenth century, in which there was no trace of Pulcinella. The history of puppets and that of the live theatre have overlapped down the centuries.

International Directory of Puppet Theatres. Compiled by T. E. HOWARD for the British Section of UNIMA, the international puppetry organisation (1968). Approximately 150 theatres, mainly European, arranged alphabetically by countries and towns, including Austria, Belgium, Bulgaria, Czechoslovakia, Denmark, France, Germany (FRG and GDR), Hungary, Netherlands, Norway, Poland, Rumania, Sicily, Sweden, Switzerland, United Kingdom, U.S.S.R., Yugoslavia, India, United States, Canada. Intended mainly for visitors who wish to know where they can find easily places where performances of puppets are given. Revised edition will be issued when sufficient additional addresses available. Enquiries: British Section, UNIMA, The Educational Puppetry Association, The British Puppet and Model Theatre Guild (addresses under these entries).

International Federation for Theatre Research. Joint Secretary-General: Ifan Kyrle Fletcher, 22 Buckingham Gate, London, S.W.1. The Federation consists of public or private organisations which devote all or part of their activities to theatre research. Officially inaugurated at the international conference on Theatre History held in Venice, 1957. In 1963 opened international institute for theatre research at the Casa Goldoni, Venice. Publishes a quarterly journal.

International Theatre Institute. Founded 28th June, 1948; a non-governmental organisation under the auspices of UNESCO; international secretariat in Paris, with national centres in over 50 countries. Aims: To promote international exchange of knowledge and practice in the theatre arts, to encourage their development and thus assist better understanding and co-operation between peoples. Activities: international exhibitions and symposia and international theatre weeks. Annual award of three fellowships; congresses. Publications include *World Theatre*, which has had two special puppet issues (No. 5, Volume 14, 1965, and No. 2, Volume 15, 1966). The Bharatiya Natya Sangh, which is also the Indian National Centre of the ITI, published *Puppet Theatre Around the World* (1960) with assistance from UNIMA, the international puppetry organisation. British Centre office for ITI: 10a Aquinas Street, London, S.E.1.

Interpreter. Puppet-showman's assistant – or the showman himself (with assistant in the booth) who stands in front of the show and explains the action, possibly talking to the puppets. A clear picture of his function can be gained from Ben Jonson's *Bartholomew Fayre* (printed 1631), in which a puppet show is actually introduced into the fairground scene and the 'motion master' (puppeteer) stands in front, giving a running commentary on the play, which is a caricature of the story of *Hero and Leander*. Elsewhere he says he is 'the voice of them all'. In *Don Quixote* (1605–12) Cervantes describes Master Peter's Puppet Show with a boy standing in front of the stage and holding a white wand with which to point out the various characters while describing the action of the play. The frontispiece to *A Second Tale of a Tub* (1715), a satirical pamphlet by Thomas Burnet, shows 'Robert' Powel also interpreting with the aid of a wand. Shakespeare uses the term in *Hamlet* (Act 3, sc 2): 'I could interpret between you and your love if I could see the puppets dallying.' The street showman interviewed by Mayhew in *London Labour and London Poor* (1851) said he worked in front of the booth, speaking and playing music on the 'pandean' pipes, using four voices for the dialogue. One possibility is that the earlier Italian players literally needed interpreting to the spectators – and the Punch 'voice' can be very indistinct and need interpreting. The 'front man' or 'bottler' also functions as coin collector. The same technique is seen in contemporary shows such as Harry Corbett's 'Sootie' – as the latter does not talk openly, his words being relayed by the performer; in the American television long-run 'Kukla, Fran and Ollie', Fran is the lady who talks to the puppets from the front. In Paul Gallico's *Love of Seven Dolls*, 1954 (basis of the film 'Lili') the puppeteer realises the value of having the orphan girl Mouche talking to the puppets, as a crowd attracting gimmick – although Mouche herself at first unaware of any audience. Some contemporary puppetry takes the further step of mixing humans and puppets on the same stage, but here the function of intermediary is discarded.

Introducing Puppetry, by Peter Fraser (Batsford; Watson Guptill, N.Y., 1968). Technical manual illustrated by 78 line-drawings of great clarity and detail. Sections on shadow, rod, and hand puppets, marionettes, special 'effects', costume, theatre, play-production methods; list of suppliers of materials, bibliography.

Inverarity, R. Bruce. American puppeteer who became Director of the University of Washington Puppeteers, producing plays and variety; experimented with surrealist constructions. Author of *Manual of Puppetry*, q.v. (Binfords and Mort, 1936), begun as a notebook, containing technical instructions and an interesting section of 'Marionettiana'. Carried out research into AMERICAN INDIAN ceremonial figures, with some drawings in his *Movable Masks and Figures of the North Pacific Coast Indians* (Cranbrook Inst. of Science, 1941).

Irving, Washington (1783–1859). Born in New York, son of an Englishman; writer whose story of *Rip van Winkle*, q.v., has had many puppet productions, e.g. by Tony Sarg in the United States, Miles Lee in his Mews Theatre in Edinburgh, and as the opening performance of the Japanese Puppet Theatre PUK in Tokyo.

Italy. 'Yorick' (P. C. Ferrigni), in his *Storia dei Burattini* (Bemporad e Figlio, Florence, 1902), of which an English translation appeared in Craig's *The Mask* (Vols. IV–VII, 1911–14), says that during more than 300 years the marionettes have maintained their position in the national theatre that and their repertoire would shame that of the better prose theatres. He also says that documents relative to the puppets of Italy are much scarcer and more incomplete than those relative to all other nations, and this although Italy was the birthplace of European puppetry. Ferrigni says that the Italian history is really that of the puppetry of the whole world 'neither more nor less' – which ignores the independent origin of Oriental and American Indian (pre-Columbian) puppetry. That puppets came to England from Italy is recorded in Pepys' famous *Diary* and in early account books (fees paid for pitches for booths), but that other puppets already existed in England is well established by Speaight in his *History of the English Puppet Theatre* (Harrap, 1955). The Italians also set up stage in Paris – but what must be kept in mind is that everywhere a great deal happened that was *not* recorded. There is also the problem of terminology – and of translation of terms which, understood well enough in the days when they were commonplace, are now obscure. Italian/English dictionaries and Italian encyclopaedias are to blame for some of the confusion as to *types* of puppets, presumably because of lack of technical knowledge on the part of the compilers, sometimes because quite obviously the same source material has been used. Ferrigni establishes the difference between 'BURATTINO' (hand puppet type) and 'FANTOCCINO' (marionette). In spite of this there are some instances in this particular translation of misunderstanding on the part of the translator. That Craig himself, for all his enthusiasm for puppets and contribution to twentieth century scholarship on the subject, was capable of mixing his terms is seen in some captions to Javanese rod puppet illustrations (in *The Marionnette*, 1918–19) described as 'marionettes'; and elsewhere in *The Mask* a Japanese BUNRAKU type is also called 'marionette'. Ferrigni makes it clear that the name 'burattino' existed

prior to its use by one of the masked actors of the COMMEDIA DELL' ARTE
and it is quite likely that the comedian based his acting on that of the
puppet and so acquired its name too. (This is seen in the study of Indonesian dance-drama and Japanese live theatre.) 'Burattino' probably
derives from 'buratto' a kind of cheap coarse cloth originally used for
sifting flour and suitable for the body or cloak of a hand puppet (and
for curtaining the booth). Earlier the terms 'magatelli' and 'fraccuradi'
were used – the first being a reference to the 'magic art' which made it
possible for the puppets to perform in surprising ways, and the second
being related to a child's slit-pea-pod toy puppet. In Rome and Naples
the names 'pupi' and 'pupazzi' were used, derived from the ancient
Latin (showing the source of English 'puppet' – probably via French
'poupée'). Another name for the marionette type was 'mastitiettate' –
with a stiff wire to the top of the head, and strings or thin wires to the
limbs. Ferrigni says a clear etymology, backed by documentary evidence,
exists for 'marionette': he quotes a book by Giustina Renier Michel,
Origine delle Feste Veneziane (Milan, 1829), with its account of the famous
'feste delle Marie' (tenth century onwards) celebrating the rescue of
maidens carried off by Saracen pirates – the annual procession of beautiful girls being replaced (for reasons of rivalry and economy) by 'the
wooden Maries' (Marie di legno). Ferrigni sees the origins of Italian
puppets – as elsewhere – in the Church use of animated effigies in various
dramatic presentations, especially as some were horrific: torture and
martyrdom were matters of fact, but 'stand-ins' (puppets) were necessary in some scenes. He also mentions (following Magnin *Histoire des
marionnettes en Europe*, 1852) the 'two Sicilians' seen by Girolamo CARDANO
(mentioned in *De Varietate Rerum*, Nuremberg, 1550), who 'worked
wonders by means of two little figures threaded through the breast by
one single string' – and apparently more impressive than others with
several strings. These were the marionettes à la planchette type, and were
later seen in France and England; operated by a string looped around the
performer's knee, passing through two or even three figures, and attached
to a short post at the end of a plank on the ground, moving to music.
Ferrigni sees Italy, particularly Florence, as the place in which new
vitality in the drama became evident in the fifteenth century 'after the
long lethargy of the Middle Ages'. Yet: 'No single name, no indication,
no title of a scenic play, has reached down to us through the sure and
safe channels of contemporary annals.' He mentions Don Lorenzo de'
Medici, son of the Grand Duke Ferdinando I, who loved to have performances in his private puppet theatre. He gives the name of a famous
mathematician-geometrician, Federico Commandino, who was also
celebrated as a maker of marionettes. From the early appearances in the
'MYSTERIES' and other religious dramas the puppets gradually devoted
themselves to farces: they had to make a living . . . Ferrigni is certain
that improvisation of dialogue was common practice even before the
appearance of the live actors in the commedia dell' arte, and that some
at least of the characters were puppets first. He mentions the device for
'counterfeiting the voice' of the fantoccini; a 'tube' used inside the mouth
– and some of the early English showmen seem to have had a similar
variation of the 'SWAZZLE'. He mentions the Brioccis who took their
puppets to Paris in 1590, and others who went to Spain, and Gavazza,
the inventor of the 'ombre Chinesi' – which became the French
'OMBRES CHINOISES' – an adaptation of the Chinese shadow puppets.
Giulio Goldoni, father of Carlo the playwright, had a small marionette

theatre which obviously influenced the boy's interest in the drama. The poet Pier Jacopo Martelli of Bolgna (1666–1727) wrote puppet farces which he called 'Bambocciate'. When the commedia declined the stock characters 'returned' to the puppet stage and appeared in every village all over Italy, and marionette theatres were constructed 'by the hundreds' in the cities, giving pantomimes, dances, caricatures, parodies. Local characters were born, Pulcinella at Naples, Gerolamo at Milan, Gianduia at Turin, Stentorello at Florence, the Dottore at Bologna, and Brighella and Arlecchino at Venice. In the nineteenth century many Italian puppeteers emigrated to the United States – and some of the 'FANTOC-CINI' appeared in England. In the twentieth century Vittoria PODRECCA (who greeted his audiences in a dozen or more languages) toured the world with his Teatro dei Piccoli, with a repertoire of variety items, opera, folk dancers, clowns, acrobats, burlesque items, and gave a strong impetus to the contemporary revival. (Podrecca illustrations in Beaumont *Puppets and Puppetry*, Studio, 1958).

J

Jack and the Beanstalk. Folk tale with many variants; in 'top ten' as panto-mime or puppet play, usually hand type but may introduce live Giant. Theme: boy exchanges cow for bag of magic beans which angry mother throws on the garden, producing gigantic beanstalk; boy climbs to top, takes gold (or golden eggs) and possibly the egg-laying hen or goose – while the Giant sleeps, descends and chops down beanstalk, killing Giant.

Jacob, Georg (1862–1937). German orientalist and shadow-theatre expert; compiler of the most important bibliographies relating to oriental shadow-theatre: *Das Schattentheater in seiner Wanderung vom Morgenland zum Abendland* (1901), 2nd enlarged edition (1902), *Bibliographie über das Schattentheater*; a more detailed bibliography divided into centuries, eleventh–twentieth (1906), *Erwähnungen des Schattentheaters in der Welt-Litteratur*; an Addenda (1912); enlarged edition (1925); in 1936 finished a typewritten bibliography in possession of Jacob M. Landau, author of *Studies in the Arab Theatre and Cinema* (which has considerable material on shadow theatre); see Arab Theatre.

Jacob, Max (1888–1967). Outstanding German puppetmaster, founder of the Hohnsteiner Puppenspiele (formerly the Hartenstein troupe, 1921), whose style and technique became the criterion for all German hand-puppet players. In 1956 awarded the Federal Cross of Merit, First Class, for distinguished service to the Federal Republic. For many years the highly regarded President of UNIMA, the international puppetry organisation, on the work of which he contributed an article to *The Puppet Theatre of the Modern World* (compiled by an UNIMA editorial board). At an UNIMA Praesidium meeting (May, 1968) it was proposed that a fund in memory of Max Jacob and of the Czech puppeteer Josef Skupa be set up with the object of establishing scholarships or bursaries for young puppeteers to travel and study in other countries; it was also agreed to set up Archives to collect material about the life and work of Max Jacob.

Jacquard Puppets. English company directed by John Carr, O.B.E., early member of the British Puppet and Model Theatre Guild. Repertoire includes *St. George and the Dragon* (hand puppets), *Peter and the Wolf*, Prokofiev (marionettes), and the *Moth Ballet* (marionettes).

Jacques. One of the various French folk puppet characters associated with Lille and speaking the local patois; faithful servant type – and good with the stick.

James, Henry (1843–1916). American novelist, critic, biographer (*Novels and Tales*, 26 vols., 1907–17, U.S.A., and 35 vols., London, 1921–23). On an occasion when obliged to watch some rather tedious puppets, said: 'An interesting example of economy, economy of means and economy of effect!' (Cecil, *Life of Max Beerbohm*).

Jan Klaassen. Netherlands folk puppet character, early seventeenth to end of nineteenth century, who with his wife Katrijn were popular in regular squabbling episodes; eventually relegated to plays for children.

Japan. The first Japanese puppet shows of which there are any records are those of the tenth–eleventh century gypsy-like people known as 'kugutsu', who travelled from central Asia; little is known as to the type of puppet, but they would have been fairly primitive. In extreme contrast, the type of performance developed from the end of the sixteenth century, which eventually came to be known as the Bunraku, q.v., is unique in style: since the company's visits to Europe in 1967–68 there are signs of influence on Western companies. The earlier puppeteers had used a stage which concealed the performers: THE BUNRAKU-ZA in Osaka has the operators in full view of the audience. The puppets used from about the thirteenth century were each operated by one man, using two hands; those of the Bunraku require three operators each, except for minor characters. The Bunraku heads have movable eyes, eyebrows and mouths; the operators do not speak the dialogue, this, and a sort of running commentary on the events on the stage, is provided by a narrator on a rostrum at the side of the stage – with a musician helping to create the appropriate atmosphere. A great deal of the success of the new form of puppet theatre was the advent of a great playwright, Chikamatsu Monzaemon, q.v., whose plays were also adopted by the actors of the live theatre (Kabuki), many of which are still played in both theatres. The Bunraku suffered a decline for a time, but has come to be regarded as a national heritage and receives Government support. Its technique requires a life-time of dedication and training. Other forms of puppetry exist in contemporary Japan, however. There is a simpler form, related to the Bunraku, practised on Awaji Island, q.v., and which was acclaimed on its visit to the U.S.S.R. in 1958. There is also the Kuruma-puppet, q.v., and the Noroma, q.v. String-operated puppets (marionettes) have been known in the larger cities since feudal times – and some, such as the company of Sannosuke Takeda, have made television appearances. In 1925 the theatre PUK, q.v., was established by Toji Kawajiri and, after his death, was directed by his brother Taiji Kawajiri: both hand puppets and marionettes were used – but activities were suppressed during World War II, re-organised after 1946; repertoire includes items from European sources: Andersen, Gogol, Maeterlinck, Goethe, as well as those based on Japanese, Czech and Russian folklore. A considerable amount of literature is now available in English, including the following (details in separate entries): Dunn *Early Japanese Puppet Drama*; Watanabe *Bunraku: Japanese Play*; Keene and Kaneko Hiroshi, *Bunraku: the Art of Japanese Puppet Theatre;* Ernst and Haar, *Japanese Theatre in Highlight*; Scott, *Puppet Theatre of Japan*; Malm, *Japanese Music and Musical Instruments.* See also BUNRAKU-ZA.

Japanese Music and Musical Instruments, by William P. Malm (Tuttle, Rutland, U.S.A.; Tokyo, Japan, 1959). Interesting data on the BUNRAKU puppet theatre, with photographs of the narrator in action; also on the SHAMISEN, musical instrument used as accompaniment to the narration (gidayu-bushi). Also on the folk puppet play on Sado Island.

Japanese Theatre in Highlight. A Pictorial Commentary by Francis Haar; text by Earle Ernst; introduction by Faubion Bowers (Tuttle, Tokyo, 1952). Includes 54 photographs of the three forms of theatre, the Noh, Kabuki, and the BUNRAKU (puppets); history of the Kabuki and Bunraku closely interwoven, the influence of the puppets on the live actors seen in the fact that the latter still study the movements of the puppets.

Jarry, Alfred (1873–1907). French eccentric, Bohemian (nineteenth century 'beatnik'), small-part player, secretary and scene-shifter at the Théâtre de l'Oeuvre (Paris), theatre-theorist and playwright. He mixed with the avant-garde artists in the cafes, died in his thirties from too much absinthe and an inadequate diet, victim of delirium tremens. Some surrealists regard him as the founder-member of the movement; the currently popular 'theatre of the absurd' and 'theatre of cruelty' were foreshadowed in his play *Ubu Roi*. The play began as a schoolboy satire of an unpopular physics master at the lycée in Rennes, whose name was Hébert, of which 'Ubu' was a corruption. The production of the re-worked version employed masked actors and man-size marionettes, and was full of shocks from the opening utterance of 'merde' onwards. See UBU ROI *re* contemporary productions on both live and puppet stage. Jarry's ideas on theatre are included in *Selected Works of Alfred Jarry* (Methuen, 1965). French publications: *Ubu sur la butte* (play in two acts and a Prologue for); *Ubu roi* (Sansot, Paris, 1906); *Ubu enchaine: suivi de Ubu sur la Butte* (Fasquelle, Paris, N.D.).

Javanese Shadows. It is necessary to keep an open mind as to 'origins' – which are usually unavoidably obscure – and although, by the nature of the plays based on the Hindu epics (*Mahabharata* and *Ramayana*) which make up the Javanese repertoire, India would seem to be the source, it is possible that the Javanese *type* could have been indigenous and the Indian material grafted on. Certainly the *style* of the shadow figures (as well as the three-dimensional rod puppets) is unique, and the performances have a ritualistic rather than a purely entertainment character – being derived either from initiation rites at which the national history and myths were handed on, or to ancestor worship. Traditionally the spectators were divided according to sex, the men sitting on the same side of the screen as the operator and the puppets, the women seeing only the shadows on the other side; hence the dispute as to whether it is strictly a 'shadow' show. Mellema, linguistic advisor of the Royal Tropical

Institute, Amsterdam, in his authoritative *Wayang Puppets* (Koninklijk Institute, 1954), states that the term 'wayang' does *not* mean shadow-play, that this is an error due to faulty European perception; 'wayang' refers to the puppet (flat or rounded) and a 'wayang show' is one employing puppets as actors. The puppet itself, however, is regarded as 'a materialised silhouette of a ghost' – of a Javanese ancestor. The shows last from sunset to dawn and still retain their ritualistic function, being given at marriages, births, or in relationship to illness – and the Dalang (who both controls all the characters, provides the dialogue and conducts the orchestra of percussion instruments) has somewhat the role of priest who is intermediary between audience and the ancestral spirits. To distinguish one type of performance from another, the word 'wayang' is qualified by a term indicating the type of puppet – or even a human actor, with or without mask – or the source-material of the plays; these are dealt with in the entries under Wayang. The flat figures used in the so-called shadow shows are known as 'Wayang kulit'; kulit = leather, the figures being cut from animal skin which has been treated to give it a translucent quality; designs are cut away by chiselling before the figures are painted and gilded, and every detail is predetermined and has its exact significance. The whole system of symbolism is dealt with in Mellema's work, with diagrams of the various designs related to characterisation – and which the apprentice-cutter and painter must study, no variations being permissible. As the total number of characters in a performance may be well over a hundred, and as they are necessarily two-dimensional, the ability to distinguish them (both for the performer and the audience) depends on precision in design and finish. Curiously, in Bali, where the same form of shows are given, the puppet makers are allowed some individual freedom within the traditional symbolism. Figures vary in size from about 2-ft. to 2-ft. 6-ins.; they are set into a main rod of buffalo horn, with thinner rods attached to the hands. Whether the style is due to a taboo as to representation in realistic terms, or to sheer artistry in the two-dimensional medium, the extended line of the shoulders and the slim elongated arms, the delicate tracery of head-dress and costume, have a perfection which is rare – and which ensures definition on the shadow side of the screen. Examples are to be seen in the Ethnographic Department of the British Museum (on the same screen as the Chinese examples) and in the Liverpool Museums. A major collection is to be found in Munich. There is a good chapter in Blackham *Shadow Puppets* (Barrie and Rockliff, 1960), which also has a valuable list of museums in various countries.

Jekyll (Dr) and Hyde (Mr). Novel by Robert Louis Stevenson, on the theme of dual-personality, the evil element eventually overcoming the good, resulting in murder and then suicide. Has had some puppet adaptations.

Jelutong. Wood from Malaya, Borneo, Phillipines; easy to carve; soft texture, straight grained, light biscuit colour.

Jerusalem Delivered (Gerusalemme Liberata). Epic poem (originally *Il Goffredo*: Godfrey of Bulloigne) masterpiece by Torquato Tasso (1544–95) at the end of the Renaissance, on the theme of the Crusades. Original English translation by Edward Fairfax (Jaggard and Lownes, London, 1600); contemporary edition, Centaur Press, 1962. Episodes are still included in the performances of some of the Sicilian marionette theatres, but are regarded as less straightforward than Ariosto's (1473–1533) *Orlando Furioso*.

Jigging puppets. (*a*) Simple flat-figure type with body and head in one piece, swinging arms, legs jointed at hips and knees; operated by short rod to centre of back and performs on table or on plank on seated operator's knee; (*b*) another term for the 'marionettes à la planchette' (seventeenth–nineteenth century) operated by a horizontal string running from the performer's knee to a short post at one end of a plank on the ground, and *through* the chest of one or more figures performing on the plank – a form of one-man show leaving hands free for musical instruments (bagpipe, pipe and drum). Enthusiastic account of the accomplishments of this type was included in CARDANO's *De rerum varietate:* Nuremberg, 1557). Illustrations in von Boehn *Dolls and Puppets* (Harrap, 1932), Baird *The Art of the Puppet* (Collier-Macmillan, 1965) and elsewhere.

Joey. A clown, especially in the circus or pantomime and in Punch and Judy. Name derives from that of the famous clown Joseph Grimaldi (1778–1837). Like many other terms, it also has slang meanings, e.g. in the Forces: the Senior Royal Marine Officer in the Ward Room, and, in the Old Lag's language: parcel illegally sent in or out of prison.

Joan. Just when this name for Punch's wife was first used has not been pin-pointed by the scholars; literary references are often merely to his 'wife' and it is possible that 'Joan' and 'Judy' (or 'Judith' originally?) were in use simultaneously with different showmen. Henry Fielding (1707–54) in *Tom Jones* (1749) mentions 'his merry wife Joan' – in a complaint that a certain puppet performance did not include Punch and his wife. Speaight, *History of the English Puppet Theatre*, q.v., mentions early playbills of Bartholomew Fair and Southwark Fair in the Harvard Theatre Collection (*c*.1700) with specific references to 'Joan'. The name did not appear on the bills of the showman Martin Powell, q.v., although his Punch – then still in the marionette form (as illustrated in the frontispiece to *Second Tale of a Tub*, q.v. – certainly had a wife, referred to in *The Tatler*, No. 115 (1710) as of the 'scolding' type. The name Joan is used again in Fielding's *The Author's Farce* (1730), where the character of Judy is recognisable: Punch says she is 'the plague of my life' and has 'a thundering tongue'. Sir Walter Scott (1771–1832), q.v., mentions Joan in *Bride of Lammermoor* (1818); Westmacott in *The English Spy* (1825) mentions 'Old Punch and his wife Judy'.

John and Marsha. A recording of an item which consists solely of the repetition of the two names, with somewhat suggestive variations of intonation (Capitol, U.A.P., 1–496); one of the most successful of the sophisticated items of French puppeteer Georges Lafaye, the characters being represented by a Top Hat and a Feather Boa – and the imagination of the audience.

John Wright Marionettes, now known as the Resident Company of the Little Angel Theatre. John Wright came to England from South Africa via Rhodesia and the Congo in 1946 after some experience of puppeteering in his home country in the form of work in the University Little Theatre, Cape Town; the Central Library, Johannesburg; the Arts Centre, Pretoria. Set up workshop in Studio House, Hampstead Hill Gardens, London (1947), with performances to Audience Club members formed under auspices of the Hampstead Artists' Council; also formed mobile company and toured many parts of the British Isles, five to seven people, with 18 marionettes and (1953) 27 in. figures. Worked in three London theatres: the Watergate, the Riverside (Festival Gardens) and twice in Lyric Theatre, Hammersmith. Toured Holland and Germany (1952), Denmark and Germany (1953). Engagements in 1954 included Dartington Hall and the Edinburgh Festival (fringe activity) and tour of Scotland for Scottish Division of the Arts Council. Left Hampstead at end of 1954 and without a headquarters for four years. Toured Southern Africa, travelling 14,000 miles by road and playing 144 centres (as far as South West Africa and Southern Rhodesia, ending November, 1955. Most of 1956 in Holland, Germany, Yugoslavia, with further tour of Southern Africa, 1957, Southern Rhodesia, Northern Rhodesia (now Zambia) and Nyasaland (Malawi), 1958. John Wright re-established headquarters in England, leaving two members of company (Margaret and Timothy Heal) in charge of small fit-up working the schools in Rhodesia, with educational show 'The History of Drama' (commissioned by the Educational Authorities). Jane Tyson who had worked with the Company since 1950, except for short intervals, joined the Salzburg Marionette Theatre (1959). Company virtually disintegrated, the Heals settling in Rhodesia, Jill and Aiden Higgins (author of *Felo de Se*) temporarily in Johannesburg; one staunch member, Lindie Parker, remained, with whose help Company successfully reformed, winning a Gold Medal (first award for small Companies) at an International Festival in Bucharest (September, 1960). Earlier in same year, John Wright purchased the Ansell Hall, a bomb-damaged temperance hall in Islington, London, reconstructing this in form of small marionette theatre, opening its doors to the public as The Little Angel Theatre in November, 1961. Company then became the Resident Company of the Little Angel Theatre. Tours also continued: 1964 and 1965, Germany; 1965 and 1967, Scotland; 1967, Belgium; several in England (including four for the South West Arts Association) and two return visits to Africa (1963 tour for Arts Council of S. Rhodesia; 1966 season at Johannesburg Civic Puppet Theatre). Other work includes participation in Films: 1946 *Foodland Fables*, 1949 *Britannia Mews*, 1950 *Tales of Hoffmann*, 1954 *Supersonic Saucer*, and numerous short films, documentaries, excerpts. Television Plays: 1948 *Briar Rose* (BBC), 1950 *The Little Mermaid* (BBC), 1954 *Lancelot the Lion* (BBC), 1964 *The Little Mermaid* (Rediffusion), 1966 *Mak the Sheepstealer* (ABC), 1967 *The Marsh King's Daughter* (Rediffusion); innumerable short programmes, demonstrations, talks, including 'Late Night Line Up' (1967, BBC). Foreign television: Denmark, Germany, Holland, Luxembourg, Roumania, Southern Rhodesia. (See also THE LITTLE ANGEL THEATRE.)

Johnson, Samuel, Ll.D. (1709–84). English lexicographer and dominant figure in eighteenth century literary world as recorded in Boswell's *Life of Johnson* (1791) and in which there is an account of an incident when Oliver Goldsmith, q.v., broke a shin in trying to show his superiority to puppets; on another occasion Gilbert Cowper, who was short and stout, called Johnson the 'Caliban of literature' and in turn was dubbed 'the Punchinello'. Entries regarding puppets in Johnson's famous *Dictionary of the English Language* (1755) are interesting if somewhat inadequate (e.g. no entry for 'marionette'); says the word was formerly 'popet', 'like the Teutonic poppe' – quotes Chaucer's use of this in *Sir Thopas* (where the meaning is different); his definition 'A small image moved by wire in a mock drama; a wooden tragedian' has been repeated in many lesser dictionaries. Includes 'puppetmaster, puppetman, puppetplayer', but not 'puppeteer'; cites Shakespeare's use in *Cymbeline* as a word of contempt ('Thou an Egyptian puppet . . .') and gives the adjective 'puppetly'; 'puppetry' has the definition 'Affectation. A word of contempt'. – citing Marston *Scourge of Vill.* (1959) 'adorning female painted puppetry'. Has a reference to the 'RAREE-SHOW', but not to the 'GALLANTY' – which helps to date usage of these terms.

Joints. Connections of articulated parts of a puppet either to the main part (body), e.g. upper arm to shoulder, or to other movable parts, e.g. fore-arm to upper-arm (elbow), lower leg to thigh (knee). The effective functioning of the whole figure and of the parts depends on the method of construction, the material used, the method of control, the latter being regarded as an integral feature of the puppet. The simplest type of joint is that used on flat figures, such as the 'jumping jack' whose limbs move in grooves in the body and are connected by a single string, the limbs moving sideways in one plane, or the shadow figure whose limbs also move in one plane but in profile; the overlapping parts of the shadow figures are held by knotted thread which acts as a pivot. The pivot joint can also be used with three dimensional figures, but limits the movement to backwards and forwards. Hinged joints also have their limits, e.g. a metal hinge (or leather) behind and connecting upper and lower leg (knee) will have movement backwards only. A tongue-and-groove joint in two wooden parts is in effect a pivot joint and will need a stopper if movement is to be in one direction only. A figure which is required to walk may be jointed differently to one which has to ride a horse; the legs of a soft stuffed puppet might splay enough when mounting, those of a wooden figure (to have enough side play) would probably be suspended on a piece of wire let into the sides of the body, bent under it and passing through the crutch. If the foot is to move up and down, a tongue at the bottom of the lower leg (ankle) is let into a groove in the foot and held by a pin (pivot action). All joints must work freely; costume should not restrict action. The arms can be attached to the shoulders by cord running right through and knotted, giving some sideways movement. Inter-locked screw-eyes – one in each piece being joined – can be used where a free range of movement is required; used indiscriminately, the movement can be difficult to control. Head and neck of a wooden figure can be in one piece or the neck can be a separate part set loosely into the head and into a hollow between the shoulders, wire pivots or screw-eyes modifying the range of movement. The points at which strings are attached influences movement range, e.g. a string fixed to the palm of a hand, to the back of the hand, or to the edge (thumb side) of the hand – if the wrist is loosely jointed – gives different range of gesture. This applies also to the rod puppet worked from below, with rods controlling the hands. The neck of the rod type can be a strong metal spring. A rod puppet with legs may use similar construction to that of the marionette, but the strings pass upwards from the knees to the body and then downwards. With all joints it is important that they are soundly constructed of durable materials, being the parts which receive maximum wear. Joints such as the ball-and-socket are for the expert craftsman. Textbooks usually have adequate diagrams and instructions, but it is best to experiment with as many types of joint as possible before actual construction is begun – and then be able to choose the joint for the job. At the same time the discovery of movement possibilities may give ideas for actual characters – particularly comic ones.

Joly, Yves. Contemporary French puppeteer whose work acclaimed at international festivals. Some of his items have only the live hands as puppets (*Jeux des mains*): hands become flowers, fish, octopus. Also uses umbrellas and parasols which become humans of different types. In *Tragédie de Papier* he uses flat paper cut-outs in a melodramatic manner: one figure is cut in half by scissors – by the villain – and another goes up in smoke; new puppets needed for each performance. This is puppetry at its most basic and highly sophisticated.

Jonson, Ben (1572–1637). English dramatist, several of whose works contain valuable historical material on the puppetry of his day. Shakespeare, incidentally, was in the cast of his *Every Man in his Humour* (1598). *Bartholomew Fayre* (1614), one of his masterpieces, has an actual puppet show within the play, a burlesque of the classic *Hero and Leander*, with the 'motion-master' (puppet-master) Lanthorne Leatherhead standing in front of the booth and providing a running commentary. (There was a revival of this by the Old Vic in 1950, the puppetry being in the hands of George Speaight.) The showman mentions a number of other productions. In *Every Man Out of his Humour* (1600), 'a comical satire', the character Sogliardo 'comes up every term to learn to take tabacco and to see new Motions . . .' and there are further references to some of the plays mentioned by Leatherhead. *A Tale of a Tub* (1596–97), 'a comedy', is of particular interest as being probably the earliest description of a shadow show in England (although of a primitive type) and in showing that the term 'motions' also applied to more than one type of puppet, and to the items performed: 'The First Motion' and the Second, etc., being short scenes. In *Cynthia's Revels*, satire on Court characters, there is a Palinode in which the Chorus repeats 'Good Mercury defend us' – from various things, including 'courting of puppets'. In *Epicaene* (or *The Silent Woman*, 1609) there is a reference to a 'French puppet'. (Complete collection of the PLAYS, introduction by F. E. Schelling, in the 'Everyman' Series, 2 vols., Nos. 489–90.)

Joruri. Chanted narrative with musical accompaniment used in the Japanese BUNRAKU puppet theatre, narrator and musician at side of stage.

Joseph, Helen Haiman. American puppeteer, teacher and author, contributor to *Theatre Arts* (periodical) and the *Encyclopaedia Britannica*; her *Book of Marionettes* (1929), q.v., is a popular history (largely based on Magnin, q.v.). Early puppet productions with the Cleveland Playhouse (1915), forming professional company about 1925, touring and later developing shows for commercial advertising. Wide repertoire has included items from Yeats and Maeterlinck, Shakespeare, and most of the popular fairy tales.

Judy. The name of Punch's wife. Origin uncertain. Judith was a popular feminine name at one time, Judy being the abbreviated form. Joan also had its vogue and was in fact the earlier name for Punch's spouse. Judy is undoubtedly the better name for speaking through a SWAZZLE. In the vernacular many names acquire the final -y sound (listen to children in street or playground). The ending -ith is weak from the elocution angle. *Toby, Joey, Sooty, Timmie*, have good carrying power as sounds (see entry *re* NAMES). Judy's character, like Punch's, evolved. What was the name of the Italian Punchinello's wife, if he had one, when he was a marionette and just arrived in London? With the change to hand puppet there would be an active change of character. In the eighteenth and nineteenth century versions of the play Judy's ghost returned to haunt Punch, but seems to have been 'laid' in the twentieth century versions. In the performance Judy's voice is that of the normal male voice of the operator. The name has various dialect and Forces interpretations.

Juggling puppets. Usually marionettes of the trick type with special stringing controlling one or more balls tossed upwards and landing on head or hands of puppet. Technique: Inverarity *Manual of Puppetry* (Binfords and Mort, 1936), Nelson & Hayes *Trick Marionettes* (Puppetry Imprints, U.S.A., 1935). Sergei Obraztsov, Soviet puppetmaster, describes hand puppets seen in China, juggling with plates and plate-spinning (in *The Chinese Puppet Theatre*: Faber, 1961).

Jumping Jacks. Flat wooden or cardboard jointed figures with limb movements controlled by a single string, popular in the eighteenth century. In Germany they were known as Hampelmann or Zapelmann and were produced by the traditional wood-carvers: very decorative contemporary examples available. Sheets of parts for cutting out and assembly, made of paper, which could be mounted on card, became a vogue in France – where they were known as 'PANTINS' – and were also popular in fashionable London. POLLOCK'S TOY THEATRE shop has original specimens for sale. A variation of the jumping jack was the 'jigging' puppet, operated on a table or a short thin plank on seated performer's knee, controlled by a rod to the back, having a normal up and down knee action, whereas that of the Jack is sideways from the hips. Batchelder, in *Rod Puppets and the Human Theatre* (Ohio University, 1947), has a photo-illustration and a diagram of a vertical rod specimen. *Make Your Own Dolls*, by Ilse Ströbl-Wohlschläger (Batsford, 1968), has illustrations and diagrams. Illustration of a German example in Whanslaw and Hotchkiss *Specialised Puppetry* (Wells Gardner Darton, N.D.).

Jungle Book, by Rudyard Kipling (1865–1936); first edition, 1894 (also *Second Jungle Book*); various editions and reprints; paperback edition, Macmillan, 1966. Fable-stories of Mowgli, child adopted by Wolf family, taught jungle lore by Baloo the Bear and Bagheera the Black Panther. Puppet adaptation by the Moscow Central State Puppet Theatre; also a Disney cartoon. See *Mowgli*.

Junkdump Fair. Puppet play written by Goethe (*Das Jahrmarksfest zu Plundersweilern*: 1769), an English translation of which is included in McPharlin *Repertory of Marionette Plays*.

Just View of the British Stage. Engraving by William Hogarth (1697–1764) with sub-title 'Three Heads are better than one' and the caption: This print represents Rehearsing a new Farce that will include two famous entertainments, Dr Faustus and Harlequin Shepherd, etc. Scene: three men seated at a table (A.B.C., theatre managers Wilks, Booth and Cibber); one has a jumping-jack held by a headstring (Punch), one a Harlequin, the other a Scaramouch; it is not clear whether the control is a thick cord or a rod. There are 'ropes' or nooses suspended over the heads of the men, by which the Muses are to assist them perform *The Hay Dance* 'in ye air'. This type of control (of the puppets) is also seen in Hogarth's *Credulity, Superstition, Fanaticism*.

Juvenile Drama. The Toy Theatre of the Regency and Victorian era, with its famous 'Penny Plain, Twopence Coloured' sheets of theatrical characters to be cut out and mounted on card and pushed on to the small stage, with vigorous melodramatic dialogue to make up for lack of action. A. E. Wilson, in *Penny Plain, Two Pence Coloured* (Harrap, 1932), traces the first play (*c.* 1811) to German Toy Theatre of late eighteenth century Augsburg engravers. Also popular in Vienna about that time. George Speaight's *Juvenile Drama*, q.v. (Macdonald, 1946), is the standard history on this branch of puppet theatre; he discounts the theory of Wilson and traces origin of English printed sheets to theatrical portraits of eighteenth century actors and actresses (in their favourite roles, costumes, poses). Speaight's authoritative and well-documented study lists English and foreign publishers from 1876–1937. Pollock's Theatres of contemporary manufacture and old and new sheets of characters and playscripts are obtainable at POLLOCK's little shop in Monmouth Street, London, W.C.2, which also has a Toy Museum. Examples of theatres can be seen at the Victoria and Albert Museum, q.v., which also has the Gabrielle Enthoven theatre collection; the British Museum has the Ralph Thomas collection of prints and various library items under publishers; the London Museum has the Jonathan King collection.

Juvenile Drama: a History of the English Toy Theatre, by George Speaight (Macdonald, 1946). Authoritative, impeccably documented book by an acknowledged master-performer and historian; author's Note says the sub-title might suitably have been 'The story of an obsession'. Every aspect is dealt with: origins, Regency and early Victorian theatre, Juvenile Drama publishers, the artists, the Toy Theatre in the home, performing the plays, portraits and tinsel . . . the decline and survival and revival . . . and Collecting. The Appendix lists the publishers, plays published, published collection and bibliography. (2nd. ed. 1969 Studio Vista).

K

Kalyb the Witch, and other Plays, by Morris Cox (Macmillan, 1952), in the 'Puppet Plays for Schools' series for hand puppets. Three items with traditional characters and themes – (1) *Kalyb the Witch,* (2) *King George and the Dragon,* (3) *Food from Lubberland.* Notes on characters and their origin and on production. No fees for non-professional performances.

Kami-shibai. Small paper theatre, type used by itinerant one-man show in Japan. Audience attracted by noise of wooden clappers. Contemporary showmen use bicycle for transporting theatre mounted on carrier. Figures move in grooves while showman provides the dialogue.

Karagheuz. Alternative spelling of 'Karagöz', q.v.

Karagöz. Principal character of the traditional Turkish shadow theatre: literally 'black eye' or the 'black-eyed one', this being one of his outstanding features. In Tunis he is known as 'Karaghouz' and as 'Karakouche' in Algiers, becoming 'Karaghioz' in Greece. Characteristics not unlike those of Punch, somewhat Rabelaisian, always having plenty of topical material. A bald head under a turban is a guarantee of laughter when exposed, and he has a thickish black beard. His boon companion and stooge is Hacivad and there are a number of other characters typical of Istanbul. Figures are cut from tough translucent skin stained with coloured dyes, height 12 to 15 ins., usually jointed at waist and knees, some characters having one jointed arm, joints being held by knotted gut. Control is by a short, thickish rod inserted in a socket at the top of the back, with extra rod if movable arm. Dancers have extra knee sections. As is vital in all folk plays, Karagöz always comes out on top in his adventures. Good chapter with black and white illustrations in Blackham *Shadow Puppets* (Barrie and Rockliff, 1960). English translation of excerpt from Théophile Gautier's *Constantinople* (1854) in Inverarity *Manual of Puppetry* (Binfords and Mort, 1936), in which a performance is described. The Pitt Rivers Museum, Oxford, has specimens in its collection. See also next entry.

Karagöz: Its History: its characters: its mystic and satiric spirit, by Professor Sabri Esat Siyavusgil (Turkish Press and Tourist Department, Ankara, 1955). Authoritative well-illustrated study with many reproductions of characters and scenery in colour.

Karius and Baktus, by Thorbjørn Egner, translated from the Norwegian into Danish by Paul Steenstrup (Gyldendal, 1958). Unpublished English transcript by Elizabeth Cockcroft, E.P.A. Library; Danish puppet production by Jytte Abildstrom. Amusing story of boy with dental trouble – and the characters who inhabit his mouth, and what happens when in desperation he cleans his teeth; happy ending, at least for the boy.

Kašparek. Puppet character who appeared on the scene in Czechoslovakia around 1815 and became the national favourite. In 1928 he was introduced into a public health film. In 1947 he was immortalised by sculptor Jan Jiřikovsky, part of the Matěj KOPECKY Memorial at Koloděje nad Lužnici, a broken comedian's drum beside him. (The original puppet is now in the National Museum in Prague.)

Kasper (Kasperle, Casper). Traditional German cousin of Punch, superseding the original Hanswurst in the eighteenth century, possibly of Austrian origin. He appears in countless hand puppet plays, is a much more genial character than Punch, a great friend of children (who often have to help him) and has the essential quality of always succeeding – but not too quickly. Something of his qualities can be appreciated from Baumann *Caspar and His Friends*, q.v., translated by Joyce Emerson – with a foreword by George Speaight and line illustrations by Wanda Zacharias (Dent, 1967) – ten plays for puppets.

Kathputli. The marionettes of Rajasthan, India. Head and body carved in one piece, stuffed arms, no legs – but long, pleated skirt reaching to ground; control is often by a single string attached to the top of the head and the back of the waist, passing over the manipulator's hand; a second string sometimes attached to both hands. The absence of legs and the minimum stringing in fact allows a great many swift and graceful actions that would not be possible if legs were added and extra strings.

Keats, John (1795–1821). English romantic poet; in *Otho the Great*, a Tragedy in five Acts, 4, 2, 103: 'Erminia's last new puppet – Furious fire!'

I

Kemble, Kenneth. English puppeteer, member of the famous theatrical family; has small permanent puppet theatre in Woodbridge, Suffolk, performances at week-ends; also performs in schools. Theatre has plush seats, Greek columns and pictures of renowned predecessors (including the great Sarah Siddons: nineteenth century). Writes own scripts. Audiences include children from United States Air Force base. In 1967 made and gave 25 puppet heads in response to appeal from the Italian Institute of Culture, towards replacement of those lost by Florentine puppeteer in the flood disaster.

Ketch, Jack. Traditional name for the hangman in the Punch and Judy show, named after an executioner mentioned in *The Plotters Ballad* (1678).

Key puppet. Complex type of rod puppet supported by harness around operator's waist and shoulders, with lever or pedal control of strings which pass upwards, developed by Geza BLATTNER, Hungarian puppeteer domiciled in France. An earlier experiment with this type was made for Signoret's 'Petit théâtre' in Paris. Technique: Batchelder *Rod Puppet and the Human Theatre* (Ohio State University, 1947).

Kharagiosis. Greek equivalent of Turkish 'Karagöz', q.v., traditional shadow theatre – and also its main character, who is more of a satirist and less of a buffoon than his Turkish ancestor. The Greek shows are given in the open, the screen being wide (up to 15 feet), the figures larger but otherwise similar to the Turkish, with one technical development: a hinge in the region of the shoulder, and to which the control rod is attached at approximately right-angles, allows for quick reversal of direction of the figure without need for removal from screen. Beaumont *Puppets and Puppetry* (Studio, 1958) has three pages of photo-illustrations showing theatre, audience, back-stage operations. Blackham *Shadow Puppets* (Barrie and Rockliff, 1960) has short section on this type. Sotiris Spatharis *Behind the White Screen* (London Magazine editions, 1967), q.v., is an interesting autobiography of a famous Greek shadow player.

Kilim Arasi. 'Between carpets': a type of improvised puppet stage found in Azerbaijan, U.S.S.R.; two men hold a folded carpet which conceals the operator of hand puppets.

Kingsley, Charles (1819–75). English author of *The Water Babies*; a puppet theatre production by The Hogarth Puppets.

Kipling, Rudyard (1865–1936). English author, born in Bombay; *Plain Tales from the Hills, Puck of Pook's Hill, the Jungle Books*, the last mentioned has been source of large-scale puppet production at the Central State Puppet Theatre, Moscow (see *Mowgli*); *How the Elephant got His Tail* has also had puppet adaptations.

Klee, Paul (1879–1940). Swiss painter whose work had important influence on twentieth century art; taught at the Bauhaus (Weimar, Dessau), q.v., for ten years; admired the marionettes of Paul Brann and made hand puppets for son Felix and joint-plays; reproductions in colour in Baird *Art of the Puppet* (1965) – an Eskimo, a self-portrait and a 'Ghost of a Scarecrow'. Paintings include 'Puppet Show' (Puppentheater, 1923) in the Berne Museum collection; a drawing 'A Performing Puppet' (1923) and 'Costumed Puppets' (1922) which has figures and costumes composed of musical symbols and spiral elements.

Kleist, Heinrich von (1777–1811). German dramatist, poet, novelist; published essay in German newspaper *Berliner Abendblätter, c.* 1810 (*Uber* *das Marionettentheater*), comparing the relative merits of live dancer and marionette, the latter knowing nothing of weight or matter, its lifting power (strings controlled by the puppeteer) being greater than the force of gravity. Conclusion: 'Only God and the marionette can be perfect.' Essay partly philosophical and insisting that the ability to contemplate and transmit the Infinite eludes self-conscious mankind. Any practising puppeteer knows that the marionette itself must be perfectly made, balanced, manipulated, before it can live up to Kleist's verdict (*'can* be perfect . . .'). Various English translations: Foresti in Craig's *The Marionnette* (Florence, 1918), McCollester *Theatre Arts* (N.Y., 1928), Jelas *Vertical* (N.Y., 1941), Beryl de Zoete in *Ballet* (London, June, 1946) reprinted in the *Puppet Master* (B.P.M.T.G., Oct., 1946).

Koninklijk Instituut voor de Tropen, Amsterdam, Holland. Institute has unique collection of Indonesian shadow puppets. Publishers of *Wayang Puppets: Carving, Colouring, Symbolism,* by R. L. Mellema, 1954. (Royal Tropical Institute, Dept. of Cultural and Physical Anthropology, No. 48.)

Kopecky, Matěj (1775–1847). Famous Czech puppeteer who has become something of a legendary character; two volumes of his 'Comedies and Plays' were published in 1862 and a memorial in his honour was unveiled at Tyn nad Vltavou in 1905; a sculpture of the figure of his puppet Kašparek, by Jan Jiřikovsky, and of a cracked comedian's drum, was unveiled in 1947 at Koloděje nad Lužnici (the puppet itself is in the National Museum in Prague). A set of gramophone records, Fragments from the 'Comedies and Plays of Matej Kopecky' in accordance with the book text of 1862, were made by the group of Antonin Kopecky.

Kreymborg, Alfred. American poet and author of non-naturalistic puppet plays; *Lima Beans* has had American and English productions (in *Plays for Puppets*, Harcourt Brace, Secker, 1923).

Krylov, Ivan Andrejevich (1768–1844). Russian fabulist, some of whose writings have been adapted for the puppet stage. Penguin Books edition with Russian and English text, translation by Bernard Pares, published 1942. The translator's introduction mentions the monument set up in honour of the writer in the Summer Garden of St Petersburg (Leningrad): the seated figure, deep in thought, is surrounded by lively reliefs of the animals which appear in the fables.

Kuchi horse. Simple type of marionette used in Rajasthan, India. Constructed with only two joints, with a continuous string attached to the two ends, looped over the performer's hand, and one string to the head of the rider. As with the human characters, there are no legs, this fact being concealed by a decorative skirt similar in effect to that of the medieval war-horse. The simple construction and stringing give a surprising range of movement; a group take part in a ballet to rhythmic drumming.

Kugutsu. Oldest form of puppetry in Japan, ninth–twelfth centuries, so-called because practised by tribe of nomads known as Kugutsu (main occupation hunting); no details recorded as to type of puppet.

Kuklapolitans, The. Name of American puppet troupe in the record-breaking category for television appearances; created by Burr Tillstrom, highly experienced puppeteer (especially with hand puppets); the characters are Kukla, Fran and Ollie – Fran being the human who stands in front of the stage, sings and helps out sympathetically in the fantasy situations of Kukla (childlike in character and voice) and Ollie (Oliver J. Dragon, relative of the crocodile in the Punch and Judy show). Ollie, incidentally, is a vegetarian. Much of the popularity of the programme is due to the element of off-the-cuff topical material mixed in with the songs. Other members of the team are Beulah Witch, Fletcher Rabbit and Madame Oglepuss – names which show shrewd assessment of importance of sounds. (Kukla: same as Russian word for puppet.) Illustrations in Baird *Art of the Puppet* (Collier-Macmillan, 1965).

Kuruma. A type of puppet found in Japan in the villages near Tokyo and operated by solo performer sitting on a box; one hand is put in the puppet's head and the other into its right hand, its leg movements being controlled by the performer's own legs.

L

Lacquer. Paint or varnish with shellac base. Also loosely used term for various high gloss finishes with quick drying by evaporation. Hair lacquer as used with some styles of coiffure can be sprayed on puppet hair also.

Lafaye, Georges. Avant-garde French puppeteer who has made strong impact on mid-twentieth century developments. Introduced the 'black theatre' technique, now widely used, in which the figures seem to be floating in light. Item *John and Marsha*, in which the whole of the dialogue consists of repetition of the two names in a variety of intonations, the characters are represented simply by a top hat and a feather boa – in an amorous pas-de-deux. A strip-tease item has an erotic giant balloon and human hands.

Lafleur. Popular local puppet character speaking the Picardy patois and associated with Amiens, France (nineteenth century); theatres in which he performs known as Les Cabotins. Character: that typical of most folk puppets – fond of good living, not *too* honest, against injustice, against the gendarmerie. Particularly effective with the feet. Interesting account in Gervais *Marionnettes et marionnettes de France* (Bordas, 1947).

La Fontaine, Jean de (1621–95). French poet, fabulist, member of the Academie Française. Fame rests on his *Contes* and *Fables* (*Contes* derived from Boccaccio, q.v.) (*Fables*, 12 volumes, 1668–94). Items adapted for puppets include *Fox and Grapes, Hare and Tortoise, Town Mouse and Country Mouse, Wolf and Stork. Oeuvres Completes,* editions du Seuil, 1965, includes 237 fables; also in 'Everyman' series, Dent, in Edward Marsh translation.

Lago, Roberto. Mexican puppeteer and director of the Teatro el Nahual, Mexico City. Active teacher of puppetry, writer. In 1945 undertook literacy campaign for Ministry of Education, using mobile theatre, performing in parks and squares. Repertoire includes wide variety of plays, songs, dances; folklore basis. Wrote text for delightful small book, *Mexican Folk Puppets*, q.v., with illustrations by Lola Cueto (1941).

Lambert, Eugene. Irish puppeteer, ventriloquist, husband of Mai and father of ten children, all in the puppet profession; Finnegan, q.v., his ventriloquial partner, is the more famous of the two. In an article in *Woman's View* (June, 1967) Eugene said Finnegan has his own peculiar opinions on everything and is never afraid to come out with them. Eugene was formerly a qualified refrigeration engineer, took over from Terry Hall ('Lenny the Lion') as vent act with a touring company. Several of the children take part with their parents in a weekly television puppet show, *Murphy agus a chairde* ('Murphy and his Friends'); the eldest son is a promising magician and takes part in television shows in Irish.

L'Amfiparnasso (literally 'On the lower slopes of Mount Parnassus'), second of four so-called madrigal-comedies, in which all parts sung, fore-runner of opera; composed by Orazio Vecchi (published 1597), who said that understanding was intended to be by ear alone. Parallel plots with COMMEDIA DELL' ARTE buffoonery. Marionette version by the LANCHESTER MARIONETTES with voices of New English singers; new sub-title 'Crabbed Age and Youth', puppets based on woodcuts of the 1597 edition. Lanchester performance at London's Wigmore Hall, 13th December, 1946. English translation by Prof. E. J. Dent.

Laminate. Construction by layer method using such materials as thin wood, fibre glass and polyester resin, strips of paper and paste. Hollow puppet heads may be built up layer by layer over a plasticine model (as distinct from the 'pulp' method). Number of layers depends on material used and size of head, larger heads usually needing more substance; plaster 'FILLER' reinforced with muslin needs fewer layers than paper-strip variation.

Lanchester Marionettes. English company established in Malvern, Worcestershire, 1936–49, Director Waldo S. Lanchester. Visited Paris Exhibition 1937 and were first English puppets on French Television. Played before King, Queen and two Princesses at Buckingham Palace, 14th December, 1938. Worked for E.N.S.A. in War years 1941–43, thereafter for C.E.M.A. (afterwards the Arts Council for Great Britain), 1943–58, including 15 visits to Scotland. Productions: 1947, *L'Amfiparnasso*, Italian madrigal-opera by Orazio Vecchi (1597), sung and recorded by New English Singers; special performance on occasion of International Puppetry Conference, London, 1963, at the Guildhall. 1949, *Peter and the Wolf*, Prokofiev, produced and performed until 1958, assisted by Jack Whitehead both in carving and travelling for a year. 1951–58, repertory included *Shakes v. Shav*, by George Bernard Shaw, specially written for this Company; *Underwater Ballet* and *Grand Circus*; 1952, *Philemon and Baucis*, Haydn's Puppet Opera, produced for King's Lynn Festival, recorded by Harry Blech Orchestra and the Mozart Singers. From 1954–56 assisted with carving and travelling by the late Frank Rose. Various television appearances, B.B.C. and I.T.V., 1954 and 1956. Film *Magic Strings* made by John Stewart of Malvern (35mm. Commercial), shown in most News Theatres and as a 'short' all over British Isles. Film (16mm. Kodachrome, silent) *The Creation of a Marionette*, produced and directed by Douglas Fisher, made in Lanchester Workshops and concluding with a performance.

Lanchester, Waldo S. English puppeteer; one of the pioneers in early days of the British Puppet and Model Theatre Guild; former co-director of the *London Marionette Theatre* at Hammersmith, London, with the late Mr Harry Whanslaw (1927–34); Director of the *Lanchester Marionette Theatre* assisted by wife Muriel; together ran the first Marionette Theatre licenced for public performances at Malvern, Worcestershire (1936–49). For the 1949 Malvern Festival, G. B. Shaw wrote them a puppet-play, *Shakes v. Shav*. Author of *Hand Puppets and String Puppets*, first published in 1937, now in 11th edition (Dryad, 1967). Puppet film *The Creation of a Marionette* produced by Douglas Fisher (1945). Moved to Stratford-upon-Avon in 1951 and established the Puppet Centre. Organised Puppet Exhibition at Midlands Art Centre for Young People, Cannon Hill, Birmingham (1964).

Lang, Andrew (1844–1912). Scottish author noted for series of Fairy Tale books (Blue, Green, Yellow, etc.). Made English translation of French chant-fable *Aucassin et Nicolette* (anon., *c.* 1200).

Language teaching. Various independent experiments have been made in the use of puppets in teaching of foreign languages and more recently in the teaching of English to immigrant children. A formal experiment was carried out by the Nuffield Foundation Foreign Languages Teaching Materials Project (Leeds University) and a Course produced on the teaching of French in primary schools (*En Avant*). A booklet was published on the practical aspects of class-room puppetry for the benefit of teachers taking the course, supported by tape-recordings providing dialogue by native speakers, adults and children, to accompany three short puppet films: *Le gateau de Fleon*; *Le Crime de Boupah*; *L'épicerie de Boupah*. Spanish and Russian versions are envisaged. The British Council film library also has two short films: *Hare builds a House* and *It's never too late to learn*. In the United States puppets were made by Bil Baird for an educational film *Patapouf* for first-grade French. Puppets have been used in some German schools for teaching of English. The main principle is the linking of the spoken phrases with the action – i.e., audio-visual aid. A teacher with a prefabricated puppet can use the traditional French song *L'Alouette*, naming the beak, the tail, the wings, etc., during the assembling of the bird. A language lesson takes on a new aspect for children when there are puppets to watch and perhaps converse with or use.

Laplapperpapp. Amateur group in Stuttgart, Germany (leader: Anni Weigand); international award winners, using large tubular-head puppets in satirical items.

La Serva Padrona (*Maidservant as Mistress*), by Giovanni Battista Pergolesi (Pergolese, 1710–36): 'opera buffa', which has remained an international favourite and is in repertoire of the Salzburg Marionette Theatre (and others). Three characters (bass, soprano and mute) with string quartet. Theme: Servant tricks master into marriage helped by disguised Mute (second servant pretending to be rival lover).

Latshaw, George. American puppeteer; past President of the Puppeteers of America; Member of the Governing Board of the American Educational Theatre Association; Chairman of the Puppetry Committee of Children's Theatre Conference; member of the Advisory Committee of the American Centre of ASSITEJ (International Children's Theatre organisation); Consultant in Children's Theatre for the Association of

Junior Leagues. Before forming own company worked with some of the leading American puppeteers such as Burr Tillstrom, Walton and O'Rourke. Professional credits include: appearance with the Dallas Symphony Orchestra; production with the Detroit Symphony (*Billy the Kid*, Aaron Copland music); for some productions used adaptation of Japanese Bunraku technique, figures up to 9-ft. tall; responsible for the character 'Carrot Top' in the *Lili* film starring Leslie Caron and Mel Ferrer (adapted from Gallico *Love of Seven Dolls*); has delightful *enfant terrible* Wilbur. TV appearances include Children's Theatre series for NBC, adaptation of Thurber's *Quillow and the Giant*. Published version of *Pinocchio* for live actors and marionettes (Coach House Press, Chicago). Guest artist at the international festivals in Britain, 1963 and 1968.

Lazy Jack and Other Plays, compiled by Kenneth Watson (Macmillan, 1955). In the 'Puppet plays for Schools' series; 12 plays by various age-groups of children, and valuable notes on production. These are offered as examples of children's work rather than as scripts to be used, but the same stories can be used, and re-worked by similar age-groups. Titles: *Lazy Jack, Jack and the Beanstalk, Sam the Snatcher, Little Red Riding Hood, The Clever Peasant, The King Who Liked Jam-puffs, Robinson Crusoe, The Adventures of Robinson Crusoe, The Forgetful Genie, The Story of Hingo the Horse, Sinbad the Sailor, Dick Horsenden and His Cat.*

Lazzi. Italian term for comic 'stage business' in the COMMEDIA DELL' ARTE improvised comedies.

Lead (metal). Used by puppet-makers for weighting parts of marionette as required; available in various forms: dress weights, fishing weights, lead shot, lead covering of electric light flex, sheet lead; cut with metal shears.

Left-handed Punchman. The chief characteristic of Punch, technically, is that he stays on the showman's hand throughout the performances: the other characters come and go, in turn, on the other hand; there is unbroken continuity of action, Punch dominating the scene. Usually, at a performance, or in a photograph or drawing, Punch appears 'stage right', i.e. on the showman's right hand. The painting by Benjamin Robert HAYDON, 'Punch or May Day' (1828: in the Tate Gallery), reproduced in several books, including Speaight *History of the English Puppet Theatre* (Harrap, 1955), shows Pike's booth, with an inscription 'Original Punchinello'; Punch is undoubtedly on the left hand.

Leg bar. Part of a marionette control, for attaching and controlling leg strings; may be detachable for use by other hand, held on hook or by clip until needed (on vertical type) or can be of the 'rocker' type attached to (or set in a slot at top end of) vertical type or front end or AEROPLANE type. In walking movements with detached bar this requires care in maintaining correct relationship with main part of control; with the rocker-bar the leg strings give a 'mark time' action and the forward movement comes from the main control.

L'Enfant et les Sortilèges. Little French opera, words by novelist COLETTE, music by RAVEL (1916), 'fantaisie lyrique en deux parties'. First scene is a Child's Room; second is In the Garden. The child is in open revolt, refusing to do his lessons, being rude to his mother, pulling the cat's tail, breaking the teapot, etc. The room darkens and the inanimate things come to life, the boy, exhausted, is in the armchair; there is a duet between two cats, the walls vanish, the scene changes to the garden.

Owls, bats, frogs, trees, take part; the boy calls 'Mama!' Among others, puppet production by the CARICATURE THEATRE, Cardiff.

Le Sage (Lesage), Alain-René (1668–1747). French novelist and dramatist; wrote over 100 farces and parodies for Comedie Française, satires on Louis XIV society, and puppet plays for the Paris fairs.

Let's Look at Puppets, by A. R. Philpott (Muller, 1966). One of a series of small books intended to give children easily assimilated information on selected subjects and a broader appreciation of the origin, history and variety of things discovered in daily life. Profusely illustrated in the margins by drawings by Norma Burgin; covers the main countries (briefly) and traditional and contemporary puppets, conveying a good deal of technical information about the different types and touching on television and films. Advice is given on how to track down puppets when travelling, and a useful list of books for further reading.

Lewis, Shari. American puppeteer with some popular television characters, including 'Lamb Chop' and 'Hush Puppy' (hand puppets). Co-author with Lillian Oppenheimer (founder of American 'Origami' Centre) of *Folding Paper Puppets* (Stein and Day, 1962; Muller, 1964).

Libraries. Major collections of puppet books are in the Munich City Theatre Collection (Puppentheatersammlung der Stadt, München, Germany) and the Detroit Institute of Arts, U.S.A., also the McGill University, Toronto, Canada. Contact should be made with local or national puppetry societies (BRITISH PUPPET AND MODEL THEATRE GUILD, the EDUCATIONAL PUPPETRY ASSOCIATION, the PUPPETEERS OF AMERICA). *Performing Arts Collections* (which see) lists libraries and museums throughout the world, arranged by continent and country, giving details as to opening hours and facilities. The British Museum library holdings are good, but a Reader's Ticket must be obtained. The Westminster Central Reference Library, St. Martin's Street, W.C.2, adds all important new books as published, with much related material in the theatre section.

Lighting. Theatrically has two functions: to make visible and to contribute to the creation of mood or 'atmosphere'. Technically: lighting facilities vary, particularly with puppet theatres, mobile or permanent, and must be related to dimensions of stage, proximity of the puppets to light source, positions of the operators. Lighting equipment may come from the professional suppliers or be home made; electricity may come from mains or generator; the use of colour filters may be desirable. Degree of intensity of light is partly determined by the size of the puppets (scenery, etc.) to be illuminated, as, unless using opera glasses, the audience may see little of the smaller detail of puppet features, costume, smaller movements; this makes it essential to test such detail under stage-lighting conditions during the preparatory period. Another consideration is heat, which may affect paint and costume. Puppet stages in some European countries today are as large as those of the live theatre; the puppets are in scale with the stage – which is why generalisations about lighting schemes are inadvisable, but position of spotlights and other lighting equipment is important: as far as possible the light must not fall on the eyes of the manipulators, a risk which is greatest with below-stage operators. Usually the general lighting should not be 'flat', shadows must be cancelled out or used deliberately; in a production of *Peter Pan* a shadow of Peter's own shadow would be disastrous. In a marionette stage the lighting equipment will probably be in the wings of the stage, but

Hand-and-rod puppets made by Midland Art Centre students (Birmingham) under John Blundall

Above: Nancy Green and Mexican Pete, hand puppets by Pantopuck (A. R. Philpott)
Below: Animal hand puppets designed and made by John Blundall

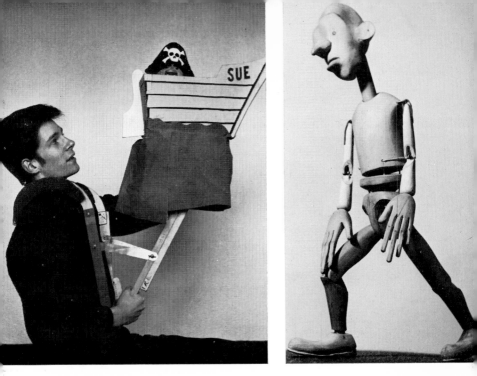

Above left: Harness to support boat (with hand puppet)
Above right: Marionette by Chris Leith for *A Christmas Carol*
Below left: Timmo Tarin, hand puppet by Violet Philpott
Below right: Rag picker, marionette by Derek Francis for *A Christmas Carol*

Above: Peter and Grandfather, from *Peter and the Wolf*. Rod puppets by John Blundall
Below: Muffin the Mule, marionette by Fred Tickner for the Hogarth Puppets

may also be situated in front of the proscenium. Lighting for a floor-show item may be two spotlights on stands, adjusted to throw most of the light on to the puppet (unless it is an act which involves an open relationship between puppet and puppeteer. In general: good lighting can improve the best of performances, bad lighting can ruin the act, and superb lighting will only make a poor show look worse.

Lighting equipment. If possible a lighting expert should be consulted. A large theatre will have a technician as part of the personnel, the members of a small company may need to be jacks-of-all-trades and this will involve an understanding of lighting equipment, electrical circuits, possibly switchboards and dimmers. If equipment must be home-made, then it is essential that safety precautions are taken in the construction and installation. Extra precautions may be necessary where performers are children. Most technical books on puppetry have chapters on lighting and equipment and there are numerous books on theatre lighting principles and practice; reference library copies could be consulted. Some equipment suppliers, such as the Strand Electric, occasionally have demonstration-lectures for technicians. Strand Electric issues a periodical, free, dealing with lighting installation ('*Tabs*'). Articles deal with many aspects, even insurance.

Lime wood (Tilia Europaea) or Linden. Soft, light, much favoured by wood-carvers.

Linseed oil. A 'drying' oil obtained from flax seed (same plant providing linen fibres). Has distinctive smell and is used for grinding of paint pigments and as paint medium; also ingredient in varnishes and some emulsions.

Literacy House. In Lucknow, India; founded by Dr Welthy H. Fisher. Centre has an educational puppetry unit; work includes preparation of puppets and puppet kits for sale to schools and field organisations; training of teachers and field workers in making and manipulation of hand puppets; production of plays and puppet literature. Mobile teams used to spread literacy and popularise Insurance among rural people.

Little Angel Theatre, The. Marionette theatre in Islington, north London; converted in 1960–61 from bomb-damaged Temperance Hall; opened to public in November, 1961. Owned by Potheinos Ltd., a non-profit-distributing company governed by a Council of seven people: Noel Benjamin, William Empson, Alan Judd, George Speaight, Sir Basil Spence, Frank Wills and John Wright. Theatre is occupied by a Resident Company of puppeteers. Director: John Wright; Art Director: Lyndie Wright; Secretary: Mary Edwards. From small beginnings the Theatre rapidly gained a considerable and appreciative clientele. Present policy is to perform at week-ends, three shows on Saturdays and one on every Sunday. Shows given daily or twice daily during school holidays. Special performances for schools during term-time, some bookings arranged by the Greater London Council, others by direct contact with schools. Performances in the Theatre totalled 378 in 1966. Theatre closed from April, 1967, for enlargement, redecoration and re-equipment, funds being contributed by the Michael Marks Charity Trust, the Arts Council of Great Britain, the Greater London Council, the London Borough of Islington and many private individuals; 22,000 cubic feet added to the existing 18,000 cubic feet; new seating installed, new stage and bridges built, considerable additions to lighting and sound equipment. Resident Company usually consists of six people. Entertainment is offered under two headings: (1) For the very young (3–7 years), with repertoire of six plays and mime programmes; (2) for older children and adults, with repertoire of 12 plays and many mime and short items. Company originally used marionettes only (27 in. figures), but later produced rod, rod-glove and shadow puppet shows with success. Various guest companies and individual artistes have performed in the Theatre, including: Violet Philpott, Glyn Edwards, George Speaight, Barry Smith, the Caricature Theatre, Wolfgang Manthey's Company, and the Indian Folk Art Group (Bhartiya Lok Kala Mandal, Rajasthan). *Friend of the Little Angel*: subscription of 5/- per annum gives registration as a 'Friend' of the Theatre, giving mailing list and certain other facilities – but, regardless of this, the Theatre is open to the public at all times except Sundays, Christmas Day and Good Friday. Seating capacity: 100. Booking is by telephone: 01-226 1787. Address: 14 Dagmar Passage, Islington, London, N.1.

Little Dwarf Writer. An educational puppet play by Mane Bernardo, Buenos Aires; young audience participates and learns about materials, each puppet being associated with, e.g., *rag* doll, *lead* soldier, *wooden* horse, *fur* cat, *paper* boat. The visual-aid approach can be extended to other subjects, including foreign languages.

Little Prince, The, by Antoine de Saint-Exupéry (1900–43). Parable for children and adults by professional airman-poet. After forced landing in Sahara desert, awakens to find small boy who asks him to draw a sheep for him to take back to the star Asteroid B-612 and tells about life on various other worlds visited. Katherine Woods English translation, Heinemann, 1945; Penguin edition (Puffin Book), 1962, and reprints. Has had a number of puppet adaptations.

Liturgical plays. Religious 'visual aids' of the tenth to thirteenth century Roman Catholic Churches, realistic presentations (in Latin) of the Life of Christ, during the main festivals (Easter, Christmas). Later given in vernacular; Lives of Saints added; then Devils and comic elements – and transferred to the market place. Subsequent evolution gave the form to the 'miracle' and 'mystery' plays ('cycles'), which were later reflected in the biblical plays of the medieval puppet stage.

Living marionettes. Also known as 'humanettes' or 'bib' puppets. Performer's own head appears as the puppet head – either over a curtain or through a hole in the backcloth of the stage. Puppet body (usually stuffed) suspended from performer's neck; limbs worked from rear by short rods.

Lofting, Hugh (1886–1947). Author of the *Doctor Dolittle* books for children; formerly a civil engineer building railways in Canada and West Africa. The first stories were in the form of illustrated letters to his own children during the War. Some of the stories have been adapted for the puppet stage – and one for a LOTTE REINIGER silhouette film. *The Story of Doctor Dolittle*, *The Voyages of Doctor Dolittle*, *Doctor Dolittle's Circus*, and eight or nine other titles have been published by Jonathan Cape, and several have appeared in the Puffin Books series.

Lok Kala Mandal. Institute for Research and Experiment in Indian folk-theatre, folk dance, puppetry; situated in Udaipur, Rajasthan, India; established 1952. Director: Shri Devilal Samar. First centre to revive and organise puppetry on scientific basis; responsible for two All-India

Puppet Festivals; represented India in the Second International Festival held in Bucharest (1960) and received award in the traditional class at Bucharest in 1965. Activities include publishing of books, production of documentary films, on various aspects of puppetry and on folk theatre; research (tracing the puppet tradition back for 2,000 years). Established Folk Lore Museum, Puppet Theatre, and Open Air Auditorium. Puppets used are purely the traditional type ('Rajasthan style'), the oldest and most developed of all extant varieties, with own presentation and production techniques; there is no European influence.

London. Places of interest to the puppet-minded include the following (details under individual headings): The LITTLE ANGEL THEATRE, Islington (John Wright's puppet theatre); the BRITISH MUSEUM (Ethnographic Department); the BETHNAL GREEN MUSEUM; the HORNIMAN MUSEUM; the VICTORIA AND ALBERT MUSEUM; the headquarters of the BRITISH PUPPET AND MODEL THEATRE GUILD (meetings advertised in '*What's On*'; the headquarters of the EDUCATIONAL PUPPETRY ASSOCIATION (Monday evenings during school-term periods, or by appointment); the various London Parks during the summer vacation period (details in *Open Air Entertainments* (bookstalls, parks, library reference rooms). St Paul's Church, Covent Garden (area with a good deal of puppet history), venue for the PUNCH TERCENTENARY celebrations in 1962 as recorded on a plaque outside the church.

London Gazette (1702). No. 3823/4: 'No permission shall be given for acting plays – or exposing any Poppets or other things that may disturb the Fair.' One occasion when the actors could not say the puppets were being unfairly favoured.

London, Impressions of, by Sergei OBRAZTSOV (Sidgwick and Jackson, 1957). 'On what I saw, learned and understood during two visits to London.' Shrewd, friendly, humorous observations by internationally renowned puppetmaster from Soviet Union, with illustrations by the author. Obraztsov has often expressed verbally his fondness for the English capital, but also has his criticisms. Very little about puppets.

London Labour and the London Poor, by Henry Mayhew (1812–87) (Griffin Bohn, 1851); sub-title *Cyclopaedia of the Condition and Earnings of Those That Will Work, Those That Cannot Work, and Those That Will Not Work*; three volumes (4th added in 1862); records as near verbatim as possible – with spelling to match the speech – of interviews with every type of person met in the streets, including entertainers, with illustrations. Volume 3 is of particular interest to puppeteers, including showmen with Punch and Judy, the Fantoccini (marionettes) and the 'Chinese Shades' (shadow puppets). The Punchman bought his stage – and puppets – from 'Porsini', who, like 'Piccini' in Payne Collier's *Punch and Judy*, lived in Coal Yard, Drury Lane, and died in St Giles Workhouse, although at one time was taking £10 a day; he claimed to have introduced the 'swazzle' (for the Punch voice) into England, had a stuffed puppet dog and a character whose name was 'Nobody', as well as a 'Merry Andrew' and a 'Blind Man'. The new owner of the outfit gave Mayhew demonstrations of his skill with the swazzle and a run-through of the whole performance; the best pitch was said to be Leicester Square (still notable for its street performers – *not* Punch). He also explained the 'broken Italian-English' language, which he felt superior to Cockney slang. There is an interesting technical note from the Fantoccini performer who had informed Mayhew that Fantoccini was the proper title of the 'exhibition of dancing dolls', although it had lately changed to 'marionettes'; he mentions problems of performing Quadrilles with *four* marionettes simultaneously 'as much as I can hold at once' (and business did not justify having a second performer); the stage was a good deal wider than the Punch booth. There have been various contemporary editions, some abridged, including those of Spring Books (1949), edited by Peter Quennell, issued under the titles *Mayhew's London*, *Mayhew's Characters*, and *London's Underworld* (which was originally Volume 4). The dozens of other characters interviewed are as interesting as the entertainers.

Long Vacation in London, The, by Sir William Davenant (1606–68). Poem written *c.* 1640, describing popular entertainments of the day; mentions 'man in chimney hid' – i.e. a hand puppet booth – and 'puppets that act our old Queen Bess'; the performer 'Through nose expoundeth what they say' – probably using some kind of 'swazzle'; 'Old Sodom and Gomorrah Lewd' was also in the programme.

Look at Life. Colour film in this series by the Rank Film Organisation (August, 1967) contained a number of brief glimpses of contemporary British puppetry and puppeteers; shown in some 1,000 cinemas at home, also abroad.

Lorca, Federico Garcia (1899–1936). Spanish poet, shot by Franco followers. Had Toy Theatre when young, no plays, so wrote his own; at 24 gave performance of a thirteenth century Mystery Play on a stage erected in a doorway, using cut-out cardboard characters. Collaborated with composer de Falla at various festivals, and performed a puppet play at a children's event (mss. lost), *La nina que riega la albahaca* (Girl who waters the basil plant). There have been various productions of his play, e.g. Tandarica Theatre, Bucharest, at the Third International Puppet Festival in that city, *Don Cristobal's Three Spouses*, text adapted by Valentine Silvestru. Don Cristobal featured in all the traditional Spanish puppet plays. Another item, *The Love of Don Perlimplin and Belisa in the Garden*, is described as 'an erotic lace-paper Valentine in four scenes'. In a translation by James Graham-Lujan and R. L. O'Connell of *Los Titeres de Cachiporra*, a tragi-comedy with 22 characters, the title becomes *The Billy Club Puppets* (in *Five Plays*, Secker and Warburg, 1965; Scribner, 1941). Enquiries *re* performances of latter to Samuel French, 26 Southampton Street, London, W.C.2. *Theatre of Garcia Lorca*, by Robert Lime (Las Americas Publishing Co., N.Y., 1963), has extensive bibliography.

Love of Seven Dolls, by Paul Gallico (Michael Joseph, 1954), author of *The Small Miracle*, *The Snow-goose*, etc. Theme: orphan girl, Bretonnaise, about to throw herself in river, passes an apparently deserted puppet booth, out of which appear Carrot Top and other characters who talk to her; she is unaware of the onlookers who gather. The showman realises the box-office value and employs the girl, which leads to romance. The puppets were begun while the showman was a prisoner of war – and it is known that puppets were in fact used in some British and some German P.O.W. camps. The film of the book had the title *Lili* and was immensely successful, starring the young Leslie Carron and Mel Ferrer, with attractive and lively puppets by American puppeteers Walton and O'Rourke. There have also been stage versions – musicals – based on the story.

Love of (for) Three Oranges, by Carlo Gozzi (1720–1806). Originally a story for children, but has become one of the favourites as play for the puppet theatre. Prokofiev wrote a musical score commissioned by the Chicago Civic Opera (1925). Theme: prince cursed by witch has to fall in love with three oranges *and* have his love requited by beautiful princess who emerges from large orange; happy ending.

Lupi, Father Mariantonio (1695–1737). Italian Jesuit priest, biographical material elusive, whose dissertation on references to puppets in Greek and Roman classic literature was probably earliest attempt at puppet history (*Sopra i burattini degli antichi* in Vol. 2 of *Dissertazioni lettere ed altre operette* (Zaccaria, *c.* 1720). He cites Herodotus, Xenophon, Aristotle, Apuleius, Horace, Petronius Arbiter, Antoninus, Favorinus, Aulus Gellius and provided basis for first chapter in Magnin *Histoire des marionnettes en Europe* (1852); a French translation of Lupi appeared in *Journal étranger* (Jan., 1757) and English translations in Inverarity *Manual of Puppetry* (1936) and Craig *The Marionnette* (June, 1918).

Lyon (Lyons). Town in the south of France and birthplace of the national favourite puppet character Guignol, q.v. There is a small but interesting puppetry museum in the rue de Gedagne (in the old part of the town). The Musée Gedagne is open daily except Tuesday, but closed between 12 and 2 o'clock. Performances are given in the Théâtre Guignol Morguet, directed by E. Neichthauser, but closed in August. This is at 31 quai St Antoine.

Lysistrata. Comedy by Aristophanes (*c.* 450 – *c.* 385 B.C.). Theme: Women go on strike against their husbands until the latter decide to end war with Sparta. (Lysistrata = She who disbands armies.) Rod puppet adaptation by the Central Puppet Theatre, Prague, directed by Dr Jan Malik.

M

McGill University, Montreal, Canada. Library holdings include important puppet collection of Rosalynde Stearn.

McPharlin, Paul (1903–48). American puppeteer, director, scenographer, instructor, publisher, author. Prime-mover of twentieth century developments in U.S.A. Organised Marionette Fellowship at Evanston, Ill. (1928), and another at Detroit (1929); ran puppetry class at Teachers' College, Detroit, 1933, and at Wayne University, 1934; edited *Puppetry Journal* for the PUPPETEERS OF AMERICA organisation and *Puppetry*, an international Yearbook of Puppets and Marionettes (1930–48); edited a *Repertory of Marionette Plays* (1929), wrote other titles in the Puppetry Imprints series and edited others. Author of monumental *History of the Puppet Theatre in America:* 1954 *to now,* but did not live to see this published, the final work being done by his wife Marjorie Batchelder McPharlin, herself author of important puppetry books.

Mabinogion, The. Eleven stories of the Arthurian period, including four independent Welsh tales, of which *Culhwch and Olwen* has had a puppet production by the Caricature Theatre, Cardiff, directed by Jane Phillips. *Everyman* edition of the English translation by Gwyn Jones and Thomas Jones replaces the Lady Charlotte Guest translation of 1849.

Macaulay, Thomas Babington, 1st Baron Macaulay (1800–59). British author, *Lays of Ancient Rome,* etc. In his *History of England* (xiii, III) wrote: 'Scotland would have been a smaller Poland with a puppet sovereign . . . an enslaved people . . .'

Machinae gesticulantes: anglice a Puppet-Show, by Joseph Addison (1672–1719); a poem in Latin hexameters written during his college days; English translation by George Sewell in *Works,* Bell, 1885 (for a complete bibliography of the different editions consult Speaight *History of the English Puppet Theatre*). Craig reproduced the Latin in *The Marionnette* (August, 1918); Speaight gives an English version (85 lines). This is of particular interest to puppeteers both as to the type of performance, the character of Punch at that time – being neither the Italian Punchinello nor the character in Punch and Judy – but probably suited to the rough and coarse taste of the contemporary audiences – and such technical devices as using a wire mesh across the proscenium to help create the illusion that the puppets were self-operating. Could it also have been a defence against objects thrown by some of the tougher members of the audience? (an activity not unknown in the twentieth century!).

Mad Mullinix and Timothy, Dialogue between, poem by Jonathan Swift (1667–1745), q.v., in which the world is said to consist of puppet-shows 'where petulant, conceited fellows perform their parts as Punchinelloes'. There is a long passage giving a vivid description of a Punch show and mentions his 'rusty voice', mentions Solomon, the Witch of Endor, Faustus, the Devil, Punch sitting on the Queen of Sheba's lap, the King of Spain and St George and the Dragon.

Madden, Cecil Charles, M.B.E. Theatre Playwright, Translator, Adaptor: First Producer/Director of BBC television at Alexandra Palace (1936); Creator of 'Picture Page' first TV Topical Magazine; Head of Childrens' TV Programme (1950); Assistant to Controller (1951–64). Present President, British Puppet and Model Theatre Guild.

Madrigal comedy. Play set to music; Italian COMMEDIA DELL' ARTE in madrigal form. Earliest and most famous example is Orazio Vecchi's *L'Amfiparnasso* (1597), q.v. Marionette production by the Lanchester Marionettes, q.v., with the New English Singers.

Maeterlinck, Maurice (Polydore-Marie Bernard) (1862–1949). Belgian poet and dramatist, symboliste, best known for his *Blue Bird* (*L'Oiseau Bleu*), which was first produced at the Moscow Art Theatre by Stanislavsky, and has had puppet adaptations. It has been questioned whether the three little plays 'for puppets' (1894) were really intended for puppet production, but *Interior (Interieur)* and *The Death of Tintagiles (La Mort de Tintagiles)* have both been produced in puppet theatres.

Magazines. The official journal of the British Puppet and Model Theatre Guild is *The Puppet Master,* a quarterly issued to its members; that of the Educational Puppetry Association is *Puppet Post,* issued twice a year to members; the Puppeteers of America issue *Puppetry Journal* six times a year to members; back numbers of these three are usually available for a time. *Harlequinade* is a privately circulated open-forum type of periodical, with no fixed dates of issue, available from C. C. Somerville in Colwyn Bay, Wales. Another privately circulated item is *Perlicko-Perlacko* (in German), a review of current affairs, occasional technical articles, available from Dr Purschke, Frankfurt. *Loutkař* is the Czechoslovak periodical, monthly, available at Czech bookstalls or by overseas subscription; well illustrated. The Pelham Puppet firm issues *Pelpup News* to its young Club members (anywhere). The Deutsches Institut für Puppenspiel (Bochum, Germany) publish a quarterly *Figuren Theater* to subscribers anywhere. (Addresses given under individual entries.) Also see '*Magical Digest*'.

Magic. Frazer, in his *Golden Bough*, mentions shadow plays and puppet shows in Java and China given to evoke rainfall. The puppets of the AMERICAN INDIANS were used in religious rites and ceremonies; illustrations of these are given in McPharlin *The Puppet Theatre in America* (Harper, 1949) and Baird *The Art of the Puppet* (Collier-Macmillan, 1965). The concept of theatre is itself linked with magic, with illusion – and magical 'effects' are possible in some types of show. The use of 'black theatre' with puppets apparently moving in space by themselves is a contemporary development of the stage magician's art. The hand puppet stage has its own possibilities, the booth can be a ready-made conjuror's outfit, the important thing being that the magic must work! There can be the comic magician whose magic never works – but a technical hitch (e.g. in a transformation scene) in what is a highlight in a performance can ruin the whole show. OBRAZTSOV, the Soviet puppet-master, has recalled his disappointment when taken as a child to see a play with a magic horse – which did not really fly – adding that when he had his puppet theatre the horse certainly did fly, this being a technical possibility. In addition to technical magic there are the possibilities of psychological magic, as when one character taps the ground with his stick and immediately his opponent is 'frozen'. In *The Magic Gloves*, an original play performed by Violet Philpott, the magician himself is turned into a black cat by a rival (witch). The puppets were hand puppets; the cat was already on the performer's hand, *inside* the magician, and a method was found for flicking the magician off and leaving the cat on stage. There is also the effect, well known in the live theatre, of the character who cannot see something which is quite visible to the audience. The performer who is already a stage magician can transfer many of his acts to the hand puppet booth, although he will have to learn to work with his hands in the high position – and with the puppets on his hands. Experiment will prove that the puppet stage has its own magical possibilities.

Magic Flute, The (Die Zauberflöte). Fantastic opera in two or four acts, music by Mozart, book by Emanuel Schickeneder and Gieseke (1791). Scene: Egypt. Time: Antiquity. Allegorical fantasy on the adventures of a prince and an imprisoned damsel (includes serpent and fairies). Prince is given magic flute which averts danger. Papageno is a strange being in birds' feathers – a bird-catching disguise. This opera is in the repertoire of the Marionette Theatre at Salzburg, Mozart's birthplace. Lotte Reiniger made a silhouette film *Papageno*, a fantasy on the bird-catcher (1935).

Magic Tower and Other Plays, by A. R. Philpott (Macmillan, 1952), in the 'Puppet Plays for Schools' series; no fees for non-professional performances. Three original items for hand puppets: (1) *The Magic Tower*, (2) *The Princess and the Dragon-fly*, (3) *Santa's Workshop*. Approximate acting time, 20 minutes each item.

Magical Digest. Monthly magazine of all Entertainment: Magic, Ventriloquism, Puppets. Published and distributed by Oscar Oswald, 7a Duke Street Hill, London, S.E.1.

Magnets. These have various possibilities on the puppet stage; can be fixed (small type) to marionette hands where metallic objects are to be picked up, or for temporary holding of removable object (e.g. King's crown). Source: electrical, radio, spare-part suppliers.

Magnin, Charles (1793–1862). French historian, drama critic. Author of *Les origines du théâtre en Europe* (1838) and of the work which has been the basis for all subsequent puppet histories: *Histoire des marionnettes en Europe depuis l'antiquité jusqu'a nos jours* (Lévy Fréres, 1852: revised and corrected 1862), which first appeared in serial form in *La Revue de deux Mondes*. Only English translation is that of the chapter on English puppetry, contained in Volume 14 of *Sharpe's London Journal* (1848–49). The need for critical reading due to later research has been pointed out by Marjorie Batchelder and others. The lack of any illustrations is underlined by the work of his successor in the historical field, MAINDRON (1838–1907), whose *Marionnettes et guignols à travers les âges* (Felix, Paris, 1900) is largely a commentary on the *Histoire*, with additional material on French puppetry and some brief chapters on that of the East, and an interesting array of illustrations. Magnin also made a French translation of the plays of the Saxon nun HROSTWITHA (*c.* 930–1000), some of which were performed at M. Signoret's 'Petit théâtre' and seen by Anatole FRANCE.

Mahabharata. One of the two great epic Hindu poems, known throughout Asia and the source of many traditional puppet plays, the other being the *Ramayana*. The *Mahabharata* is the longest poem in the world, having 220,000 lines. Reputed author Krishna Dwaipayana. Date of composition given by various authorities as between 500 B.C. and 50 B.C. A Javanese prose version was made between eleventh – fourteenth centuries. Content is religious, moral, philosophical, but the story related to the 'great war of the Bharatas', which occurred about 900 B.C. Characters include gods, demons, giants, royalty, magical monkeys. Not only have these epics dominated the various forms of theatrical production in India and Indonesia in the past, but the first decade of Indian cinema had films almost entirely based on this course material. An issue of the UNESCO 'Courier' (December, 1967), with 12 pages in full colour, is devoted completely to a survey of the arts which have been influenced, including sculpture, the shadow theatre, dance-drama and film.

Maile, Stanley. English puppet-maker. First started making puppets for the London Marionette Theatre in the 1920's, and produced many amusing figures such as The Danse Macabre devils and skeletons, the 'Mahogany Woman' (a semi-nude rather daring for the period, with interesting wood graining on the breasts) and the newspaper cartoon characters Strube's Little Man, The Hon. Bob, Mr. Thake, etc. Joined the Hogarth Puppets as a full-time puppet-maker in 1946 and created many wonderful figures, including several of Muffin the Mule's 'friends' – Katy the Kangaroo, Grace the Giraffe, Hubert the Hippo, etc. (Died 1955).

Maindron, Ernest (1838–1907). French man-of-letters, reconstituted the archives of the Academy of Sciences; author of *Marionnettes et guignols à travers les âges* (Felix, Paris, 1900), partly a commentary on the earlier work of MAGNIN (1793–1862), *Histoire des marionnettes en Europe*, with an important contribution of additional material on nineteenth century French puppetry, and brief introduction to some Eastern. His volume also valuable for its illustrations, lacking in the Magnin.

Mak the Sheepstealer. The introductory episode to a mediaeval Miracle Play written around the end of the fourteenth century, the Second Shepherd's Play in the Towneley Cycle which presented the adoration by the shepherds at Christ's Nativity. Mak having stolen a sheep hides it in a cradle and pretends it is his wife's new-born child – a curtain-raiser for the more serious material that followed. A puppet version of this was produced at the Little Angel Theatre in London, director John Wright. See *Old England at Play* for text (Harrap, 1943).

Make Your Own Dolls, by Ilse Ströbl-Wohlschläger (Batsford, 1968). Attractive small book with ideas, technical diagrams and photographs (some in colour) of finished dolls, toys, puppets and jumping-jacks, using various methods and materials. An inspirational book.

Make-up. Theatrical disguise, tracing to primitive dance-drama, including use of paint and masks. In the theatre the function is not only that of disguise but also 'projection' – an exaggeration of detail to ensure that the characterisation reaches the audiences in the back seats. Modern stage lighting has a bleaching effect, so that colours, lines, shading need to be intensified if the desired effect is to be seen by the audience. The same principles used in stage make-up are applied in the creation of puppets – the make-up being permanent. If the puppets are small, the degree of intensification, both of detail modelling and painted details, will need to be increased. In contemporary puppetry there is a trend towards extremely simplified (stylised) heads as a means of projection, but the principle of exaggeration applies even when 'realistic' heads are required, i.e. it is the effect *at a distance* which is important – and the effect under stage lighting conditions. A puppet which looks fine when seen in close-up will be ineffective at a distance. The make-up of puppets for television is a job for a specialist, as with the live film-actor. There are books dealing with stage make-up, and usually chapters in any book on acting – but the technique involves the use of grease-paint, of little use to puppet-makers. The same principles apply in the design of stage scenery.

Malik, Dr Jan. Secretary-General, UNIMA (Union internationale de la Marionnette), since 1933; State Prize Laureate, and for many years Director of the State Central Puppet Theatre, Prague; responsible for various modern stage developments; produced Sophocles *Oedipus the King* (1933); author of the popular puppet play *Miček Fliček* (Story of a Football), which has been translated and produced in Rumanian, German, and Flemish; edited the Czech puppetry magazine *Loutkova scena* (The Puppet Stage) from the autumn of 1940 (monthly), which was suspended in 1941 after six issues; author of *Puppetry in Czechoslovakia*, q.v., contributor of important survey 'Tradition and the Present Day' in the UNIMA book *Puppet Theatre of the Modern World*, q.v.

Making a Start with Marionettes, by Eric Bramall (Bell, 1960). Author is Director of the Harlequin Puppet Theatre, q.v., particularly well known for his marionette Cabaret. The book deals with all aspects and gives instructions and diagrams for two methods of marionette construction: (1) tennis-ball head, stuffed body and dowel limbs; (2) all wood, but not involving carving; construction of stage and settings, planning

K

Variety items, preparing a play and production; photo illustrations. This book can be linked with the same author's *Expert Puppet Techniques* (Faber, 1963), which is also concerned with marionettes.

Man. Monthly record of Anthropological Science, published by the Royal Anthropological Institute of Great Britain and Ireland, 21 Bedford Square, London, W.C.1. Occasional articles on puppetry, e.g. on the Wayang of Java and Bali (September, 1957).

Manipulation. Dictionary definition: to operate or work by means of the hands (same root as 'manual'). Manipulation of puppets may be directly by hand (hand or glove puppet) or by rod or hand-and-rod technique, or by strings (marionette) or by a combination of techniques. *Performing with puppets*, irrespective of type, demands *more* than manipulation of figures as a whole or of their heads and limbs individually: all action must be significant dramatically. The puppet is an added element for the actor to master and the study of manipulation must be associated with purpose, never become mechanical. Observation of puppeteers during performance from a privileged back-stage position or by means of documentary films will give an appreciation of the degree of concentration required and of the identification with the character portrayed by the puppet; manipulation as such must become a natural means of expression. Textbooks usually give hints on manipulation – one French book gives a hundred exercises for hand puppets, akin, say, to Czerny's piano exercises – but unless these are related to *performance* are of little help. Books cannot show movements. The theory of 'practising in front of a mirror' has its dangers, as it involves a division of attention, apart from reversing the positions of the puppets. It is important to perform in as comfortable a position as possible; it is important to have puppets that handle well – a hand puppet must be of correct fit, the stage itself must not impede action; as far as possible all rehearsal should be under performing conditions.

Manual of Puppetry, by R. Bruce Inverarity (Binfords Mort, 1936). American puppeteer, director of University of Washington Puppeteers. Comprehensive technical instruction on hand puppets and marionettes, construction, manipulation, and chapters on puppet tricks and trick puppets; illustrated by diagrams. Section entitled *Marionettiana* with historical notes, texts of early puppet show advertisements, English translations of Lupi *Marionettes of the Ancients*, Gautier *Karagheuz* (from *Constantinople*); extract from Dickens *Italian Pictures*, on the marionettes of Genoa. Title misleading for Munsterberg *Japanese Marionette Plays and the Modern Stage*, but interesting; the 'three man' BUNRAKU type is described. For the student intending to do Punch shows there is instruction on making the essential 'voice' instrument (the 'SWAZZLE').

Marceau, Marcel. Internationally famous French mime. In Preface which he wrote for Tankred Dorst's *Geheimnis der Marionette* (Hermann Rinn, 1957) he sees close relationship between certain aspects of puppetry and human mime; mentions the much-copied marionette pianist of Podrecca's Teatro dei Piccoli, and the three-man puppets of the Japanese Bunraku theatre; sees the marionette as lyrical and the hand puppet as dramatic; sees possibilities of 'almost alive' stage properties – and finds Meschke's productions (Stockholm Marionette Theatre) come nearest to his ideal, visual fantasy dominating the performance; dreams of a theatre relating traditional commedia dell' arte (Italian), the Japanese Kabuki (live actors) and Chinese mime – with contemporary themes. Dorst's book has historical and theoretical material and a number of photo-illustrations; author also of *A Trumpet for Nap*, of which an English version produced by John Wright at 'The Little Angel' Theatre in London (1968).

Mariage de la Flûte, Le. Item in repertoire of Hungarian puppeteer domiciled in France, Gera Blattner (founder of the Arc en Ciel Theatre), music by Alexandre Tansman, theme by Alexandre Arnoux: violin and 'cello as rivals for love of lady flute; they fight a duel with their bows and the violin wins. Of particular interest for style of puppets – marionettes whose bodies are musical instruments, self-playing. (Illustration in Beaumont *Puppets and Puppetry*, Studio, 1958.)

Marionette (definition). Normal dictionary definitions are usually inadequate technically, e.g. 'A jointed figure suspended by strings from a control.' The main distinction of the type is that *operation is from above*: this includes the heavy, armoured type found in Sicily and elsewhere, the main support being a strong iron rod to the head, a thinner rod to the sword arm, a cord to the shield arm. In one part of India there is a type where the supporting strings are attached to a hoop around the perform-er's head, and downward rods to the hands; there are also Indian marion-ettes where a single string looped from the top of the head to the back of the waist has no 'control' but passes over the operator's hand. Contempor-ary marionettes include abstract shapes, ready-made objects (e.g. in advertising films), supple, *jointless* creatures – fish, cobra – as well as jointed human and animal characters. Flat cut-out shadow figures may also be suspended on strings. The most important element is the *dramatic function*, this being true for every type of puppet. The perfect definition covering every variant of 'marionette' has yet to be composed – but the lack of it does not stop any of them from functioning.

Marionette (etymology). Origin of name uncertain; various theories offered by scholars. Name seems to have been in regular use by seven-teenth century, but first literary reference so far traced is in Guillaume Bouchet *Les Serées* (*c.* 1600), but it occurs as an affectionate term in a thirteenth century French pastorale *Jeu de Robin and Marion* (Marion-nette). Derivatives from Latin 'Maria' include: Marion, Mariotte, Mariole, Mariola, Mariolette (statuette), Marotte, Mariott, Mariette ... At one time Paris had its 'rue des marionnettes' where objects of piety were sold, including 'marioles' – 'little Maries' or figurines of the Virgin. The Virgin appeared in the Nativity 'cribs' in many countries in the Middle Ages, and sometimes the figures were given movement: another possible source for the word. In the tenth century Venice had an annual Festa delle Marie in memory of maidens carried off by pirates in 944; for social reasons (perhaps related to those of the Beauty Queens of the twentieth century) wooden figures or 'Marie di legno' were sub-stituted for the living representatives in the processions. Frish (*Lexicon*, 1741) gives 'Morio, Morione' as mediaeval Fool's name. Greek and Roman terms referring to 'string operated' figures have no connection with 'marionette'. Contemporary French usage is as generic term for 'puppet' – often mistranslated. French for English 'marionette' is 'marionnette à fils' = puppet with strings. The other types are as clearly defined. German 'marionetten' refers to string-type (hand puppet = handpuppen). An Italian variation 'fantoccini' (Fr. fantoches) also adopted in England in nineteenth century, but more especially for trick marionettes. With an international puppetry association it should be possible to coin terms for universal use.

Marionette, The, by George Merten (Nelson, 1957). Companion volume to *The Hand Puppets.* On the making and operating of string puppets; various methods of construction in detail, illustrated by diagrams and photographs; manipulation and making of controls; building stages and lighting; play production; two short plays.

Marionette control. Also referred to as 'crutch' or 'perch'. A handling device to which strings are attached rising from various parts of the marionette anatomy. The more the number of strings the greater the need for some form of main control: types with only one to three strings (some varieties in India) may be managed without a control – but there is always the problem of change-over. Early Venetian type had a 'turnip' control with leather tabs attached to which the top ends of the strings were tied. Some Chinese marionettes have 20–40 strings, which employ all the operator's fingers. The simplest form of control is a single bar of flat wood, either with drilled holes for attaching the strings, or with small screw eyes or metal staples. The next variety consists of two separate bars, leading on to a cross shape (with optional removal of the cross-piece). The two main types in use today (with many variants) are the vertical and the horizontal, the latter known as 'aeroplane'; these consist of a main handle with various cross-pieces. There may be a 'rocker bar' for the leg strings, having a see-saw movement, lifting the knees alternately; this can be fixed to the front of the control or set in a slot; or there can be a detachable leg bar, operated by the other hand, giving an extended range of movements. Alternatively, the detachable bar can be used for the hand strings. The vertical control may have stiff wire projections with loop end to take 'run through' arm strings. Another extension, at the rear and base of the control, is for the spine string, used when the figure makes a bow. Performers usually have individual preferences for type of control, but it may need varying for special actions. Many movements are obtained by tilting the control rather than pulling a string. In puppet ballet or opera it may be necessary to have the characters close together; too large a control may give problems overhead. Experiments have been made with converted coat-hangers, plywood triangles with various extensions, and all-wire controls. Temporal *Comment construire et animer nos marionnettes,* q.v., has illustrations of 15 controls.

Marionette in Motion, by W. A. Dwiggins (Handbook No. XII, Puppetry Imprints, Detroit, 1939). Analytical study of the 'Püterschein' counter-balance system of marionette control, the law of gravity relative to the control from above, of limb movements from fixed points, construction of control and arrangement of strings. Explanatory diagrams. Not necessarily the final word on the subject, but worth testing.

Marionettes and Rod Puppets, by H. W. Whanslaw (Religious Education Press, 1953): Book 2 of *Bible Puppetry.* Includes rod type and rod-marionette (similar control to traditional Sicilian); making the various parts and controls, stages, lighting, decor; the dramatising of stories; *Ruth,* a play for marionettes.

Marionettenbühne München. Marionette theatre in Munich, established in 1934 by Hilmar Binter; repertoire originally for children, fairy tale plays; present repertoire includes a number of operas and operettas and comedies.

Marionettes, by Pierre Gauchat (Eugen Rentsch, Zurich, 1944. Limited) edition, English text, on the work of the Zurich Marionette Theatre, puppets carved by Carl Fischer; illustrated by beautiful coloured lithographs and photographs. Résume of each play illustrated: *Bastien and Bastienne* (Mozart), *The Star Child* (Oscar Wilde), *Abu Hassan* (Weber), *Caliph Store* (Hauff), *La Serva Padrona* (Pergolese), *The Town Musicians of Bremen* (Grimm). Some original drawings for the puppets also reproduced, and photograph of unusual type of control.

Marionettes, composition by Eduard Poldini (1869–1957), q.v., originally for piano, later orchestrated.

Marionnette. French term equivalent to English generic 'puppet'. The French term for the English 'marionette' (puppet with strings) is 'marionnette à fils'; for the English 'glove' or 'hand' type the French is 'marionnette à gaine (sometimes 'à main') or simply 'guignol' (taking the name of the most popular French character of that type). Other types are also given distinctive additional words; see subsequent entries. A contemporary French author, Paul-Louis Mignon, in his admirable *J'aime les Marionnettes* (Editions Rencontre, 1962), gives both 'marionnette' and 'poupée', e.g. 'marionnette à fils' and 'poupée à fil' – the latter being clearer for the English translator. There has been a tendency for the translator without technical knowledge merely to omit one of the n's – giving the significance of the English string-puppet when the generic term was intended. Even Gordon Craig, q.v., used the French spelling for his periodical, *The Marionnette*, but used the term 'marionette' in his captions to illustrations of Javanese rod puppets. See separate entry for etymology.

Marionnette à fils. French term for puppet controlled from above by strings (English: marionette, string-puppet). An interesting alternative is given by Paul-Louis Mignon in *J'aime les Marionnettes* (Editions Rencontre, 1962): 'La poupée à fil', which is less confusing for the English reader – although the generic term 'marionnettes' is used in the title. Remarks also apply to the following entries.

Marionnette à gaine. French term for 'hand puppet' (occasionally given as '*à main*'); not from '*gant*' (glove), but from '*gainer*' (to sheath, encase clothe tightly). Type is also popularly known as '*guignol*', taking the name from that of the national favourite character Guignol. (See previous entry *re* use of 'poupée.')

Marionnette à tige. French term for rod puppet controlled from below stage, with other rods to arms. See previous entry *re* use of 'poupée'.

Marionnette à tringle. French term for rod puppet controlled from above stage; main rod to top of (or passing through) head, rod to one arm (Sicilian knights), optional strings to other arm and legs. See previous items *re* alternative use of 'poupée'.

Marionnette, The: Tonight at 12.30 (Florence, Italy, Box 444, 1918: Volume 1). Edited, published and largely written and illustrated by Edward Gordon CRAIG (1872–1967), actor, designer, theatre theorist and puppet enthusiast. The magazine ran for 12 issues – erratically dated, the first being 1st April; No. 2 appeared or at least was dated March; No. 3, May; No. 4, January. As he used the pseudonym 'Tom Fool' as author of some puppet plays, the 1st April may be significant. The individual issues had delightful coloured covers, one being in gold. A bound edition contained an index and shows the wide range of his interest and research at a period when the 'revival' had hardly begun. For his short plays he returns to the Elizabethan word 'MOTION', e.g. 'A Motion for Marionnettes: 7 scenes: an Interlude from the *Drama for Fools*, by Tom Fool: *Mr Fish and Mrs Bones*.' On History: 'Who knows the history of man? Nobody. Who knows the history of marionettes? Nobody.' Although there has been a tremendous amount of research there is *still* an enormous amount of history that can probably never be known. No. 2 includes the second 'motion': *The Tune the Old Cow Died of*. No. 3 had *The Gordian Knot*. Occasionally there is a slip of the pen, e.g. in referring to Javanese *rod* puppets as 'marionettes'. There is a translation of KLEIST's famous essay '*On the Marionette Theatre*'. No. 4 has an illustration 'Behind the scenes in a Japanese Puppet Theatre,' by Shokosai Hanbei (1800). No. 5 has the first English translation of Corrado Ricci's *The Burattini of Bologna* – which clinches the matter: ' It is needless to say that BURATTINI have nothing in common with marionettes' – a fact which even Italian encyclopedias sometimes overlook. There is also Father Mariantonio LUPI's famous 'Dissertation' from *Storia Litteraria della Sicilia* on the early references to puppets in Greek and Roman classics. No. 6 has the most popular of the shadow plays *Le Pont Cassé* – and a quotation from Anatole France, who had 'an infinite desire to see marionettes replace living actors'. Craig got into trouble with the theatre world with his own concept of the 'ÜBERMARIONETTE' which would supplant the bad actors. No. 7 contains Théophile Gautier's chapter on the Turkish KARAGÖZ shadow show (from *Constantinople*, 1856) and a reproduction of a N. African shadow figure – and a good deal about the Javanese Wayang Purwa, Gedog, Kelitik, Golek and Beber. No. 8 contains an excerpt from Dickens' *Pictures from Italy*, dealing with shows seen at Genoa – and another N. African shadow figure (a man on horseback, falcon on hand). A further shadow in No. 9, a four-sail battleship with bowmen. Also an excerpt from Stendhal on the puppets of Rome. No. 10 has a translation from the French of George SAND on the puppet theatre established at her chateau in NOHANT. No. 11 has a further shadow, an Ostrich attacked by an Eagle. He points out Magnin's confusion of 'marionettes' and 'burattini' (hand puppets) in his *Histoire des marionnettes en Europe* (1852), which later writers have also done, and that 'Yorick', who 'ransacked' Magnin 'through excess of imitation fell into the same error'. (*Storio dei Burattini;* Florence, 1902.) Craig could not be aware of the contemporary developments of course when stating that marionettes are 'the imitation of man' (they can be many other things) as compared with the burattini (hand puppets), which are 'caricature'. The third of the 'motions' was *The Three Men of Gotham*. No. 12 included, surprisingly, a chapter from the *Book of Tea* and Joseph ADDISON's *Machinae gesticulantes Anglice: a puppet show*, in the original Latin. Incidentally, No. 3 contains a valuable list of the puppet references in Craig's other publication *The Mask*, which was devoted to the art of the theatre.

Marionnettes à la planchette. Origin not known, probably Italian. 'Jigging' puppets performing on a plank on the ground, controlled by a horizontal string looped round the performer's knee, passing through the chest of the figure (or two or three figures) and hitched to short post at other end of plank. This technique left both hands free for playing bagpipes or pipe and drum. A number of illustrations exist and have been frequently reproduced in puppet histories. Hogarth's engraving *Southwark Fair* (1735) shows small bagpiper performing, the string is looped around his *foot*, attached at the other end direct to the plank (no post); a glove puppet booth is also shown, and a banner with Punchinello (good reproduction in Baird *Art of the Puppet*); several prints in von Boehn *Dolls and Puppets* (1932, 1965). A lithograph after sketch by Carle Vernet (1820) shows dog as extra attraction. Cardanus, an Italian scientist, in his *De Varietate Rerum* (1557), gives an enthusiastic description of a performance, being amazed at the movements obtained by a single string compared with marionettes seen elsewhere. A distant relative is the African 'TULUKUTU', q.v. (from Zambia: specimen in possession of the author), consisting of two simple figures sharing one pair of arms, string from each figure operated by big toes of a boy seated on ground with legs outstretched, thighs slapped to give rhythmic movement while other boys chant. There is also some obvious connection with a type of 'peg' puppet known in London into early twentieth century, with string attached to leg of a chair. No details available of another African type operating over heads of audience.

Marionnettes et Guignols: les poupées Agissantes et Pailantes à travers les Ages, by Ernest Maindron (Felix Juven, Paris, 1900). Eight colour plates and 148 black and white illustrations. A history, largely a commentary on Magnin's *Histoire des Marionnettes en Europe* (Levy Freres, 1852), but with useful additional material on French developments and some brief chapters on puppets in the East. Chapters on: puppets of the Middle Ages, puppets in other countries, English puppets, German, Spanish, those of Bruxelles and Anvers; Karaguez, Chinese, Javanese, Burmese. Particularly valuable for the illustrations (none in the Magnin volume).

Marionnettes et Marionnettistes de France, by André-Charles Gervais (Bordas, Paris, 1947). Author one of the puppeteers in Gaston Baty Theatre. Emphasis on hand puppets. Chapters on puppeteers, puppets, audience, and an elementary grammar of hand puppet manipulation with detailed exercises. Second part is well-illustrated account of work of the leading French puppeteers of the period, including Raphard's *Guignol des Tuileries*, Chesnais *Comédiens de Bois*, Desarthis *Théâtre du Luxembourg*, Marcel Temporal *Bonshommes Tempo*, Baty *Marionnettes à la Française*, Blattner *Arc-en-Ciel*; four theatres in Lyons, nine provincial groups (e.g. Roubaix and Amiens marionettes). Part three is 72-pp. bibliography of French books on puppetry, historical and technical; Guignol and Polichinelle, Lafleur and other types; educational and toy theatre and shadow shows, and books on foreign theatres. Impressive supplement of play-titles in repertory of French puppet theatres, Raphard, e.g. has 111 titles.

Marot, marotte. Originally the mediaeval Fool's stick or sceptre, a short rod topped with a small head in cap and bells. Some contemporary puppeteers, especially in France, have developed a simple form of rod puppet from the basic marotte, adding shoulder pieces with cord arms, hands, costume, the rod running through a tube to give rotary head movements. Andre Tahon in particular has demonstrated delightful group possibilities. Technique: Temporal *Comment construire et animer nos marionnettes* (Bourrelier, 1955, 2nd edition).

Maschere. Italian term for the masked actors of the COMMEDIA DELL' ARTE, such as Arlecchino, Brighella, who were possibly descended from the characters of the Atellan farces of early Roman times, although there is a gap of about a thousand years between the two; the reappearance of a type of theatre (perhaps modified) could be due to a continuity not recorded or simply to the recurrence of human traits (to be comic, satiric, etc.) in successive generations.

Mask. (French *masque*, Italian *maschera*): origin obscure. Although there are differences, there is a close relationship with the puppet, which has been called 'the complete mask'. The mask is a form of disguise which has been traced to the most primitive times – but its precise function varies, the purely theatrical being the final development. In its earliest development it was used by hunters and in rituals and ceremonies; it has taken diverse forms and been made from a wide range of materials: wood, metal, ivory, bone, horn, stone, feathers and fur, paper, cloth, etc. It can be very simple or elaborate and ornate – carved, covered with mosaic – have added wig. It usually has the double function of influencing both the wearer and the onlooker. It has been used in initiation and healing ceremonies and by secret societies, and taken grotesque form when worn by the warrior. It has survived in festivals such as the Mardi Gras carnival. It was used in the Greek and Roman theatres, in the medieval Mysteries (for characters such as devils, demons, dragons, and the abstract 'deadly sins', and was adopted by the Italian 'improvised comedy' players in the Renaissance – by such stock characters as Pantalone, Arlechino, Scaramouche, Pulcinella half or full-face, made of leather). The traditional Noh drama of Japan has some 125 named varieties, strictly traditional in design, made of wood, coated with plaster, painted and gilded; the Tibetan type are carved fantastically and painted; the Chinese have papier-mache type for religious drama, but in the secular use make-up and paint to a mask-like consistency. The Javanese for the dance-drama developed from the eighteenth century shadow-plays use face masks held by the teeth on a strap. A contemporary Polish puppet theatre has used complete basketwork figures with the actors inside. Whether the actor uses a mask (which also influences the rest of the body, may even appear to change its size) or uses a puppet, there is a temporary identification with the character represented. It is also possible for a puppet to wear a mask as a disguise, calling for a subtle psychological adjustment on the part of the puppeteer. The main difference between the mask and the puppet is that (normally) the puppet is seen by its operator as well as by the audience, the 'control' is to some degree remote, whereas the masked actor becomes his own puppet. Normally both the masked actor and the puppeteer are hidden – only the new character is seen. Many of the same processes can be used by the mask-maker or the puppet-maker, but the factor of relative size calls for careful study of modelling and colour. The stronger the modelling (carving) of the features the more the face can *change* expression with the changes of light and shadow when in movement. This is true for both mask and puppet. Teschner said that his marionettes had no expression – and not even any eyes: 'I leave my heads almost unfinished and leave the eyes empty. I leave it to the lighting to give magic to the faces of my puppets.' Masks vary: some have immense eyeballs (the wearer must have somewhere else to look through), but the eyeless type are akin to statues without eyes – light and shade gives expression. A book which is worth the study of all puppet-makers is W. T. Benda *Masks* (Wapton-Guptill, N.Y., 1944), which has 68 illustrations and a full description of the making technique, with a full discussion of mask-psychology. It is not necessary to adopt the process, a long and tedious one except for the born artist, but an understanding of the principles involved in design is a good starting point for the puppet-maker.

Mask, The. Periodical published by Gordon Craig from Florence Italy, in the period 1908–29 (with some gaps); 15 volumes. Whilst mainly concerned with matters concerning the live theatre there are important contributions relative to puppets, e.g. an English translation of Ferrigni's *La Storia dei Burattini* (*History of Puppets*), originally published in 1902, appearing in serial form in Vols. VI–VII, 1911–14; No. 6, 1913–14, has an article on *Puppets in Japan*. Craig provided an index to the *Mask* puppet material in his *The Marionnette* (No. 3, May, 1918).

Masking. The screening-off of parts of stage not to be seen by the audience, involving the checking of SIGHT-LINES. Sometimes used when one character passes in front of another and obscuring him.

Masks and Marionettes, by Joseph Spencer Kennard (Macmillan, Y.N., 1935). On the origin of the COMMEDIA DELL' ARTE, famous players and companies; scenarios; the playwrights GOLDONI and GOZZI (some of whose plays have had and continue to have puppet productions); section on Italian marionettes, with illustrations, and on their origin and travels abroad. As with other authors who quote from MAGNIN and MAINDRON and other sources, author confuses some terms, e.g. 'burattini *and* fantoccini', as being those 'worked and moved by wires': burattini are specifically hand puppets, fantoccini are marionettes. Also gives term 'bambocci' as Italian term for the French 'MARIONNETTES À LA PLANCHETTE, operated on a horizontal string running from operator's knee through chests of figures and to a short post.

Master Peter's Puppet Show (*El retablo de Maese Pedro*). Musical score by Manuel de Falla (1876–1946) based on the puppet episode in Cervantes' *Don Quixote*, q.v. Publisher: J. W. Chester, London, 1923.

Matchbox puppets. Simple type which can be made by very young school children. The lid of the box forms the neck in which two fingers are placed; a face is cut from card and stuck on, with crayoned eyes (or gummed paper features), cotton-wool, etc., for hair. The simplest costume is a piece of cloth with three holes, one fitting round the neck, the child's own fingers protruding through the others for the puppet hands and able to handle small objects. The matchbox lid is also used in a more advanced form of 'junkbox' puppet, as the neck of a pulp-flowerpot head or one created from a plastic 'squeezie' bottle.

Materials. Beginners and experts alike may find inspiration for creation simply by seeing and handling materials of different nature and wide range of textures and colours. Experienced makers tend to become magpies, collecting and storing all manner of materials for later use; ready-made objects also. Costume material can suggest character; the relationship of costume between the various puppets in a production must be considered and also be checked against scenery: particularly important if a small stage is in use and the puppets close to any scenery. Hair materials such as wool, silk, string, fur, hemp, also contribute to characterisation. Sometimes quite inexpensive materials can be effective under stage lighting. If coloured lighting is to be used then this must be tested against the chosen materials, or curious unintended effects may follow. A further important consideration is that of stiffness or flexibility of materials; this can vary with the same material on different sizes of puppets. In the case of the string puppet the risk of costume material catching in joints must be examined. There are no fixed rules; experience (experiment) is the only teacher. Small samples are usually of little use for testing – as with wallpaper. The only criterion is theatrical effectiveness. The creative designer sees possibilities in all kinds of things, e.g.

paper, cardboard (flat or in tube form), 'Nature' objects such as roots, driftwood, pinecones, fern fronds, coloured-headed pins, beads, buttons, bottle-tops, metal foil, pieces of glass and coal, wood shavings, various kinds of wire, raffia and straw-plait – preferably stored in clearly labelled boxes or plastic bags.

Matt paint. Type that dries without shine (gloss), non-reflecting. Also known as 'flat' or 'flatting'. All paints have some degree of shine while wet.

Mayhew, Henry (1812–87). Sociologist and popular journalist, originally trained for the Law; one of the original proprietors of the periodical *Punch*. Important contribution to literature: *London Labour and London Poor* (three volumes, 1851, and a fourth added in 1862), which he described as 'the first attempt to publish the history of a people, from the lips of the people themselves – giving a literal description of their labou r their earnings, their trials, and their sufferings, in their own "unvarnished" language'. With two assistants he interviewed thousands of people in the London streets, including entertainers – strolling players, musicians and a Punch and Judy showman from whom he obtained the text of the play verbatim (Vol. 3), which Speaight (*History of the English Puppet Theatre*) regards as more authentic than that of Payne Collier (*Punch and Judy*). Mayhew has been re-discovered in recent years and selections have been published by Spring Books, edited by Peter Quennell: *Mayhew's Characters* includes an interview with a showman who gives a lively description of the 'Chinese Shades' or 'Lez Hombres' – i.e. Ombres Chinoises, a shadow show given at night on a Punch stage with a white cloth across the proscenium and candle light.

Medium. The binding ingredient in paints which holds pigment-particles together. Ingredient which acts as a DILUANT, such as turpentine, is not a medium.

Meister des puppenspiels. Series of profusely illustrated booklets published by the Deutsches Institut für Puppenspiel, Bochum, Germany, each dealing with one puppet company or theatre (various European countries). Text usually in German, some in the language of the country of origin (e.g. two in English: Hogarth and Harlequin). Order of publication does not necessarily follow the numbering. (1) Albrecht Roser's marionettes (Germany); (2) Carl Schroder's hand puppets (Germany); (3) the Hanneschen of Cologne (German Rhineland); (4) Obraztsov and the Central State Puppet Theatre of Moscow (USSR); (5) Therese Keller's hand puppets (Switzerland); (6) Augsburger marionettes (Germany); (7) The Hogarth Puppets (England); (8) Oestreich-Ohnesorge (Germany); (9) Salzburg Marionette Theatre (Austria); (10) Vermeire marionettes (Netherlands); (11) Tandarica Theatre (Rumania); (12) Ljubljana Theatre (Yugoslavia); (13) Die Hohnsteiner, hand puppets (Germany); (14) Die Hohnsteiner, 2nd group (Germany); (15) Eric Bramall's Harlequin Theatre (Wales, Gt. Britain); (16) Hurvinek and Spejbl theatre (Czechoslovakia).

Melodrama. Operatic form in which singers use recitative, or in which entire text spoken; popular in Victorian era, but contemporary revivals tend to evoke laughter rather than tears in the sentimental passages. It is a form asking to be burlesqued by marionettes or rod puppets.

Meschke, Michael. Swedish puppeteer, director of the Stockholm Marionettentheater; studied with Harro Siegel, Jean-Louis Barrault and Marcel Marceau; extensive repertoire (see Stockholm).

Mester Jakel. The Danish cousin of Mr Punch. Not mentioned in Magnin's *Histoire des marionnettes en Europe* (1852). For those who read Danish there is *Mester Jakel*, by Svend Smith (Arnold Busck, Copenhagen, 1945), with 22 illustrations, some in colour, and five short play-scripts. Denmark seems to have only a slight tradition of puppetry, but there are signs of contemporary activity, and the country is one of the strongholds of the Toy Theatre.

Metaphor. Figure of speech in which one object is likened to another, e.g. man as puppet of the gods, king as puppet of his government. Examples abound in the works of poets and prose writers, see specimen entries: Arbuthnot, Bacon, Browning, Coleridge, Donne, Gale, Keats, Macaulay, Shakespeare, Shelley, Spenser, Tennyson, Thackeray, Vaughan, Wordsworth. See also Concordance.

Methods. Usually refers to the crafts involved in making puppets rather than to styles of acting or producing. Choice of method may be a matter of degree of craft-skill, or a matter of expense (cost of materials) or, ideally, be determined by the individual puppet to be made. The final test is successful function during performance. Methods and media are inseparable – although if a designer feels he will get the desired effect by cutting cloth with a chisel he will use this method. There is no substitute for experience when it comes to handling tools, but some expert tuition may mean a longer life for the tools. The basic problems are the same for the professional, the amateur, the educationalist. There are plenty of textbooks describing techniques, usually with diagrams or step-by-step photographs; but no book can show movements, either of tools, paint-brushes, sewing machines – or of puppets in action. Often the method for making one puppet, working with new materials or using old materials in a new way, is a matter of sheer experiment, trial and error, undoing, re-doing. If there is any choice of materials then their different possibilities should be explored. The head of a mouse carved from wood will have a different character to one made from stuffed velvet. Very large heads may need to be made from lightweight materials, e.g. POLYSTYRENE. A head which may have to suffer hard knocks during performance may need to be made from FIBRE-GLASS. There are many ways of making marionette joints; the beginner will not be able to make a ball-and-socket joint unless already a skilled craftsman; the selection is mainly determined by function, the way a part is to move. Methods of control of any type of puppet must also be related to function; after experience it is possible to plan this from the beginning, being part of the concept of the finished puppet. Industrial developments have made many new materials available to the puppet-maker and designer, especially in the field of plastics. It is, for instance, possible to make FLEXIBLE moulds for casting, instead of rigid Plaster of Paris type, and this gives a degree of 'UNDERCUTTING' of features which would be a problem with the traditional method. Tools such as a 'heat gun' have been developed for creating shapes in blocks of polystyrene, as used in display work. The maker who cannot afford one will heat up old files or other improvised tools. Methods are means; they are of little value without vision.

Memoirs of Bartholomew Fair, by Henry Morley, LL.D. (1822–94) (Routledge, 1892, 4th edition; 1st, 1857). Has interesting puppet references; mentions a pamphlet *An Agitator Anatomised* (1648) which notices the puppet playing in the Fair, and an undated advertisement stating that the memory of the old MIRACLE PLAYS and MORALITIES was 'being cherished' among the puppets. From the *Ancient Song of Bartholomew Fair* – quoted in Vol. 4 of d'Urfey's *Pills to Purge Melancholy* – gives the line 'For a penny you may see a fine puppet play' and, in another verse, mentions three items which appeared regularly together: *Patient Grisel, Fair Rosamond*, and *The History of (Chaste) Susanna*. PEPYS records seeing LADY CASTLEMAINE (the King's Mistress) coming away from a performance of *Grisel* (30th August, 1667). Flockton, who flourished in the second half of the eighteenth century, was one of the regulars at the Fair; Morley calls him 'the Prince of showmen' (and his puppets were known as 'the Italian FANTOCCINI). In 1797 some of the puppet showmen were prosecuted for allowing the puppets to talk! (This was due to rivalry with the live theatre, and the Licensing Act.) The play-bill of Crawley's puppet shows at the Fair mentions the *Creation of the World* and *Noah's Flood* – which were also among the popular items of puppet showmen's repertoire.

Mexican Folk Puppets. Text by Roberto Lago, coloured drawings by Lola Cueto (Puppetry Imprints, U.S.A., 1941); includes traditional and modern and some toy puppets (dimensions not given). Author and artist, both leaders in the puppet field in Mexico.

Mexico. In an introductory note to an Exhibition, Professor Roberto Lago, puppeteer and teacher, mentions a legend given in an MS. left by Fray Bernardino de Sahagun (died 1590), which tells of a necromancer named Tlacavepan or Ocexoch who astonished the Toltecs in a market square at Tianquiztli by making a small puppet dance on his hand (no technical details). This was before the Spanish adventurer Cortes arrived with his private entertainer in 1524, who did sleight-of-hand and manipulated puppets to the sound of music. The French invaders with Emperor Maximilian introduced 'guignols' (hand puppets) and these were adopted by showmen who travelled on mules. An attractive small book by Lago and illustrated in colour by Lola Cueto (*Mexican Folk Puppets*), q.v., shows various traditional and some toy types. There is a chapter on the aboriginal puppets in McPharlin *Puppet Theatre in America*. A strolling player (contemporary) mentioned by Lago, Francisca Pulido Cuevas, who makes two grotesque figures – Woman and Devil – dance zapateados and jarabes on a board on the ground, controlled by a horizontal stick in one hand, with a thin chain each end, while playing harmonica held in other hand – is shown in an illustration accompanying an article in *World Theatre* (Vol. 14, No. 5, 1965). The ingenuity of this technique is a parallel of the early European marionnettes à la planchette, operated by a horizontal string through the puppet (or puppets) and hitched to a short post and to the knee of the puppeteer-musician.

Midlands Art Centre for Young People. Site: Cannon Hill Park (14 acres of parkland), south of Birmingham. Purpose: 'not only to provide new facilities ... but also to act as a starting point – a stimulus for greater cultural activity in the home and the hundreds of communities served by the Centre'. Sponsored by the Cannon Hill Trust, Director John English. A ten-year foundation programme involves the building of three theatres: (1) large: seating 500–1,000, for plays of any period, music, opera, ballet; (2) studio: seating 300, for puppetry, films, ballet, music; (3) an outdoor arena theatre. Building work began in March, 1963; by 1967 Arts Club workshops and studios in full-time use, followed by library, discussion rooms and recital theatre. By Spring, 1966, more than 100,000 visitors had signed the book in Foyle House, and within six months of the opening of the studio building more than 2,000 family memberships registered (parents with children under 15) and a thousand Arts Clubs members, aged 15–25. The studios and workshops offer the services of over 50 professional artists and craftsmen; the resident theatre designer and puppetmaster is JOHN BLUNDALL, Council Member of the Educational Puppetry Association and member of the British Section of UNIMA, the international organisation. The actual designing and construction involves young architects, technicians, craftsmen, college and school workshops. Social facilities include swimming pools and squash courts. Work-camps (international) are run in co-operation with Scouts and Guides and other organisations. Professional theatre and puppet companies are being formed. This is a project which needs repeating in all the major cities of Britain.

Midsummer Night's Dream, book adapted from Jiří Trnka's famous puppet film (Grand Prix award at the Cannes Film Festival, 1959); story retold in simple form for children by Eduard Petiska; illustrated by photographs and designs from the film, in colour (Artia, 1960).

Mikado, The. Gilbert and Sullivan comic opera (1885); has had several marionette adaptations, including that by the Harlequin Theatre during the international puppetry Festival at Colwyn Bay, 1968. Complicated libretto concerning romantic intrigues at Court, the problems of town councillors and the Lord High Executioner, with mock-Japanese names such as Ko-Ko, Yum-Yum, Nanki-Poo; happy ending. In Act 1: 'If you think we are worked by strings, Like a Japanese marionette, You don't understand these things; It is simply Court etiquette.'

Milne, A. A. (Alan Alexander) (1882–1956). English novelist, dramatist, essayist, one-time assistant to the editor of *Punch*. Well known for his children's books, such as *Winnie the Pooh*, which has had puppet productions, e.g. *Bil Baird's Marionettes* (U.S.A.) with music and lyrics; characters such as Eeyore, Kanga, Rabbit, Tigger, Mice, Owl, Moles, Spiders, Cows, Butterflies, right for puppets. Also puppet versions of *The King's Breakfast*.

Mise-en-scène. French term. The putting together by the Producer of everything that makes up the stage picture: scenery, lighting, actors.

Mr Punch, by Philip John Stead (Evans, 1950). Excellent study of the historical aspects, with chapters on Punch in Italy, France, his naturalisation in England; about Punchman, Piccini, the Italian whose performance provided the text for Payne Collier's *Punch and Judy* (1828), q.v., and the street performer interviewed by Mayhew (*London Labour, London Poor*, 1851, q.v.) and who had purchased some of Piccini's figures; the text as given by the Mayhew 'professor' (q.v.); some interesting notes about Dog Toby. Speaight (*History of the English Puppet Theatre*, 1955) disagrees with Stead as to the possible French influence on the Punch show – Punch did go to France and *could* have influenced the French – one of the many historical blind spots unlikely to be removed by fresh evidence.

Moir, David Macbeth (1798–1851). Physician; writer (under pseudonym 'Delta'); wrote for Blackwood's *The Life of Mansie Wauch, Tailor in Dalkeith*, in which occurs the interesting reference to 'Punch and *Polly* and *puppie*-shows' – 'puppie' being a dialect form for 'puppet'.

Modelling stand. Simple construction on which to shape plasticine heads as preliminary phase to casting or direct application of final medium. Materials: (*a*) wood for base, five or six inches square and about half to one inch thick; hole drilled in centre to take a screw; (b) piece of broom-handle or similar wood (approximately 1 in. diameter) nine or ten inches long; (c) screw, long enough to pass through base and enter 1 in. or more into the upright post. Plasticine is built up around top of post, proceeding downwards to chin and neck, the post providing a solid core for the modelling. The stand leaves both hands free for the work, but can also be lifted and turned about when checking details. If the cast from the model is by the 'direct' method by applications of layers of paper and paste, muslin and plaster, etc., then the drying out is done on the stand. It is possible to make a plaster mould, for casting internally, by (a) application of Plaster of Paris over the model, first inserting card or tin 'SEPARATORS' for easy removal in two pieces, or (b) by placing stand horizontally over cardboard box or other container into which plaster is poured to half-depth of model, allowed to set before casting second half. For removal of head made by direct method: turn stand on edge, base and top of head resting on table, cut through with craft knife, reverse and cut other side, remove and rejoin. Plasticine *stays* on stand ready for fresh modelling.

Modelling. Shaping by building up as distinct from carving or cutting away. Puppet heads are either solid, hollow or partially hollow. Solid heads are usually created by direct modelling in chosen medium such as paper pulp or plastic wood. Hollow heads are made over a preliminary clay or PLASTICINE (plastilene) model or in a plaster mould made from the model. The degree of modelling at the plasticine phase depends on whether the final shell is to be built up directly over the model or in a mould; for the latter full detail is done at the plasticine phase and the cast will be a replica same size as model; for the former a minimum of detail is done at the plasticine phase and allowance must be made for the thickness of medium to be applied *over* model, the thickness depending on type of medium, layers of paper and paste, muslin and plaster, etc. Here the final detail is modelled *in the medium itself*, and when dry the shell is cut in half and removed. The plasticine is then ready for immediate re-use. For this type of work plasticine is preferable to wet clay, the wet slowing up the drying-out phase. With the casting method from the fully detailed model, replicas can be made from same mould if required, and the process is by applications of medium *inside* two halves of the mould, which are then removed for joining. With the mould method it is also possible to cast a hollow rubber head, the two halves of the mould being tied together and liquid rubber poured in. There is an advantage in work with school children in the 'direct' method, applications of paper and paste layers over the model; the actual casting is begun sooner, the modifying of the shape proceeds during the applying of the layers and, being in the air, the drying process is speeded up; there is also no problem of storage of plaster moulds or additional cost of the plaster. The best tools for shaping plasticine where the minimum of detail is to be done are the fingers; for fine detail as required in the casting method, modelling tools are available from craft shops, supplied in wood, wood with wire ends, plastic, and in a variety of shapes. Plasticine modelling is best done on a MODELLING-STAND (described elsewhere) which allows the model to be studied from all angles, leaves both hands free for the work and, most important, work can be checked *from a distance* – as the finished heads will be seen on a stage at a distance. Modelling also *includes the hair* (if any) of the character. This is sometimes part of the paper or plastic wood head, but is usually more effective if added in form of wig, this having contrast in texture and movement. The wig material should be tested at the initial modelling phase, being part of the final shape.

Model theatre. Term loosely synonymous with 'toy' theatre (e.g. name of the British Puppet and Model Theatre Guild, originally the British Model Theatre Guild), but some authors of textbooks on the making of 'model' theatres stress the difference in function of two types: (1) the Toy Theatre as associated with 'JUVENILE DRAMA' and the 'Penny plain, twopence coloured' *performances*; (2) the Model Theatre, scale model reconstruction of a real theatre, for the use of theatre producers, scenic designers, actors, in the working out of technical and production problems. Techniques: Anthony Parker *Build your own Model Theatre* (Stanley Paul, 1959); Roy Smith *Three Model Theatres* (Nelson, 1960); the latter deals with those of different periods.

Morality Plays. A form of religious play developed in the fifteenth – sixteenth centuries, supplanting the earlier 'MYSTERIES'; dramatised allegories dealing with Man's fall and redemption according to the Christian religion; characters represented abstract qualities such as Vice, Virtue, Conscience, etc. As the term implies, didactic in purpose, but usually with some 'light relief'. Best known of the surviving Moralities is *Everyman* (*c.* 1500), possibly derived from a Dutch version. Some scholars see traces of the Morality in the Punch and Judy play; certainly many of the plays of Biblical origin found their way on to the medieval puppet stages, whose main function was entertainment, so that comic elements would be essential.

Moppet. One of many dialect forms of 'puppet'. American puppeteer Jim Henson has created a group of characters known as 'muppets', which have made regular television appearances.

Monro, Harold (1879–1932). English poet born in Brussels; chiefly remembered as founder of the *Poetry Review* (1912); established his Poetry Bookshop in Devonshire Street, Theobalds Road, London, W.C.1 (1913), which became the centre for all interested in this branch of literature; Edith Sitwell and other eminent writers gave readings of their works. The February, 1921, issue of a monthly *Chap-Book* contained Gordon Craig's essay *Puppets and Poets*, q.v. The Bookshop also became the place where the first monthly meetings of the British (Puppet and) Model Theatre Guild, q.v., were held. In 1926 H. W. Whanslaw, q.v., and Waldo Lanchester, q.v., gave special performances of *Ali Baba*. Monro's *Collected Poems* were published in 1933 with an introduction by T. S. Eliot.

Molière, Jean Baptiste Poquelin (1622–73). French actor, dramatist; lifted farce to the level of classic tragedy. Many of his plays have appeared on the puppet stage, particularly in France, and it would be interesting to know just what happened when the character Guignol took a hand, as is indicated by some of the titles in the repertoire of the Théâtre Guignol lyonnais (listed in Gervais *Marionnettes et marionnettistes de France*, Bordas, 1947): *L'Avare et Guignol, Le Médicin malgré lui*. The last also produced at the Polish theatre 'Arlekin' at Lodz. Adolphe Thelasso, in Revue Théâtrale (1904) mentioned Turkish 'Karagöz' shadow puppet items based on *L'Avare, Le Tartuffe*, and *Les Fourberis de Scapin*. The Japanese puppet theatre PUK, Tokyo, has adapted *Amphitryon*.

Mold, mould. Optional spelling for hollow casing in which anything is shaped. For puppet-head making the mould is usually made of Plaster of Paris from a clay or plasticine model and is divided into two sections. On removal from the model the inside is allowed to harden off, given a coat of lubricant as a separator to ensure easy removal of final cast which is formed inside the mould from layers of paper and paste, plastic wood, or other media. The half moulds can also be tied together and used for casting heads from liquid rubber, poured in at the open neck end (see RUBBER). A modern development is the FLEXIBLE MOULD, which allows a certain amount of 'UNDERCUTTING' of features such as nose, chin, ears, the mould stretching during removal. Some puppetmakers make a mould for each head, preferring to do all detail in the initial model, this being reproduced in the cast – but the mould is particularly valuable for mass-production of same head (as in pottery making) and some makers cast a number of basic shapes and add the features after removal from mould. Parts of limbs for marionettes can also be mould-cast. Technique: many text books include, e.g., *Introducing Puppetry*, by Peter Fraser (Batsford, 1968); *A New Art of Papier Mache*, by Desmond MacNamara (Arco, 1963); *New Materials in Sculpture*, H. M. Percy (Tiranti, 1962).

Modern Puppetry, by A. R. Philpott (Michael Joseph, 1966), in the series 'Blishen Books', gives an initial glimpse of modern trends in puppet entertainment and then approaches the practical aspects along the lines of the personal tuition given to hundreds of students over a period of 20 years, backed by professional experience; although a good deal of technical information – with diagrams – is provided, there are no 'patterns'; the reader is encouraged to explore and experiment, to develop original work right from the start, to master the simple before attempting the complex; every aspect is discussed; a bibliography is provided, addresses of suppliers of materials, addresses of puppetry organisations.

Modern. Reference to things of the present time and which, if they continue to exist, become traditional. The connotation of 'contemporary' as synonymous with 'modern' – but simply meaning 'existing at the same time' – overlooks the surviving traditional forms.

Mordant. Fixing agent used in dye process.

Morice, Gerald. English journalist and authority on puppetry (historical, traditional, contemporary). Co-founder (with H. W. WHANSLAW) of the British Puppet and Model Theatre Guild (1925) and its first Secretary and (later) Press Officer; Editor, 'Wartime Bulletins' and 'The Puppet Master' (1950–52). Member of UNIMA and Founder Patron of the British Section, UNIMA (as Joint International Committee of B.P.M.T.G. and E.P.A.). Member of the UNIMA Praesidium for several years, organised study tours of continental puppet theatres (pre-war and post-war). *World's Fair* columnist since 1938 ('Punch and Puppetry Pars'). Regular contributor to *The Stage* on puppetry and other subjects. Broadcasts and television appearances and articles in the Press at home and abroad; substantial part of activities over a very long period. Co-director with GEORGE SPEAIGHT of 'The Old-Time Marionettes', a reconstruction of a traditional nineteenth century travelling company, the Clowes-Tiller Puppets, the old figures being carefully refurbished and given, in part, new settings by Reginald Woolley (designer for the Player's Theatre, London) in a partially 'FANTOCCINI' programme created in Festival of Britain Year, at the Riverside Theatre in London's Battersea Pleasure

Gardens during whole of August, 1951; subsequently seen, in excerpts, at the Christmas Market in the Mansard Gallery of Messrs. Heal's, Tottenham Court Road, London. Translator of the repertoire of the SALZBURG MARIONETTES (not all of the 13 pieces translated have received presentations in English, but most of them were used during the Marionettes' two visits to Britain and the several visits to the United States in the immediate post-war years). Arranged the 1936 JUVENILE DRAMA exhibition at the George Inn, Southwark, South London, in honour and on the occasion of the 80th birthday of Mr Benjamin Pollock, the Toy Theatre publisher, immortalised by Robert Louis Stevenson in his essay 'Penny Plain, Twopence Coloured' (which originally was printed in *The Magazine of Art* and then included in his volume Memories and Portraits), when he wrote: 'If you love art, folly, or the bright eyes of children, speed to Pollock's . . .', the Exhibition being sponsored by the B.P.M.T.G.

Morley, Henry (1822–94). Scholar, editor, originally trained as doctor; produced cheap reprints of the English classics and wrote a history (*English Writers*, 11 volumes, only reaching Shakespeare). Author of *Memoirs of Bartholomew Fair*, q.v. (1857), which contains interesting puppet references.

Moscow. The Central State Puppet Theatre, directed by SERGEI OBRAZTSOV, a leading figure in the world of puppetry, is regarded as a 'must' for every visitor to that city, even if not already interested in puppets. The problem is to obtain a ticket, especially if some new production is opening. Established in 1931, it has become one of the leading centres of puppetry, with a wide and ever-expanding repertoire, involving over 200 people, actors, playwrights, sculptors, musicians and technicians, and constant experiment in new methods. The technique grows with each particular production, mainly variations on the rod type, but also items which introduce live actors alongside the puppets. In *Mowgli*, based on Kipling's *Jungle Book* story, some of the animal characters are large and require two or three operators each. In the play *Two Nil in Our Favour* 30 replicas of the main character are used, each capable of special action. In *The Devil's Mill*, the mephistophelian character, in order to court both maid and mistress, turns into two identical lovers (in Beau Brummel style costume). In *The Divine Comedy*, a satirical version of the biblical *Genesis*, God and the Archangels are played by live actors, Adam and Eve, the Serpent and other characters being puppets; Eve is produced by a surgical operation on modern lines. There are special programmes for children, *Aladdin, Puss in Boots, The Wizard of Oz, Doctor Dolittle*, and various Hans Andersen items; it is part of the social system that regulates programmes to age groups. The Central Theatre has its own puppet museum and is also a training centre for actors and directors. (Illustrations: Beaumont *Puppets and Puppetry*, Studio, 1958; Baird *Art of the Puppet*, Collier-Macmillan, 1965.)

Motif-Index of Folk-literature, by Stith-Thompson (Rosenkilde and Bagger, Copenhagen, and Indiana University Press, 1955): 5 vols. and Index volume. A classification of narrative elements in folk tales, ballads, myths, fables, medieval romances, jest books, local legends, and other sources. All the elements have been collated according to type, such as those in which the main character is 'the youngest son' or where 'magic' comes into the title, and sub-divided, e.g. where magic is result of rubbing an object. An inexhaustible supply of themes which can suggest original

L

plays. The puppeteer or the teacher who lacks ideas should skim through these stimulating volumes.

Motion. Sixteenth–seventeenth century colloquial term for puppet *or* puppet-show, but also having many other meanings (all related to movement in one sense or another, mechanical, emotional, mental), as seen in many instances in Shakespeare's plays. Occasionally both terms used in *same* phrase, e.g. 'O excellent motion, O exceeding puppet!' (*Two Gentlemen of Verona*, Act 2, sc. 1). Term sometimes applied to live dancers in the Elizabethan masques. In the *Winter's Tale*, Act 4, sc. 3, there is a reference to an actual puppet play: 'He compasseth a motion of the Prodigal Son.' The *type* of puppet is rarely indicated, but Ben Jonson provides two clear examples: (1) in *Bartholomew Fayre* (1631), in which an actual show is introduced by a 'motion master' and in which the type of booth and puppets are almost certainly of the hand puppet variety, and (2) in his *Tale of a Tub* (1633) with another play-within-a-play, brief shadow-puppet items of some primitive form. Davenant mentions the 'motion men of Norwich, Op'ra puppets' in his *Playhouse to Let* (1668). Gordon CRAIG revived the term for the short plays published in his *The Marionnette* (1918), q.v., calling them 'Motions for marionettes'. Interesting correspondence in modern usage 'motion pictures' and 'movies'.

Motions for Marionnettes, by 'Tom Fool' (Gordon Craig, Florence, 1918). Three short plays for puppets ('motions') included in issues of *The Marionnette*: *Mr Fish and Mrs Bones* (April), *The Tune the Old Cow Died of* (March), *The Gordian Knot* (May).

Mourguet, Laurent (1745–1844). French puppeteer who established small theatre in Lyon and evolved the most popular character 'Guignol'. According to Paul-Louis Mignon, *J'aime les Marionnettes* (1962), Mourguet was given a 'Girolamo' – popular puppet in Milan – by an Italian from a small town called Chignolo. A puppet named Gnafron referred to the Gerolamo as 'Chignol'; the latter lost his strings and became a hand puppet 'Guignol' – and has since given the name to *all* hand puppets in France. (Formerly, 'Polichinelle', q.v., had been the national favourite.) Another theory as to the origin of the name is quoted by Baird in *Art of the Puppet* (1965) that of a local phrase '*C'est guignolant!*' – the height of amusement! – but the etymology is not forthcoming. ('Guignolet' = a sweet cherry liqueur.) Both theories are mentioned in Maindron *Marionnettes et Guignols* (1900).

Movement in Two Dimensions, by Olive Cook (Hutchinson, 1963). Study of animated and projected pictures of the pre-cinematic era; chapters on Mirrors and Magic; Peepshows and Panoramas, Far Eastern Shadows, Karagöz, The Chinese Shades, Dissolving Views, Living Models, The Persistence of Vision; bibliography. Illustrations include Hand Shadows, Shadow puppets from Java and Bali, Turkish Karagöz, Greek shadow-theatre and two action photographs. Interesting material regarding 'persistence of vision', the factor involved in the illusion of movement when a number of 'still' photographs showing various *phases* of movement are projected on to a screen, whether of the cinematic or stop-motion method of film production.

Mowgli. Play based on Kipling's story in the *Jungle Book*, produced at the Central State Puppet Theatre, Moscow, director Sergei Obraztsov. Theme: Mowgli is little boy reared by wolf family, befriended by other jungle creatures who teach him the ways of the jungle. Puppets are ideal for animal characters. The larger animals (with moving eyes, mouths, ears, tails), such as tiger Shere-Khan, about three feet long, and Python Kaa, ten feet long, require two or three operators each (below stage). Superb jungle settings. Disney Studio made a cartoon film version.

Mozart, Wolfgang Amadeus (1756–91). Austrian composer. Hermann Aicher, director of the famous Salzburg Marionette Theatre, says in a souvenir booklet: 'The SALZBURG Marionettes have always had two powerful guardian angels. They are the glowing and harmonious beauty of Salzburg, and its genius Mozart, who has become our genius, too.' The repertoire includes several of his operas: *Apollo and Hyacinth, Bastien and Bastienne, Don Giovanni, The Magic Flute, The Abduction from the Seraglio,* and others, and a ballet *Eine kleine Nachtmusik.* Some of these items have also been adapted to the puppet theatre by the Zurich Marionettes and other companies. Lotte REINIGER's silhouette films include *Ten Minutes with Mozart,* ballet to *Eine kleine Nachtmusik* (1930) and *Papageno,* a Fantasy on the birdcatcher from *The Magic Flute.* The Central Puppet Theatre in Prague has presented a shadow-show version of *Apollo and Hyacinth.*

Muffin the Mule. World-famous marionette character of The Hogarth Puppets; carved by Fred Tickner for the Hogarth Puppet Circus (1934); starred with Ann Hogarth (manipulator) and Annette Mills (pianist-singer) in B.B.C. television series 1946–54. Films of these programmes have been shown in many countries, and Muffin has appeared live on television with Jan Bussell (guitar) and Ann Hogarth (manipulator) in Russia, Poland, Germany, Luxembourg, Holland, Canada, Australia and France. Exact replicas of Muffin can be seen in museums in Moscow and New York. Toy Muffins are available in shops. Stories about him by Ann Hogarth in the *Muffin Annuals* (1951–54) have been translated into Russian and Latvian. Various Muffin stories published by the Brock-hampton Press.

Multiple control. Groups of marionettes can be operated by solo performer, or by one member of a group, using specially constructed control, design related to actions required. Hoop with cross-bars can have four or more figures attached, dancing in a circle, armstrings bunched in one hand for raising and lowering in unison. A row of Can-Can dancers may be suspended from an extended horizontal control. The same principle can be adopted for control of underwater creatures *from below,* using horizontal bar with stiff wire supports for the figures – or for a group of fish, etc., on a shadow screen, from above or below.

Multiple marionette. A five-headed figure, with connecting shoulder line, only two arms, strings to legs, used in *A Small Play about Europe,* by Professor Weiss (Switzerland), illustrated in Helen Binyon *Puppetry Today* (Studio Vista, 1966), with the caption 'The Public'. There have also been three- and five-headed hand puppets, small heads on individual fingers, e.g. group of baby chicks.

Multi-production. Replica puppet heads may be needed for reasons other than commercial mass-production; a variety show may require a line of identical chorus girls, a play may need twins or triplets, replacements may be anticipated when there is to be unavoidable wear and tear during performances, or basic shapes for modification as individual characters may be regarded as economical. The technique for such reproduction is usually that of casting from MOULDS (Plaster of Paris, Vinamold, etc.) made from clay or plasticine models. It is also possible to begin with wooden or rubber balls as basic heads to which features are added.

Multi-purpose stage. A number of puppeteers and companies have experimented with stages adaptable for various types of puppets, but usually there must be sacrifices due to the varying needs of different types. A primitive kind has been used in schools, made from a clothes-horse, curtained (three-sided); operators are inside for hand or rod puppets, or a screen can be mounted for shadow-show; stage reversed and equipped with internal table as marionette floor, table at rear for the operators. McPharlin published *A Plan for Folding Stage adaptable for Puppets, Marionettes, and Shadows* (1934). The 'Universal' *Theatre* to be built in Prague will, it is anticipated, successfully accommodate every type of production. *Exploring Puppetry*, by Stuart and Patricia Robinson (Mills and Boon, 1967), gives variation of the school design.

Multiple set. Stage setting with three or more localities for ACTING AREAS.

Mumbo-Jumbo and other Plays, by A. R. Philpott (Macmillan, 1954), in the 'Puppet Plays for Schools' series (for hand puppets). No fees for non-professional performances. Two original items and one based on an old folk-tale: (1) *Mumbo-Jumbo*, (2) *The Little Red Sledge*, (3) *Lucky Hans*. Approximate acting time 15 minutes each.

Mummers' or mumming play. Folk drama of Death and Resurrection involving a number of stock characters such as St George and the Turkish Knight, sometimes Father Christmas or Punch; from medieval times and especially in rural areas (occasional contemporary revivals). St George is popular as a hand puppet item, having plenty of slapstick. An acting version is available in paperback (Puffin Book), *St George and the Dragon*, by Diana John (with *Punch and Judy* in same volume); there is a puppet version *King George and the Dragon*, by Morris Cox, in the Macmillan Puppet Plays for Schools series (see bibliography).

Munich. In 1858 Joseph Leonhard ('Papa') SCHMID took over a small theatre which became the first permanent puppet theatre and was to have many repercussions elsewhere, e.g. Anton Aicher, founder of the famous SALZBURG MARIONETTE THEATRE, was among those inspired by it. Count Franz POCCI, Director of the Court Musicians and later Lord High Chamberlain, wrote many comedies for this theatre which have become German classics. In 1900 the municipal authorities built a special theatre for Schmid and in 1950 honoured his memory by naming a street after him. Another important landmark was the establishing of Paul Brann's Munich Artists' Puppet Theatre in 1905, where plays by MAETERLINCK, MOLIÈRE, GOETHE and others, as well as operas, were produced. Today there is still the marionette theatre at No. 29a Blumenstrasse, and there are two or three students' theatres, and, apart from the fact that Munich has been the venue for an international festival, the city has become a Mecca for puppeteers drawn by the magnificent puppet theatre collection (Puppentheatersammlung der Stadt München: Jakobsplatz 1); the museum has over 5,000 puppets of all types from world sources, and a vast collection from the Orient; the library has more than 4,000 publications dealing exclusively with puppetry, including numerous scripts in MSS., and archives of printed matter, slides, press cuttings, photographs, phonographic and magnetic tape recordings, films – with library facilities for anyone interested in puppetry. Ludwig Krafft, former Director of the Collection, prepared a profusely illustrated volume (black and white and colour plates) published by the Akademie für das Graphische Gewerbe, 1961, *München und das Puppenspiel*.

Muppets. The 'pure puppet' creations of American puppeteer Jim Henson, television favourites, two of whom are pictured in Baird *Art of the Puppet* – 'Wontkins and Will', large-eyed, large-mouthed, fuzzy creatures.

Murray, Gordon. Puppetmaster, film and television producer, author, puppetmaker. 1952: Marionette productions, with Alan Judd, of *The High Toby* (Priestley), *The Rose of Auvergne* (Offenbach) at Broadstairs and Boltons Theatre, London. 1955: Rod puppets, with Alan Judd, at the Soho Fair, London, *Up the River* (Herve) and *Spoiling the Broth* (Offenbach). 1955: Joined BBC Children's Television as puppet producer. BBC Productions: 1955: *The Bird of Truth, The Queen's Dragon.* 1956: *Toytown* series. 1957: *The Emperor's Nightingale, Beauty and the Beast.* 1958: *The Winkleburg Armourer, The Petrified Princess* (Arnell Opera). 1959: *The Emperor's New Clothes, King of the Golden River.* 1960: *The Crumpot Candles, The Magic Tree.* 1962: *The Dancing Princess.* 1956–65: the *Rubovia* series (26 plays). 1965: Left BBC staff to become free-lance TV film producer, using stop-motion system. 1966: *Camberwick Green* series for BBC's 'Watch with Mother' programmes. 1967: *Trumpton* for BBC. 1968: making new series for BBC.

Museums. The enthusiast in search of puppets will try even the smallest and most remote museum hopefully. Except for specialist collections, puppets tend to find themselves in ethnographic museums or ethnographic departments (e.g. as in the British Museum) – and sometimes in private collections (e.g. that of the Hogarth Puppets). Puppetry associations usually have collections, but not necessarily on permanent display or on view to the public except on special occasions (e.g. British Puppet and Model Theatre Guild Exhibitions, display usually augmented by temporary loan material). The Bethnal Green Museum (E. London) – which mounted a joint British and Polish display in 1963 – now has a permanent exhibit with an international flavour (including material formerly at the Victoria and Albert Museum). The Horniman Museum in S.E. London has a small varied collection, including some oriental and a Polish szopka. The Edinburgh Museum of Childhood has a growing collection; the Toy Museum at Rottingdean in Sussex has a small selection. For a major collection it is necessary to go to Munich (Puppentheatersammlung der Stadt München), where there are puppets by the thousand from world sources and a special library exclusively devoted to puppet literature, with archives of slides, photographs, films and other material. The Theatre Museum connected with Kiel University has special collections of oriental material. Sometimes in countries where there are State Puppet Theatres, e.g. in Moscow, U.S.S.R., a museum may be attached to the Central theatre. There is an important collection in the Musée internationale de la marionnette in Lyon, France. A major collection in the United States is at the Detroit Institute of Arts, an active puppet centre. It is envisaged that a Directory of Museums with puppet exhibits will eventually be compiled and published, probably by the British Section of UNIMA (the international organisation), which has already issued a preliminary edition of a Directory of Puppet Theatres. In the meantime, enquiries should be made from any national puppetry organisation, national section of UNIMA, or Public Library; the last mentioned may have or be able to obtain a copy of *Performing Arts Collections* (see individual entry), which is an international handbook listing museums and libraries with theatre material – often including puppets – arranged under countries. For an extensive list of museums with Shadow material refer to Blackham *Shadow Puppets* (Barrie & Rockliff, 1960).

Music. The place of music in the puppet theatre could well be a theme for discussion at some international conference. In some traditional forms of puppetry it would be as unthinkable to omit the music as it would be to omit the words from Shakespeare's plays (although, in fact, TRNKA, the Czech puppet-film maker, *did* omit the words from his version of *Midsummer Night's Dream*, and added music). The GAMELAN orchestra of Indonesian puppet shows, mainly of the percussion type, is an integral part of the performance. The evolution of the unique Japanese Bunraku 'three man' puppet art stemmed from the collaboration of the great playwright CHIKAMATSU ('Shakespeare' of Japan), a virtuoso narrator, Takemoto Gidayu, and the introduction of the three-stringed SAMISEN (from Ryukyu). Music plays an important part in Chinese shows, providing 'background' to the dramas, the instruments being Chinese guitars, fiddles, flutes, clarinets, gongs, bronze bells, drums and rattles. There are puppet theatres which produce operas – the SALZBURG MARIONETTE THEATRE being the most famous. Operas are rarely written for puppets, although HAYDN wrote some operettas for Prince Esterhazy's private puppet theatre in Hungary, and opinions vary as to whether they are appropriate in the puppet theatre, however superbly produced. TESCHNER, whose unique 'FIGURENSPIEGEL' (gold-framed concave-lens proscenium) is preserved in the Austrian National Library, felt that human speech was out of place in the puppet theatre, and that music should be scaled to the size of the puppets – and took on a musical-box quality. Bertolt Brecht's *Threepenny Opera*, a contemporary version of Gay's *Beggar's Opera*, had German jazz music by Kurt Weill. The modern music of STRAVINSKY and Bartok, for the ballets *Petrouchka* and *The Wooden Prince* produced by the Hungarian State Puppet Theatre, was not written with puppets in mind (except that the Russian traditional puppet Petrushka *did* influence Stravinsky). A special arrangement of the same composer's *Histoire du soldat* was made for Michael Meschke's puppet theatre in Stockholm. The Punch and Judy show does not have music during the show, but there is traditionally drum and panpipe or other music to attract the audience, and some of the outdoor Guignol theatres in Paris have accordion overtures. The Czech composer Smetana wrote two amusing overtures for puppet plays, and Professor Skupa's early puppet repertoire included a number of musical items – some serious and some burlesque. The piano-act has become a stock item with marionette performers since Podrecca introduced his burlesque of the eccentric Russian maestro Vladimir de Pachmann. Obraztsov, the Soviet puppetmaster, in his solo performances, gives a series of short songs accompanied by puppet mime. Music may be introduced during the course of a hand puppet play; if a character feels moved to burst into song or, like the German Kasper, wishes to dance with the princess – and may even ask the audience to sing to a folk tune. Puppet folk-dances have been successfully introduced with rod puppets, hand puppets, marionettes. At the surrealist level, and which is only possible with the puppet medium, characters in the form of cellos, violins, flutes, produce music by playing on themselves. Where the puppets, or the puppeteers, may fail is in attempting 'musicals' – even with the top singing stars on tape – for the sheer personality power of the humans will be lacking. Experiments have been made with electronics and musique concrète, which certainly have affinity with the puppet theatre. What is required is a unity of all the elements of any production. If the puppetry is not of the same standard as the music, then the music instead of covering up the weakness will only expose it. A splendid Wagnerian outburst should not be necessary with a hand-puppet version of a well-known folk tale. There are musical versions of such tales, e.g. *Hansel and Gretel*, which have been adapted to puppet production. Ideally the puppeteers and composers collaborate on material specifically for the puppet theatre; rarely will a genius appear who is puppeteer, playwright, puppet-maker, scenic designer, costumier, *and* composer – the nearest may have been Acciajuoli, mentioned by Baird in *Art of the Puppet*, who wrote the first marionette opera (Florence, 1670) and was 'designer-poet-mathematician-producer' in the one person.

My Profession, by Sergei Obraztsov (Foreign Languages Publishing House, Moscow, N.D.). Autobiography of internationally famous Soviet puppet-master, director of the Central State Puppet Theatre, Moscow. The qualities required to achieve mastery of the puppet art are here revealed, perhaps the most vital being the ability to analyse results of work done, to understand audience reactions, to be self-critical. Readers who have been fortunate enough to see the solo performances of Obraztsov will appreciate the numerous photo-illustrations, recalling the quality of the performance. His meetings with the last of the traditional Petrushka players, whose puppets are now in the museum attached to the theatre, and with the Efimovs whose experiments with rod puppets had repercussions not only in Obraztsov's theatre, but throughout Europe and in America, are of particular interest, as are the photographs of that other great Theatre phenomenon STANISLAVSKY.

Mystery Plays (Mysteries). No connection with modern fiction. Development from the liturgical (church) drama and consisting of a series of scenes based on biblical subjects, various episodes being the concern of different Trade Guilds and presented on special platforms or 'pageants' (on wheels) set up at various points in the town. 'Miracle' plays are particularly concerned with legends of the Saints.

N

Names. A rose might *smell* as sweet by any other name, but would not *sound* the same. The theatrical importance of names is seen in the adoption of professional stage-names, e.g. 'The Beatles'. In the early twentieth century only foreign-sounding musicians or ballerinas could hope to attract audiences, e.g. Marks had to become Markova; due partly to an association of ideas (Pavlova), partly to the concept that only foreign artistes were in the star category, but largely because of the impact of the *sounds* of the names. In the realm of puppets it would be impossible to improve on the name and sound 'Punch' for that character. The sound of 'Ju-dy' displaced the earlier 'Ju-dith' and 'Joan' – both weak-sounding – and 'Ju-dy' is more effectively produced with the aid of the Punchman's SWAZZLE. This applies also to 'To-by' and 'Jo-ey' (Clown): the sounds carry well and have dramatic quality. Such characters as 'Sooty' and 'Andy Pandy' depend a good deal on their names (sounds) for their appeal. The simple two-syllable words are the first used by young children: 'Ma-ma' (later 'Mum-my'), 'Da-da' ('Dad-dy'), 'Dog-gy', 'Ted-dy' and so on. The German popular puppet is 'Kas-per' (or 'Kasperle'); the French favourite is 'Gui-gnol'. The Russian 'Petrush-ka' is virtually two-syllable in pronunciation, and would be weak if reduced to 'Petroush'. The Czech national favourite (a little boy) is 'Hurv-inek' – two-syllable in effect – and his father is 'Spej-bl'. It is the actual *sound* rather than any precise number of syllables that is important. Titles for books are chosen carefully to help sell them. Titles of stories such as *Hansel and Gretel, Snow White and Rose Red* – which can become play-titles – have immediate appeal and could not be bettered. 'Joan' acquires strength if transformed into 'Joan of Arc'; 'Robin' is weak in sound, whereas 'Robin Hood' is strong, as is 'Orlando'. 'Patient Grizel' (Ital.: Grizelda) from the *Decameron* stories reappeared in Chaucer, Dekker and other authors, was mentioned as a puppet play (Pepys' *Diary*); it would have been weakened in appeal had the title been 'Patient Mary'. A quick look through a Dictionary of Fictional Characters gives evidence of authors' search for effective names which, inseparable from 'character', must have the right dramatic power as *sound*.

Nang, The. The shadow play of Thailand (Siam), one of its most ancient art forms and which, according to H.H. Prince Dhaninivat Kromamun Bidyalabh Bridhyakorn, came from India via Sumatra, Java and the Malay Peninsula. The performance with the large cut-out scenes against a long white screen illuminated by firelight has dance characteristics which may have influenced the development of the Khon (classical dancing). There is no action of individual characters, these being static within the elaborately incised scenes, cut from buffalo, bear or tiger hide, supported by two rods. The pamphlet by Bridhyakorn is *The Nang*, in the Thailand Culture Series, No. 12, published by the National Culture Institute, Bangkok, is in English and illustrated. There are some references in Busch *An Introduction to Modern Siam* (van Nostrand, 1959, 2nd edition). See also under Thailand.

Narrator. Story-teller, as distinct from actor. Exact function varies, e.g. in Sicily, with a sword as his sole 'prop', will gather an audience and give a dramatic narration on the same traditional themes presented at puppet plays in the theatre; in the Japanese BUNRAKU puppet-theatre, the narrator-chanter sits at one side of the stage (with a samisen-player to provide musical emphasis) providing commentary on the puppet action, the thoughts of the characters, all dialogue. From the Middle Ages onwards many puppet shows had an 'interpreter' *in front* of the stage – although it is not always clear whether any dialogue was spoken from within the stage – an example being given in Jonson's *Bartholomew Fayre*, q.v., in which a puppet show occurs within the play; in Cervantes' *Don*

Quixote, q.v., this practice of having an 'interpreter' in front is seen again. In modern performances the Narrator may be off-stage and invisible, either talking about the scene as it unfolds or explaining what happens between one scene and the next. Occasionally a Narrator will be in front and directly address the audience. In the traditional Javanese shadow-show the puppet-master (DALANG) not only narrates and provides all dialogue, but also operates a large number of the characters single-handed. There is the possibility that wandering showmen crossing national boundaries, e.g. Italy into France or into England, would need a translator-interpreter in order to get over the initial language problem. Whatever the reason and whatever the method or style, this theatrical CONVENTION is accepted by the audience – but sometimes amateurs (and professionals!) employing a Narrator are revealing a weakness in the production: if the Narrator tells the audience that the hero is killing the dragon while both are off-stage the audience will feel frustrated.

Nativity play. Presentation of the story of the Birth of Christ. Since the Middle Ages, throughout Europe, the Nativity has been performed with every type of puppet, beginning with the simplest Church 'cribs', which developed into a form of small stage still seen in Poland (SZOPKA), the architecture of which is related to church design. A performance by very young children in school, using hand puppets, naive and sincere, can be as moving as any by a professional company. In his *Bench Book*, H. W. Whanslaw mentions a play having 15 to 20 group-scenes, presenting biblical scenes, preserved in the Museum at Verviers, Belgium, the puppets being converted from ordinary dolls.

Needlework Puppets, by Brenda Morton (Faber, 1967). Detailed pattern instruction book on making hand puppets with needlework heads.

Netherlands, The. As elsewhere in Europe, the earliest shows were those of the ambulant showmen, the first recorded show being that given at the Court of Jan de Blois in Dordrecht in 1363. The dominant character in the popular shows was named Hans Pickle – or Pickled - herring–a parallel to the German Hanswurst or Jack Sausage, essentially crude in type, and later supplanted by Jan Klaassen (as Hanswurst was by Kasperle). Jan had a wife Katrijn, and they appeared in episodic quarrels and, towards the end of the nineteenth century, developed into shows for children. A general revival of interest in puppets, as in the rest of Europe, took place after World War I. A theatre using the rod type of puppet was established in 1923 by Bery Brugman, presenting operas. Fairy tales began to find a place in the repertoire for children, especially that of Henri Nolles. Further developments took place after World War II and, among others, Quido van Deth founded a hand puppet theatre; some formed mobile companies. In addition to a number of experiments by artist-puppeteers there were developments within the schools. Practical puppetry courses were begun, including those at the Free Academy of Plastic Arts, the Hague, where some of the lecturers were puppet-masters. A Royal Association for the Dutch Puppet Theatre has been founded. A periodical, *Wij Poppenspelers*, is published by Nederlandse Vereniging voor het Poppenspel, Amsterdam. A book on theory and technique, *Het Moderne Poppenspel*, by Rico Bulthuis, was published by Uitgeverij Heijnis N.V., Amsterdam (1961).

Neurospastos. Greek word for puppet (from 'neuron', a cord made of sinew); there is no precise evidence that the method of control was similar to that of the modern marionette; some of the small jointed terracotta dolls (female) found in Athenian tombs (neurospasta) have the vestige of a head rod, a miniature version of that of the large Sicilian puppets still in use. Archaeologists may yet come up with a full-size puppet and miraculously preserved 'cords'.

New Materials in Sculpture, by H. M. Percy (Tiranti, 1962). Handbook for craftsmen and colleges. Details of new materials and techniques which are revolutionising whole field of sculpture and which are being explored by puppet-makers also. The polyester resins and the vinyl group of plastics are reasonably easy to use and require no special equipment; what working instructions are necessary are provided in this small book. Apart from working in plaster or flexible moulds, direct modelling in polyester resin-glass fibre (of the type used for insulating) has been found practical. It is also possible to work with fibre glass direct over a plasticine model (without use of mould). Thirty-five reproductions and glossary. Note: Tiranti's are suppliers of materials and tools: 72 Charlotte Street, London, W.1.

'New' Puppetry. Phrase coined by ERIC BRAMALL, director of the Harlequin Puppet Theatre, Colwyn Bay, N. Wales; definition for anti-conventional approach, or 'purist' movement with accent on the 'puppetesque' qualities of puppets. Experiments included performances with figures 12-ft. high with special methods of control and audience required to participate *mentally*.

Ningyo. Japanese term for 'puppet' (literally: *doll*). *Ningyo shibai* = puppet drama. The term 'Bunraku' – although loosely used for 'puppet' – applies only to the three-man type of the BUNRAKU theatre.

No Strings Attached. 16 mm. colour film, sound-optical track, showing all aspects of puppet play production as seen through the eyes of the performers. Can be hired on application to the Principal, College of Education, St Andrew Street, Aberdeen, Scotland.

Nohant. The location of the famous chateau of George Sand, q.v.; small village near La Chatre about 200 miles south of Paris; the puppet theatre and about 100 of the hand puppets made by George's son Maurice are preserved and can be viewed. Jan Bussell describes a visit in *Through Wooden Eyes*, q.v. Incidentally, a certain much-used Guide Book refers to George's son as her 'brother'.

Noises off. Theatrical sounds produced off-stage, such as wind and rain, thunder, car back-firing, aeroplane, train wheels and whistle, chimes, birds singing, dogs barking, horse galloping; artificially produced by special equipment (often very simple, e.g. coconut shells for hooves) or from tape or disc recordings. Textbooks on theatre techniques usually include practical details, and some puppet manuals give instructions for home-made equipment. See next entry.

Noises Off, by Frank Napier (Garnet Miller); good small book on techniques of producing stage effects; author one-time stage director of the Old Vic Theatre.

Noroma. Japanese term meaning 'stupid' puppet, applied to a primitive type found on the Sado island and controlled by the performer's hands around the puppet body.

Nose, The, by Nikolai Vasilyevich Gogol (1809–52), q.v. This has had puppet productions – whereas it would be somewhat difficult to perform it on the human stage. Theme: a Nose suddenly leaves its owner and has a marvellous time riding around in a carriage, dressed in the height of fashion. (See chapters on puppet heads and noses in Philpott *Modern Puppetry*, Michael Joseph, 1966.)

Notes and Queries. A medium of intercommunication for Readers, Writers, Collectors, Librarians (sub-title originally read 'for Literary Men, Artists, Antiquaries, Genealogists, etc.'); first issued as a weekly publication, Volume 1, November, 1849 – May, 1850 (Bell, London, 1850); war-time issues from 1942 were bi-weekly; monthly from 1953. Volume 14, December, 1967 = No. 12/No. 212 of continuous series. British Museum Reading Room has bound copies each indexed; additional indexes bound separately. Valuable source for research material and, via the *Queries* columns, new material. Regular features over a long period included Proverbs, Phrases, Shakespeariana; correspondence, sometimes extensive and both 'entertaining and instructive', has included surprising number of puppet items, some from puppetry notables such as George Speaight, Gerald Morice, and the American Paul McPharlin (in period preceding publication of his *Puppet Theatre in America*, and some from purely scholastic correspondents. Wide range of puppet topics, e.g. etymology of name of Punch (eliciting material about social gatherings in France, 'Punch patriotique' and 'Punch d'adieux', i.e. Punch as a drink), and etymology of 'silhouette', traced to French minister of State, with a wealth of detail on portrait-silhouette cutting techniques. The origin and meaning of 'Pantin' – the jumping-jack type of toy figure which was in vogue with ladies of fashion in Paris and London. Items on Punch and Judy show in Egypt, Punch with two left legs (in a Tenniel illustration for the *Punch* periodical) and an interview with a 'swatchel cove' (Punch showman). 'Puppets' as a term for coal-wood or 'faggots'; the origin of *Puss in Boots*; the 'Penny Plain' of Skelt and Webb; the first use of the name Judy as Punch's wife; the marionettes of the Patagonian Theatre at Exeter 'Change. Some Public Library Reference Rooms have current issues. Notes or Queries for publication should be addressed to J. C. Maxwell, English Faculty Library, Manor Road, Oxford.

O

Oberammergau. Bavarian village (south Germany) renowned for its Passion Play performances (from 1634) given every tenth year; also as a great wood-carving centre. The Museum (Langsches) has a collection of eighteenth–nineteenth century 'jumping jacks', q.v.

Obraztsov, Sergei. People's Artist of the Soviet Union, Director of the State Central Puppet Theatre, Moscow. Vice-President of UNIMA, the international puppetry organisation. Internationally famous for his solo performances as well as for the wide range of productions of his theatre (with a personnel of around 200 actors, sculptors, musicians, technicians); has a passion for fresh experiment with each production and has been largely responsible for the widespread contemporary development of the rod puppet. Some items in the theatre's repertoire, such as the *Divine Comedy* (satire on *Genesis*, by Isidor Stok), mix live actors with the puppets. In his own repertoire are items requiring varied techniques, in which the characters mime to his singing. *We were Sitting Alone by a Murmuring Brook* (Tchaikowsky) employs the bare hands with wooden ball heads, male and female, with minimum of features, the unclad hands being amazingly expressive. For *The Lullaby* (from Mousorgsky's *Children's Album*) he uses no stage; the puppet is a life-like baby which is disinclined for sleep; through an opening in its nightie the flesh shows; when it is finally asleep and the puppetmaster moves silently away, the audience is hushed, too. In the item *Fill up that glass*, with the music of a gypsy folk song, the live hand lifts the bottle which repeatedly fills the glass; the large, flexible head becomes more and more grotesque after each drink, and the tempo increases. (A rubber tube inside the neck conveys the liquid to a container below stage.) Another universally appreciated item has a bored Tiger who eventually swallows the Tamer, of which Obraztsov says, in his introduction, this ensures that everybody gets their money's-worth – whereas it is very rare at a real circus to see the Tiger as the victor. This puppetmaster's autobiography *My Profession* (Foreign Languages Publishing House, 1950) has the directness and self-criticism of the genius who began as an art-teacher, a singer (many of his items burlesque bad singers) and an actor. The photographs of the great Stanislavsky watching an Obraztsov performance are significant. In his article *Some Considerations of the Puppet Theatre* (in *The Puppet Theatre of the Modern World*, published for UNIMA by Henschelverlag, Berlin, 1965, and in nine languages, English edition Harrap, 1967) he finishes by asking 'Why should I not cherish this dream?' – i.e., of the puppet theatre presenting works 'full of passionate conviction' and dealing with topical issues. In his *Chinese Puppet Theatre* (Faber, 1961), which is part of a larger work on the Chinese Theatre, a record of his experiences in that country, he confesses to being surprised at the skill of the performers – and even comes upon a tiger-taming act. He came to the conclusion that in the Chinese Puppet Theatre every object is a work of art in itself. Obraztsov has visited Britain many times (has performed within the framework of the Edinburgh Festival) and has a fondness for London, which is revealed in a small book *Impressions of London* (Sidgwick and Jackson, 1957).

Occupational therapy. Treatment method for patients suffering from some physical or psychiatric disability. Many Training Schools for student therapists include puppetry in the syllabus. Assessment of the individual needs of each patient determines choice of craft (such as basketwork, dressmaking, woodwork) which may contribute not only to physical rehabilitation but also to the development of a hobby or even a profession. Puppet-making – choice of type of puppet and method – is also related to individual needs and may lead to group work and social benefits. The Association of Occupational Therapists issues a journal, *Occupational Therapy*, which has occasional articles on puppetry and puppet book reviews. (Correspondence: 251 Brompton Road, London, S.W.3.)

Odyssey, The. Homer's epic story from the ancient Greek world – where the destinies of men were in the hands of immortals, oracles, nymphs, enchantresses, giants and monsters; the adventures of Odysseus encountered on his return from the Trojan Wars, told in ten episodes with silhouette figures and settings inspired by Greek vase paintings and sculptures. A Firebirds Film production, each episode approximately 13 minutes' duration; 16 mm. black and white composite optical sound prints.

Oedipus Rex. Opera-oratorio by Stravinsky, based on Greek myth; libretto by Cocteau (after Sophocles). A special production was presented by the League of Composers and the Philadelphia Orchestra (1931), directed by Leopold Stokowski, with massed choir, and puppets 10-ft. tall made by Remo Bufano to designs of Robert Edmond Jones; puppets controlled partly from above, by operators on a bridge 40-ft. up, partly from below (operators clothed in black). Theme: Oedipus ('swollen foot'), son of King Laius of Thebes, is left to die (with spike through feet) so that a prediction will not come true; is found by a shepherd; later unwittingly kills his father, marries his mother Jocasta, thus fulfilling the prediction; mother hangs herself, Oedipus blinds himself. (Illustrations of the puppet production in Beaumont *Puppets and Puppetry*, Studio, 1958.)

Oil colours. Concentrated pigments in drying oil, usually in paste consistency in tubes. These can be obtained either at an artists' suppliers or the decorators' oil-and-colour merchants. Used in paste form are slow drying. For puppet painting it is usual (and more economical) to mix the colour with a small quantity of decorators' 'flat white' (household undercoating). The colours are inter-mixable and it is best to invest in the more intense shades rather than the pale tints; the latter cannot be increased in intensity, but the former can be reduced by addition of white. The names of the colours vary between different manufacturers; the labels should be ignored and the actual colour inspected. The paste can be reduced to correct brushing consistency by the addition of turps – and brushes can be cleaned (immediately after use) in turps, turps substitute (white spirit), or soap and warm water (and then thoroughly rinsed).

Old England at Play, by Lynette Feasey (Harrap, 1943). Pocket-size book of old plays adapted for young players, including the Coventry *Nativity* Play, the farcical-comedy of the *Yorkshire Shepherds* (or *Mak the Sheepstealer*), *Noah's Ark*, *St George and the Dragon*, the morality play *Everyman*, and *Punch and Judy*: short introductory notes to each. Some reproductions from old prints.

Old Time Marionettes. Famous Victorian troupe founded 1873 by Tiller and Clowes; discovered during World War II by GERALD MORICE and GEORGE SPEAIGHT in a Lincolnshire village; renovated and presented at the Riverside Theatre, Festival Gardens, London, in 1951, in a programme of Victorian music-hall songs and trick items.

Omar Khayyam (*c.* 1050–1123). Persian poet, mathematician, astronomer, famous as author of the *Rubaiyat* (English translation by Edward Fitzgerald and others); in it human life is compared with 'a magic shadow show played in a box' – and indicates the possibility of a type of entertainment similar to that of the 'motions' in Ben Jonson's *Tale of a Tub*, q.v., with painted figures made to revolve by the heat from a candle. *Persian Poems*, an anthology in the 'Everyman' series includes two versions of Fitzgerald *Omar*.

Ombres chinoises. French term for a form of shadow show popular in the eighteenth–nineteenth centuries, but being more closely related to the silhouette-portraits than to the exquisitely cut and coloured and mobile Chinese shadows. There is no record of who first introduced them and they also appeared in Germany and Italy. Later in England the Punch and Judy showmen adopted the idea, converting the proscenium of the booth into a shadow screen by stretching white calico sheeting across it, giving shows at night by candle-light, and calling the show a 'gallanty', q.v. Mayhew, in his *London Labour and London Poor*, q.v., interviews a street showman, who informs him that 'the proper name of my exhibition is *Lez Hombres*, or the shades', and that 'we calls it the Chinese galantee show'. The showman did not mention France or the intermediary source. Dominique Seraphin (1747–1800), born into a travelling showman's family, opened a shadow theatre in Paris in 1776, moved it to Versailles and, in spite of success there with the nobility, moved back to Paris, eventually sold the theatre, bought it back again and introduced marionettes as a fresh attraction. Olive Blackham, in *Shadow Puppets* (Barrie and Rockliff, 1960), mentions a performer named Ambroise who performed in Paris in 1772 and in London in 1775.

Ombromane, ombromanie. French term for hand shadows. An interesting set of illustrations showing how to make a variety of amusing shadow creatures from hand-shapes is given in *Les Théâtres d'Ombres*, by Denis Bordat and Francis Boucrot (L'Arche, 1956).

O'Neill, Eugene (Gladstone) (1888–1953). American playwright: *The Hairy Ape* (1922), *Emperor Jones* (1921), q.v., which has had puppet adaptations.

Open Air Entertainment. Annual publication of the Greater London Council: detailed guide to the summer season entertainments in the London parks – date and time for every performance – opera, ballet, symphony concerts, dancing, concert parties, fairs, horse shows, exhibitions, pop groups, tennis, zoos, motor-cycle races, etc. During the schools vacation (August) anything up to 200 puppet performances, including many Punch and Judy shows; also children's play parks which include puppetry among the activities. Booklet available from most bookstalls in the parks, or by post from Parks Department, Cavell House, 2a Charing Cross Road, London, W.C.2.

Opera (from Italian '*opera in musica*': a musical work; Fr. *opéra*, Ger. *oper*). Drama set to music, vocal and instrumental, with arias, duets, trios, choruses, recitative links, costume and scenery. First work in this form: *Dafne*, by Italians Jacopo Peri and Giulio Caccini (1594). Many puppet companies have adapted operas or included excerpts in their repertoire, outstanding being the SALZBURG MARIONETTE THEATRE, with items such as Mozart's *Bastien and Bastienne*, *Apollo and Hyacinthus*, *The Magic Flute*, *Don Giovanni*, and others, and some by Gluck, Offenbach, Pergolesi. The term 'Punch's Opera' (or 'Op'ra Puppets') occurs in historical literature, but with little indication as to the amount of singing or what musical accompaniment was provided.

Optical effects. Moving clouds, flames and other effects are obtained in the theatre by use of a special projector.

Oriental Theatricals, by B. Laufer (Field Museum of Natural History, Chicago, 1923). Interesting data regarding masks and Chinese shadow puppets, with some illustrations, in the museum's holdings.

Origami. Traditional art of paper-folding in Japan. The only material: paper. No paste, no scissors. A contemporary development is the application to paper puppets. American puppeteer Shari Lewis co-operated with Lillian Oppenheimer to produce book *Folding Paper Puppets* (Stein and Day, 1962), including about 20 items with step-by-step diagrams; basic rules given and transcript of an actual lesson in the folding technique.

Oswald, Oscar. Supplier of Punch figures, ventriloquial dolls, second-hand books on magic, Punch and puppets; publisher of the 'MAGICAL DIGEST', monthly magazine on magic, ventriloquism and puppets.

Our Lady and the Juggler. Story by ANATOLE FRANCE, English translation available in Harrap's Bilingual Series (1948), translation by Margaret Weale (*Le Jongleur de Notre Dame*). McPharlin in *Puppet Theatre in America* mentions various productions with puppets. Theme: A poor juggler in the time of King Louis in France, and who could toss six brass balls and catch them with his feet, was impressed by the works of devotion of a group of monks, decided to perform his tricks in front of the altar of the Holy Virgin; is discovered by disapproving monks – but the Virgin steps down and wipes away the sweat from his brow. Moral: Blessed are the pure in heart, for they shall see God.

Overcasting. Another term for 'direct' casting, i.e. building up a hollow head over a clay or plasticine model – as distinct from mould casting, which involves the extra process of producing a mould from the model, either of Plaster of Paris or one of the modern flexible moulding substances. In the mould method the full detail of the features are in the model prior to casting; in the overcasting method a minimum of detail is given, features being gradually built up in the actual casting material. Some makers use 'dividers' – pieces of thin stiff card or tin – inserted in the model at a line running from under one ear and over the highest point of the head and down to bottom of neck on other side. The cast is built each side, giving removable halves. Alternatively, the cast can be made without division and then cut open with a craft knife, which gives a more exact join. For repeats of any one head – as in mass-production – the mould method is used. Where time is an important factor, as in school work, the 'direct' method has advantages, the pupil can begin making the actual head much sooner, modify it as it grows over the model – and the problem of finding storage space for moulds does not arise.

Oxford Companion to the Theatre, edited by Phyllis Hartnoll (O.U.P., 1967, 3rd edition), 1,088 pp. text, 176 plates (some puppets); extensive puppet material by GEORGE SPEAIGHT. Select list of books (58 pp.).

P

Paddle control. Chinese marionettes of the Ming dynasty had paddle-shaped control as seen in silk painting showing children performing with small puppets on low platform.

Paints. Colouring media for use on paper, plaster, wood, etc. Second function, with some types, is protection of surface coloured. Water-colour types are not washable; surfaces (including puppet faces) which may need to be cleaned should be painted with washable types (oils or emulsions). For theatrical work a choice must be made between 'flat' or 'gloss' types – i.e. which do or do not shine and reflect light. Puppet faces which are shiny will lose in detail seen at a distance, because of the bouncing light. The handling of paints and mixing of desired shades can only be learned by experiment with actual colours; colour *names* vary between different manufacturers and it is safest to examine actual paint in tube or tin. The 'flat white' ('flatting') used by decorators can be tinted with tube oil colours and is very serviceable for puppet work. Tube oil colours (artists' or decorators') are in thick paste form and can be thinned to desired consistency by addition of TURPS or TURPS SUBSTITUTE; some colours are more opaque and some are translucent; some are affected by strong light (e.g. stage lighting). Some emulsion paints can be tinted with oil colours, some with poster or tempera powder colours (check with supplier). The modern (plastic by-product) Polymer and Acrylic colours are quick drying and hard wearing. Small tins of lacquer or enamel (gloss) are useful for details such as eyes and lips. Metallic paints (for stage props such as crowns and weapons) need to be stirred during use. Fluorescent paints have theatrical possibilities (used in 'BLACK THEATRE' technique). See also BRUSHES and COLOUR, POLYMER COLOUR.

Pal, George. Hungarian artist, puppet-film maker (Holland, England, U.S.A.); *Aladdin, Sinbad* and others, including advertising items; wooden marionettes, wire-jointed, using STOP-MOTION animation technique.

Palm Leaf puppets. Examples of shadow-type made by Malaysian children in the Pitt Rivers Museum collection, Oxford; reproduction in Blackham *Shadow Puppets* (Barrie and Rockliff, 1960).

Palmer, Ray DaSilva. English puppeteer, director of the 'DaSilva Marionettes' and the 'Little World Theatre', Wisbech, Cambridgeshire. Interested in puppets as a child, mostly as sideline to Magic. Elected to the Magic Circle as its youngest member (1951). Married in 1954, wife Joan a dancer, emigrated to Canada (1955) and lived there for seven years. Presented 'English Punch and Judy Show' on a semi-professional basis in different parts of Canada and the United States, bread-and-butter job being expert 'taster' for General Foods. Appeared at the Puppeteers of America Festival (1957) with *Punch and Judy* and was impressed by scale and presentation techniques of the American shows; started creating own puppets and became known as 'The DaSilva Marionettes'. Returned to England (1962) as full-time professional puppeteers and, in addition to experimental developments with production techniques, acquired the only *portable theatre* in Britain, canvas-covered scaffolding structure seating 200, used in summer season at Morecambe (1967). Also developing 'Puppet Theatre in the Round', with audience on all sides as in circus. For repertoire, *see* DA SILVA MARIONETTES.

Pandanean pipe. Another term for Panpipes, q.v.; showman interviewed by Mayhew (*London Labour and London Poor*); insisted it was the correct term and that the instrument was first brought to Britain by the Romans.

Pan-pipes. One of the oldest known musical instruments; origin mythically attributed to the god Pan. A series of pipes of graduated length (wood, bamboo) joined side by side; when blown across the open top ends produces a scale (lower ends closed). Known in China, Egypt, Greece, Islam, Java, South America, Turkey, South Africa, Peru, Bolivia, Burma, most European countries; performers sometimes reach virtuoso standards, as in Rumania (where the instrument is slightly curved). The Greek name 'syrinx' also occurs (being the nymph turned into a reed by Pan). Early illustrations of street puppet-shows have the 'front man' (the musician-cum-collector) with a set of pipes tucked into the top of his shirt, leaving hands free for playing drum. Illustrations in *Ancient and Oriental Music*, edited Egon Wellesz (Oxford University Press, 1957).

Pantin. Small cut-out figure (paper mounted on card) with similar method of assembly and control as the wooden JUMPING JACK. Vogue in France in eighteenth century among Society, as a toy for adults, transferred to London. Printed sheets with coloured characters for cutting out, such as Arlequin, Scaramouch, and burlesque figures, were sold; some are still available from POLLOCK's Toy Theatre shop in London. As with other puppet names, the etymology remains uncertain. It has been connected with a district of the same name, an industrial area on the outskirts of Paris, which had a reputation for its dances. Eleventh century orthography: Penthinum or Pentin. Spellings such as 'pantine' and 'pantein' have been used. Construction: head and body in one piece; arms usually one piece (sometimes one fixed arm); legs two-piece. The movable parts are connected by a single thread controlled from below, plus a supporting head string. A contemporary example was provided by one of the British Rail Transport posters.

Pantomime. Originally 'player of every part': one-man entertainer in ancient Rome; sometimes used as synonymous with 'mime' (acting without speech). Contemporary use is for burlesque fairy-tales in the Christmas season: *Cinderella, Babes in the Wood*, etc.

Pantopuck the Puppetman. Professional name of A. R. Philpott, puppeteer, playwright, author and editor; Vice-Chairman of the British Section UNIMA committee; member of the Council of the Educational Puppetry Association, London, and instructor at E.P.A. evening and vacation Courses; editor of *Puppet Post* and the E.P.A. Newsletter for many years; editor of third edition of *The Puppet Book* (Faber, 1965) and *Eight Plays for Hand Puppets* (Garnet Miller, 1968), both compiled by the E.P.A. Book Committee. Author of *The Magic Tower and Other Plays* and *Mumbo Jumbo and Other Plays* in the Macmillan series of puppet plays for schools (1954) and *Puppet Diary* (Macmillan, 1952), a puppet's-eye view of travels with a handcart (pre-world war II). Contributor of technical articles to many educational journals and of the therapy and hand puppet chapters in *The Puppet Book*. Author of *Let's Look at Puppets* (Muller, 1966) for children and *Modern Puppetry* (Michael Joseph, 1966) on the new approach to techniques. Lecture-demonstrator at Colleges of Education and in schools, including tours in Leicestershire, Derbyshire, Yorkshire. Contributor of papers at international puppet conferences on the educational and therapeutic aspects of puppetry (Brussels, Brunswick, Karlovy Vary, Rome, Budapest). After television appearances in 1932 (in the basement of Broadcasting House), preference confirmed for live audiences; sessions on the 'Young India' programme (1944) re-confirmed. Career began in the mid-1920's (after some years of office life), in partnership with artist friend Morris Cox, who could have become a supreme puppet-

M

master, but preferred to found an outstanding private press (*The Gog-magog*), publishing his own prose and poetry. Highlight of career: spotting the performing and playwriting talents of wife Violet, q.v., during her apprenticeship days.

Panchatantra, translated by Arthur W. Ryder (University of Chicago Press, 1956; Phoenix Books, 1964). 'The Five Books', translated from the Sanskrit, original authors unknown; possible source of some later fables by Aesop and La Fontaine. Tales grouped in five types: Loss of Friends, Winning of Friends, Crows and Owls, Loss of Gains, Ill-considered actions. Creatures introduced include: ass, cat, cow, elephant, frogs, jackal, lion, mice, ram, snake, heron, plover, sparrows – which have distinct possibilities with one or other type of puppet. In his introduction the translator draws attention to a characteristic use of epigrammatic verses by the actors in the various tales, from sacred writings and other sources and which in English beast-fables would be the equivalent of the animals justifying their actions by 'quotations from Shakespeare and the Bible'.

'Papa Schmid.' Joseph Leonhard Schmid (1822–1912). German pup-peteer, founder of first permanent theatre for puppets in Munich (1858), taking over the tiny Heideck Theatre – one of the turning points in puppet history. Count Franz POCCI (1807–76), writer of children's stories, and who became the most important official at Court, wrote many plays which have become puppet 'classics' (such as *The Three Wishes*) specially for this pioneer, whose work influenced many companies. In 1900 the municipal authorities built a special theatre for 'Papa Schmid', whose memory is honoured by a street named after him in Munich.

Paper-folding technique. See *Origami*.

Paper puppets. In his chapter on Indian puppetry, in *Puppet Theatre Around the World* (1960), Balwant Gargi describes a show with paper puppets operated by threads, presumably flat-figure marionettes, by a solo performer who must be 'conjuror, juggler and actor-producer all in one'. What the warriors, devils, wrestlers and animals lack in action is apparently compensated by the liveliness of dialogue and sound effects. A modern development, stemming from its use in display work, is paper scupture; examples of marionettes in this style by Margaret Hoyland are among the illustrations in Beaumont *Puppets and Puppetry* (Studio, 1958). Interesting examples of children's work are reproduced in Batchelder and Comer *Puppets and Plays* (Faber, 1959). French avant-garde puppeteer Yves JOLY uses cut-out figures in his melodramatic item *Tragedie de Papier* (one figure is cut in half and one goes up in smoke . . .). Another French artiste, Georges LAFAYE, creates symbolic figures from folded newspapers, using these with the 'BLACK THEATRE' technique. Small children also make folded paper creatures. Animated paper-sculpture figures have been used by Halas and Batchelor (*Top Dog*) for television. The traditional Japanese art of paper-folding (Origami) has been adapted to puppets by Shari Lewis, American puppeteer. Tech-niques for puppets from paper bags, paper plates, paper strip and paper pulp – also paper costume – in Robinson *Exploring Puppetry* (Mills and Boon, 1967).

Papier mâché. Strictly refers to pulped paper which is mixed with paste or glue-size to form a modelling medium; can be used for solid heads, either by direct building-up on a stand or inside a mould. Also loosely used to include the paper-layer method in which narrow strips are pasted around and across a plasticine model. Techniques in many puppet textbooks. Also: Desmond MacNamara, *A New Art of Papier Mâché* (Arco, 1963), with section on puppets.

Papier Mâché, A New Art of, by Desmond MacNamara (Arco Publications, 1963). Textbook by professional sculptor who experimented and developed new methods and applications of an age-old art; illustrated by many photographs and diagrams, indicating new scope for sculptors, display artists, film and television designers, puppeteers and schools. Contents: historical introduction, modelling, plaster casting, lamination (layer method), modelling in pulp, head-casting by lamination and pulp overmodelling; theatrical properties, costume accessories, stage animals; simple hand puppets and marionettes, more complex puppets, giant puppets, heads for ventriloquial figures; hollow cast core for multiple production of heads.

Parody. A literary or dramatic work which imitates another in order to ridicule it. As a verb: to burlesque.

Parting agent. Any lubricant which prevents adhesion of plastic or other casting material to the inside of the mould.

Pastoral. Romantic poem or play with a rural setting in which the main characters are shepherds and shepherdesses.

Patient Grizill. Puppet play mentioned by Samuel Pepys in a *Diary* entry for 30th August, 1667, which was seen by LADY CASTLEMAYNE, q.v., at Bartholomew Fair. Henry Morley also mentions the play in his *Memoirs of Bartholomew Fair* (1857), in which he quotes verses dated 1665 describing puppet entertainments of the period: 'Patient Grizel here, Fair Rosamond there, and the History of Susannah.' If the puppet showmen were Italian then the plot of the play was probably taken direct from Boccaccio's *Decameron* (1471), q.v. A number of authors used the plot (Chaucer, Petrarch, Dekker, and others), which remained a favourite as story or play for several centuries. The spelling of the name varies: Grissel, Grissil, Grissill, Grizell, Griselda, etc. There was a *Commodye of pacient and meeke Grissil*, compiled by John Phillip of London, and a *Meke and pacyent Gresell*: Tom Warton, *History of English Poetry*, section xv (*c.* 1770), mentions 'Patient Grizill' and 'a stage of the lowest species . . . a puppet show'. Rocker (1603) refers to the play as the 'Pleasant Comodie of . . .'. The story is of a husband who tests his wife's fidelity – and of virtue finally rewarded. He pretends to kill their two children, to take another wife, and then turns the heroine out of their home, destitute; she accepts all without complaining – and the husband relents. The twentieth century theatre would surely give it melodramatic form.

Pattens. Special footwear to give added height to performer. Also referred to as 'buskins' and 'clogs'. Where performers in a group vary in height, operating from below-stage, thick cork can be attached to shoes. Chief operator in the 'three man' BUNRAKU puppet theatre uses hollow box-like variety (Umanori) with bamboo-mat soles, silent; this is to accommodate operator of the puppet feet, who works kneeling or stooping.

Patter. Showman's term for the quick-fire talk – 'dialogue' – between the various characters – or for a conjuror's words to the audience before or during a trick.

Pavliha. Name of Jugoslav puppet character in the KASPER tradition and who appears in every hand puppet play.

Pedal puppet. Type developed for use in Henri Signoret's 'PETIT THEATRE' in Paris (1888), conceived by Edmé Arnaud and elaborated by M. Bellée; figure, operated from below stage, mounted on iron rod fitted into a base, controlling strings for legs and arms descending to pedals (levers). BLATTNER (Arc-en-Ciel theatre), q.v., developed a mobile variant requiring a harness to leave hands free for manipulating. Alternative terms: piano, key.

Pedroff (Pierre) et ses marionnettes. Director: Pierre Borig, Swiss puppeteer; member of the Association suisse des marionnettistes, the E.P.A. and the B.P.M.T.G., and the Pelpup Club. Has interesting and growing collection of puppets; welcomes contacts (correspondence preferably in French): 16 avenue G. Motta, 1202 Geneva.

Peep-show. A simple form of portable entertainment, eighteenth–nineteenth centuries, which could be set up in the market square or fairground, consisting of a box mounted to a convenient height for viewing the interior through a peep-hole (or 'small orifice'), usually fitted with a magnifying lens, containing a small exhibition of pictures, cut-out figures, scenery, etc. Mayhew, in *London Labour and London Poor* (III, 1861), in one of his many intriguing interviews with street entertainers, was told 'Being a cripple, I am obliged to exhibit a small peep-show'. Dickens mentions one in *Our Mutual Friend* (1865) which showed scenes from the Battle of Waterloo 'and every other battle of later date'. Old prints of the period sometimes show simultaneous viewing by several customers; the proprietor would sometimes have a musical instrument such as a hurdy-gurdy, q.v. Technique (illustrated), Robinson *Exploring Puppetry* (Mills and Boon, 1967).

Peep Show, The, by Walter Wilkinson (Bles, 1927, several reprints). English showman's account of his travels with a stage and puppets on a handcart, the people he meets, camping problems, performances, views on life and a mode of travel hardly possible in the 1960's. Up to the late thirties it was possible for the present author to cross Wilkinson's trail and be mistaken for him, and in the meantime the latter was exploring fresh fields and writing a whole series of books, including *Vagabonds and Puppets, Puppets into Yorkshire* – and Lancashire, Scotland, Wales and America (American editions by Stokes).

Peg puppets. (Not to be confused with 'peg dolls'). Miniature variation of the MARIONNETTES À LA PLANCHETTE, operated by horizontal strings, one from one figure and attached to chair-leg, one from other held or looped around ankle; type of peg is the one-piece variety (not modern spring type or split wood), the fork being cut off to form legs, wooden garden labels or small pieces of plywood for arms, attached by knotted thread through small holes; the two figures share one pair of arms. Amusing actions obtained by holding both strings and experimenting; suitable for small children. Also see TULUKUTU, African variation.

Pegasus Book of Puppets, by Jan Bussell (Dobson Books, 1968), with illustrations by the author, notable puppetmaster (Hogarth Puppets); practical book with a life-time of experience behind it, on making all types of puppets (glove type, marionettes, shadows) from elementary to professional, and on manipulation techniques, stages, scenery, lighting, show-production.

Pelham Puppets. Commercially produced puppets made by Pelham
Puppets, Limited, at Marlborough in Wiltshire, established by Bob
Pelham in 1948 with four employees. First string puppets designed for
children and available in toy shops. Initial problem to be overcome:
tangling of strings. Pelham introduced an anti-tangle device which had
immediate effect on sales; device patented. Type of control was decided
by two factors: ease of handling by child, ease of packing; instructions
and aids for handling were provided. To encourage formation of groups
and the pooling of talents a Club was formed in 1949, application forms
being incorporated with the instruction sheet, a life-member subscription
of 2/6 being charged. A magazine was produced on a Gestetner duplicat-
ing machine, every month for 50 consecutive months, given up for a
short time (due to costs) and later issued in a new format twice a year –
Pelpup News. Membership rose, to 22,000 – as did the cost of printing;
in 1966 a charge of 2/6 per annum was instituted; membership dropped
but subsequently rose to the 10,000 mark, members being in almost every
country in the world, with high percentage in America. Television is felt
to have stimulated interest, as has puppetry in education. Development
of local groups has been encouraged.

Pelpup News. Magazine issued to members of the Pelham Puppets Club
(see PELHAM PUPPETS); international circulation averages 10,000, issued
twice a year. Includes instructional articles and illustrations, news, plays,
photographic competitions, playwriting competitions, correspondence
columns, photograph-reproductions. Application forms for membership
incorporated in the instruction sheet supplied with Pelham Puppets, on
sale in most toy shops.

Penny Plain, Twopence Coloured, by Robert Louis Stevenson (1850–94), an
essay on the Toy Theatre or Juvenile Drama (*Magazine of Art*, April,
1884), providing the best publicity line in the language. R.L.S. himself
influenced by boyhood sessions with a Toy Theatre, retained his enthusiasm in later years and visited various London publishers of the printed
sheets of characters. The name of POLLOCK's, the last of the publishers,
is still to be seen over a small shop (and museum) in Monmouth Street,
London, W.C.2, and both old and newly printed sheets can still be
purchased.

Penny Plain, Two Pence Coloured: a History of the Juvenile Drama, by A. E.
Wilson (Harrap, 1932). Foreword by Charles B. Cochran; 83 illustrations. Cochran confesses a boyhood passion for the Toy Theatre; he and
Aubrey Beardsley, the artist, ignored the printed sheets and put on dramas
of their own devising. (The vogue for Beardsley's work, in the late 1960's,
would make those characters and scenery into collectors' items.) Cochran
'as a remote descendant of William Blake' was excited to learn from this
book that Blake had played a part in the designing. Wilson says that
Robert Louis STEVENSON contemplated writing a book on the Toy
Theatre. Ralph Thomas, a London lawyer, whose collection of prints is
now in the British Museum Print Department, writing in *Notes and
Queries* (August, 1908), mentioned acquiring 5,000 distinct prints
published between 1811–50, and many of Wilson's facts came from a study
of these. Another well-known illustrator actively connected with print
publishing was George Cruikshank (who illustrated *Punch and Judy* with
the Payne Collier text). Goethe, Dickens, Ellen Terry, and even Winston
Churchill are named as Toy Theatre enthusiasts. George Speaight
(*Juvenile Drama: History of the English Toy Theatre*, Macdonald, 1947

disagreed with Wilson as to the origin of British prints (Germany had earlier examples), and it is the privilege of historians to have theories based on inadequate evidence; moments of origin are rarely recorded. Once the vogue occurs, the market expands – and some 50 publishers were involved at the height of J.D. popularity (*c.* 1830); some even cut the prices!

Pepys, Samuel (1633–1703). English statesman and diarist (*Diary*: 1660–69). A number of entries about visits to puppet shows during period 1661–68 at Bartholomew Fair, Covent Garden, Lincoln's Inn Fields, Southwark Fair, Moorfields, including the first reference (9th May, 1662) to 'Punchinello' (now recorded on a plaque outside St Paul's Church, Covent Garden, which was unveiled on the occasion of the Punch 'Tercentenary' celebrations in 1962). Pepys used a variety of spellings for Punchinello (e.g. Policinella, Pollincinella). An entry about 'Holofernes *and other clockwork*' seen at Lincoln's Inn (6th August, 1663) is of interest, and the title of a play at Bartholomew Fair (30th August, 1667) *Patient Grizill*, q.v., shows derivation from Boccaccio's *Decameron*, q.v. (probably through later versions of the story). On another occasion he mentions *Whittington* – but as his *Diary* was originally in a form of shorthand or cipher, the entries were not so much for the benefit of later scholars as for his own pleasure – and are mostly devoid of technical data. He does not specifically say that the common use of 'Punch' as a term for 'all that is thick and short' (including someone's fat child . . .) is an abbreviated form of Punchinello. Its use as a name for a Suffolk horse may have had an independent origin.

Perch. Term sometimes used for the control to which the strings of a marionette are attached.

Performing. In the theatrical sense: acting. The actor with and the actor without a puppet have the same function: the presentation of a character in some kind of stage environment. The actor on the human stage uses his own body as a kind of puppet which takes on the physical characteristics of somebody else, both in appearance and manner of moving, behaving and talking 'in character'. The puppet is physically created for one specific role and remains the same character on or off stage, needing the actor to give it life by a transference of energy or motor power. The puppet may be human, animal, or some fantastic creature, and if it needs vocal power the actor also provides this. The differences between acting with and without a puppet are partly technical, partly psychological. It is not enough for an actor to identify with a character internally unless it is expressed outwardly, but in the case of the actor-with-puppet any expression off-stage (not seen by the audience) is wasted; it needs to be transferred to the puppet. This demands constant focus of attention on, and self-identification with the physical puppet as well as with the 'character' as such. The difference between merely 'manipulating' a puppet and *acting* with it is evident when, to the audience, the character seems to determine its own actions – even if the means of control such as rod or string are visible. The chief actor of the Japanese 'three man' puppets is visible to the audience; all expression is withdrawn from his face and transferred to the puppet, this becoming so supremely alive that the actor is forgotten. With any type of puppet its anatomy (construction) determines its potential range of movement; this range must be discovered by the actor before maximum action and expressiveness can be attained. The range will differ with each puppet even if the same method of construction has been employed. Physical factors such as weight and costume can influence manipulation. The hand puppet would seem to be the easiest with which the actor can identify, the live hand being literally inside it, and OBRAZTSOV, the Russian puppet-master, whose solo items are with hand puppets, has called the hand 'the soul of the puppet'; this will only be true if the actor is utterly identified with the puppet character. If the hand inside the puppet merely 'beats time' to the speech, no matter how perfect the built-in characterisation, the audience will not be convinced of its life. In such shows as Punch and Judy, the French Guignol plays, the German Kasper plays, the phenomenon of 'AUDIENCE PARTICIPATION' is evidence that the audience accepts the 'life' of the puppets; but, providing the actor has mastered his art, the audience will be as much involved in the performance even if it is not of the type evoking open participation.

Performing Arts Collections. An International Handbook (Editions du Centre National de la Recherche Scientifique, Paris, 1960); comprehensive list of Libraries and Museums with theatre collections, arranged under countries and giving opening times, facilities (typewriting, photography, microfilm, etc.). Many references to puppetry collections, approximate number of volumes, MSS., photographs, exhibits, colour-slides, etc.

Performing Rights Society, Ltd., 29–33 Berners Street, London, W.1. An association of composers, authors and publishers of copyright musical works, established to collect royalties for the public performances and broadcasting of such works and their transmission by diffusion service; also to restrain the unauthorised use thereof. The operations of the Society extend only to copyright musical works. It is not concerned with the performance of non-musical plays or sketches, nor with operas, musical plays or other dramatic-musical works.

Pergolesi (Pergolese), Giovanni Battista (1710–36). Italian opera composer; his *Maidservant as Mistress* (*La Serva Padrona*) has remained in international repertory, and is a popular item with puppet theatres, e.g. the Salzburg Marionette Theatre and the Zurich Marionette Theatre.

Periodicals. See individual entries for the following: *Billboard, Czechoslovak Puppeteer* (*Loutkař*), *Figuren-Theater, Harlequinade, Magical Digest, Open Air Entertainment, Pelpup News, Perlicko-Perlacko, Puppet Master, Puppet Post, Puppetry Journal, Stage, Theatre Notebook, UNIMA-France, Woodworker, World's Fair.*

Perlicko-Perlacko. Small, privately circulated, puppetry review edited and published by Dr Hans R. Purschke at Frankfurt/m 21, Hadrianstrasse 3, Germany. Back issues available.

Perrault, Charles (1628–1703). French poet and collector of traditional tales (*Contes de ma Mère l'Oye*: 1697), source of many pantomimes, ballets, puppet shows, e.g. *Sleeping Beauty, Red Riding Hood, Blue Beard, Puss in Boots, Cinderella,* etc. Contemporary translation by Geoffrey Brereton available in 'Penguin' Classics series, and many individual items in various illustrated editions for children.

Personality puppets. Puppet characters based on real human counterparts. A group of English performers in Oswaldthwistle (Lancs.) included Pavlova and Shirley Temple in variety acts (1937). Rufus Rose, in the U.S.A., presented Fred Astaire and Ginger Rogers (photograph in Beaumont *Puppets and Puppetry*). Charlie Chaplin, The Beverley Sisters, the Beatles, are among the notables to appear on puppet stages – but it is probable that puppets succeed better in burlesques of *types* rather than of highly successful individual artistes. See also POUPÉES DE PARIS and TEATRO DEI PICCOLI.

Peter and the Wolf. Musical fairy tale for children by PROKOFIEV, each musical instrument and theme related to the various characters (and teaching orchestral timbres): Peter, strings; Grandfather, bassoon; Bird, flute; Dog, oboe; Cat, clarinet; Wolf, three horns. Has had a number of puppet adaptations. BIL BAIRD American puppeteer, extended the theme to include mythology, with additional Prokofiev music lyrics, for songs, 40 or 50 puppets and one live actor. Various recordings available of the original work.

Peter Pan, by J. M. Barrie. Modern fairy tale which has become a perennial in the theatre. In the puppet theatre the Aberdeen Puppet Players, associated with the Aberdeen College of Education, have produced this famous story, first published 1904. An edition by Hodder and Stoughton (*c.* 1910) has 24 illustrations by Arthur Rackham which capture the fantasy and have definite puppet characteristics.

Petit Théâtre, Le. Puppet Theatre founded in Paris by the poet Henri Signoret and which survived from 1888 to 1892 with a largely literary following (including Anatole France, who thought the puppets had 'a divine awkwardness'); the puppets had a remarkable method of control, being mounted on rods fixed in a base moving on rails below stage, movements of limbs by strings attached to pedals; dialogue was spoken by separate group of performers. A diagram of the mechanism is given in Batchelder *Rod Puppets and the Human Theatre* (Ohio State University Press, 1947). Repertoire included Aristophanes *The Birds*, Shakespeare *The Tempest*, Cervantes *The Vigilant Guardian*, Hrotswitha *Abraham*, and items by Signoret's contemporary Maurice Bouchor *Noël*, *Tobias*, and the *Legend of St Cecilia*. The English translations of Anatole France *On Life and Letters* (Lane, 1914–24, 4 vols.) record several visits to the Theatre (vols. 2 and 3).

Petrouchka. Burlesque scenes in four tableaux, by Igor Stravinsky and Alexandre Benois; scenery and costumes by Benois; choreography by Michel Fokine; first performance by Diaghilev's *Ballets Russes* in Paris, 1911. The music was originally conceived as a piece for piano and orchestra. The composer, in seeking a title for it, realised that the subject was really the Russian puppet Petrouchka; Diaghilev saw the possibilities for ballet. The Hungarian State Puppet Theatre, Budapest, have successfully transferred it to the puppet stage and in 1968 it was presented at both the Aldeburgh and Bath Festivals. The scene was old St Petersburg in the carnival time which preceded Lent; a Fair is being held in the square, with side-shows, including a puppet booth. The puppet-man produces three characters, a doll-like Ballerina, Petrouchka and his rival the Moor; the latter kills Petrouchka with his scimitar and the showman lets the horrified crowd see the sawdust falling on the snow. Petrouchka's ghost arises above the booth and the showman runs off.

Petrushka (Petrouchka). 'Little Peter': name of the traditional Russian folk-puppet character, relative of Punch; appeared at country fairs and in city courtyards from eighteenth century; adopted by post-revolutionary government in early propagandist programmes. In his book *My Profession*, Obraztsov, the Soviet puppetmaster (Director of the Central State Puppet Theatre, Moscow), tells of his meeting with the last of the Petrushka-men, Ivan Afinogenovich Zaitsev, who had some trick marionettes as well as hand puppets (now in the theatre's museum). Although there were many puppet theatres in the Soviet Union, ZAITSEV was the first puppeteer to receive the title Merited Artist. See also Petrouchka (Stravinsky).

Petrushka. Puppet ballet film, a B.B.C. School Television production (May, 1968), part of a series on 'Making Music'; production by John Hosier and Maddalena Fagandini, puppets designed and made by Alan Platt; stop-motion technique employed by Bob Bura and John Hardwick. *Guardian* critic expressed view that this was the most imaginative British use of puppets seen on television. (Screened in both black and white and colour.)

Phase puppets. Term related to the technique used in animated film production (STOP-MOTION); each camera shot is of one phase of a movement (one 'frame'). Projection of a sequence of frames at correct speed gives apparent motion on the screen.

Phillips, Jane. Welsh puppeteer, Director of the Caricature Theatre, Cardiff. Early interest in puppet club at Howell's School, Llandaff. Inspired to professional career in puppetry through Jan Bussell's book *The Puppets and I.* At 16 joined Cardiff Art School, then became apprentice for five years with The Hogarth Puppets. Free-lance for next five years in films, television, theatre, as puppeteer-actor, working with John Wright, Lotte Reiniger, Olive Blackham, Jan Bussell. Juvenile lead in '*The Water Babies*', large-scale marionette show at Lyric, Hammersmith. Acted in Torchy Films, pilot film of 'The Goon Show' and other T.V. puppet series. Joined B.P.M.T.G. 1959 and Editor of its magazine *The Puppet Master* in 1960, eventually changing the format and including many photographs. Influenced by Obraztsov and French puppeteer Marcel Temporal adopted rod puppets, returning to Wales 1962. Performances in Welsh for B.B.C. Welsh T.V., lecturer on Puppet Theatre at Cardiff College of Music and Drama. Became member of E.P.A. and UNIMA. Trained group of students for performance at first International Festival in Colwyn Bay, 1963. Full-time professional company 1965 commissioned by Commonwealth Arts Festival to present full-scale production of Welsh legend '*Culhwch and Olwen*'. In 1966 company established as non-profit distributing company registered as a Charity: The Caricature Theatre Ltd., and appointed Director.

Philpott, A. R. See PANTOPUCK THE PUPPETMAN.

Philpott, Violet M. English puppeteer, wife of present author; director of the Charivari Puppets; member of the British Section UNIMA committee and of the Council of the Educational Puppetry Association. Instructor at the Stanhope Evening Institute (adult education); Puppetry Instructor, Rose Bruford College of Speech and Drama. Demonstrator at Colleges, schools, clubs; frequent guest-artiste at London's only puppet theatre, 'The Little Angel' (Islington); participant at the international festivals in Colwyn Bay (1963 and 1968), Karlovy Vary (Czechoslovakia, 1964), Bucharest (Rumania, 1965); German tour following appearance at the annual 'Puppet Week' at Bochum (1963). Performances at the Arts Theatre, London, for the 'Unicorn' Children's Theatre Club (1968). Inveterate experimenter with all types of contemporary materials (polystyrene, plastic foam, etc.) and techniques. Responsible for large-scale productions at the E.P.A. Headquarters and the Stanhope, in group work with hand, rod, tubular-head puppets. Inimitable solo performer of original plays. Contributor of technical and other articles to the E.P.A. Journal Puppet Post and the B.P.M.T.G. Puppet Master. Expert photographer and re-touch artist.

Phonographic Performance Ltd., 62 Oxford Street, London, W.1. In operation since 1934 and controls the public performance of virtually all gramophone records manufactured today. Its membership includes all the leading record companies and its Constitution gives it power to authorise the use of their records in theatre, music halls, etc., and to collect fees on behalf of its members. The licence of the Phonographic Performance Ltd. is required wherever records subject to its control are used for overture, entr'acte, effects or background music during a production, or as part of any individual item in a programme, e.g. miming acts, puppet shows, etc. Licence tariffs available on application.

Phosphorescent Paint. Useful for stage ghost effects; invisible in ordinary daylight, glows in the dark. Obtainable from theatrical suppliers.

Piano act. Usually a marionette item, but the Moscow Central State Puppet Theatre has amusing rod-puppet version in its *Unusual Concert* programme. First introduced by Vittorio Podrecca with his Teatro dei Piccoli and thought to be a burlesque of the famous Russian pianist Vladimir de Pachmann (whose little eccentricities were just right for puppets). It soon became a stock item with every English marionette company, although synchronisation with recordings is rarely as effective as the unity achieved by Podrecca's live pianist and puppet. Tony Sarg and others in the U.S.A. and Professor Skupa in Czechoslovakia developed similar acts, in some cases the piano itself becoming a puppet (the logical outcome on a puppet stage).

Piccini, Signor. Italian puppet showman thought to have been 82 when he performed for an audience consisting of George Cruikshank (artist) and J. Payne Collier (writer) with the publisher Septimus Prowett, who had commissioned illustrations and text for the small book *Punch and Judy,* q.v. (1828), which had many editions, the earlier now being collectors' items. The showman was well known in the London streets and lived in 'a low public house', the King's Arms, in Coal Yard, Drury Lane; died in St Giles Workhouse, 1835. The performance was given indoors, a first floor window having to be removed to allow entry of the showman's booth. Collier's transcript of the play has been questioned by Speaight and others and is probably a composite effort based on various shows as well as being polished for its literary public. See also *London Labour and London Poor.*

Pickleherring. One of various food-names given to clown or buffoon types in Germany and the Netherlands, sixteenth-seventeenth centuries; chief character in a series of plays called 'Pickelhäringspiele' in Germany. English itinerant players sometimes included comedian 'Pickelhering'.

Picture-frame screen. Simple construction for shadow shows. Glass removed from ordinary picture-frame and replaced by translucent material – white sheeting, parchment, architect's tracing linen – stretched taut and fixed by drawing pins (thumb tacks). Frame can be mounted on pair of wooden feet to stand on table, fixed across a doorway or to portable posts. Proportions of frame governs scale of figures.

Pigments. Prepared colouring media, of earths, minerals or vegetable origin, varying in their nature, quality, affinity or otherwise with other colours, in their opacity or translucence, in their suitability for use on different surfaces (e.g. wood, plaster, metal). Books on art-techniques usually give some guidance – but only personal experience with actual colours of various types can give the ability to choose the right paint for each job. It is still possible to obtain the raw materials from oil-and-colour merchants and to mix these as did the classical artists, but for general purposes the ready-to-use paints in tubes and tins give economy in *time*. It is, however, best to ignore the names on the labels and to examine the actual colours. Also see PAINT and COLOUR.

Pigs. First mention of a pig in a puppet show seems to be that in *The Spectator*, q.v., 16th March, 1711, in a reference to Martin Powell's, q.v., performance in Covent Garden, q.v., in which he introduced a 'well disciplined' pig which danced a minuet with Punch. Anderson, in *Heroes of the Puppet Stage*, q.v., mentions a pig which could distinguish playing-cards and numbers and was named Toby! The Dalibor 'Pinky and Perky' piglets have had long television lives. The story of the *Three Little Pigs* who leave home to build themselves houses of (*a*) straw, (*b*) wood, (*c*) bricks, and get into trouble with the Big Bad Wolf, is a favourite with hand puppet performers.

Pike. English Punchman, originally an apprentice of the Italian PICCINI (whose show provided the basis for Payne Collier's *Punch and Judy*, with Cruikshank illustrations). Pike's show was held in high regard by the showman interviewed by Mayhew, as recorded in his *London Labour and London Poor* (1851) and who stated that Pike was the first to introduce a live dog Toby. A painting by Benjamin Robert Haydon (1828) with the title 'Punch, or May Day' (now in the Tate Gallery) shows Pike's booth with the inscription above the proscenium 'Pike, original Punchinello' and the audience near Mary-le-Bone Church.

Pilgrim's Progress, by John Bunyan (1628–88); earliest editions 1678–88, frequent new editions, e.g. Oxford University Press (1960) and in the Everyman Library series. The title continues 'from this World to that which is to Come,' the theme being allegorical and dealing with the life of a Christian in search of redemption and final attainment of eternal Paradise. Many of the characters with whom he has contact are abstractions, as in the MORALITY plays: Evangelist, Obstinate, Mr Worldly Wiseman, Sloth, Hypocrisy, Charity, etc.; the places too have names such as Vanity Fair, Plain of Ease, Doubting Castle, the Delectable Mountains. Among various puppet productions, and at extreme ends as to scale: that of the Toy Theatre version by the Goldsmith's College, q.v., London, and the version in Welsh (*Taith Y Pererin*) by the Caricature Theatre, q.v., Cardiff, commissioned by the Welsh National Theatre Company for the 1967 Royal National Eisteddfod held at Bala in North Wales, later toured in Welsh and English. The puppets for this production were large figures held by black-clad operators (similar to the Japanese Bunraku) with live hands as puppet hands.

Pin-hinges. Two-piece type used for joining sections of portable puppet-stage framework. Removable pin permits separation of sections for transport and storage and ease of handling. Pin tied to one section to avoid loss. Variation of the two-piece hinge is the 'reflex mirror hinge', one half lifting off a fixed pin; useful for small interchangeable stage doors.

Pinocchio (Avventure di Pinocchio: storia di un burattino), by C. Collodi (Carlo Lorenzini). Classic story for children, originally in serial form.

Theme: adventures of a puppet who comes to life. Author's pen-name taken from the village of Collodi, where there is a statue of Pinocchio in his honour. A special postage stamp issued in 1954. Many puppet companies have adapted the story, some using human actor as the wood-carver who creates the puppet. Disney's cartoon film modified the charac-ter, turning him into a 'well-meaning boy led astray by other characters'. English edition, *Pinocchio: the story of a puppet*, C. Collodi (Dent, London; Dutton, N.Y., 1911, and many reprints).

Pipe and Tabor. Two musical instruments (one Wind, one Percussion) played simultaneously by one performer; first known in twelfth century in Northern Spain and South of France, used as folk-dance accompani-ment; also used by itinerant performers of the MARIONNETTES À LA PLANCHETTE (as seen in old French prints) – but not consistently, some using a form of bagpipe. The pipe was of the three-hole type which could be held and played by one hand; the drum varied in size and shape, but was usually shallow in relation to diameter and was suspended either from the shoulder or the left arm, drumstick in right. References in English literature often have the spelling *tabour*. Whether a musician first invented the horizontal string control for the puppets – passing through their chests and attached at one end to a short post (usually fixed in a plank), the other end looped round one knee of the performer (leaving both hands free for music-making), is not known. The use of the hori-zontal string technique, with puppets on a table and operated by *two* performers (no musical instruments), one at each end of table, is seen in a twelfth century woodcut in the Codex of Herrad von Landsburg (reproduced in Baird *Art of the Puppet*). In the same volume is a two-page illustration, 'highly conjectural', from a nineteenth century engraving and showing a possible variation of the planchette figures as found in Roman ruins; one man operates four figures on the horizontal string, a second plays a double pipe. A further illustration (from a nineteenth century French lithograph) shows planchette operator (two figures) with bagpipe.

Pipe cleaners. Among the many everyday things that have unconven-tional use in puppet-making, e.g. fantastic hair or moustaches, antennae.

Pitch. Showman's term for the site on which to erect booth and perform; same sense as in 'cricket pitch' – performing area, and to 'pitch a tent' or erect it on chosen site.

Pito. Spanish term for 'swazzle', q.v.

Pivetta. Italian term for 'swazzle', q.v.

Plaster-bandage ('Pariscraft'). Tough thin gauze impregnated with Plaster of Paris, supplied in various widths, originally for surgical purposes. When wetted can be moulded to shape, setting hard in a few minutes. Has been used by some puppet-makers using the lamination process of building heads over plasticine models – but cheaper and superior variety for puppet work is ordinary gauze, bookbinding muslin, open-mesh bandage, impregnated with PLASTER 'FILLER' during the laminating (this having greater bonding quality). An initial layer of damp tissue paper over the plasticine simplifies removal of the cast and leaves model clean for re-shaping. See also ALABASTINE METHOD.

Plaster 'fillers.' Modern filling media for cracks and holes in walls or ceilings contain strong bonding agents. They are available under various trade names (Alabastine, Polyfilla, Templaster, etc.) in household size packets; are used by some puppet-makers for construction of hollow heads made over plasticine models and reinforced with open-mesh muslin. Unlike the traditional Plaster of Paris, which sets very quickly, the new media give ample working time and are extremely tough when set. SEE PREVIOUS ENTRY.

Plaster Moulds (Molds). The pottery-maker's technique adapted for casting of puppet heads or other parts. Model is first created in plasticine (or clay); the mould is made of PLASTER OF PARIS (obtained in powder form) mixed with water to a thick, creamy consistency, either applied directly over the model and built up to required thickness (varying with size of head), making half moulds separately, or can be made by pouring plaster around the head in a box or deep tray (half at a time). Thin metal or card 'dividers' can be pushed into the plasticine at the half-way line around the head. Plaster of Paris is quick-setting, the mould being removed when evaporation has completed the hardening process. The making of the final head is done inside the mould, which is first coated with vaseline or some other medium to ensure easy removal, and layers of paper and paste, muslin and paste, muslin and PLASTER 'FILLER', or plastic wood, built up, reproducing the features from the impression in the mould. Some makers use the mould process for creating individual heads; the process is particularly valuable where repeat heads required (as in mass-production).

Plaster of Paris. Partially dehydrated GYPSUM. Used in building industry and for making moulds for casting pottery or hollow puppet heads. Also used as a filler in the plastics industry. Mixed with water, sets rapidly.

Plastex; Pariscraft. Trade names in United States for PLASTER-BANDAGE, used by some puppetmakers, a development from its use in surgical casts. Plaster-impregnated gauze is dipped in water and built up over the clay or plasticine model, or inside a mould, requiring several layers; cut open and removed when set.

Plastic. Greek *plastikon*: moulded; any substance which can be shaped by modelling or moulding – wet clay, plasticine, dough.

Plastic foam (polyurethene). See FOAMED PLASTIC.

Plastic paint. Type suitable for use on rubber surfaces. When dry retains some of chemical and physical properties of the base ingredient, synthetic rubber or resin.

Plastic scenery. Three-dimensional as distinct from scenery painted on flat surfaces.

Plastic wood. Mixture of wood 'flour' and clear lacquer or varnish and containing a solvent; primarily used as a 'filler' for wood surfaces and supplied in tins and tubes. Highly inflammable. Used by some puppet-makers for heads and marionette parts, either by direct building up or by making over a plasticine model or inside a mould made from model. Shrinks during drying; modelling best done in thin layers. Addition of castor oil slows drying. When hard can be cut, filed, sand-papered, painted, and is extremely tough.

Plasticine (Plasticene, Plastilene). Modelling clay needing no water and remaining malleable during use and when stored; originally developed by William Harbutt, sculptor and teacher at the Bath School of Art; formula said to be secret and handed down by word of mouth. Widely used as modelling medium by professional artists and in schools and by many puppet-makers. Preliminary model is made on a MODELLING-

STAND (wooden base with central post about 8–10″ height), being gradually built up around the wooden core, detail added in form of small
pellets; or an over-size model can be made and then features produced
by cutting-away as in carving. If a cast is to be made by the 'direct'
method (i.e. without first making a mould), applying layers of paper and
paste, muslin and paste plastic wood, etc., over the actual model, a
preliminary layer of damp tissue paper serves as a parting agent ensuring
easy removal. If a MOULD is made from the plasticine model, a coat of
vaseline or other medium is applied. Plasticine adhering to the fingers
is removed by a rough, dry cloth; does not adhere if fingers are kept moist.
In World War I pilots used plasticine to plug bullet holes in planes.

Plasticizer. Substance, liquid or solid, added to a 'film' material such as
paint to give elasticity.

Plastics. In modern industry refers to various organic materials which,
under heat and pressure, can be caused to 'flow' and moulded into
desired shapes. Modern artists are exploring the possibilities in sculpture
and crafts, e.g. use of fibreglass reinforced resins. Standard book on
techniques: Newman *Plastics as an Art Form* (Pitman, 1965). Also see
NEW MATERIALS IN SCULPTURE, Percy (Tiranti, 1962).

Plastics as an Art Form, by Thelma R. Newman (Pitman, 1965). Monumental study of art possibilities with all types of plastics, profusely
illustrated; details and photographs of processes and artists at work;
detailed on chemical and technological aspects; extensive bibliography;
list of manufacturers and suppliers and trade names. Glossary.

Plato (*c.* 422–348 B.C.). Greek philosopher and prose writer. In his last
work *The Laws* (I.664) asks if human beings should not be regarded as
puppets of the gods, their playthings, or perhaps were created with some
other purpose.

Playbills. Posters advertising entertainments. Early examples are usually
in private collections or specialist museums and provide evidence of shows
of their period. The earliest known English playbill is an advertisement
for 'John Harris's Booth at Bartholomew Fair' – which mentions the
'merry humours of Punchinello' and says the figures are as large as two-
year-old children. The original is preserved in the Harvard Library
Theatre Collection and has been reproduced in several puppet books,
e.g. Speaight *History of the English Puppet Theatre* (Harrap, 1955), who
gives the date as '*c.* 1700', and Baird *Art of the Puppet* (Collier-Macmillan,
1965), who places it 'before 1660'.

Playboard. Shelf running across top front edge of hand puppet booth and
on which stage props may be placed; Punch uses it as a seat and it is used
as a support for the hangman's GALLOWS. If shelf projects it may spoil
sight-line for low-seated audience close to stage, when puppets retreat
from front line. A modern variation is the optional playboard, or interchangeable sections of shelf, designed for the technical requirements of
different productions: e.g. a sea-scene, with cut-out waves, requiring
maximum room for manoeuvring boat, has shelf removed (it is held in
normal position by two short projections of plywood fitting into slots
under the top cross-rail). With the detachable shelf it is possible to fit
SLIDING-SLOT devices on vertical rails connecting top and middle cross-
rails, by which flat scenery (tree, bed) can be raised or lowered. With the
playboard (or section) fixed along the *inside* of the framework, parts can
be cut away for 'trick' items, e.g. a jack-in-the-box, the puppet actually

popping up through the hole in the shelf matching the hole in the bottom of the box (and box clipped to shelf). To maintain the rigidity of the framework large plywood triangles are bolted at top front corners, also serving as shelves.

Playing with Punch, by Frank Baker (Boardman, 1944). Includes a new play and the Payne COLLIER transcription of the Punch and Judy play; a 'fantastic essay' on Mr Punch's theatre; an account of a trip in Scotland and the Orcades, and some historical notes. Illustrated by drawings.

Plays for Marionettes, by Maurice Sand; English translation by B. & E. Hughes (French, 1931). SAND used, and his mother expressed preference for, *hand* puppets. The original French 'marionnettes' should be translated 'puppets' and is the generic term; the French distinguish technical differences by adding '. . . à fils' (strings, marionettes in the English sense) or '. . . à gaine' (hand type). Titles include: *Rose-Queen of Vire-mollet* (a satire on municipal councils and beauty contests), *The Flageolet*, and *The Clemency of Titus* (a parody on classic plays).

Plays for puppets. No international survey has yet been made of plays performed, although this would be a possibility in view of the existence of an international puppetry organisation (UNIMA) with many National Sections. Speaight *History of the English Puppet Theatre* (Harrap, 1955) and McPharlin *Puppet Theatre in America: A History: 1524 to Now* (Harper, N.Y., 1949): both performed remarkable feats of scholarship in tracking down performances of the past and listing these. An analysis of these and of other material such as contemporary posters, programmes, news-clippings, published plays, can only lead to a cautious approximation as to the 'top ten' – and of course leaves out of account the traditional plays in European countries and the East; for instance, a perusal of the repertoires of a number of French puppet theatres listed in Gervais *Marionnettes et marionnettistes de France* (Bordas, 1947) shows a preponderance of plays which include the character Guignol (even if the title indicates *Robinson Crusoe*, *Blue Beard*, or other item among the favourites in Britain and America). In Germany there is a similar situation, with the character Kasper (Kasperle) appearing in countless hand puppet plays. In Sicily the plays are traditional, often in serial form lasting months, and concern the adventures of Christian knights and Infidels in the days of Chivalry. In India and Indonesia the two epics *Mahabharata* and *Ramayana* dominate. Although countries such as Germany, France and Czechoslovakia have a large number of published plays, for technical and other reasons puppet theatres or companies usually do their own adapting of the chosen source-material (fairy or folk tales, legends, etc.). The Faust story has been in the repertoire of most large companies at some time or other, and might easily top the poll for Europe and America – has even been played in Japan (a country with its own puppet 'Shakespeare' – see Chikamatsu Monzaemon). Usually all that exists of medieval plays are the titles, mostly derived from the Bible and reflecting the 'Mystery' and 'Morality' plays (and with Punchinello or one of his derivatives intruding and gradually becoming dominant). There is in fact a close parallel between the favourites of the live theatre and the puppet theatre in the late nineteenth and twentieth century material, the same sources of material for pantomimes and puppet plays. Numerically, because there have always been more Punch and Judy shows than other forms of puppetry, in Britain and America, these would probably head the list. A complete survey of amateur productions would probably confirm that of the professional, giving the following (very approximate order, based on all material examined): *Aladdin and his Magic* (or *Wonderful*) *Lamp*; *Hansel and Gretel*; *Cinderella*; *Jack and the Beanstalk*; *Red Riding Hood*; *Sleeping Beauty*; *Snow White*; *Rumpelstiltskin*; *Ali Baba and the* 40 *Thieves*; *Beauty and the Beast*; *The Three Wishes*; followed by *Alice in Wonderland, Little Black Sambo, Peter Rabbit, Pinocchio, Puss in Boots, Rip van Winkle, The Three Bears, Treasure Island* – and a number of these reappear in European repertoires. Whether the choice is mainly that of the puppeteers or of their audiences, and what the varying qualities of the productions have been like, can hardly be estimated. Hundreds of other items, including some from Shakespeare and other live theatre playwrights have been adapted for the puppet stage – but ideally plays for puppets should be written with particular types of puppet in mind. Relatively few in English have been published; even less are strictly 'original' items.

Plays for Puppets, edited by Jan Bussell (Faber, 1951), includes *The Surprising Story of Alfred, Warder of the Tower*, by L. du Garde Peach; *The Four Little Goats*, by Jan Grabowski; *The Brigands of the Black Forest*, by (anon.) traditional French; *The Cat and the Kingdom*, by Dorothea Bussell; *The Strolling Clerk from Paradise*, by Hans Sachs; *Fly-by-Night*, by Jan Bussell and Edith Lanchester; and *Three Wishes*, by T. Maynard Parker. Introduction and production notes with each play.

Plays for Puppets, Marionettes and Shadows: Producer's Guide to, by Paul McPharlin (Puppetry Handbooks No. 3, 1932); an annotated list of about 100 items.

Plays (Twelve) for Puppets, by Jan Bussell (Pelham, 1964). Plays written specifically for Pelham Marionettes; characters recognisable in the Ruth Granger illustrations.

Plays for shadow shows. The technical possibilities with the two-dimensional screen and black-and-white or coloured figures illuminated from the rear influence the choice of material for productions. In the traditional shows of the East the themes are derived from religious sources, legends, history – and demand special training of the performers. Once the technical scope of this form has been explored then various literary sources can be considered; a wide range is indicated in Blackham *Shadow Puppets* (Barrie and Rockliff, 1960), Appendix 1, with sections on Fables, Animal Stories, Poetry, Folk Songs, Humorous Verse, Cautionary Verses, Nonsense, Myths, Legends, Folk and Fairy Tales – and miscellaneous items which might at first thought seem to offer no hope. There is also a reminder about the protection of authors' works by the Copyright Law.

Plays without People, by Peter Arnott (Indiana University Press, 1964). A study of puppetry as serious drama, especially as possible in Colleges. Discusses all aspects of production (*Faust*, etc.).

Play-writing. The great playwright George Bernard Shaw said that those who *can, do*; those that *can't, teach*. It is certainly true in the realm of writing for the puppet theatre; far more adapting is done than original writing. To write for the puppet theatre the playwright must first have a close acquaintance with puppets, even with a particular type of puppet, and possibly for a particular puppet theatre company. What little response there has been for the 'poets' to come forward and use their talents on behalf of the puppets has been defeated because the poets have not first studied the possibilities of the puppets and their technical requirements. A few outstanding solo artistes make their own puppet characters and their plays as part of a unified process, and then do their own performing. This is not possible when it comes to large-scale group work – although, ideally, if a theatre can have its own resident play-wright, or several who are prepared to work closely with the company, then the development of the play can be checked as to technicalities during the writing. A musician must know the scope of the instruments he is to write for, even if he cannot play all of them himself. There can be no recipe for writing a successful play; no school of playwriting can give its students the vital ingredient needed for original work. Working in with puppeteers the playwright can see his characters materialise in a way rarely possible in the human theatre, as the puppets are made precisely for their particular roles, although there is still the problem of finding actor-manipulators who will identify with those characters. The Lanchesters created marionettes of Shaw himself and Shakespeare and then requested a play in which these could be used; result, *Shakes versus Shav*, a slapstick farce with a leaven of Shavian wit. This approach is sometimes followed in educational puppetry – individual children or older students first creating puppet characters (with no pre-conceived relationships) and then going the 'so many characters in search of a play' route, often with surprisingly interesting results. This way ensures that everyone is thinking in terms of actual puppet characters – not of human characters who may or may not adapt successfully for the puppet stage. Discussions take place at the international level about puppet 'drama-turgy' – i.e. the creating of a repertoire specifically for the puppet theatre and related to particular age-groups of audiences. Jean-Loup Temporal, a lively contemporary French puppeteer, in an article included in *Puppet Theatre Around the World* (New Delhi, 1960), said the word did not exist in his language – and proceeded to discuss his own work and experiments and conclusions in the hope that these would contribute towards 'a more precise definition of the common laws which could provide the basis on which to elaborate a dramaturgy for contemporary puppet theatres'. Those 'common laws' can, in fact, only be discovered experimentally or by a constant study of puppets in action – puppets of a particular type (technically). So many things are possible on the puppet stage which are beyond the scope of the human theatre. What human actor dressed up can be as effective an animal character as a puppet made for the part? How can *objects* come to life, in a fantasy, except in the puppet theatre? The hand puppet, the rod type, the marionette, the shadow figures, each have their own range of possibilities – and their limits. 'Rules' can only be related to what the particular types of puppet, and even the individual puppet, *can* do. The playwright for puppets must think in terms of puppets from the start.

Plumb line. A builder's device for testing accuracy of vertical surfaces or lines, consisting of a length of twine and an attached weight. Useful also for basic experiments in marionette control, varying the length of string and weight and studying its movements when induced by finger, hand or arm movements. Children will see immediate possibilities and begin adding features (wire, legs, feathers, etc.) and so begin creating fantastic characters.

Plumber's tow. Fibre obtained from flax or hemp, supplied in large hanks. Natural colour light straw, easily dyed. Useful for theatrical wigs

N

or puppet hair. Obtainable from rope and canvas dealers, ironmongers, theatrical suppliers.

Plywood. Thin sheets of wood (veneers) bonded together with grain running at right-angles to neighbouring layer (three or more, sometimes of equal thickness, sometimes with a thicker middle layer); various woods are used and sometimes special facings. Heavy types specially bonded to resist moisture are used in the building industry. Apart from the more obvious uses such as stage and scenery construction, plywood has been tried for large cut-out shadow figures. Shapes are cut with fretsaw or jigsaw, but the $\frac{3}{16}$ in. variety can be cut with a craft knife and steel straight-edge if straight cuts required; e.g. corner pieces for right-angled framework construction are first cut in squares or rectangles of required size (4 – 6 in.) and then cut diagonally, cutting the *two* outside layers, snapping the middle layer. These are nailed and glued to the rails, giving completely rigid corners.

Pocci, Count Frank Graf (1807–76). German author of children's stories and 46 comedies for 'Papa Schmid's' Puppet Theatre in Munich, over 30 of which are in the Salzburg Marionette Theatre repertoire. Some items translated into other languages; English version of *Casper among the Savages* included in McPharlin *Repertory of Marionette Plays*.

Pod, Captain. English puppet-show proprietor who first exhibited in 1599; references in Jonson *Every Man out of His Humour* (1600): 'Rather let him be Captaine Pod and this his Motion . . .' and Johnson *Bartholomew Fayre* (1614), Act 5, sc. 1: ' O the Motions that I, Lanthorne Leatherhead, have given light to, in my time, since my Master Pod died', and Jonson *Epigrammes* (No. 97): 'See you yond' Motion? Not the old Fa-ding, nor Captayne Pod, nor yet the Eltham thing, But one more rare, and in the case so new.'

Podrecca, Dr Vittorio (1883–1959). Italian puppeteer, founder-director of world-famous theatre, the Teatro dei Piccoli of Rome. Member of UNIMA since 1929, Member of Honour (in Memoriam), 1960. Bernard Shaw wrote to him expressing his regard for puppets; letter reproduced in von Boehn *Dolls and Puppets*, q.v.

Poe, Edgar Allan (1809–49). American poet and writer of stories of the supernatural, some of which have supplied themes for puppet productions, e.g. *The Gold Bug, The Mummy, The Masque of the Red Death*. His *Tales of Mystery and Imagination* (45 stories) available in 'Everyman' Edition (Dent).

Poesjenellenkelder ('Puppets of the cellar'). Puppet theatre in cellar, St Nicholas Plaats, Antwerp, Belgium; performances occasionally given with folk puppets operated by iron rods. Photo-illustrations showing auditorium, stage, back-stage and performance in *Puppetry* (Year Book of the Puppeteers of America, 1946–47).

Poetry Bookshop. Established 1913 in Devonshire Street, Theobalds Road, London, W.C.1, by Harold Monro (1879–1932), founder of the *Poetry Review*. Poets, e.g. Edith Sitwell, reading their own works became one of the attractions and the early meetings of the British Puppet and Model Theatre Guild, q.v., were also held there, with performances by those who achieved eminence in the profession, such as 'Whanny' (H. W. Whanslaw, q.v.) and Waldo Lanchester, q.v.

Poland. Illustrated magazine with occasional interesting articles on puppet theatre developments. Published in Polish, English, French, German,

Spanish, Swedish; issued by the Polish Interpress Agency, Warsaw. Individual copies in English, or subscriptions: B. Swiderski, 6 Warwick Road, London, S.W.5, and from some newsagents. American edition: Select Magazines Inc., 223 Park Avenue South, New York 3, NY. 10003.

Poldini, Eduard (1869–1957). Italian-Hungarian composer of operas and fairy-tale pieces for children; best known for piano pieces such as *Arlequinades, Poupée Valsante, Marionettes* (also orchestra version).

Polichinelle. Name of French puppet character derived from Italian *pulcinella* (Neapolitan *polecenella*), introduced to Parisian audiences about 1630 by Jean Brioché or Briocci, gradually acquiring French temperament and appearing in a great many plays as the main character, together with equivalents of the Beadle, Hangman, Devil, in the English Punch and Judy play; although normally unmarried, becomes involved with a Mère Gigogne in one episode, her dowry being an incredible number of children. Like Punch, originally a marionette, at some time became a hand puppet (giving more effective use of the baton or stick). An illustration in Maindron *Marionnettes et Guignols* (1900), reproduced from *Magasin pittoresque* (1834), shows a marionette type with a short head-rod to the top of which are attached strings controlling the limbs. Illustrations in Baird *Art of the Puppet* (1965) in colour show: (*a*) a hand-puppet booth with Polichinelle using his stick, two victims, a devil, a live cat (caption says 'dog'); (*b*) a Polichinelle *pantin* (coloured paper cut-out parts for assembling; (*c*) an example with large wooden head supported by internal rod. Costume varies but each has variant of the tricorne (three cornered) hat, a hump on the back, a paunch; the rod figure has legs. Duranty, playwright turned showman, performed Polichinelle plays of a rather literary nature, later published in *Théâtre des Marionnettes du Jardin des Tuileries* (1863). A new character, Guignol, first introduced in Lyon by Laurent Mourguet, eventually displaced Polichinelle, to the extent that the popular term for hand puppets in France is 'guignols'.

Political puppets. In his small book on *Puppetry in Czechoslovakia* (Orbis, 1948), DR JAN MALIK mentions a plaque placed in the lobby of the Citizens' Assembly Rooms in Pilzen in 1928 to the puppet hero Kašparek for his part in pre-revolutionary cabarets – and which was removed by the Nazis, later replaced and tells how Kašparek 'helped to demolish the Austro-Hungarian Empire'. In 1966 the ban-the-bomb brigade (CND) marched to Trafalgar Square, which became a vast auditorium for 18-ft. tall puppet characters representing Mr Harold Wilson, Mr Lyndon Johnson and the Rhodesian 'rebel', Mr Ian Smith. The 'play' was amusingly satirical; the puppets designed by *Private Eye* cartoonist Gerald Scarfe (flat cut-outs with moving eyes and mouths, built by art students). Mock *Pinky and Perky* (T.V. piglets) were presented to Mr Wilson, who was finally daubed with red paint and set on fire. The weekly political series on Anglia T.V. *Under the Clock* was introduced by appearances of puppet personalities created by Polish sculptor Stefan Baran (in fibreglass), including Harold Wilson, Quintin Hogg, Jo Grimond, Barbara Castle and others, with a background of the Houses of Parliament. Another Baran item has satirical figures of de Gaulle, Khrushchev and other international figures (shown at a Society of Portrait Sculptors exhibition, London, 1964). *The Bread and Puppet Theatre* of New York was described by Irving Wardle (of *The Times*) as 'the most political of all the off-off Broadway groups'. It has its own press and prints pamphlets about napalm and so on, some of its street puppets being up to 30-ft. tall, requiring three operators with poles. Political satire has been one of the sources of Greek Kharagiosis (shadow plays) and some scenes are reproduced in Beaumont *Puppets and Puppetry* (1958) from a play celebrating the liberation of Greece from Axis domination – and Satan's reception of Hitler and Mussolini.

Pollock's. Name synonymous with Toy Theatres or Juvenile Drama. The business still trading under this name was founded by Benjamin Pollock (1856–1937), who was the last of the publishers of the sheets of characters for the miniature theatres popular in Regency and Victorian days. The original shop was in Hoxton Street, London, was damaged during the air-raids of World War II, continued for a time in the hands of his daughters (until 1944), was taken over by a company of toy-theatre enthusiasts and re-opened in John Adam Street, Adelphi, W.C.2 – and now has premises at 44 Monmouth Street, W.C.2 (proprietor, Mrs Fawdrey). In addition to the 'PENNY PLAIN, TWOPENCE COLOURED' sheets (about which ROBERT LOUIS STEVENSON wrote so delightfully) there are new stages and plays, puppets, pantins, toys and seasonal material at Christmas and Easter. A small but intriguing Museum fills several rooms and is worth a visit by nostalgic adults and historians with or without children.

Pollock's Toy Museum. Part of the premises occupied by Pollock's Toy Theatre shop, proprietor Mrs Fawdrey, at 44 Monmouth Street, London, W.C.1; permanent exhibition of miniature stages and original sheets by West, Green, Redington, and stage sets for Juvenile Drama; also toys, games, dolls, dolls'-houses, gollywog books, magic lanterns and coloured slides, 3-D peepshows. Shop has constantly changing array of purchaseable items.

Polly. Female character sometimes introduced into the nineteenth century Punch and Judy show – usually when Judy has been disposed of – to cater for Punch's amorous proclivity. In the Payne Collier text from PICCINI's performance (*Punch and Judy*, Prowett, 1828) Punch sings from Gay's *Beggars' Opera* and dances with the mute Polly; there was a Polly in Gay's opera. Collier quotes another version in which Polly has some dialogue with Punch. There is a reference to 'Punch and Polly and puppie-shows' in Moir *The Life of Mansie Wauch* (1828) – 'puppie' being a Scottish variant of 'puppet'. Polly is also the standard name for puppet Parrots in various contemporary hand-puppet shows.

Polymer. Substance formed by joining simple molecules to form larger. Process used in plastics manufacture.

Polymer colour. Twentieth century development, emulsion based paint; can be used direct on unprimed semi-absorbent surfaces such as paper, card, hardboard, plaster, plywood, or fine-woven fabrics; fast drying; opaque and non-fading and optional flat or gloss finish; thinned with water or special medium; brushes easily cleaned. Range of intermixable colours in see-through tubes. Particularly valuable when speed is important.

Polystyrene. Lightweight white thermoplastic produced by polymerisation of styrene, familiar in form of ceiling tiles, display material, packaging. 'Self-extinguishing' variety may be cut and shaped by the 'hot wire' method or by heat-gun – or improvised tools used with gas ring. Available in large blocks which can be cut with saw, sculpted by heat method or craft-knife and rasp. Surface can be toughened by one or more layers of torn brown paper and thin, hot glue or by a layer of 'Celastic' (plastic impregnated cloth). Some quick-stick adhesives have a solvent effect on polystyrene and should be tested. Resin-based paint suitable for direct painting; emulsion can be applied over paper surface or 'Celastic'. Some suppliers (e.g. Shell Chemicals) have pellets and expandable beads for shaping by mould process. Various trade-names such as 'Styrofoam' and 'Mardel'. Consult trade directory for addresses.

Polystyrene resin. Clear, colourless, thermoplastic moulding substance made by polymerisation of styrene.

Popet. Given by Samuel Johnson (*Dictionary of the English Language*, 1827) as the former spelling for 'puppet' and giving as example 'This were a popet in an arme . . .' from Chaucer *Prologue to Sir Thopas*. His definition: 'A small image moved by a wire in a mock drama.' In the early usage it is essential to study the context, as reference could be to a 'doll' and sometimes used metaphorically.

Poppentheatre 'Hopla'. Puppet theatre in Mechelen, Belgium, directed by Louis Contryn; repertoire includes de Falla *Master Peter's Puppet Show*.

Poppet. Early English standard term for 'doll'. Contemporary use: term of affection – and a form of confectionery.

Popular Entertainments through the Ages, by Samuel McKechnie (Sampson Low, 1931; Stokes, N.Y., 1932); on the history and development of various forms of entertainment, illustrated from old prints. Chapter on *Punch and Judy*, and the Payne Collier text of the play. Reproduction of Robert Austin's *The Puppet Master* (from *Masters of Etching* No. 25) with a showman retouching the paint on a group of figures (with head and hand wires). Account of various Fairs.

Portable theatre. Portable *auditorium* (as distinct from portable stage). *See* PALMER, Ray DaSilva.

Postage Stamps. As yet, Britain has not issued a stamp with Mr Punch as the motif. The following list of foreign stamps has been compiled by T. E. Howard (Committee member of the British Section of UNIMA) from actual specimens and checked against *Gibbons Simplified Whole World Stamp Catalogue* (1968 edition). *Czechoslovakia*: 1959, 10th Anniversary of Young Pioneers' Movement. Series of four designs showing activities of the Movement. The 30 haleru value is described as 'Girl with Doll', but both the appearance of the figure and the way it is being held indicate it is a puppet; colours violet-blue and yellow. 1961 'Czech Puppets': 30 haleru 'Manasek Doll' (red and yellow) 40 h. 'Dr Faustus and Caspar' (sepia and turquoise) 60 h. 'Spejbl and Hurvinek' (ultra-marine and salmon) 1 koruna: Scene from 'Difficulties with the Moon': Askenazy (green and blue) 1 k. 60 h. 'Janasek' of Brno (red and blue). *Italy*: 1954, 'Carlo Collodi' (author) Commemorative: 25 lira, 'Pinocchio' (red). *Java (Netherlands Indies)*, 1943, Japanese Occupation of Netherlands Indies, a pictorial series, includes: 5 sen 'Wayang Puppet' (green). *Rumania*, 1960, 'International Puppet Theatre Festival, Bucharest': multi-coloured designs show puppets: 20 bani 'Globe and flags in form of Puppet': 40 b. 'Petrushka'; 55 'Punch': 1 leu 'Kaspar': 1 leu 20 b. 'Tandarica'; 1 leu 75 b. 'Vasilache'. *Turkey*, 1967, 'International Tourist Year': multi-coloured. Series of four, two of which are puppets: 50 kurus 'Karagoz and Hacivat' (puppets), 100 k. 'Karagoz' (puppet). Item contributed by W. C. Meaocck, member of the above-mentioned Com-

mittee: *Japan*, 1966: multi-coloured designs, 15 yen 'National Theatre':
25 yen 'Kabuki': 50 yen 'Bunraku'.

Potheinos. Earliest named European puppeteer, in Athenaeus *Deipnoso-phists*, I.i.19.E (*c.* 230 A.D.), about whose puppets there has been much conjecture; was allowed to perform on Athenian stage previously used for the plays of Euripides. GORDON CRAIG, in an article in *The Mask* (Vol. 2, Nos. 4–6) suggests puppets were life size or larger, because of the size of the theatre. Speaight (in *History of the English Puppet Theatre*: Harrap, 1955) thinks the theatre must have been that of Dionysus, but that it would be a mistake to think this evidence of any high regard for puppets. Baird (in *The Art of the Puppet* Collier-Macmillan, 1965) thinks the puppets were probably of the type used in Sicily, large figures whose main control is an iron rod to the head, operated from above (reflected in the jointed figurines found in ancient tombs). Note: Potheinos Ltd., company owning the 'Little Angel' Theatre (John Wright's marionettes) in Islington, London.

Poupée à fil. Alternative term (French) for 'marionnette à fils', 'puppet with strings'; used by Paul-Louis Mignon in *J'aime les Marionnettes* (1962); less confusing for the English reader. See remarks under MARIONNETTE.

Poupées de Paris. Spectacle at Seattle World's Fair, 1962; production by Sid and Marty Krofft, modelled on Paris Lido revues and Folies Bergere; puppets 3-ft. tall: seven male (wooden) and 131 female (rubber-and-plastic); Balmain costumes; star characters represented Mae West, Charles Boyer and Liberace, with recordings; a swimming pool, fireworks, rain; Grand Guignol touches in giant Bat attacking a 'stripper'. Seen by 50,000 spectators in six months.

Powder puppets. No extant description of construction – possibly 'pyrotechnic' (mechanically operated by gunpowder); Obraztsov, in his *Chinese Puppet Theatre*, q.v., says mentioned by Chinese historian Sun Kai-Ti.

Powell, Martin (flourished 1710–29). English (possibly Welsh) showman, most celebrated puppeteer of his day, performing first at Bath and then in London (St Martin's Lane and Covent Garden); there is a good deal about him in the *Tatler*, q.v., and the *Spectator*, q.v., including a letter purporting to be from the Sexton of St Paul's Church (Covent Garden) complaining of the loss of congregation (and collection?) due to timing of the puppet show by the church bell. Presented mock-operas in competition with the Italians at the Haymarket. Extensive repertoire, including *The Children in the Wood, Dr Faustus, Friar Bacon and Friar Bungay, Robin Hood and Little John, Mother Shipton, Mother Goose*, and seems to have helped establish the Punch show in its later form (one item included a 'tuneful warbling pig of Italian race' which danced with Punch). The frontispiece to *A Second Tale of a Tub, or the History of Robert Powel the Puppet-show-man* (1715), q.v., shows a marionette stage with Punch and (presumably) Judy (or 'Joan'), perspective scenery and footlights, and a dwarfish hunchback showman standing in front holding a wand; as the object of the satire in this pamphlet was *Robert* Harley, Earl of Oxford, it is probable that it is the latter's head on Powell's body. Both Magnin (*Histoire des marionnettes en Europe*, 1852) and Speaight (*History of the English Puppet Theatre*, 1955) devote a considerable amount of space to this showman, who must have had several assistants.

Press, Percy. England's 'uncrowned king of the Punch and Judy showmen'; Vice-President of the British Puppet and Model Theatre Guild;
member of the International Brotherhood of Magicians (British Ring
No. 25); member of the Inner Magic Circle (with Gold Star); Hon.
Member and Past President of the Home Counties Magical Society.
Hon. Member: London Sketch Club; member of Equity/VAF and the
Concert Artistes' Association. At school, top for Art and Elocution and,
according to Form Master, born 'to be a clown'. Advised by doctor to
seek an outdoor job when health affected by Mezzotint Engraving colour-
mixing. Early experience in Music Hall sketches and Variety. Developed
conjuring act from tricks learned during schooldays from a penny book
on Magic. Formed partnership with comedian (Carlyle and 'Robinson')
playing Working Men's Clubs and Smoking Concerts. Experience in
'busking' between engagements; first summer season as al-fresco magician
at Exmouth (1921). Bought a ventriloquial doll for 7/6 ('my first introduction to puppetry'); influenced by Punch showman Sam Bridges,
met at children's parties, and by a window display of Nancy Henry glove
puppets; and became a dedicated Punch and Judy showman. First
performance lasted five minutes – not having mastered the use of the
'swazzle' for Punch's voice. Shows at Exeter during the Easter Fair, with
a Market Grafter friend to do the 'bottling' (collecting) more successful.
Joined the 'Guild' during its period at the famous 'George Inn' in Southwark. In 1935 a 17-weeks' engagement at Swanage with five or six shows
a day gave the necessary experience and mastery of the 'call' (swazzle).
Various summer seasons preceded engagement with E.N.S.A. in 1940
– with Mr Punch in Battle Dress, Judy in NAAFI costume, Clown as Army
Cook, Beadle as the 'Red Cap' – and the Hangman became Hitler.
Shows everywhere to all branches of services and civil defence, in Music
Halls and as speciality turn in Pantomimes. In post-war period returned
to seaside seasons, becoming established at Hastings from 1948. Prestige
engagement during the Festival of Britain, 1951, with highly successful
shows in the Festival Gardens, Battersea Park (joined by the late Bruce
MacLoud). Post-war Winter engagements mainly at private parties,
from Royalty downwards and annual visits to the Mansion House for the
Lord Mayor of London Children's Party. December, 1955, beginning of
annual seasons at Madam Tussaud's – proving a great additional
attraction to the Waxworks and the Planetarium. Other activities include
Broadcasting: Punch in 'In Town Tonight' (1935) and war-time broad-
casts with Bebe Daniels, Jack Warner, Air-Raid Shelters with the late
Ed Morrow direct to America, etc. Television appearances for B.B.C.,
I.T.A., America C.B.S., French T.V. and German T.V. Extracts of
Punch included in Feature and Documentary Films, including *Oliver*
(Romulus Films). Two sons, Percy Junior and Leslie, both highly
experienced Punch operators.

Press fasteners. Two-piece metal fasteners used on garments, also available attached to tape (by the yard) and can be used for removable wigs
on puppets, one piece of tape glued to head, one inside wig. A larger type
can be used for removable curtaining on portable puppet stages, a series
of fasteners being arranged around the top edge of the framework,
matching series along top edge of material.

Preventive puppetry. Term covering plays with (*a*) 'Safety First' themes;
(*b*) dental themes: prevention of decay and toothache; (*c*) immunisation
themes, diphtheria and polio; also plays for maladjusted children to pre-

vent neuro-psychosis in adult life. Welsh specialist, R. A. Hoey, M.R.C.S., L.R.C.P., used puppets extensively (plays having titles such as *The Iron Lung*) and published articles in Health Education journals; convinced that puppets the best medium in work with pre-school-age children. English Keith-Blair Puppets perform regularly for local authorities, including Road Safety and Safety in the Home items. Jytte Abildstrom, in Denmark, has an item *Karius and Baktus* with an amusing dental-decay theme. Various hygiene campaigns helped by puppets in Australia, India, Mexico.

Priestley, J. (John) B. (Boynton). Notable English writer. In the *New Statesman* (1st April, 1966) said: 'Now I come to think of it, the happiest men I have met, belonging to several different countries, ran marionette or puppet theatres'. Wrote a play for the model theatre (modern Pollock's), *The Old Toby*, with sketches of characters and scenery by famous theatrical designer Doris Zinkeisen.

Primary colours. In theatrical lighting these are *blue, green, red*; those of pigment colours are *blue, yellow, red*.

Primer, or priming. The first coat of paint applied to a surface as preparation for subsequent coats.

Proctor, Romain (1899–1961). Eminent American puppeteer; one-time President of the Puppeteers of America organisation and Vice-President of UNIMA, the international organisation. Had great affection for London and was saddened when the red buses vanished from the streets on the occasion of a strike.

Producer. Stage director in charge of rehearsals of play, lighting plan, decor. English and American usage as to function varies; in the States the 'producer' is concerned with finance and general management; the 'producer' (English variety) is the 'director'. Confusing in theatrical literature.

Professional. One who earns an income from career as performer and/or creative artist or technician, as distinct from the amateur who devotes himself without concern for monetary reward. Secondary meaning: the quality of a performance by one who has mastered the art and which may apply to either professional or amateur: a critic may refer to the work of some professionals as 'amateurish'. Most professionals begin as amateurs. Theoretically, it might seem that the professional devoting his whole time to the art should reach a higher standard than the amateur; in practice many professionals lament the fact that they are too busy earning a livelihood to be able to experiment and develop as freely as the amateur (this refers to the self-employed professional; see below). There are differences of inherent talent both among professionals and amateurs. Professionals actually fall into one of two categories: (1) State employed, (2) self-employed. (1) applies only to those countries in which culture and entertainment are the concern of Government Departments; initial training may also be provided, grant-aided students attending a special school for intending puppeteers, e.g. as in Prague, Czechoslovakia, which has a four-year Course covering all aspects, with eventual specialisation as performer, creator, technician, director or producer, playwright. Training may be at a school attached to a particular puppet theatre, as in Moscow. Successful students have an assured full-time employment with a theatre, a mobile-group, or in a television studio or film-making centre. Future development of the personnel is then the concern of the

Harlequin: marionette designed and made by Jan Bussell

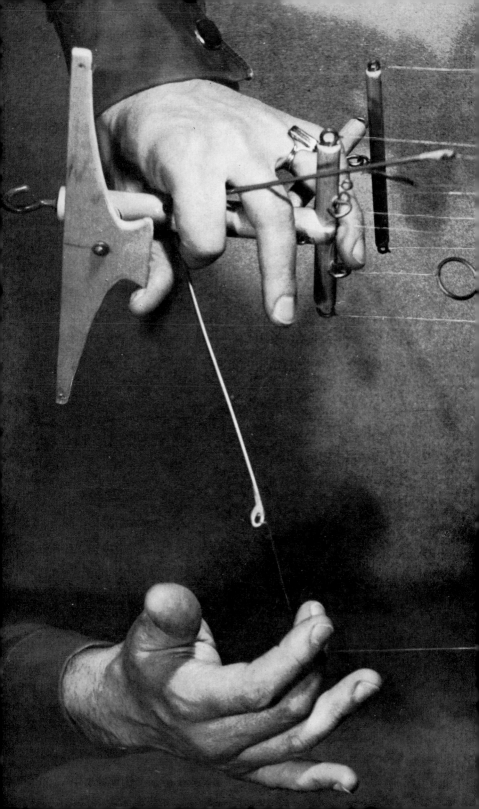

Opposite: Marionette control (with rocking leg-bar) demonstrated by Derek Francis
Above: Hero and Leander from *Bartholomew Fair*. Rod puppets carved by John Wright
Overleaf: Dougal and Florence, stop-motion puppets for the B.B.C. Television
production of *The Magic Roundabout*

Director. (2) In countries where a career in puppetry is a matter of self-employment or working for an established company – large or small – the only guarantee of earning capacity is by the law of supply and demand – the quality of the work has to create the demand; a good agent can also help. (1) it is an established fact that in most State-controlled theatres the annual number of spectators runs into millions, comparing perhaps with the millions who see occasional puppet items on television elsewhere. The theatres are to that extent self-supporting. (2) Professional engagements may be given by local Municipal authorities, e.g. the seasonal shows in London Parks (August) often free to audiences of children, box-office for special shows for adults, with around 200 performances in the season, approximately 50% Punch and Judy shows and the balance divided between five or six small companies. Puppet shows are also a familiar attraction at many English seaside resorts, Punch shows on the beaches, companies in theatres. Engagements are sometimes put out to Tender, and this may be a gamble from the performers' point of view: small audiences, small takings. Engagements may also be obtained from local Arts Councils, Arts Societies, or from local education authorities for shows in schools and children's libraries. Fees vary enormously: the authority may have its fixed terms, or the fee *may* be related to the reputation of the individual or group, the size of the group, the distance to be travelled, the length of the performance, or to a flat rate for a series of performances. Another field (rare in the State-controlled countries) is the private performance in the home, in the clubs, Sunday Schools and so on. Here also the fee may be relative to reputation, etc. A factor which enters into self-employment considerations is that of time and money required for preparation of shows, possibly cost of special workshop premises, maintenance of a van, etc. (3) Another category is that of the 'semi-pro' – the part-time puppeteer who has another main profession as source of income. The full-timer puppeteer may complain that the semi-pro can afford to undercut and therefore take engagements which the full-timer regards as his by right. Not only does the professional begin as an amateur, he usually begins as a semi-pro.

Professor. Showman's term for the Punch-and-Judy performer (introduced late nineteenth century). The assistant who plays the music to collect a crowd and sometimes talks with Punch is known as the 'bottler' – whose main function is to collect the money from the spectators.

Profile. In acting, the position in which the performer's right or left side is turned to the audience. On the two-dimensional shadow puppet screen the characters are normally in profile, although with some modern developments it is possible to have them full face.

Profile Art, by R. L. Mégroz. (Art Trade Press, 1948.) A study of profile and silhouette from the Stone Age to Puppet Films, with over 200 illustrations; section on work of Lotte Reiniger.

Projected Puppetry. A concept put forward by INTERMEDIA, q.v., and stated as 'the projection of two and three dimensional translucent and opaque puppets is an art form which has points of relationship with both puppetry and motion film and when used in combination with dancers or actors it has points of relationship with dance and the theatre'. Although INTERMEDIA mentions the 'relatively small scale' of puppets as an economic advantage, this ignores the trend for large and even larger than life puppets – and may to some extent invalidate experiments; *scale* can be an important element of impact on audiences. Performances may be (*a*) for an audience, seated in normal fashion, performers at one end of hall; (*b*) with action taking place in every direction; (*c*) with the audience swivelling around on their seats; (*d*) with the audience lying horizontally while watching the action on the ceiling; (*e*) in some cases the members of the audience might participate 'kinetically' by walking through the performance; (*f*) for audiences with their heads in individual box-screens (and walking into various beams of projection). It is admitted that artists are unlikely to come up with great performances with the new media until they have had a chance to become familiar with its creative nature – and one of the functions of INTERMEDIA is to assist in providing this opportunity.

Projected scenery. Effect produced by light projected on to theatrical gauze and having quite different dramatic quality and scope to painted scenery; not a substitute for the latter. Technical problems involved: (*a*) back projection: light source must not be visible; (*b*) front projection: actors must not intercept the projection.

Projection lantern. Theatrical lighting equipment similar to high-wattage spotlight, fitted with special lenses for projecting 'effects' (clouds, flames, water, etc.) on to stage back-cloth or gauze curtain from prepared slides.

Projector. Lighting equipment for directional illumination (as distinct from 'flood' or diffused lighting).

Prokofiev, Sergei Sergeivitch (1891–1953). Soviet Russian composer; like Stravinsky, associated with Diaghilev's *Ballets Russes*. His symphonic fairy-tale *Peter and the Wolf*, q.v., has become extremely popular with puppet theatres; Bulgarian State Puppet Theatre (Sofia) took top award at an international festival for their production of this item. His *Cinderella* ballet, based on Grimm's *Ashputtel*, has also been adapted for puppets.

Props. Stage properties, including (*a*) furniture, carpets; (*b*) items such as vases and clocks; (*c*) items carried by actors (watches, walking sticks); (*d*) things handled by actors, such as tea-cups, lanterns. In the puppet theatre, too, everything except the fixed scenery and the puppets. The term is also applied to the man responsible for seeing that the props are available as required, kept in good condition, stored.

Proscenium. The opening in the front wall of the 'picture frame' type of stage. Familiarly: 'pros'. Modern theatres sometimes dispense entirely with the proscenium and so do some marionette theatres; this exposes (*a*) the above-stage machinery for lowering and raising scenery, (*b*) the marionette operators. Also, the traditional type of Punch booth has top (roof) and sides – useful for out-of-door shows – but which limits the viewing from the side seats (particularly the front rows) in wide halls; the open-front stage has additional action possibilities.

PUK Puppet Theatre. Name is abbreviation for 'La Pupa Klubo', which is Esperanto for Puppet Club; established 1929 by Toji Kawajiri, first performance included Washington Irving's *Rip Van Winkle* (marionettes); later Andersen's *Emperor's New Clothes* and other hand puppet plays added, including Hasek's *Good Soldier Schweik*; silhouette plays were also developed; after World War II Kawajiri became Secretary to the Japan Council of Puppet Troupes; in 1949 Goethe's *Dr Faust* produced and repertoire continued to add plays of European origin as well as from Japanese folklore and other sources: Maeterlink's *Blue Bird*, Gogol's *Nose* and an adaptation of Molière's *Amphitryon*; 35th anniversary programmes included *Peter and the Wolf*, adapted from Prokofieff, and a *Shakespeare Fantasy* celebrating his 400th anniversary.

Pulcinella. One of the 'stock characters', q.v., of the commedia dell' arte, q.v., born in Naples, and from whom stemmed the French 'Polichinelle' and English 'Punch' – Pulcinella having become Punchinello (with a variety of spellings). Whether his origins go back to the earlier Roman mimes or not, which the scholars disagree about, is perhaps unimportant: burlesques of the same human types are likely to occur at any time. Duchartre, in *The Italian Comedy*, q.v., sees him as a dual personality combining characteristics of his predecessors 'Maccus' and 'Bucco' (who were opposites) and such features as the beak nose, paunch, hump. Even the voice was based on that of Maccus, who used a 'pivetta' – an instrument related to the English Punchman's 'swazzle', q.v. Whether his way of walking, a 'hen-step' as Ducharte has it, gave rise to the name (Maccus 'the hen': Pullus Gallinaceus: Pullicinello, Pulcino, Pulcinella, etc.) that author says 'has not as yet been corroborated'. Speaight, author of *History of the English Puppet Theatre* (1955), is obviously right in regarding Punch as a genuine English development, and the name has an English ring to it.

Punch. Famous English periodical, first issue dated 17th July, 1841, subtitled 'or The London Charivari' (as distinct from a satirical paper published in Paris); founded by Henry Mayhew (author of *The London Labour and London Poor*) and Mark Lemon, assisted by Landells, an engraver. The original cover illustration by A. S. Henning showed a group in the Cruikshank-'Phiz' style watching a Punch and Judy show, top-hatted 'bottler' standing by the booth with his drum and panpipes. Early contributors included William Makepeace Thackeray, John Tenniel the artist, and Phil May caricaturist. Later covers showed Punch as a writer, still with his Dog Toby.

Punch (character). It is behaviour that shows character. Behaviour on the puppet stage is largely determined by the construction and method of control of the puppets. There are therefore *technical* reasons why Punchinello who arrived from Italy in the form of *a marionette* would behave somewhat in a different manner from the later Punch as a *hand puppet*. The marionette might well sit on the lap of the Queen of Sheba – at the time when Punch/Punchinello was merely an intruder in the biblical or other plays – if the operator was careful not to tangle the strings (or kink the wires) of the two characters; but only a hand puppet would be capable of the slapstick associated with Punch. There are even degrees of violence (some present-day showmen have eliminated the hanging scene, even though it is the executioner who suffers). Walsh, in *Heroes and Heroines of Fiction* (Lippincott, 1914), says that Punch 'strangles' his infant son – the sex of the child is rarely indicated. Brewer, in *The Reader's Handbook* (Chatto, 1934), calls Punch's stick 'a bludgeon' – with which he 'knocks out the brains' of his wife. With present-day showmen the knockabout farce is fairly light-hearted, not vicious. Both Brewer and the author of another Reader's Encyclopaedia, Benet (Harrap, 1948) state that the play is an 'allegory' in which Punch 'triumphs' over *Slander* (the Dog), *Disease* (Doctor) and the Devil (*Death*) – and historians have seen possible connections with the earlier 'morality' plays (in which the characters were abstract *qualities*). Duchartre, in tracing the history of Punchinello-Punch (in *The Italian Comedy*, Dover, 1966), says the Neapolitan original only gave rein to 'all the cold-blooded ferocity' which he had stored up in his nature, upon arriving in England in the seventeenth century; apparently he also became a great seducer of young girls, and not only throws the baby out of the window but kills both his mother-in-law and father-in-law – relatives which the present-day Punch never seems to possess. It will be seen that Punch's character has (*a*) evolved, (*b*) been different in the performances of different showmen in any one peiiod, (*c*) is probably modified by the evolution of his public. Historians tend to discuss Punch as though there were only *one* of him – and at one time that would have been true (although where and when the phenomenon occurred has not been recorded). Actually, of course, audiences do the same: there *is* just the one Punch, the one they are watching. At the seaside in the summer they can see him day after day (never getting older) – although he may also be in forty or fifty other resorts at the same time (like Father Christmas in the store bazaars). Character is also seen in the relationship *with the audience*: in 'audience participation', q.v., in the good-natured argument '*Oh, no I never! Oh yes you did!*' Not only Punch but also Judy and the Baby and all the other victims of his stick reappear day after day – and are thus immortal. Speaight (in his *History of the English Puppet Theatre*) sees Punch as 'essentially English' with some 'minor and incidental accretions' from Italian and French sources; Stead (in *Mr Punch*) thinks the play to be of Italian or possibly French derivation and 'worked upon by the native tradition'. Speaight suggests that, having disagreed, it is best to agree to enjoy the next performance.

Punch (**origin**). How much the present-day Punch owes to the first Italian 'Punchinello' – apart from his name, and even that is not absolutely certain – there just is no evidence to prove one way or another. An entry in the *Oxford English Dictionary* (1933) begins: 'Now chiefly dialect; of uncertain origin; no words certainly related found outside English.' Further on the probability of derivation from Punchinello is admitted. *The English Etymological Dictionary*, by the Rev. W. Skeat (O.U.P., 1882), says the name is a contraction of Punchinello and cites *The Spectator* No. 14, in which *both* forms are used. 'Punchinello' is a corruption of the Italian 'Pulcinello' and, like Shakespeare's spelling of his own name, had no standard spelling; Pepys in his *Diary* uses several variants and other writers added further spellings: Polichinello, Polichinelle, Policinello, Pulcinello, Pulchinello, Puntionella, Punchonella, Punchanello, Punci- Punchi- Ponchiello, and even Pugenello. If as a character he was of Neapolitan origin, then he would be Polecenella – from which the French 'polichinelle' would also derive. *New English Dictionary* (Oxford, 1909) gives usages up to 1860 (Ponchinelli). In the *Vocabolario Napoletano* (1789) the name is said to be a corruption of 'Puccio d'Aniello' – a peasant of Acerra, whose face served as a model for the mask; there was also a buffoon at Naples with the name Paulo Cinella. Pianigiani, *Vocab. Etymol. della lingua Ital.* (1907) cites Quadrio and Baretti: Pulcinella is a diminutive of Pulcina '*chicken*' and Pollecenella is dim. of Neapolitan Pollecena, 'the young of the turkey-cock': a resemblance is seen between the nose of the Punchinello mask and the hooked bill of the bird. Skeat says the literal sense of Italian Pulcinello is 'little chicken'; that 'chicken' is a term of endearment; that derivation gives (1) a little boy, (2) a puppet. Brewer (*Readers' Handbook*, 1934) gives: Pullicinella, a wag of Apulia. The *Oxford Companion to English Literature* (2nd ed., 1937) says that Pulcinella 'is said by Italian authors' to have been invented by Silvio Fiorillo, a comedian (*c.* 1600) for use in the

Neapolitan impromptu comedies in imitation of the peasants of Acerra, near Naples. It adds: 'The character of Punch may be in part derived from the Vice of the old Moralities.' For a detailed study of the evolution of Punch, anglicised or utterly English see Speaight *History of the English Puppet Theatre* (1955). The Italian original was a *marionette*; at some time a change-over to the livelier hand puppet occurred; the costume changed; Walsh *Heroes and Heroines of Fiction* (Lippincott, 1914) describes it as follows: 'A three-pointed cap terminating in a red tuft, a white woollen shirt and drawers, the skirt besprinkled with red hearts and fastened with a black leather girdle, the drawers and sleeves trimmed with fringe; a linen ruffle encircles the neck.' A present-day Punch would regard that as straight from swinging London's Carnaby Street.

Punch and Judy, by Dion Clayton Calthrup (Dulau, 1926). Interesting historical notes; diasgrees with Magnin as to Punch's paunch, seeing it as a development from a doublet of Italian style ('Peascod-bellied') rather than the heavy cuirass worn by a Gascon officer of the guard of Henri Quatre period. Also records conversation with a showman.

Punch and Judy, by John Payne Collier, with illustrations designed and engraved by George Cruikshank; an account of its origin and of puppet plays in England (S. Prowett, London, 1828). Small book commissioned by the Publisher containing text based on the performance of an aged Italian showman who lived in the vicinity of Drury Lane; illustrations from sketches made during the performance, the audience consisting of the publisher, author and artist; the text as published probably not verbatim, possibly some admixture from other performers, possibly amended for the 'gentle reader'; see Speaight *History of the English Puppet Theatre* on this topic). Much of Collier's other literary work was suspect. Most showmen are individualists and not only develop their own versions of the Punch and Judy play, but may introduce variations (and topicalities) at every performance; even the number of characters involved varies, so that there can never be one final authentic fixed script. (Many later editions, e.g. Bell & Sons, 6th ed., 1881, and some in America.)

Punch and Judy, Opera by English composer Harrison Birtwhistle: 'A piece for 12-foot high puppets – with loudspeakers in their mouths'; libretto by Stephen Pruslin. First performance: Aldeburgh Festival, 1968.

Punch and Judy, as presented annually at the Annisquam Village Fair, Cape Ann, Mass., U.S.A., with an Introduction and bibliography by S. Foster Damon (Barre Publications, 1957). Successive generations of young performers give the show; text of the play included.

Punch and Judy characters. The number of characters in any performance will partly depend on the length of the show; entries, exits, stage business all take *time*. The number of characters available varies from one showman to the next; very little is known as to when any particular character was first introduced, and the fact that there is a close parallel with some of the characters in the French plays is probably due to the logical development of the drama; the folk element requires that the hero (even if he is a villain) should be in trouble with the Law – and overcome the Law, represented by the Beadle, the Constable or 'Hofficer of the Law', the Hangman (Jack Ketch, named after a real hangman who was a bit of a bungler) and, as in the old Morality play, even the Devil himself. Murder is the best possible reason for bringing in the Law; so there must be at least one character to be disposed of, but dramatically it is better to have several. The first victim is the Baby, which Punch is supposed to be minding and which provides a comic element when he is teaching it to walk; but there would be no development if the Baby was not thrown out of the window. Then Judy (or Joan as she was formerly called; Judy is a better *sound* when uttered through the showman's swazzle) is naturally annoyed, gives Punch a beating with his own stick, only making it worse for herself. Comic relief may now be called for, and so the Clown and Sausages and Frying-pan are introduced, or some 'business' with the Negro. The Dog Toby? Many present-day Punchmen do not have one; some have a puppet dog. *If* the Dog does appear, then his former owner must also come on the scene to claim him. Judy's Ghost may be conjured up – but fare no better than the rest. The Beadle/Constable will be added to the corpses, whereupon the 'business' of counting them begins – with lots of variations. Punch may nod and one character hits him, then returns to his place; audience participation now occurs with Punch's question 'Was it *this* one?' and slick changing of places. Then of course there is the Crocodile with the wide-open jaws. At one time Punch had a hobby-horse named Hector. Eventually the Hangman arrives, sets up the gallows; Punch plays dumb, then induces the executioner to put his own neck in the noose. Finally, there can be the Devil, who in early times, as in the Morality, would carry Punch off. According to Speaight *History of the English Puppet Theatre* (Harrap, 1955), the largest recorded cast totalled 16 characters. A pair of boxers are sometimes introduced as a sort of interlude. Some of the old-time showmen disapprove of any short weight performances; some of the contemporary performers adjust to the requirements of a particular engagement – and at least one has been reported as omitting the Hangman since the No-Hanging Bill was introduced.

Punch and Judy on Ice. Performance at the Silver Blades Ice Rink (1967) by English showman Terry Herbert.

Punch and Judy (origin of the play). If the play could be traced to a single author, in the form in which it is known today, it might be possible to see a definite connection with some earlier play – such as a medieval 'morality', q.v. The theory put forward by J. R. Cleland (article in the *Puppet Master*, q.v., July, 1948) is that the play's origins can be found in the teachings of the Ancient Mystery Schools and as a survival of a Morality; he parallels the characters neatly with a scheme of existence which involves Man with a physical body and an etheric body, with Punch as a spiritual 'aspirant', with the Dog Toby as a representative of the 'astral' plane, with the main action that of Punch overcoming various 'tests' and finally overcoming even Death and the Devil. The various killings are seen to be symbolic of the elimination of undesirable human traits in Punch the Aspirant. That puppet shows existed before the arrival of Punchinello (direct from Italy or via France) is certain and there is literary evidence enough to show that the religious plays were transferred to the puppet stage, probably very much modified – certainly so when Punch (as played by English showmen) intruded into the lay versions. A playbill mentions 'The Merry Humours of Punch' (relative to shows at Bartholomew Fair, *c.* 1700): *not* 'Punch and Judy' or 'Punch and Judith' or 'Punch and Polly'; Punch dancing in the Ark or sitting on the lap of the Queen of Sheba, these were normal antics – but there seems to be no evidence of 'a Punch play' as such; there is also a dearth of information about the early Italian items in which 'Punchinello' (Pulcinella, etc., q.v.) appeared. Did later Italians bring the play and, if so, what of its antecedents in Italy? The play may or may not be a Mystery or a Morality; its origins are certainly a mystery. Speaight has followed every trail in his *History of the English Puppet Theatre* (Harrap, 1955), and his documentation is as impeccable as the state of historical data allows; he makes no claim to have pin-pointed the precise 'premiere' of the Punch and Judy play of the period when its action and dialogue began to be recorded. It seems unlikely that an *original script* by an earlier showman will come to light.

Punch and Judy (script). How many of the earlier showmen ever used (or had) a script? How much English was known and used by the Italian showmen who brought their Punchinellos to this country? Was there any connection between the use of an 'interpreter' in front of the stage with the language problem – a problem which faces present-day performers with audiences including a high percentage of immigrants. Like ballads and folk-tales, passed on orally, the early showmen would probably be apprentices acquiring the knowledge of the action and dialogue by seeing and hearing, rather than by reading; would later have their own shows and make their own variations. The showman interviewed by Mayhew, as recorded in *London Labour and London Poor* (1852), mentioned the acquisition of a stage from an old performer. If Piccini, the aged Italian whose show provided the basis for the Payne Collier *Punch and Judy* with the Cruikshank illustrations, had had a script, Collier could have borrowed that rather than make notes during the performance. The final printed script, in any case, appears to be a composite one including some material from another showman's performance (why? if there was such a thing as a fixed traditional script). A first-hand study of a number of present-day shows proves the use of the same basic plot and characters (not always identical), but a fairly flexible dialogue which may vary somewhat in different performances by the same showman. It is interesting to compare the variants (which must have some foundation) in various encyclopaedias and other reference books. For instance, Walsh *Heroes and Heroines of Fiction* (Lippincott, 1914) states that the Baby is a boy, that after the killings Punch is borne off by the Devil, whereas in Brewer *The Reader's Handbook* (Chatto & Windus, 1934) the Baby is a girl, Punch is shut up in prison by an Officer of the Inquisition, escapes with a golden key, overcomes Slander (in the shape of a Dog), Disease and Death (in guise of Doctor and Devil). Various authors have seen Morality Play ingredients reappearing in the Punch show – but neither of these works gives any source for their information. The tendency for contemporary authors to reproduce the Piccini-Collier version can be misleading as to present-day performances.

Punch line. In dialogue, a line giving special emphasis for comic or dramatic effect.

Punch, or May-Day. Painting by Benjamin Haydon (1786–1846). English historical artist, q.v. Two-page colour reproduction in Baird *Art of the Puppet* (1965); black and white detail in Speaight *History of the English Puppet Theatre* (1955). Scene: near Mary-le-bone Church, London; crowd watching Punch and Judy show (one boy is picking a pocket); name on facia board is 'Pike', who was referred to by showman interviewed by Mayhew (*London Labour and London Poor*, 1856) and was possibly first to use live dog Toby. Also seems to have been left-handed, as most Punchmen use Punch on the right hand.

Punch Tercentenary. On Saturday, 26th May, 1962, the 300th anniversary of Punch was celebrated at the place recorded as that of his first appearance in England: Covent Garden, London, 1662, according to the famous Diary of Samuel Pepys (entry for 9th May): 'Thence to see an Italian puppet play, that is within the rails there, which is very pretty, the best that I ever saw.' The last phrase is significant – and frustrating for the historian – and it must be appreciated that 'Policinella' (various spellings in different entries) was not the Punch we know in the twentieth century. Pepys took his wife on another occasion and still found it 'very pleasant', and on 8th October of the same year Signor Bologna performed for the King at Whitehall and was rewarded with a gold chain and medal. In 1961 the Society for Theatre Research, the British Puppet and Model Theatre Guild, and Prebendary Clarence May, Rector of St Paul's Church, Covent Garden (the Actors' Church), worked out a plan for the 1962 celebration, which included a Service of Praise and Thanksgiving, a subscription list was opened to pay for a commemorative inscription on the portico wall, and invitations were sent to all the Punchmen in the country – some 40 of whom attended with their families, some with Dog Tobys. The full attendance was around 400, including most of the well-known puppeteers, some general public, the Press, the Cine camera operators, Television and Radio recorders. Percy Press, the Guild Chairman, read the Lesson, and the preacher had Mr Punch in the pulpit – and welcomed the Tobys, too. Outside, a gigantic booth had been erected, into which the Punchmen entered, with music from the drums; one Punch appeared, chatted with a Clown, banged the playboard with his stick three times – and up shot a swarm of Punches, then their Judies ('Kissy, kissy, kissy!'); they dance; a Dog Toby appears and goes through his routine; a giant birthday cake is put on the playboard, the candle explodes, the cake emits Crocodiles, Dragons and Snakes. Finally one of the Punches pulled the cord which unveiled the plaque on which is inscribed *Near this spot Punch's Puppet Show was first performed in England and witnessed by Samuel Pepys, 1662* – and all the Punches cry 'That's the way to do it!' Many other puppet showmen played in the area later – and the famous Martin Powell even timed his show against the tolling of the church bell – reducing the congregation. The celebration may be repeated, perhaps before the 400th anniversary. As a record for its members, the Guild issued a special number of its *Puppet Master* devoted to Punch, with articles on his history, on the special event, articles on and by the 'Professors', excerpts from some of the letters and telegrams received from all over the world, a special item on the Codmans (fourth generation Punchmen), illustrations of the scene in and out of the church, illustrations of Punch's cousins in other countries and one of the marionette Punch (his original form) specially made for the occasion by Waldo Lanchester.

Punch: the Immortal Liar, by Conrad Aiken, in *Selected Poems* (Secker, 1920, N.Y., 1933). Poet says that he too is a puppet, that Punch is a symbol of him and he himself is a symbol, 'a puppet drawn out upon strings'.

Punch's Playhouse. Situated in the Strand, London, in the year of the Great Exhibition (1851) and mentioned by Edward Stirling in *Old Drury Lane* (Chatto, 1881); says that a Charles Read wrote several plays for Punch *adapted from French sources*. This is interesting in the light of the disagreement between historians SPEAIGHT and STEAD over French influences, and Speaight mentions a text of *'Polichinelle'* (Punch's French cousin), which turned out to be an apparent translation of the script recorded by Payne Collier (*Punch and Judy*, 1828) – complete with the Cruikshank engravings! Polichinelle appeared in a great many plays, as did Punch in the days prior to the evolution of the Punch and Judy play as now performed. *Some* approximation could occur in the light of simple dramatic logic, but conscious piracy in the puppet world is not limited to Punchmen.

Punch's Voice. Reference in Gould *Dictionary of Medicine* (1894) to 'a ringing tone' – like that of Punch – and sometimes to be observed among the insane!

Pupazzo. Italian term for puppet; plural: *pupazzi*. Presumably from Latin *pupa*, girl, doll, puppet. Related to pupazzettare 'to caricature'. As with other terms, sometimes loosely used for more than one type, but mostly for hand puppets with wooden heads and hands. Context sometimes a guide.

Puppet (definition). Perfect definition eludes theorists, historians, puppeteers, dictionary-makers. It is easier to state what a puppet is *not*: it is not a 'doll' – although some puppeteers refer to their puppets as 'dolls'. Dolls are for personal play; puppets are essentially theatrical in function. Helen Binyon (in *Puppetry Today*) gives: 'Man-made actor, inanimate object to which human beings have found a means of giving an appearance of life.' Paul McPharlin (*Puppet Theatre in America*): 'Theatrical figure moved under human control.' Margareta Niculescu, Director of the Tandarica Theatre in Bucharest: 'A plastic picture endowed with ability of acting and presenting somebody' (in a paper on *Metaphors as Puppet's Means of Expression*: at an international conference). Gordon Craig (in *Puppets and Poets*): 'The actor's primer.' Webster's *New School and Office Dictionary*: 'A small doll or image, especially one moved by wires in a mock drama; one who is under the influence and control of another.' Bil Baird (in *Art of the Puppet*): 'An inanimate figure that is made to move by human effort before an audience.' Sergei Obraztsov, Soviet puppetmaster (in an article in *The Puppet Theatre of the Modern World*): 'The puppet is a plastic generalisation of a living being: man, reindeer, dove.' In practice, puppeteers are not much concerned to define 'puppet'; they are more concerned to create each puppet with its individual personality, i.e. to give it *definition of character*. Walter Wilkinson, English puppeteer and author of *The Peep Show* and other volumes, says the idea that puppets are inanimate creatures controlled by human beings is incorrect and that the position is exactly the opposite: the showman is at the mercy of his puppets.

Puppet (dialect form). Popular etymology results in transference of names, adoption as pet-names, with subsequent multiple meanings of the original or its variants. This is seen in Shakespeare's plays in the use of the term 'motion', q.v., which appears frequently and with a great variety of meanings (all related in some way to movement, physical, emotional, mental), not always too clear even from the context. The early form of 'poppet' has often been used as a term of affection, retained this (especially of children) in the North and Midlands and has had something of a revival in this sense. There is some overlapping between 'puppet' and 'puppy' (latter possibly from French 'poupee') and in dialect 'puppie' can mean 'puppet'; in the North a 'puppy show' could be a puppet-show, having nothing to do with dogs. In Carew *Estienne's World of Wonders* (1607) the situation is reversed: 'Great curres (dogs) . . .

O

and the little puppets (puppies).' In German the same source is seen in 'puppe' and 'puppen': 'puppenspiel', a puppet-play. 'Poppin' was an East Anglian variant. 'Puppet' is also dialect name for the Red Poppy and the term for the handstock of a lathe.

Puppet Diary, by Pantopuck and His Puppets (Macmillan, 1952). On the author's (A. R. Philpott's) adventures with a stage and puppets loaded on a little push-cart in leisurely pre-war English countryside. Illustrations by R. G. Leffingwell. Text in simple puppet-English.

Puppet (*etymology*). The Middle English form was 'popet' or 'poppet', which possibly came via French 'poupette' (known in 1583) from the common Latin source: *Pupa*, girl, doll, puppet; Romanic *puppa*; Italian sixteenth century *puppa*, doll, especially one worked by strings; English variants include 'poopet', 'poppette' and 'poppit' and dialect forms often have meanings unrelated to dolls or puppets; see Puppet (dialect).

Puppet Films, List of, compiled by T. E. Howard for the British Section of UNIMA, the international organisation; covers 16 mm. black and white and colour films for hire in Great Britain; approximately 80 titles from 12 countries (revised edition in preparation) arranged in categories: Documentary, Fictional, Stop-motion, Silhouette. Details of running times, hire fees, with brief notes on subject content, name and address of each distributor.

Puppet Master, The. Official journal of the British Puppet and Model Theatre Guild, quarterly; articles on technical and other aspects, news, correspondence, book reviews, illustrations; some issues have directory of puppeteers. Special issues, e.g. 'Punch Tercentenary: 1662–1962; Hastings Festival, 1966. Membership details from Hon. Secretary, B.P.M.T.G., 90 The Minories, London, E.C.3.

Puppet Post. The official journal of the Educational Puppetry Association (London), edited by A. R. Philpott. Wide range of articles, technical, educational (including therapy), international news, book reviews, correspondence. Circulated to members twice a year (March and September). Membership details from Hon. Secretary, E.P.A., 23a Southampton Place, London, W.C.1.

Puppet, types of. Classification is by (1) operating position – (*a*) from above stage, (*b*) from below, (*c*) from side or rear; (2) method of control – (*a*) direct, using only the operator's hand, (*b*) remote, by means of strings, rods, combinations of these, (*c*) shape, flat or rounded; (3) types which do not fit into a single category, mainly hybrids. (1*a*) Types operated from above may be controlled by strings, rods, or a combination of these; if by strings only, usually referred to as 'marionettes' or 'string puppets'; a large and heavy variety found in Sicily has an iron rod attached to the head (through it), a thinner rod to the sword-arm, a cord to the shield-arm, and a variant of this type is found in Belgium (no controls of limbs); in India there is a type which has supporting strings attached to a hoop worn around the operator's head, downward rods to the hands; marionettes with complex controls sometimes require two operators. (1*b*) Types operated from below include the 'hand' (or 'glove'), which has live hand inside the figure (a variant has two hands inside); 'hand-and-rod' with hand inside controlling the head, and rods to the hands; 'rod puppet' with long internal rod to head and rods to the hands (internal or external); large puppets may require two operators;

a Rhineland variant has a rod reaching to the floor, a rod to one arm, free-swinging legs; in Thailand a small rod type has strings running downwards; Teschner (Austria) evolved a strings-through-rods variety. (1c) Flat figures can be small Toy Theatre cut-outs, pushed on from the side of the stage, or larger versions of these: flat marionettes; and shadow figures behind an illuminated translucent screen (controlled by rods or strings). Rounded construction can occur in any type – even in contemporary shadow-figures. (3) The live hands can be transformed into puppets (Yves Joly, France); the live hands can become puppet hands, as part of the hand-and-rod type (with short internal head rod, and one puppet-hand) or, with second operator, as part of larger rod type; small finger-puppets (fingers becoming puppet-legs, with or without strings to hands); puppet-head worn on operator's head, live hands as puppet-hands; the three-man puppets of the Japanese Bunraku, combination of hand-rod-string control. Variations in the individual types of controls are dealt with under the relative entries.

Puppet Plays, by Alfred Kreymborg (Martin Secker, 1923). Preface by Gordon Craig, q.v. Titles: *When the Willow Nods, Blue and Green, Manikin and Minikin, Jack's House, Lima Beans, People Who Die, Pianissimo*. Of these the *Lima Beans* has probably been the most popular, e.g. productions by Remo Bufano, q.v., in the United States; Olive Blackham, q.v., in Great Britain.

Puppet Plays and Playwriting, by Eric Bramall (Bell, 1961). Author is Director of the Harlequin Puppet Theatre, q.v. Chapters on the essentials of the puppet play, play-making from stories, e.g. *Blue Beard, The Swineherd*, original plays (*The Voice of the Lobster, Harlequinade, The Japanese Print*) and 'pure puppetry', in which inanimate objects become animate, in which the characters may have names like Oxygen, Hydrogen 1 and 2, or The Whiskerians and Spoonerians. Interesting historical notes (but without references), e.g. that Marlowe's *The Massacre at Paris* was adapted from a puppet play, as also ('most likely') his *Dr Faustus*, that Milton's *Paradise Lost* is, in part, adapted from an Italian puppet production, and that Byron (who was interested in puppets) adapted the old puppet play *The Libertine Destroyed* for his *Don Juan*. See also Play-writing.

Puppet Plays for Schools: series published by Macmillan for hand puppets; see individual entries under the following titles: *Brer Rabbit Plays*, by Barbara Lancaster; *Kalyb the Witch and other plays*, by Morris Cox; *Lazy Jack and other plays*, by Kenneth Watson; *The Magic Tower and other plays*, by A. R. Philpott; *Mumbo-Jumbo and other plays*, by A. R. Philpott; *Silly Willy and King John and the Abbot*, by K. & L. Amaral.

Puppet Theatre and its Relation to other Branches of Art, with special reference to Film and Television. Theme for International Conference held in Warsaw, Poland, in 1962, the collected papers afterwards made available to interested members of UNIMA. Contributors: Jan Bussell, England; Lucien Caron, France; Krystyna Mazur, Poland; Gatara Mile, Yugoslavia; Marjorie Batchelder McPharlin, U.S.A.; Dr Vojmil Rabadan, Yugoslavia; Bogdan Radkowski, Poland; Harro Siegel, Germany. Among a great many other points raised was that of the competition between the live puppet show and puppets on cine or television screen. A statement by Mrs Meher Rustom Contractor from India that 'no cinema, no theatre, no television and no radio can threaten our puppets' had a response that puppetry must find more appropriate methods of

work and attain a high level of achievement in performance if it is to
survive the strong competition of the other media (Gatara Mile). In
those countries where there are State Puppet Theatres the audiences out-
number the television viewers. Ideally the aim should be highest artistic
and entertainment quality in each medium.

Puppet Theatre Around the World, published by the Bharatiya Natya Sangh,
New Delhi, 1960, which is also the Indian national centre of the International Theatre Institute. The Editors acknowledge co-operation from
UNIMA, the international puppetry organisation. This is a unique
collection of 40 chapters on both historical and contemporary puppetry,
profusely illustrated. Any summary would be impossible, the material is
so diverse. In the case of the chapters on the 'Water Puppets of Vietnam',
this is the first material available in English. The full range is indicated
by the following chapter-headings: *Puppetry Yesterday, Today and Tomorrow*,
by Joze Pengov, Yugoslav puppetmaster. *Stage Production in a Puppet
Theatre*, by Henryk Ryl, Polish Director. *A Dramaturgie for a Contemporary
Puppet Theatre*, by Jean-Loup Temporal, French puppeteer. *Indian
Puppet Theatre*, by Suresh Awasthi (General Secretary of the Bharatiya
Natya Sangh). *Impressions of Indian Puppetry*, by Balwant Gargi (excerpt
from his book on *Theatre in India*). *Puppet Show of Burma*, by U Tha Myat,
Director of the Cultural Institute, Rangoon. *Puppetry and Myself*, by Harro
Siegel, German puppetmaster. *Indonesian Puppetry*, by Satyawati Suleiman.
Thai Puppet Shows, by Montri Tramote. *Puppets and Puppeteers of Rajasthan*,
by D. L. Samar, Director of the Lok Kala Mandal Research Institute,
Udaipur. *Recent Trends in Indian Puppetry*, by Meher R. Contractor,
puppeteer, teacher. *Kathputli – an experiment*, by Miles Lee, puppeteer and
UNESCO Theatre Expert at the Asian Theatre Institute. *The Invisible
Hand*, by Mona Leo, Finnish puppeteer. '*Puppets Calcutta*', by Katayum
Saklat (contemporary developments). *Puppet Theatre of Orissa*, by G. C.
Tej (India). *Puppet Shows in South India*, by E. Krishna Iyer, Secretary of
the Madras State Sangita Natak Sangam. *Use of Puppets in Adult Education*,
by T. A. Koshy, Executive Director of Literacy Village, Lucknow.
Shadow Play of Andhra, by M. V. Ramanaurthy, authority on this type.
Impressions of Japanese Puppetry, by Kamaladevi Chattopadhyay. *Develop-
ment of Japanese Puppets*, by Yuu Yamamura, Puppetmaster of the Puk
Theatre. *Water Puppets of Vietnam*, by Lorraine Salmon. *The Working of
the Vietnamese Puppets. Puppet Theatre of Ceylon* (anon.). *Chinese Puppet Plays*,
by Li Ko-Jan. *How our Theatre was Born*, by Sergei Obraztsov, Director
of the Moscow State Puppet Theatre. *New Approaches in the Soviet Puppet
Theatre*, by Lenora Shpet. *Czechoslovakia – classical country of Puppets*, by
Dr Jan Malik, General Secretary of UNIMA. *Children's Puppet Theatre in
Czechoslovakia*, by Miroslav Cesal. *Puppet Theatre in G.D.R. (Germany)*, by
Rudolf Halbohm. *Mozart and the Salzburg Marionettes*, by Hermann Aicher,
Director of the Salzburg Marionette Theatre. *Art of Puppetry in Hungary*,
by Deszo Szilagyi, Director of the State Puppet Theatre, Budapest.
Vienna's Fadenbuehne (anon.). *Puppet Theatre in the Netherlands*, by Rico
Bulthuis. *The Comic Substance of Karaghiozis*, by Eugene Spatharis, Greek
shadow-player. *The Puppet Show in Rumania*, by Margareta Niculescu,
Director of the State Puppet Theatre, Bucharest. *Puppets in Britain*, by
Gerald Morice, Puppetry Editor of 'The World's Fair'. *Italian Puppet
Plays*, by Maria Signorelli, Italian puppeteer, director. *Glove in Hand with
George Latshaw* (photographs only). *Puppets and an Art Museum*, by Gil
Oden, Curator, Detroit Institute of Arts. *Lighting in the Puppet Theatre*, by
Michael Overman.

Puppet Theatre for Language Teaching. Booklet issued in connection with a Course for Teachers in connection with the Foreign Languages Teaching Materials Project (Nuffield Foundation, Leeds University) and the teaching of French in the Primary School. Also available are tape recordings of three short plays, with native French speakers, and related puppet films. An extension to other languages is envisaged. Spanish available.

Puppet Theatre Handbook, by Marjorie Batchelder (Jenkins, N.D.), drawings by Douglas Anderson. Excellent practical manual on all aspects: use of puppetry in education, recreation, therapy and rehabilitation, advertising, cinema and television, as a profession; chapters on planning the show, puppet construction (all types, including finger-puppets and 'humanettes', q.v.), stages (including conversion of hospital equipment), scenery, lighting, properties and special effects; play-writing and plays, production; under marionettes includes study of the counter-balance system of Dwiggins; 69 illustrations, bibliography, supplementary information on Societies, Organisations, Firms; Equipment, Films, Variety Acts.

Puppet Theatre in America: A History: 1524 *to Now,* by Paul McPharlin (Harper, New York, 1949). A monumental work, 507 pp., published after author's death, final editing carried out by his wife, Marjorie Batchelder. This is an exhaustive and well-documented account of puppetry from time of early Spanish conquest, when Cortés, the adventurer, included a puppeteer among his private retinue of entertainers; it seems probable that the Toltecs and other 'aborigines' of America already used puppets in religious ceremonies. McPharlin devotes chapters to each development which followed immigration from England, France, Spain, Italy, Germany, including the advent of the Toy Theatre and up to the early twentieth century renaissance. The book is in fact quite enlightening on early European puppetry, from which the contemporary forms have developed. The book is profusely illustrated and concludes with an 86-page List of Puppeteers, 1524–1948, and details of their repertory. A new edition with chapters on the post-1948 developments, which are considerable, is anticipated.

Puppet Theatre in Germany, by Dr Hans R. Purschke (Neue Darmstadter Verlagsanstalt, 1957); in English translation; good historical introduction, with 75 black and white photo-reproductions and four colour plates.

Puppet Theatre of the Modern World. An International Presentation in Word and Picture, compiled by an Editorial Board of the Union Internationale des Marionnettes (UNIMA), with translations by Ewald Osers and Elizabeth Strick (Henschelverlag, 1965; Harrap, 1967). Published in nine separate language editions. A total of 36 countries represented by nearly 240 photographs, high-quality reproduction, and 19 contributors to the text, notables in the field of puppetry, discussing many aspects of the art. At first glance it is the illustrations which seem the more important section; a reading and re-reading of the various texts will reveal the importance of having this collation of thought and theory and observation from some of the leaders of this puppet-generation. The word 'modern' in the title is significant, although there are references to traditional forms, some of which have survived. Dr Jan Malik, of Czechoslovakia, Secretary-General of UNIMA and director of one of the leading puppet theatres in Prague, writes on 'Tradition and the Present Day', including the problems which arise from international exchanges. Russian puppet-master Sergei Obraztsov, Director of the State Central Puppet Theatre in Moscow, probably the most famous of all present-day puppeteers, whose work has had world-wide influence, offers 'Some considerations on the Puppet Theatre' – and is still able to dream of a theatre offering works 'rich and full of passionate conviction'. German actor and puppeteer Harro Siegel (Federal Republic), who taught for many years at the Brunswick College of Visual Arts, not concerned with commercial possibilities, begins: 'In this article we shall try to deal not with theories and speculations but with facts and actual experience' ('Actor and Puppeteer'). Jean-Loup Temporal, French puppeteer and 'puppet art philosopher', asks: Where have we come from? Where are we going? Henryk Jurkowski, head of the Polish government department in the Ministry of Culture concerned with puppet theatres, writes on 'The Eternal Conflict', concluding that contemporary developments – in which Polish puppet theatres are prominent – stem from the 'natural peculiarities' of the puppet itself: 'Let it move itself.' Stefan Lenkisch, Rumanian producer and author of works on contemporary puppet art, deals with 'The Puppet as a Poetic Symbol' and says that 'no trick can help us ... no trick can make up for the artistic truth the puppet demands.' The English contribution from George Speaight, author of the standard history of puppets in England, writes on 'Tradition and Experiment', stresses the need for imaginative experiment. Maria Signorelli, Italian student of puppet history and Director of a theatre with a modern approach, has the theme 'The Vitality of a Tradition'. The contribution from Dr Erik Kolar, Dean of the Puppetry Department in the University of Prague, Czechoslovakia, has the title 'The Puppet Theatre: a Form of Visual or Dramatic Art? and regards the visual element as 'an ancillary factor subordinated to the producer's intentions'. 'A Producer's Reflections on the Roles of the Actor and the Designer' comes from Mikhail M. Korolov, Director of the Leningrad Bolshoi Puppet Theatre, one of the leading Russian theatres. Dr Szilagyi, Director of the Hungarian State Puppet Theatre, Budapest, which visited Britain in 1968, an authority on children's literature, is concerned with 'The Modern Puppet Stage and its Audience' – and is responsible for some international award productions. A second item from Britain is Jan Bussell's 'The Art of the Puppet Theatre, with Special Reference to its Position in England' (he is co-director with his wife of the well-known Hogarth Puppets). An exponent of the modern school in Japan, Taiji Kawajiri, director of the 'Puk' Theatre, points out that there are many folk-puppet groups in addition to modern marionette theatres, as well as the better-known Bunraku with its 'three man' puppets. Bulgarian Director Stantscho Gerdjikov takes the theme 'A New Art is Born' – and relates puppet developments to contemporary aesthetic trends and modern art tastes. The inimitable French puppeteer Yves Joly, begins: 'You make puppets; just like that ...' and Carl Schroder, Director of the D.E.F.A. Cartoon Film Studio, Dresden (G.D.R.), tells of a stage which is 'free-standing, open at the top, semi-circular.' So far there is only one other book which is the collective voice of a number of contemporary authorities: *Puppet Theatre Around the World*, published in India by Bharatiya Natya Sangh, which is also the Indian national centre of the International Theatre Institute, and had co-operation from UNIMA (1960).

Puppet Theatre: Production and Manipulation, by Miles Lee (Faber, 1958), with illustrations by Olivia Hopkins. Author had small Mews Theatre in Edinburgh; deals with the permanent theatre, puppet theory and the

Producer, manipulation methods, manipulation exercises, the man-
ipulator-actor, group work and rehearsals; two scenes produced; play
selection; bibliography.

Puppeteers of America, Inc. A national non-profit organisation whose
object is the improvement of the art of puppetry; governed by a Board of
Trustees elected by the membership. Consultation service on Education,
Films and T.V., local Guilds, Junior activities, Lighting, Music, Religion,
Script, Sound, Therapy. Members receive the *Puppetry Journal* at two-
monthly intervals, dealing with all aspects and current news, giving
addresses of local guilds and regional directors. Initial correspondence
to Executive Secretary, Olga Stevens, Box 1061, Ojai, California 93023.

Puppetical. Obsolete term (in some old dictionaries) meaning 'pertaining
to a puppet'.

Puppetry. (1) Branch of Dramatic Art which uses specially created figures
as characters and whose action is controlled by human actors by various
technical means; quality of performance and of the content of the
production (as in the 'live' theatre) form the criteria. (2) According to
Samuel Johnson's *Dictionary of the English Language* (Longman Rees, 2nd
ed., 1827), this was a word of contempt, meaning 'affectation'. The word
'puppet' is still used satirically by journalists and politicians of kings and
statesmen.

Puppetry. An International Yearbook of Puppets and Marionettes. The
official yearbook of the Puppeteers of America, q.v., edited by Paul
McPharlin; 15 volumes, 1930–45. Material contributed from every part
of the world, wide range of articles and illustrations, covering the progress
of the twentieth century developments as an art and in education, therapy,
advertising, films, television. Valuable documentation for the puppetry
historian. Currently the Puppeteers of America publish a two-monthly
Journal (Volume XIX, 1968).

Puppetry Fundamentals, by A. R. Philpott (an Educational Puppetry Association publication). General introduction on the nature of puppets and
puppetry; sections on puppet-making (general principles rather than
specific techniques), stages, scenery, lighting, acting, speech, the audience,
source material for shows; short list of recommended reading. Book for
the beginner – *before* beginning.

Puppetry in Czechoslovakia, by Dr Jan Malik, q.v. (Orbis, 1948). Brie
authoritative survey of the history of puppetry in the country which has
become the centre of international developments; author is the Secretary-
General of UNIMA (the international organisation), q.v., and for many
years Director of the Central Puppet Theatre, Prague. Over 50 photo
illustrations and reproductions of early prints; list of Czech gramophone
records, excerpts from plays and music.

Puppetry in the Curriculum. Bulletin No. 1 of Curriculum Series, published
by Board of Education of City of New York, 1947–48. Mainly on puppets,
marionettes and masks for elementary and junior high school years.
Chapters on evaluation of each type, photographs of children's work,
chart of suggested activities for each grade and introducing puppetry
into syllabus. Consideration of plays based on experience, on literary
sources, and effective planning of play. Practical use of puppetry in class-
room: kindergarten, 2nd, 4th, 5th and 8th grades. Section on construction, including stick figures, hand puppets, marionettes, shadows and
masks; on manipulation, costume, stages, screens and scenery. Study of

influence of puppetry on personal and social growth of child. Bibliography, visual and audial aids, materials.

Puppetry Imprints. Series of handbooks each dealing with one aspect, published by Paul McPharlin, Birmingham, Michigan, U.S.A. (1) Puppet heads and their making; (2) Puppet hands; (3) Producer's Guide to puppet plays; (4) Hand puppet primer; (5) no title; (6) Trick marionettes; (7) Marionette control; (8) Plan for folding stage adaptable for all types; (9) Posters, playbills, publicity; (10) Animal marionettes. Also: *Adventures of a Russian Puppet Theatre*, by Nina Efimova.

Puppetry Journal. The official magazine of the Puppeteers of America society, issued to its members at two-monthly intervals; technical articles, international news, photographs, correspondence, book and film reviews. (1968, Volume XIX.) Enquiries: National Executive Office, Box 1061, Ojai, California 93023.

Puppetry Today, by Helen Binyon (Studio Vista, 1966). Book which has behind it many years of successful experimental puppetry with students at the Bath Academy of Art; on designing and making marionettes, glove puppets, rod puppets and shadow figures. Good bibliography and well illustrated.

Puppets and Education. Conference held at the Villa Falconieri (European Centre for Education, maintained by the six Common Market countries, at Frascati) at the time of the 19th International Festival in Rome, sponsored by Italian Ministries of Education, Tourism and Entertainment and under UNIMA, q.v., patronage.

Puppets and Fairy Tales, by Kamil Bednar (Prague, 1958). English edition edited by Charles Časlavsky. Each page is divided into an illustration from a puppet film for children and brief outline of the story, some in colour, various types of puppets; includes *The Golden Key* (a version of *Pinocchio*), *Hurvinek among the Insects*, *Hurvinek's Enchanted Swallow*, *The Gingerbread Cottage* (version of *Hansel and Gretel*), *Cinderella*, *Princess Scribble-Scrawl*, *The Tin Soldier*, *The Kids and the Wolf*, *The House of Cats*, *Princess and the Seven Knights*, *The Little Humpback Horse*, *A Chinese Fairy Tale*. Trnka, q.v., master-puppet-film-maker, contributes a note to the effect that puppets and puppet films are not only for children, and some reproductions from *A Complicated Story* (Chekhov), *The Assembly of Women* and other of his films.

Puppets and I, The, by Jan Bussell (Faber, 1950). Autobiographical account of the experiences and travels of an English puppet-master and in which he tells about his puppets, the first heads, the first show, early tours and later journeyings, his Caravan Theatre, Television, shows located in Greece, Venice, Paris and Amiens. Then 'naval excursions' and the famous Admiral Chin-up marionette, and puppets in Belgium, India, Java. A tour in Czechoslovakia with the renowned Skupa Company. Twenty-one illustrations.

Puppets and Plays, by Marjorie Batchelder and Virginia Lee Comer (Faber, 1959). Valuable addition to the literature on puppetry in education; outcome of collaboration with classroom teachers, librarians, youth leaders, puppetry workers. Accent is on the 'creative approach' to puppet-making and play production; deals with all types of puppets and a variety of methods, including delightful creatures made from scrap material, nature objects, cardboard cones; stages, scenery and properties, music and sound, presentation techniques, audience participation, and the planning of projects. Extensive bibliography and suggested source-material; useful addresses of booksellers, suppliers, associations, periodicals. Fourty-four plates (photographs and diagrams).

Puppets and Poets, by Edward Gordon Craig (1872–1967). No. 20 of *The Chapbook* (February, 1921), a Monthly Miscellany published by the Poetry Bookshop (Harold Monro, q.v.). 'It is he who knows how to let it move and how to let it speak' who counts most as a puppeteer. He also pointed out that a puppet can change its head or even have three separate selves. Of Maeterlinck's *Drames pour marionnettes*, q.v. – which some critics have doubted as genuinely intended for puppets – he had the opinion that these were his 'earliest and best Dramas'. There is a section on the Japanese puppets with illustrations showing technical construction. An item that is now a collector's piece.

Puppets and Puppetry, by Cyril Beaumont (Studio, 1958). This book, with its 400 illustrations, photo-reproductions, is an important record of twentieth century developments by an author already distinguished as a historian of the ballet. Some of the material appeared in the earlier *Puppets and the Puppet Stage* (Studio, 1938), and there is an introductory compressed history and a chapter on contemporary work and the new uses of puppetry (advertising, education, therapy). The illustrations include many scenes, as well as individual puppets. Not every country is covered, Poland, for instance, being represented only in the section on puppet films, although having some outstanding puppet theatres. Countries: Austria, Czechoslovakia, France, Germany, Great Britain, Greece, Holland, Israel, Italy, Japan, South Africa, Soviet Union, Switzerland, U.S.A., Yugoslavia. Films: Czechoslovakia, Poland. The future historian who has access to this book and to the later volumes, *The Puppet Theatre of the Modern World* (UNIMA and Henschelverlag, Berlin, 1967; English edition, Harrap) and Baird *The Art of the Puppet* (Collier-Macmillan, 1965), will be in a much better position, pictorially, than any former historian.

Puppets and Shadows: A Bibliography, compiled by Grace Greenleaf Ransome (Faxon, Boston, 1931), in the 'Useful Reference' series No. 44. Valuable list of early twentieth century (pre-1931) publications in many countries (including bibliographies): historical, critical, modern, educational, technical, plays, shadows and shadow plays; about 6,000 titles; authors include 8 Belgian, 7 Czech, 48 English, 94 French, 21 German and 7 Italian (some with large output). It should be appreciated that there has been a great expansion of puppetry literature since World War II, some indication of which is given in the bibliography in the present *Dictionary*.

Puppets into Actors, by Olive Blackham (Rockliff, 1948). Textbook on the construction and use of marionettes: planning the figure, the various parts to be made and assembled, animal characters, costume; the crutch (control) and the stringing; movement and rehearsals; shows, the stage and lighting, scenery; choice of plays. Very clear illustrations. Appendix: (*a*) on Paper Pulp; (*b*) a Permanent Stage Structure; (*c*) Bibliography.

Puppets, Mimes and Shadows (With), by Margaret K. Soifer (Furrow Press, N.Y., 1936). On how to teach folk literature through pantomime, puppets and shadow plays. Scenarios and material from the Bible, Greek myths, English ballads, legends, Indian lore.

Puppets Past and Present. Picture Book of the Puppetry Collection in the Detroit Institute of Arts (D.I.A., 1960). Foreword by Gil Oden, Curator of Theatre Arts. The Collection has been built up from the initial acquisition of the Paul McPharlin Collection containing examples of traditional and contemporary puppets from all over the world. Proceeds from the Paul McPharlin Memorial Fund have been used to acquire, among other holdings, a complete Victorian Puppet Theatre and puppets, scripts, scenery (*c.* 1870), marionettes of various American pioneers, and marionettes and hand puppets of Remo Bufano, q.v. (1894–1948), as well as the giant rod-and-string figures he created for Stravinsky's *Oedipus Rex*, q.v. Documentary material has been contributed from various sources, and the library has over 800 volumes on puppetry as well as ballet, opera, theatre design, histories, etc. The Institute receives an annual grant from the *Detroit News* (since 1954) for the purpose of furthering puppet activity. The book has a selection of 57 photo-reproductions of items in the Collection.

Puppets' Progress, by Jan Bussell (Faber, 1953). Further biographical material and travels of an English puppet-master (following *The Puppets and I,* Faber, 1950): Why puppets? The Show; On the road; The commercial theatre; Manipulation and the screen; Television; Puppet films; Woolacombe Beach; The Tent; Australian Adventure; In the Bush; Home.

Puppy (Puppie) show. Obsolete dialect form for 'puppet'; used in North of England and Scotland. Moir in *Mansie Wauch* (1828) mentions 'Punch and Polly and puppie-shows'.

Purcell, Henry (1659–95). English composer whose *Aeneas and Dido* had puppet production by Harro Siegel, q.v., German teacher and puppeteer, who at one time toured with English dancers, players, German singers.

Pusher. Term for simple device for positioning Toy Theatre figures mounted on flat bases, and consisting of a length of stiff wire and a block of wood.

Push-on puppets. (*a*) Cut-out cardboard figures set in ends of horizontal wire controls or fixed to narrow wooden sliders moving in grooves, for use with Toy Theatre; (*b*) large-scale cut-outs mounted on long wooden battens and pushed on from wings of small 'live' stage.

Puss in Boots. Perrault's fairy tale *Le chat botté* has quite different possibilities in the puppet theatre to those of the Christmas pantomime. It has been adapted by the National Puppet Theatre of Cuba, by some of the French guignol theatres, and the Moscow Central State Puppet Theatre, the latter employing a live actor as the giant (ogre). He has puppets as prisoners in the dungeon of his castle; there is tremendous dramatic tension when the hand grasps a puppet. The Cat who calls on the giant persuades him to demonstrate his power of transformation, first as a Lion, then as a Mouse, whereupon she pounces. A new translation by Geoffrey Brereton of this and *The Sleeping Beauty, Cinderella, Bluebeard and other tales* is available in the Penguin Classics.

Püterschein system. Method of marionette construction and control based on study of gravitation and relationship of weight, the movement of parts from fixed points or fulcrums, design of control and method of stringing. Dealt with in detail and scientifically by W. A. Dwiggins in *Marionette in Motion*, q.v. (Puppetry Imprints Handbook No. XII; Detroit, 1939). Theory is that whole weight of marionette at rest is carried by the two head-strings, whereas the alternative approach whereby head is supported by the body and the body by the shoulder strings gives a different range of movements. In either case the control has to be regarded as part of the puppet. Also a section on this topic in Batchelder *Puppet Theatre Handbook*, q.v.

Q

Quand les marionnettes du monde se donnent le main ... Interesting collection of papers on various aspects of puppetry given at the Congrès International de la Marionnette Traditionnelle (Liege, 1958); text partly in English, partly French; useful notes on the many European companies and their theatres that participated in the festival of modern and traditional puppets; many illustrations.

R

Rackham, Arthur (1867–1939). English illustrator, *Grimm's Fairy Tales, Peter Pan*, etc. Illustrated Perrault's stories by silhouettes, creating effect of shadow theatre figures for each story.

Raffia. Fibre from Madagascar palm, used in mat making and basketry; good range of colours in small hanks from craft-material stockists; useful for puppet hair, grass skirts, decor. Also plastic variety with high sheen.

Raffles, Sir Thomas Stamford (1781–1826). Lieutenant-Governor of Java, creator of Singapore; established the Royal Zoological Society; collected, author of *The History of Java* (2 vols., Murray, 1817), which according to Batchelder (*Rod Puppets and the Human Theatre*, q.v.) has some inaccuracies shown by later research. The bulk of his collection of Wayang Leather Puppets, masks and gamelan (orchestral instruments) – acquired 1810–24 – was presented to the British Museum in 1859 by the executors of Lady Raffles. Some of the material is to be seen in the Ethnographic Department, the Wayang figures probably some of the earliest extant. (Also examples of Chinese shadow figures in same section.)

Rain box. Simple 'effects' equipment: box containing dried peas, rice, small beads, etc., for producing sound of rain.

Rake. Theatrical term for slope of stage floor in eighteenth–nineteenth century theatres (whence 'upstage' towards the back, 'downstage' towards the footlights) introduced partly to assist in creating scenic illusion. In modern theatres the auditorium floor is raked, degree of incline varying. Necessary to check sight-lines from various parts of the house when mobile puppet stage mounted on theatre stage.

Ramayana. 'The Adventures of Rama', the oldest Sanskrit epic poem, attributed to the Sage Valmaki (*c.* 500 B.C.) and part of the cultural tradition in India and Indonesia; MSS. vary widely, this and the other great epic, the *Mahabharata*, having been transmitted orally for centuries before being written down. Rama was the early 'superman' hero; his wife Sita has to be rescued from the Demon King; there are supernatural elements and monkey allies. Both epics have been the source of puppet plays in India, Java, Burma, Thailand, Malaya. A special issue of the Unesco 'Courier' (December, 1967) was devoted to these two works and their influence on the arts, dance-drama, shadow puppetry, with 12 pages of illustrations in full colour.

Raree Show. Seventeenth–eighteenth century term for a Peep Show. Samuel Johnson's *Dictionary of the English Language* (1827) gives origin of term as 'imitation of the foreign way of pronouncing "rare" show'; a show carried in a box; peep show, and cites Pope: 'The fashions of the town affect us just like a raree-show; we have the curiosity to peep at them.' Early exhibitors were Savoyards, but there is no evidence of *their* term for the entertainment. Literary variants: rary-show, rary-shew, raree-show-box. Sterne, *Tristam Shandy*: 'Thou didst look into it with as much innocence of heart as ever child look'd into a raree-shew-box.' Scott, *Peveril of the Peak*: 'Fitter . . . by his size and appearance for the inside of a raree-show than the mysteries of a plot.' Swift *Tale of a Tub*: 'Lord Peter was also held the Original Author of Puppets and Raree-shows, the great usefulness whereof being so generally known, I shall not enlarge farther . . .' There could be a possible connection, as suggested by N. D. Shergold in *History of the Spanish Stage* (Oxford, 1967) between 'raree' and 'reredos' or church altar-piece with carved figures (and between the Spanish 'retablo' and 'reredos' – used as word for an entertainment, *c.* 1539, wooden figures moved by clockwork, in sixteenth–seventeenth century as term for a peep show, and for the puppet show in Cervantes *Don Quixote*).

Rasp. Rough file, having separate teeth instead of grooves: quick cutting in preliminary shaping of wood or polystyrene.

Ravel, Maurice (1875–1937). French composer of mainly opera, ballet, orchestrated piano pieces: *Bolero* (1928); *L'Enfant et les Sortilèges* was written to a text by Colette, q.v., written for her small daughter and variously interpreted as 'dream of a naughty child' and 'little boy bewitched' (but neither having quite the impact of the original title: 'sortilège': magic, sorcery). There have been a number of puppet adaptations, notably that of the Welsh 'Caricature Theatre' directed by Jane Phillips, q.v.

Recordings, Use of. To use or not to use disc and/or magnetic tape recordings in puppet productions is one of the more controversial topics with contemporary puppeteers; members of audiences vary in their reactions, and this may be due to the constant acceptance of sound from radio, television and home recording equipment, i.e. a conditioning of the listener. In the days before recordings were practicable the performances were necessarily 'live' – and many of those who use recordings admit that the live performance is the ideal, and then proceed to explain why the ideal is not practicable. If it were *technically* possible to achieve identical results from the *aesthetic* aspect, then there might be no argument; this is a possibility with a televised performance, as *both vision and sound* are recorded (whether televised 'live' or pre-recorded). However, the televised show, as such, necessarily loses in comparison with the live performance, however enjoyable it may be; this will still be true even when colour-TV is universal. Discussion divides into (*a*) the use of recordings for speech (dialogue) and (*b*) their use for music and 'effects'. Discussion starts with the assumption that recordings are of equal quality and apparatus is fool-proof; in practice neither assumption is true. It must be admitted that many performances are spoiled by poor quality recording, worn discs, breakdowns; also by ignoring the need to tune the volume to the acoustics of the auditorium. There are psychological differences for the performers when acting 'live' or against a recording of the dialogue; technical differences also; the audience will not be aware of these, only of the results. An actor-with-puppet moves about with that puppet and, if speaking for it, the voice comes from the same position as the puppet; with recorded sound it comes from the position of the 'speaker' (probably amplified, and so having a different quality). In a large theatre the actor speaking for his puppet may use a portable microphone; again volume needs testing and controlling. On a very wide stage the puppets may often be some distance away from the point or points of emission of sound. In outdoor shows it is all too often obvious where the sound is coming from: the 'speakers' at the sides of the stage, *not* from the puppets. Against this could be put the example of the Bunraku, q.v., convention of having a narrator and a musician at the side of the stage (in view of the audience); as indicated earlier, the listener becomes conditioned, accepts the convention. One of the major arguments supporting the use of recordings is that of *economy*; few puppet theatres can afford a resident orchestra – unlike that of Prince Esterhazy, for whom Haydn, q.v., wrote little marionette operas. The Salzburg Marionette Theatre has recordings of its musical productions, including the vocal parts in the operas – sung in various languages (for use when touring). The whole economy of any company has to be considered, including physical *space*, but mainly the number of personnel justified by the box-office results. Small companies wishing to put on large productions resort to recordings; performers with inadequate vocal technique or range (for 'character' voices) 'borrow' voices and record them. Here again the aesthetic aspect arises: the quality of the performance must match that of the borrowed voices. In the human theatre no actor would dream of having a recorded voice providing the dialogue while miming the action; he would be cast for his ability to act *and* speak as required. *Because* the actor (invisible) in the puppet theatre *can* take far more parts than would be possible on the live stage, there is the risk that he will accept a range of characters beyond his vocal range – and resort to taped voices. There are also performers who are quite adequate when it comes to providing spoken dialogue, but who still prefer to record it; this may be psychological – an attempt to avoid any risk of forgetting the 'lines' – or it may be felt that delegating the act of speech to a recording leaves the performer free to attend more closely to manipulating. This is a misconception, in fact, as it is vital to synchronise speech and action – and this *divides* the attention between manipulating and listening. The performer who both manipulates and speaks has an advantage as to synchronisation. In the case of music, e.g. for dancing, for ballet, it may matter little to the manipulator whether the sound is from an actual orchestra or from a recording. So far, in Indonesia, there is no sign of substituting recordings for the music of the (live) gamelan orchestra backstage, during the Wayang, q.v., performances. Such a musical item as the 'piano act', q.v., a live pianist synchronising with the marionette has an advantage over the operator trying to synchronise with a recording; this is why none of those who copied the original act in Podrecca's *Teatro dei Piccoli* have managed to match the quality. Psychologically, those who manipulate to recordings of speech, even if they know the dialogue as well as the recorded speaker, have the problem of synchronising mentally and emotionally with sounds coming from elsewhere: they are the slaves of the tape. When it comes to the type of show in which there is instinctive audience participation, q.v., no amount of editing of tapes – leaving gaps for the audience to fill – can ever succeed, as it is impossible to anticipate exact responses, they vary with different audiences. In practice every user of recordings will justify such use.

Regional characters. Just as there are puppets which are associated with a particular nation – the English Punch, French Guignol (originally Lyonnais), German Kasper or Kasperle, Turkish Karagöz – there are also some more local types, usually speaking the patois of the area, e.g. the French Jacques (Lille) and Lafleur (Amiens), Italian Gianduja (Turin). Duchartre (*The Italian Comedy*, Dover, 1966) mentions Stentarello, a simpleton who used to come on stage and perform without any reference to the actual plot and action – a forerunner of the Marx Brothers – a similar line being followed by actors in Milan, Venice, and elsewhere, these being known as *rôles caratterista*, characters associated with a region. Some of the traditional types have survived, mentioned above, but there is a suggestion here for some contemporary local types.

Reinforcement. Any 'filler' used to give greater strength in plastics; also muslin used to strengthen hollow puppet head made from a filler.

Reiniger, Lotte. Internationally famous creator of silhouette films. Born Berlin-Charlottenburg, Germany (1899). Extremely happy childhood, developing passion for painting and drawing, inspired by visits with father to the Arts Academy. Liked to tell stories with the drawings and later developed passion for the theatre, continually performing with classmates. When films appeared, passion swung over to that medium. On Easter Sunday, 1915, heard lecture by Paul Wegener, great German actor and film-pioneer whose films had made a strong impression; learned of stop-motion technique and the fantastic possibilities and then had no other ambition. Wegener, at height of fame, was playing at the Reinhardt theatre and Lotte was able to attend the Reinhardt acting school and to see many notable performances; began cutting portrait silhouettes of the actors in their typical attitudes, which impressed Wegener – who had a real understanding of the visual arts – and led to her first film work (cutting out title pictures for Wegener's film *The Pied Piper of Hamelin*), and in 1919 to an introduction to a group of scientists and artists who had formed an experimental film studio in Berlin, the Institut für Kulturforschung (still in existence). Made first silhouette film in 1919, the figures being articulated directly in front of camera (unlike animated cartoons), so that the camera-work was a creative function and not a mechanical reproduction. 'I obviously had a vocation for this hitherto non-existing occupation, for I have not stopped it ever since.' Married Carl Koch in 1921, a member of the small unit, working together from then onwards in the new medium, except for period when he went to France to work with Jean Renoir. Made various silhouette films for the Institute and in 1923 had offer to produce first full-length silhouette film, based on a combination of themes from the Arabian Nights and called *The Adventures of Prince Achmed*, working on this from 1923–26 in close collaboration with the leading animation artists of the period. Most successful of the later films were *Dr Dolittle* (1927), *Harlequin* (1931), *Carmen* (1933) and *Papageno* (1935). Exhibition of work at the Victoria and Albert Museum in London and worked in England from then on. Worked on various films during the war, but unable to finish any of these. Post-war work included series of films for Children's Television in London, one of these (*The Gallant Little Tailor*) awarded first prize at the Biennale in Venice in 1955 for Television 'shorts'. Later made various films in colour and short interludes and used same articulated figures in films with coloured transparent backgrounds; also interludes for pantomimes for the theatre in Coventry. After death of husband in 1963 made only one more pantomime interlude, but now working on direct shadow-plays with manipulation by horizontal rods. (For full list of Lotte Reiniger Silhouette Films *see* SILHOUETTE.)

Release agent. Also known as 'separator' or 'parting agent': any lubricant which prevents plastic or other casting material from adhering to inside of mould.

Repertoire, repertory. Stock of plays or other items of individual performers or companies, which have been presented and can be produced when required.

Repertory of Marionette Plays, compiled by Paul McPharlin (Viking Press, N.Y., 1929). Includes items for hand puppets and shadow shows; interesting collection of translations, including *The Coq Brothers* (a sentimental comedy by Laurent Mourguet, creator of 'Guignol'); *The Death of Tintagiles* (symbolic drama by Maurice Maeterlinck), *Junkdump Fair* (Goethe), *Casper among the Savages* (Pocci), *Candidate for Trepagny* (Maurice Sand), *Cataclysterium's Medicine* (Duranty; slapstick farce), *Every Dog has his Day* (Dondo), and *Noël* (Bouchor: written for the Petit Théâtre, Paris). Excellent pre-1929 bibliography, well annotated; lists of producers in Britain and U.S.A.

Respighi, Ottorino (1879–1936). Italian composer; his '*Sleeping Beauty*' opera adapted for puppet stage by Vittorio Podrecca (Teatro dei Piccoli). Illustrations in Beaumont *Puppets and Puppetry*, q.v.

Revolve. Circular section of stage floor (occupying the central acting area) pre-set for quick scene changes, operated manually or mechanically, one set disappearing and the next taking its place. The device has also been introduced into some model theatres, but is rarely practical in puppet theatres. The Narrator in the Japanese BUNRAKU puppet theatre sits at one side of the stage on a rostrum which is equipped with a revolving section, used when a replacement Narrator is to be brought on. Experiments have been made with a revolving backscreen of an open-type hand puppet stage (by the present author) with decor back and front; the

BACKSCREEN is suspended on a length of aluminium tubing (vertical) fixed in the centre of the top cross-rail; a button-catch each end locks the centre section to the wing pieces.

Richard Teschner und sein Figurenspiegel, by Dr Franz Hadamowsky (Vienna, 1956). Author is director of the Theatre Collection at the Austrian National Library in Vienna; this monograph is not only a tribute to the life and work of a unique artist-puppeteer, it also reveals for the first time the 'secrets' of his superb techniques which evolved from a study of the Javanese wayang golek type and from a concept of puppet theatre which had no place for dialogue, but a magical use of lighting and music; the design of the stage itself with its concave-lens proscenium being the perfect setting for the dream-like productions. See also FIGURENSPIEGEL.

Rifflers. Specially shaped metallic files (eight or more) designed for work on curved surfaces.

Ring control. Special form of marionette control, having rings at the operational end of the strings, slipped on to fingers for special manipulation. Also a unique type found in India, worn on the head like a crown, supporting strings descending to the head, shoulders and spine of marionette, leaving performer's hands free to control the arms by rods (from above).

Rip van Winkle, by Washington Irving (1783–1859), attributed to 'Diedrich Knickerbocker'; a number of puppet productions include one by the Japanese theatre PUK, q.v. Theme: Rip van Winkle goes on a solitary ramble in the Catskill Mountains to escape from his wife, falls asleep, wakes up 20 years later; his wife has died, his house is in ruins, the world has utterly changed.

Road Safety. Some puppet companies include 'Safety' items in their programmes (which may be sponsored by municipal or local education authorities). Occasional articles in the *Safety Training* Bulletin for Parents and Teachers: Autumn, 1959, had 'Kerb Drill' and 'Keeping Dog on Lead'; The Keith-Blair puppets contributed 'Alice in Bomperland' (No. 89, 1960).

Robinson, Stuart. Head of the Arts and Crafts Department, City of Coventry College of Education; trained at Goldsmith's College, Central School of Art and the Slade School; alert to the values of puppetry in education; co-author with wife Patricia (teacher, lecturer, textile designer, printer) of *Exploring Puppetry*, q.v.

Rocker or Rocking Bar. Cross-piece on a marionette control, having a see-saw action on a pivot-screw; usually operated by thumb and one finger, giving a 'marking time' or walking movement by alternately lifting the puppet knees (done with one hand); optionally the bar can be removable.

Rod puppets. Usually operated from below in contemporary European and American types (derivatives of the Javanese traditional types) – but with a number of variations both old and new. The puppets may be two- or three-dimensional: e.g. children will construct figures with flat cut-out heads or painted picnic-plates mounted on flat laths. In Sicily and Belgium there are folk puppets operated from above, the figures being large and heavy; an iron rod is attached to or passes through the head, a thinner rod may be attached to a sword arm. In the German Rhineland puppet theatres, a long rod is used, reaching to the floor, supporting figure above head level, one arm swinging free, one controlled by thin rod; legs free. In South India there is a traditional rod-and-string type which, like the Sicilian, is large and heavy; support is by heavy strings from the sides of the waist and sides of the ears of the figure, attached to a padded ring worn on the operator's head like a crown; his hands hold rods (downwards) attached to the puppet hands. A group from New York use giant puppets in street shows, with internal operators, some requiring three performers with pole controls. In Java flat shadow-type figures are held against a screen by rods (operator in squatting position) and there is a three-dimensional type operated from below (rod passes through a tube to give a swivel action). Unique among European developments were the puppets made by TESCHNER (influenced by the Javanese), who developed internal controls with strings running *through* very thin rods. In Russia the EFIMOVS (sculptor husband, painter wife) carried out experiments, later extended by Sergei OBRAZTSOV (originally a hand-puppet performer, later Director of the Moscow Central State Puppet Theatre) and which have had world-wide repercussions. The simplest form of rod puppet is the medieval Fool's 'MAROT' (marotte) – a short baton or sceptre surmounted by a small head in cap and bells; this also has had modern developments, particularly in France. Extend the rod and figures with large heads, arms, costumes can be contrived; there can be a jointed neck with internal control, or the neck can be a powerful length of spring. A shoulder-piece can be mounted (rod running through central hole) and arms of cord or tape, with or without cardboard tube sections, can be controlled by thin rods (external). If the puppet mechanism becomes elaborate then two operators will be required, one for the main support and any head movements (possibly mouth and eye action) and one for the arms. Short rods (internal) can be attached to forearms. Another variation has the substitution of live hands for puppet hands (large heads). The head can also be supported and moved by one hand (in same way as hand puppet), but with rods to puppet hands (hand-and-rod type). If the figure has a three-dimensional body, legs can be attached as for a marionette and string-controlled from below. The VENTRILOQUIAL puppet (doll, dummy) has a short internal head-control, as has the 'three man' figure of the Japanese BUNRAKU theatre. Other variants include the large SIAMESE shadow-scenes (static figure cut in one piece with decorative scene) supported in two cleft rods, one in each hand, and 'double marot' type, e.g. two ends of horse each constructed around short rod. The stage for the rod types operated from below is of similar construction to the hand-puppet booth, but will usually be of greater frontage to give maximum action possibilities; more floor-space for the operators is necessary if two- or even three-man figures are used. Standard work, with extensive historical data and technical information, well illustrated, is by Marjorie Batchelder *Rod Puppets and the Human Theatre* (Ohio State University Press, 1947). Also, both technical: *Hand-and-Rod Puppets* (same, 1947), by Batchelder and Michael; *Comment construire et animer nos marionettes* (for marotte), by Marcel Temporal (1953).

Rod Puppets and the Human Theatre, by Marjorie Batchelder (Ohio State University Press, 1947). Major work on historical development of the rod puppet, its relation to the live theatre, information on use, modern developments, construction (details and diagrams); also an analysis of aesthetics of puppet theatre. Author a practising puppeteer, producer, teacher, experimentalist interested in educational and social values, as well as the professional aspects. Extensive annotated bibliography; over 100 illustrations (some rare).

Roman du bon Roi Alexandre, Li (The Romance of Alexander). Illuminated Flemish manuscript in the Bodleian Library, Oxford, text in Picard dialect; anonymous author (1338), illustrations by Juan or Jehan de Grise (added *c.* 1344); two marginal illustrations of particular interest to puppeteers, showing hand puppet booths (castelettes), with either a curved roof or curve-topped BACKSCREEN; one has a tower each end of the PLAYBOARD, one is castellated the full width of the stage; design gives the name: castelet, castelette, castello. In one there are four puppets on stage, indicating two performers (or more), the other has only two; delightfully stylised audiences. The entire MSS. was reproduced with an introduction by M. R. James (1933); the British Museum has coloured post card reproductions, and there are others in various puppet books, a particularly good full-page colour item of one in Baird *Art of the Puppet* (Collier-Macmillan, 1965).

Rootitootoot. Sound associated with Punch and any of his overseas cousins with swazzle-voices. OBRAZTSOV, in his *Chinese Puppet Theatre* (Faber, 1961), found that Chinese showmen use a 'whistle' giving the same kind of noise as the Russian PETRUSHKA, referred to by the Chinese as 'U-dyu-dyu' – while a Ukrainian puppet talking in that fashion is called a 'Vanka Ru-tyu-tyu'. The RAJASTHANI puppeteers use a bamboo-type SWAZZLE.

Rose and the Ring, by William Makepeace Thackeray, q.v.; 'A Fireside Pantomime for Great and Small Children', written while staying with a large family in Rome for Christmas, with the help of a Miss Bunch, the governess. With characters called King Valeroso the 24th of Paphlagonia, Glumboso the Prime Minister, Countess Gruffanuff, Prince Bulbo of Crim Tartary, and Captain Hedzoff, it invites puppet adaptation, and was produced by Tony SARG and others in the U.S.A.

Rossini, Giocchimo (1792–1868). Italian composer. His opera *L'occasione fa il Ladro* (Opportunity makes the Thief) had puppet production by Podrecca's Teatro dei Piccoli (illustrations in Beaumont *Puppets and Puppetry*; Studio, 1958).

Rowe, Nicholas (1674–1718). English playwright, acquaintance of Pope and Addison; in *Lady Jane Grey* (iv, i), produced at Drury Lane Theatre in 1715, has a reference to 'their puppet queen . . .'

Rowlandson, Thomas (1756–1827). English designer, etcher, caricaturist, one of many inspired by Punch; his *George the Third and Queen Charlotte driving through the Broadway*, Deptford (1785), includes what is possibly the earliest illustration of a street Punch and Judy show.

Rubber heads. Hollow puppet heads made from liquid rubber ('soft toy mix') by the casting method in a two-piece mould made from clay or plasticine model; rubber is supplied in 1-gallon tins, is poured into the MOULD (two halves tied together) through the open end of the neck, is given time to coagulate on the inner surface (half to one hour, varying with thickness) and the surplus poured back into container, which must be kept airtight. When dry, rubber cast removed; it will be flexible, which permits some UNDERCUTTING of the features. Colouring: rubber paint, flexible, obtainable from Macadam Ltd., London; or waterproof inks can be mixed with rubber solution, or powder (poster) colours mixed with emulsion. Suppliers: write to Dunlop's, Chester Road, Birmingham, for address of nearest stockist.

Rue des marionnettes. 'Street of the puppets' – in old Paris, where objects of piety were sold, including statuettes of the Virgin Mary, 'little Maries', possible source of the word 'marionnette' (which is a double diminutive), but the puppet historians vary in their opinions. The French 'Marie' derived from the Latin and gave rise to a variety of forms: mariola, marotte, mariotte, mariole, mariette, marion, marionnette. A note about this street appeared in the review *Wallonia* (December, 1911).

Rumania. Up to the early part of the nineteenth century the wandering showmen with their puppet plays, in which Vasilache featured, another of Punch's many cousins, provided one of the most popular forms of folk drama. Official support was not forthcoming for professional companies formed in first part of twentieth century, but rapid developments took place from 1944 onwards under the cultural drive of the People's Democratic State; by 1949 ten puppet theatres had been established in Bucharest, Craiova, Oradea, Cluj and elsewhere, and there are now well over 20 theatres all with their resident staff of performers and technicians; some millions of spectators attended the many thousands of performances in the first decade. Some theatres cater for national minorities by playing in German or Hungarian. Repertoire is derived both from the tales of Andersen and Grimm and from Rumanian classics – and even Jules Verne's *Five Weeks in a Balloon*. Bucharest has been the centre for three international puppet festivals; its own Tandarica theatre, q.v., directed by Margareta Niculescu, has won international awards. The Ministry of Culture offers training courses dealing with all the aspects of production. There are numerous amateur ensembles throughout the country. Rumanian puppeteers helped to establish the first puppet theatre in Cairo in 1959 (United Arab Republic). Mme Niculescu acted as Chairman of the international Editorial Board which compiled the important book *The Puppet Theatre of the Modern World*, q.v., which includes a number of illustrations from Rumanian sources.

Running or Run-through string. Double length string running from one hand to the other of a marionette, passing through a screw-eye on the control, permitting movement of either or both hands.

Ruskin, John (1819–1900). His *King of the Golden River* performed, among others, by the Tatterman Marionettes in the United States. As a boy was given some toy puppets which danced when a string was tied to the leg of a chair – apparently a variation of the MARIONNETTES À LA PLANCHETTE.

S

Sachs, Hans (1494–1576). One of the earliest German playwrights (Nürnberg), shoemaker-poet, some of whose items are still played.

Harro Siegel, German puppeteer, adapted two plays: *Cutting of Fools* and *The Devil Marries an Old Hag*. English translation of *The Strolling Clerk from Paradise* included in *Plays for Puppets*, edited Jan Bussell (Faber, 1951).

Safety Last. An approved series on Road Safety and Safety in the Home, presented by English company The Keith Blair Puppets, in conjunction with local Safety Campaign organiseis. Each show stresses one main feature, such as Kerb Drill – or Running Out Behind Stationary Vehicles – with incidental lessons on the use of special road-crossings, and a final Quiz on Road Rules. Show also features a ventriloquial parrot; special programmes for deaf children. *Kitchen Kapers* related to Home Safety scheme worked out in conjunction with Royal Society for Prevention of Accidents and local committees. Television puppeteers giving road safety instruction should remember that right is left and left is right on the screen to young viewers, so puppet may need to turn his back to the viewers to avoid confusion.

Saint-Exupéry, Antoine de (1900–43). French writer, professional air pilot. Published *Courier Sud* (1929), *Terre des Hommes* (1939), written after a crash in the desert and rescue by an Arab. Pilot in World War II, moved to the United States after Fall of France; continued writing. Flying with American Forces over the Mediterranean, disappeared. His *The Little Prince*, q.v., has had various puppet adaptations. Available in English in Puffin Books.

St George and the Dragon: Punch and Judy, by Diana John (Penguin Books, 1966). A 'Puffin' book; the first play is for live actors and is based on the old Mummers' play; it can be adapted for puppets; the second is for puppets and has instructions for making them (by Philippa Gregory). Illustrated throughout by drawings.

Saint of Puppetry. S. Simeon el Salo (Simeon Salus); Roman martyr (1st July), died 588. Lived as hermit in Sinai Desert for 30 years, nicknamed 'salus' = 'fool' on account of eccentric behaviour. Small illustration on text from South America shows the Saint holding a small branch (? olive) in one hand, a puppet on his other and holding a miniature branch. Text is a prayer in Spanish, with typical reference to the human as puppet. (None of the books of Saints consulted mention puppets, but perhaps he is Patron Saint by adoption and because of his eccentricity.)

St Paul's Church, Covent Garden. Known as 'the actors' church', built by Inigo-Jones in the heart of London in a district which has many associations with puppet shows. A letter supposedly from the Sexton of the Church, in an issue of the *Spectator*, complained that Powell's puppet show was stealing the congregation by timing his performances against the tolling of the bell. On the 26th May, 1962, a special service was held in the church as part of the Tercentenary celebrations for Mr Punch (q.v.), and a plaque on the outside wall reads 'Near this spot Punch's puppet show was first performed in England and witnessed by Samuel Pepys, 1662.' On this occasion the church was filled with Punchmen (and some Dog Tobies) and other puppeteers.

Saint-Saëns, Camille (1835–1921). French composer; his *Carnival of Animals* sometimes used as background music for puppet items; the item *Le Cygne* (The Swan) is in repertoire of the SALZBURG MARIONETTE THEATRE, in homage to Anna Pavlova, the great Russian ballerina.

Salt. Added to Plaster of Paris mix used for making moulds for casting; speeds the setting process. (Vinegar increases the setting time.)

Salzburg Marionette Theatre. Founded by Professor Anton Aicher (1859–1930) and now world-famous and fashionable; it is usually necessary to book seats a long way ahead. Present Director, son, Hermann Aicher. The theatre employs hundreds of artists, sculptors, writers, composers, singers, actors, instrumentalists and technicians; a second company makes world tours, their performances being seen by millions of spectators. Puppets are counted by the thousand and a great deal of constructional and technical experiment is carried out to attain maximum movement and control of the superbly-made marionettes; there are critics who think them *too* lifelike. Constructional developments include hollow-ring torso, sectional limbs, special stringing and design of controls. See *Salzburg Marionette Theatre*, by Gottfried Krauss, for interesting data on techniques and biographical material. The extensive repertoire includes operas, especially by Mozart, genius and 'guardian angel' of Salzburg: *Apollo and Hyacinth, Bastien and Bastienne, Don Giovanni, The Magic Flute, The Abduction from the Seraglio,* and his *Eine Kleine Nachtmusik;* Strauss operetta *Die Fledermaus*. Ballet includes Saint-Saëns *The Dying Swan* (in homage to Pavlova) and Tchaikowsky *Nutcracker Suite*. Plays total about 150 items and include Shakespeare *The Tempest* and *Dr Faust, The Wizard of Oz, Rumpelstiltskin;* special recordings have been made of programmes in English, French, Italian, Japanese, 'American' and Canadian-French. Some illustrations in Beaumont *Puppets and Puppetry* (Studio, 1958) and UNIMA *Puppet Theatre of the Modern World* (Harrap, 1967).

Salzburg Marionette Theatre, by Gottfried Kraus, photographs by Gretl Aicher (Residenzverlag, 1966). English text; interesting historical and technical material; 68 illustrations, workshops, stage scenes, close-ups of controls; repertoire for 1913–66 (operas, operettas, musical plays, straight plays, pantomime, marionette plays, ballets); impressive list of countries toured.

Samar, Dr Devi Lal. Director of the Lok Kala Mandal, Udaipur, Rajasthan, India, a research institute concerned with folklore, traditional folk dances, drama, puppets. Contributor of interesting article on the puppets and puppeteers of Rajasthan in *Puppet Theatre Around the World* (Bharatiya Natya Sangh, New Delhi, 1960); organiser of All-India Puppet Festivals; troupe took part in International Festivals in Europe and in the third Bucharest event gained award in the traditional category; visited London and gave several performances, including some folk-dance items.

Samisen (Shamisen). Japanese three-string musical instrument, approximately 3-ft. in length; belly of catskin (originally snakeskin); played by large plectrum. Tuning variable, e.g. two fourths, fourth and fifth, two fifths, to suit melody accompanied. Used in the BUNRAKU puppet theatre as dramatic background to the Narration. Earliest variety was imported from Manila and displaced the traditional biwa (4-string lute type of Chinese origin). History and technical details (including photographs) in Malm, *Japanese Music and Musical Instruments* (Tuttle, U.S.A., Japan, 1959).

Sand, George (Amantine Lucile Aurore, née Dupin, Baroness of Dudevant, 1804–76). French novelist, poetess, writer of memoirs, founder of famous puppet theatre of the Writers' Circle in her chateau at Nohant, q.v., near Lachâtre; theatre and puppets have been preserved. Son Maurice made the puppets, George the costumes – both having a preference for hand puppets; 120 plays were produced (scenarios with improvised dialogue). Author mentions the puppet activities in her *L'Homme de Neige* (Hachette, 1859) and *Dernières Pages* (Colman-Levy, 1877). Article in Craig *The Marionnette* (October, 1918), *George Sand et le Théâtre de Nohant*, by Aurore Lauth-Sand (1930).

Sand, Maurice (1823–89). Son of famous French writer George Sand, q.v. As a boy had a miniature stage with cut-out characters; later created hand puppets for the 'Théâtre des Amis' at the chateau in Nohant, q.v., where plays were given over a period of 30 years. Maurice carved and painted heads, adding glass eyes, real hair and beards, George made the costumes. Some of the repertoire published (five comedies), *Sand's Plays for Marionettes*, q.v. (Benn, 1930); title should be 'Plays for Puppets'. Illustration showing theatre and audience, from a drawing, reproduced in Baird *Art of the Puppet* (Collier-Macmillan, 1965).

Sandpaper. Technically the term is obsolete, although still in use; the term 'coated abrasive' has no sales appeal for the public. There are different types and different grades of abrasives suited to different classes of work, including flint, garnet, emery, silicon, carbide.

Sand's Plays for Marionettes (English translation). See PLAYS FOR MARION-ETTES, SAND.

Sarg, Tony (1880–1942). Born in Guatemala, son of German consul. Became highly successful illustrator in London, with rooms over the famous Old Curiosity Shop (tourist Mecca). Built up collection of old toys and acquired an interest in marionettes and, after studying perform-ances by the Holden troupe, produced his own studio shows, one of which was seen by G. Bernard Shaw. Moved to New York in 1915 and teamed with other illustrators (Frank Godwin and Mat Searle); first big touring show an adaptation of Washington Irving's *Rip van Winkle*, seeing which decided BIL BAIRD as to his own career (later worked with Sarg). Among other outstanding activities, invented animated gas-filled creatures for the Macy Parade. Author, with Anne Stoddard, *Book of Marionette Plays*.

Sawdust. Coarse variety sometimes used for stuffed cloth marionette filling; fine (wood flour) mixed with cellulose cement forms plastic wood.

Scale. Relative dimensions – as distinct from actual size. The puppet maker has to consider not only the proportions of any particular puppet, e.g. leg length against overall height, size of head against body, size of hands against face; for dramatic purposes these may be deliberately made disproportionate, e.g. a large character with tiny hands will be weakened. Other points of reference are (*a*) the overall size of the figure relative to the stage, e.g. a very wide stage will make a hand puppet look smaller than when seen in a narrow stage; (*b*) if there is a PROSCENIUM arch, the height of the puppet relative to this – a small (short) figure will make the arch seem higher; (*c*) the height of the puppets relative to each other; the primitive rule is to make the important ones larger; if a giant has to be introduced into a small stage that does not allow for much increase of height relative to the non-giants, such details as a heavy mop of hair, large ears, large nose, large hands, will help to create the effect desired; a comic and purely puppet answer might be to have the giant very long and sticking out of the top of the stage. With an open-front stage the giant can be as tall as the ceiling allows – the problem then being how to get him on and off stage. There are no problems that cannot be solved, but this requires consideration of performing conditions when planning a production and the puppets to be used.

Scaramouche (Scaramuccia). One of the many 'stock characters', q.v., created from about the middle of the sixteenth century by various troupes of the commedia dell' arte, q.v.; both Scaramouche and Pulcinella (whence Punch) were born in Naples. Duchartre, in *The Italian Comedy*, q.v., quotes Du Tralage, who wrote of Molière that 'he held Scaramouche in great esteem' and that he was the model by which Molière trained his best actors, which seems to be a reference to the actor's art rather than the character as such – which is however indicated in the very name, meaning 'little Skirmisher'; costume always completely black; a wine-women-and-song man, often taking the part of a valet, given to picking pockets; best friend, although constantly quarrelling, Pulcinella. At one time he frequently appeared with Punch, but probably made way for the English Clown Joey.

Scenario (Italian). Outline of plot of play; synopsis, as distinct from complete script. In the case of films, it is the complete plot. It was the working plan for the 'improvised' comedies (COMMEDIA DELL' ARTE), indicating the sequence of episodes, exits and entries, the main course to be followed. Hand puppet performances are often based on a scenario, this leaving the actors free to vary the dialogue and action – particularly if it is the type of show which evokes AUDIENCE PARTICIPATION, e.g. as in Punch and Judy.

Scenery. Stage setting designed to indicate the place of the action, the locale. The use of stage-sets was unknown in classical and medieval drama, and until the Renaissance performances were given against permanent backgrounds, sometimes architectural. Painted backcloths were introduced; full-scale stage settings developing with the coming of opera. A taste for realism was followed by symbolism – and in modern theatre many producers make their own conventions; monetary economy as well as design economy may be an influence. With puppet stages there are special technical factors that influence design, such as the risk of catching of strings while using marionettes. In small stages the puppets and scenery are relatively close and there must be co-operation between scene designer and costume designer; on the other hand, in some of the larger European theatres the scenic designer may be dominant – rather than the puppets. Some of the most dramatic performances are given against a black background; with the 'BLACK THEATRE' technique the focus can be entirely on the puppets and their PROPS.

Schattenspiel, das farbige, by Dr Max Bührmann (Paul Haupt, Berne, 1955). German text, with 41 photo illustrations, mainly on Chinese shadow figures – on which the author is an authority – with constructional diagram for screen and figures.

Schichtl marionettes. Transformation figures created by members of the Schichtl family, German puppeteers of late eighteenth and nineteenth centuries, popular in Central Europe; some of the younger generation visited the United States early twentieth century. Items included variations of the lady-into-balloon figure, an egg-laying ostrich (with dragon emerging from egg). Tony Sarg acquired a Schichtl figure of an owl used on a darkened stage with special lighting. The British Puppet and Model Theatre Guild has specimens in its collection, occasionally demonstrated, including a man-into-aeroplane figure.

Schiller, Friedrich von (1750–1805). German poet and dramatist; as a child played with puppet theatre, assisted by sister Christophine.

Schmid, Joseph Leonhard (1822–1912). German puppeteer popularly known as 'Papa Schmid', q.v.

Schneckenburger, Frederick (1922–67). Swiss puppeteer whose sur-realist creations at one time were regarded as the most notorious in the world, and some of them as 'vicious'. Curiously enough he used some of the same puppets in performances for children as appeared in items for the sophisticated adult audiences. Began puppet-making in 1947, carving first 40 figures with a pocket-knife. A Kasper-figure consisted mainly of a bulbous nose with a wire shape holding the eyes, a harlequin pattern costume, and white-gloved human hands. Some puppets were given distorted angular arms, and one head made in the manner of African craftwork with beads. A wide stage permitted broad movement of the rod figures, with dramatic lighting and music in keeping with the puppets. His company consisted of five players, four speakers and seven singers. In the item *Lilt of Life*, done in operatic style, a Dowager has a sequence of curious suitors, including a murderer, a plumber, with some flashbacks and flash-forwards by the Kasper figure, the doorbell rings constantly, the lady dances with the plumber; finally comes 'the sweetest of all husbands' – Death. The plumber consoles himself with the now rich Maid. A programme note for *Green and Yellow*, 'The Meadow's Green has fallen in love with the Yellow of the Sun and finds its love requited. But the meadow has gone off colour . . .' The Cow and an Old Man and Three Ladies stage a Great Revolution, which restores the status quo. The note ends: 'But then, of course, they were only Two Hands . . .' Some illustrations in Beaumont *Puppets and Puppetry* (Studio, 1958).

School for Rabbits. Hand puppet play designed to induce pre-school age children to look forward to school life; delighted adult audience at an international festival. Production by Bulgarian State Puppet Theatre, Sofia. The little Rabbits have their breakfast, sit on their potties, go to school, enjoy the experience, return home.

Schools of puppetry. Czechoslovakia established a Chair of Puppetry within the Theatre Faculty of Academy of Arts in 1952, concerned with the training of young professional puppeteers. Students receive grants for four-year course. Curriculum covers all aspects with eventual special-isation as directors, actors, writers, set-designers, lighting technicians, etc. Productions are given in the former Comedy Theatre. The U.S.S.R. established Chair of Puppetry in 1959 at the Leningrad Institute of Theatre, Music and Cinema. The four-year course has three sections. Four-year training also given at the Gorki Theatre School and the Sverd-lovsk Puppet Theatre. Technicians trained at Moscow's art-technique school. Other centres at Kalinin, Novosibirsk and Orenburg. The Director of the Moscow Central State Puppet Theatre, Sergei Obraztsov, holds one-year courses for directors and special seminars for directors already functioning. Moscow School No. 428 has had 14 groups of young puppeteers in as many years.

Scissors. Apart from their normal use as cutting instruments, their possibilities as puppets were explored by students of the Bath Academy of Art, under Helen Binyon; as a result of experiments with a variety of everyday objects held behind the shadow screen, a Scissors Ballet was produced with music composed by the students.

Scott, A. C. English author of a number of books on the theatre of the East, particularly Japan and China; Member of the Department of Speech,

University of Wisconsin. Important small book on *The Puppet Theatre of Japan* (Tuttle, 1963).

Scott, Sir Walter (1771–1832). Scottish poet and novelist. In *Bride of Lammermoor* mentions 'Punch and his wife *Joan*', name in fairly common use in eighteenth century performances. No precise evidence of first use of 'Judy'; the latter is undoubtedly the better choice from the *sound* aspect, carrying better to the ears of the audience. A 'Punch and Joan' show seems unthinkable.

Separator. Usually refers to a lubricant with which inside of mould is coated before making cast from plastic or other material, to ensure easy release; also refers to other material such as damp tissue paper used over plasticine model when puppet head cast by direct method.

Seraphin, Dominique (1747–1800). French showman, born into family of wandering players. Opened a shadow-puppet theatre in Paris, of the type known as 'Ombres chinoises', but quite different in style to the original Chinese, his figures being cardboard silhouettes giving black shadow, well articulated. Theatre (opened 1776) moved to Versailles (1781), where it was popular with the nobility, and back to Paris (1784). There was harpsichord music in the intervals. He eventually sold his theatre, bought it back and added marionettes – and a live dog. After his death members of the family maintained the theatre until 1870. There are some Seraphin shadow-figures in the Cooper-Union Museum, New York. A script of one of the plays is reproduced in Maindron *Marionnettes et Guignols* (Juven, Paris, 1900).

Set. (1) Stage scenery or 'setting' – which establishes the locale. (2) Plaster of Paris and various 'fillers' (mixed with water) are said to have 'set' when the moisture has dried out and the material has hardened; setting time varies with type of material and room temperature. Term also applies in conversion of liquid resins to solid, process known as 'curing', by evaporation of a solvent or by gelling.

Shadow Plays of Peking, translated by the distributors (Collet's Chinese Bookshop, London, W.C.1). In the Introduction the claim is made that China is the birthplace of the shadow show (initiated eleventh century), and that with the development of maritime transport the shadow show was brought to Java, Malaya, Siam and Burma (although quite different types of shadow figures were developed in these countries). Synopses of 15 plays adapted for the shadow theatre are given.

Shadow shows. The historians are agreed that these are the oldest form of puppet theatre, but are uncertain as to whether China or India was the birthplace of the art. The requirements for this type are: a translucent screen, a light source, cut-out figures placed immediately behind the screen (between this and the source of light); the audience sees the shadows on the other side of the screen. Thus it is a two-dimensional art and is in fact the forerunner of the cine-film and television, although the techniques are different. Traditionally characters were always in profile, but modern developments include figures which are full-face to the audience. Animation is usually by some form of rod, but may be by strings or springs and levers. The amount of movement of parts (head, limbs) depends on the method of construction, using overlapping sections (loosely attached by fine wire or knotted thread), with or without control rods (legs may swing freely, for instance). The size of the figures is related to the dimensions of the screen – and those of India, China, Java, Turkey,

Greece vary considerably. Oil lamps were the traditional kind, but electric light is widely used today. Daylight from a window may be used experimentally when introducing shadow shows to children. The oriental figures were cut from tough, durable animal hides, treated to become translucent, sometimes coloured, and great skill in making incised designs was developed. Sometimes the patterns were obligatory, being part of the characterisation, a means of recognition – most important when a very large cast of two-dimensional figures have to appear. Modern developments include the use of plastics – e.g. Perspex rods, which are almost shadowless – and experiments with nature materials such as fern fronds and feathers, and spatial 'depth'. The simplest form of screen is a converted picture-frame (glass removed) with a taut, translucent material stretched across it (calico, architect's tracing paper, an old roller-blind, etc.). Experiments have also been made with 'back projection' of scenery, with lantern and slides, and an interesting production by German art-teacher students involved the use of five screens set in a partition of room width, one having a washable screen on which titles were drawn and wiped off. In addition to the 'live' shows there are the delightful silhouette films of Lotte Reiniger, made by the stop-motion technique, which also achieved 'depth' and eventually colour. The most comprehensive book in English, dealing with both history in many countries, and techniques, is Olive Blackham's *Shadow Puppets* (Barrie & Rockliff, 1960). A good earlier introduction, Whanslaw's *Shadow Play* (Wells, Gardner and Darton, 1950). Authoritative on the Javanese 'Wayang' – on their carving, colouring, symbolism – is Mellema *Wayang puppets* (Royal Tropical Institute, Amsterdam, 1954). The British Museum has examples of Javanese and Chinese figures in the Ethnographical Department, and Blackham's book lists museum collections in England, Holland, Germany, the Scandinavian countries, Switzerland, France and America. (Also extensive bibliography.)

Shakes versus Shav, by George Bernard Shaw (Constable, 1950, in volume with two non-puppet items, *Buoyant Billions* and *Farfetched Fables*). Ten-minute knockabout play in blank verse, especially written for the Lanchester Marionettes (with two marionettes in the name parts for inspir-ation) and performed in the Lanchester Theatre at Malvern and in London's Festival Gardens (1950); at the Lyric, Hammersmith, 1953, Shaw said it was probably his last play and, at the first performance. 'One feels, in front of these real creatures, so extremely unreal.' The puppet voices were recorded by actors Lewis Casson (Shakes) and Ernest Thesiger (Shav); other characters: Macbeth, Rob Roy, Captain Shotover and Ellie Dunn. Text and dialogue have typical Shavian humour and turns on the dispute as to whether Shakespeare or Shaw is the greater – enlivened by some slapstick. Lanchester Puppet Centre, 39 Henley Street, Stratford-upon-Avon, Warwickshire, stocks copies of the play (special edition).

Shakespeare, William (1564–1616). English playwright, poet. Terms 'puppet' and 'motion' (popular name for puppet or puppet show) occur frequently in dialogue in the plays, mainly in metaphorical sense. Specific reference to puppet-play and puppeteer (Autolycus), who 'compassed the motion of the *Prodigal Son*' in *Winter's Tale*, Act 4, Sc. 2. As is seen by reference to the *Complete Concordance to Shakespeare* (Bickers, revised 1889), which gives 89 examples of 'motion', the exact meaning must be deduced from the context. 'O excellent motion! Fellows let's be gone . . .'

in the *Taming of the Shrew* refers to human actors. The term 'interpret' (*Two Gentlemen of Verona*, and elsewhere) is also related to puppet performances of the period; it was customary to have an 'interpreter' in front of the stage giving a running commentary on the action, introducing the characters – as is also seen in Ben Jonson's *Bartholomew Fayre* with an actual puppet performance in the fairground scene. *Hamlet*, Act 3, Sc. 2, has: 'I could interpret between you and your love if I could see the puppets dallying.' *Taming of the Shrew*, Act 4, Sc. 3: 'Belike you mean to make a puppet of me.' *Midsummer Night's Dream*, Act 3, Sc. 2: 'Fie, fie! counterfeit, you puppet, you!' *Antony and Cleopatra*, Act 5, Sc. 2: 'Thou, an Egyptian puppet, shalt be shown in Rome as well as I.' *Comedy of Errors*, Act 3, Sc. 2: 'We in your motions turn and you may move us.' *King Lear*, Act 2, Sc. 2: 'And take vanity the puppet's part.' *Taming of the Shrew*, Act 1, Sc. 2: 'Give him gold enough and marry him to a puppet or an aglet-baby' (small image). Other examples in *Titus Andronicus*, *Love's Labour's Lost*, and elsewhere. Shakespeare himself appears as a puppet in G. B. Shaw's only play for puppets, written for the Lanchester Marionettes, *Shakes versus Shav*, q.v., in which Macbeth and other characters appear, including Shaw (Shav). Many of Shakespeare's plays have been adapted to puppet theatre presentation in many countries, particularly in the Quatercentenary year, e.g. *The Tempest*, at Bochum, Germany; *Midsummer Night's Dream*, in Budapest, Hungary, using all types of puppet. Scenes from Shakespeare are popular with amateur groups. There is no evidence that the Bard wrote the *Dream* with a puppet performance in mind, although the theory has been raised from time to time. TRNKA, the master puppet-film maker of Czechoslovakia, produced the *Dream* with elegant stop-motion figures in colour, but without Shakespeare's dialogue, with music – beautiful but controversial. Pollock's Toy Theatres also celebrated 400th Birthday by re-issuing adaptations of *Richard III*, *Othello*, and *Hamlet* (the last being based on the 1947 Olivier film).

Shankar, Uday. Indian dancer, first to introduce Indian folk and temple dances to the world during the renaissance of Indian arts in the 1930's. As creative choreographer studied the movements of traditional marionettes; in some of his ballets human figures take on puppet roles. Masked dancers acting as puppets also used by the Little Ballet Troupe directed by Shanti Bardhan.

Sharpe's London Journal, Volume 14 (1848–49). Includes English translation of the section on Puppets in England (the only part translated) from Magnin *Histoire des marionnettes en Europe depuis l'antiquité jusqu'à nos jours* (1852), q.v.

Shaw, George Bernard (1856–1950). Irish dramatist and critic. In a letter to Podrecca, director of the Teatro dei Piccoli (reproduced in von Boehn *Dolls and Puppets*), Shaw said 'flesh and blood actors can learn a good deal about their art from puppets' and that a good puppet show should form part of the equipment of every academy of stage art. He also wrote to Clunn Lewis, an old-time Kentish showman (died early 1920's), the letter appearing in the *Strand Magazine* at the turn of the century, giving reasons for believing that the Puppet Show was even more interesting to men-of-letters and others concerned with the imaginative arts than to the village audience. He saw the possibility that the Cinema, instead of killing it, would lead to the revival of the Puppet Show. On one occasion he was among those present at a performance given by Tony

Sarg (who later took a leading part in the developments in the United States) at his apartment above The Old Curiosity Shop. The last dramatic work by G.B.S. was, in fact, specially written for the Lanchester Marionettes, *Shakes versus Shav*, q.v., a ten-minute piece of wit and slapstick, the central figures being Shaw himself and Shakespeare, with some characters from their own plays, and which had its premiere in Malvern in 1949.

Shell Chemicals, Ltd., suppliers of plastic powders and pellets, POLYSTYRENE and expandable polystyrene beads. Address: 15–17 Great Marlborough Street, London, W.1.

Shelley, Percy Bysshe (1792–1822). English poet; several references to puppets, e.g. *Queen Mab*, V, 71: '. . . from his cabinet These puppets of his schemes he moves at will'; *Invocation to Misery*, XIII, 3: 'like multitudinous puppets passing from a scene'; *Charles the First* (a short Drama), I, I, 37: 'Art thou a puppet moved by (enginery)?'

Shims. Another term for 'dividers' – strips of card or thin metal set into clay or plasticine model and projecting to form a central wall and separating the two halves while layers of paper, plaster, plastic wood, etc., are applied, allowed to harden, removed without cutting. Method known as 'shim casting'.

Show Book of Remo Bufano (Macmillan, N.Y., 1929 and 1941). Seven plays 'for marionettes and people'. BUFANO was one of the pioneers in the American twentieth century puppetry revival and received a Guggenheim award to study play production and puppets in Europe. There is a brief chapter on marionette-making. Plays: *Red Riding Hood, Cinderella, Rumpelstiltskin, Jack and the Beanstalk, The Three Bears, Frog Prince, David and Goliath*. Some of these come in the 'top ten' for popularity – they have also all been done with hand puppets.

Show-cloth. The predecessor of the modern poster advertising a show and consisting of a painted cloth with a scene and a caption. An example is seen in the engraving of *Southwark Fair* (1733), by William Hogarth (reproduced in several puppet books), advertising 'Punch's Opera', the upper half showing Adam and Eve and the Serpent in the Garden of Eden, the lower showing Punch trundling his wife in a wheelbarrow, heading for the flames arising from Hell. In Jonson's *Bartholomew Fayre* (1614), in which an actual puppet show is performed, the instruction is given 'Out with the sign of our intention . . . and do you beat the drum awhile' (Act V, Sc. 1). In Jonson's *Every Man Out of His Humour* (Act IV, Sc. vi): 'He will hang out his picture shortly in a cloth.'

Siamese puppets. See THAILAND.

Sicilian puppets. One of the few surviving forms of folk-puppetry, of tremendous vigour in itself, but only to be seen in an ever-dwindling number of theatres. The type of puppet, apart from the difference in size (up to two-thirds life size and extremely heavy), and its method of control (a strong iron head rod operated from above stage) is reflected in the little articulated figurines found in ancient tombs and ruins. Most of the puppets have elaborate armour and the plays are all related to the struggles between Christianity and Islam. Sicily's own history is closely linked, hence the appeal of the medieval romances and legends which make up the repertoire of the puppet theatres, which are also the stock-in-trade of street story-tellers, and which reappear on the sides and wheels of the carved and painted carts. The most famous of the present-day puppeteers is Signor Emanuele Macri, whose theatre is at Acireale, on the coast below Mount Etna. These theatres are all family affairs. They make the puppets, beat out the metalwork of the armour, give the performances – usually stripped to the waist. The play cycles can go on for months and include ARIOSTO's *Orlando Furioso*; *Gerusalemme Liberata* (30 episodes); the epic *I Paladini di Francia* (305 episodes) – all being dramatisations of the books of the same names – and all, in their turn, stemming from the *chansons de geste* of twelfth century France. How much is pure history and how much legend and romance cannot be determined, but all the action is involved with the medieval code of chivalry. Orlando, the great favourite among the characters, is immediately recognisable by his cross-eyes. He is the counterpart of the eighth century Roland, a commander under the Emperor Charlemagne, and was killed through some treachery (c. 778 A.D.). *The Song of Roland*, in English translation by Dorothy L. Sayers, is available as a Penguin Classic (1957 and re-prints to 1967). Technically, it is the relatively simple basic construction which gives these puppets their characteristic style in action. The body is of wood with a padded chest; the action of the legs is stiff and depends on the handling of the whole figure rather than on leg strings (there are none); the knight's sword is bolted to the hand and controlled by an iron rod, the arm with the shield being moved by a cord. In one of the tremendous fight scenes a hero can pile up the slain, heads can fly off and the blood flow. Hollywood could not do better. The operators need to be athletes. A closely related type of puppet – with the same source material for the plays – is to be found in Liége, but of even simpler control: a head rod and neither arm nor leg strings. Superb illustrations in colour of the Sicilian puppets, and two back-stage in black and white are included in Baird *Art of the Puppet* (Collier-Macmillan, 1965). There is now a small Sicilian theatre in Paris, at Librairie 73, boulevard Saint-Michel, the director being a one-time assistant of a noted player in Palermo. He married a Parisienne, was presented with a selection of knights and dragons, dogs and angels, magicians, horses, brigands and young heroines – and drives a taxi between performances.

Siegel, Harro. German puppeteer and teacher; had Toy Theatre when 13 years old; influenced by seeing PODRECCA's Teatro dei Piccoli marion-ettes. First public show 1927; later toured in England and Germany and the Baltic countries with English dancers, players, German singers; repertoire included PURCELL's *Aeneas and Dido* and some items of Hans SACHS, one of the earliest German playwrights. Taught at Brunswick School of Arts and Crafts and ran puppetry class; repertoire included a notable production of *Dr Faustus* and many original items. Retired to Florence. Member of the Editorial Board of UNIMA, which compiled *The Puppet Theatre of the Modern World* (Henschelverlag, 1965; Harrap, 1967), issued in many languages.

Sight lines. Spectators in different parts of a theatre auditorium have different lines of vision of the stage. Ideally every viewer sees everything that happens on stage – but there are also areas of the stage which should be out of sight (the wings, the flies, etc.). Stage planning must be related to these lines of vision, particularly from the extreme ends of rows of seats and from balcony positions. In 'theatre in the round' with the stage in the middle of the auditorium a new viewing problem arises: that of seeing the audience on the other side. Stage sets have to be designed to certain dimensions and so placed that there is the minimum of loss of viewing from any angle. The existence of a proscenium gives immediate

boundaries of vision and some modern theatres dispense with the proscenium and leave exposed all the backstage and above-stage mechanism;
if what happens on stage is sufficiently interesting, the spectators ignore
'the works'. With the puppet theatre – either of the permanent type or
the temporary (mobile) – the normal sight lines of the spectators will be
changed. If a hand puppet production is mounted in an auditorium (or
on a platform) and there is a balcony, there is the risk of the upstairs
viewers seeing down *into* the booth and seeing the puppeteers as well as
the puppets. If the auditorium has a non-sloping floor and a marionette
production is mounted on a low platform, only the front rows will have
good viewing.   If the front rows are too near the stage then an upward
glance may give a sight of the performers or at least their operating hands.
The sight lines of a narrow booth, e.g. Punch and Judy show, with side
curtaining at the performing level, only the action along the front edge
will be seen by all. Even the best sight lines can be spoiled by ladies
with large hats or tall hair-styles. Mixed audiences, adults and children,
or children of varying heights, can never have equality of viewing unless
there can be adjustable-height seating; this is a feature to be incorporated
in the Universal Puppet Theatre planned for Prague (Czechoslovakia);
mechanically movable seats have not proved practicable, portable
prismatic cushions may solve the problem. Whatever the type of production and whatever the physical limits of the auditorium, the producer
must check viewing from various points of the seating. An experiment
made by a Polish puppet theatre in which viewing was through a large
cut-away circle in a moving screen, changing the sight lines, was rather
frustrating for the viewers except those seated on the central line of view.

Silhouette Films by Lotte Reiniger: *The Ornament of the Loving Heart*
(short ballet with two figures; Berlin Institut für Kulturforschung, 1919).
Cupid and the Constant Lovers (Fairy Tale: live action and silhouettes mixed;
BIK, 1920). *The Flying Coffer* (Andersen Fairy Tale, BIK, 1921). *The
Star of Bethlehem* (nativity; BIK, 1921). *Cinderella* (BIK, 1922). *The
Adventures of Prince Achmet*, full-length film on the Arabian Nights, directed
by Carl Koch, collaboration with Walter Ruttman and Berthold
Bastosch; Music, Wolfgang Zeller (Berlin Comenius Film, 1923–26).
The Shamming Chinese (Arabian Nights tale; Comenius, 1927). *The
Adventures of Dr Dolittle* (Lofting) – 1, The Journey to Africa; 2, The
Monkey Business; 3, The Monkey's Illness (Comenius, 1928). *Running
After Luck*, silhouette part of feature film; Music, Theo Mackeben
(Comenius, 1929); *Ten Minutes with Mozart*, ballet to *Eine Kleine
Nachtmusik*, music arranged Wolfgang Zeller (Berlin, 1930); *Harlequin*:
a commedia dell' arte pantomime with contemporary seventeenth
century music: Scarlatti, Pergolesi, Lully, Baneau, Couperin, arranged
by E. W. White (Berlin Town Film, 1931); *Carmen*: parody on Bizet's
Opera, music Peter Gellhorn (Lotte Reiniger Films, Berlin, 1933).
The Rolling Wheel, film on the development of Traffic, music Peter Gell-
horn (LRF, Berlin, 1934). *The Count of Carabas* (*Puss in Boots*), music
Peter Gellhorn (LRF, 1934). *The Stolen Heart*, fairy tale (LRF, 1934).
The Little Chimney Sweep, Fantasy on the street cries of London, by Orlando
Gibbons, with contemporary English music arranged by Peter Gellhorn
(LRF, 1935). *Papageno*, Fantasy on the bird-catcher of Mozart's *Magic
Flute*, music arranged Peter Gellhorn (LRF, 1935). *Galathea*, the Pyg-
malion story, music Eric W. White (LRF, 1935). *The King's Breakfast*,
Nursery story, music Fraser Simpson, arranged Irving (facts and Fan-
tasies, London, 1936). *The Tocher*, Post Office Savings Bank Film, music

arranged Benjamin Britten, Donizetti (London G.P.O., 1937). *Dream Circus*, Fantasy on the Pulcinella music by Stravinsky; not completed (Facts and Fantasies, London, 1939). *Elisir D'amore*, after Donizetti's opera; not completed (Scalera Film, Rome, 1939). *The Golden Goose*, not completed (Berlin, 1944). Various trailers (Crown Film Unit, London, 1950). *Mary's Birthday*, colour film, music Edward Williams (CFU, 1951). Also see Television Films.

Silhouette Notes and Dictionary, by Mrs E. Nevill Jackson (Methuen, 1938), with 103 plates (10 in colour); interesting notes on the Dr Paul Kahle discovery of leather shadow figures in the Nile Valley, on the modern Greek shadow theatre of Antonios Mollas – with an estimate of 50 'karagiosi' or shadow shows, with own Trade Union, in the pre-war days. Also on Lotte Reiniger's silhouette films – for one of which (*Prince Achmet*) over a quarter of a million photos were taken and 80,000 used.

Silhouettes. Profile portraits filled in with black; black shadow figures (as distinct from translucent coloured type); modern development seen in the SILHOUETTE FILMS of Lotte REINIGER. There is an interesting note in an issue of *Notes and Queries* (22nd April, 1882) from a correspondent who supposes that the silhouette portrait went out with the coming of the daguerrotype. There is also a quotation from Isaac d'Israeli *Curiosities of Literature*, in an article on Political Nicknames, stating that the word came from the name of a Minister of State in France (1759), who could only suggest excessive economy as a remedy for an exhausted exchequer – which led to the wits cutting their coats short, using wooden snuffboxes and offering as portraits profiles traced by a black pencil of the shadow cast by a candle on white paper. There are some illustrations on the technique of making portrait silhouettes in Bordat and Boucrot *Théâtres d'Ombres* (L'Arche, 1956), and an illustration with the caption 'silhouettes à fils' showing flat figure marionettes by Geza Blattner. See also Megroz *Profile Art*.

Silly Willy and *King John and the Abbot*, by K. & L. Amaral (Macmillan, 1953), hand puppet plays in the 'Puppet Plays for Schools' series. Acting time approximately 20 and 35 minutes respectively. No fees for non-professional performances.

Simmonds, William. English sculptor, woodcarver in a Gloucestershire village. One of twentieth century pioneers of puppetry; performances in London, 1916–34. Sensitive carved marionettes, operating one with each hand, with music on the virginals by his wife. Several illustrations in Beaumont *Puppets and Puppetry* (Studio, 1958), including figures for John Drinkwater play $X = O$. (Died 1968).

Size. (Italian 'sisa', diminutive of 'assisa': painter's glue.) Thin solution of glue or gelatine used for stiffening and glazing scenic canvas. Some puppetmakers use size instead of paste in preparing papier maché.

Skeleton. Trick marionette, see Dissecting Skeleton.

Skeleton set. Scenery consisting of outline structure, leaving the rest to the audience's imagination. Some contemporary puppeteers have adopted the principle in *puppet* construction also.

Skupa, Professor Josef (1892–1957). Internationally famous Czechoslovak puppetmaster, National Artist, best known abroad for his two characters Spejbl (somewhat bourgeois father) and Hurvinek (precocious son), who were an immediate success at home with adults and children.

During World War I Skupa's shows boosted the morale of the Czech people and resistance to the Austro-Hungarian monarchy; founded the first and only professional puppet theatre in the new Czech Republic. During the Nazi occupation he again gave satirical performances, was imprisoned at Dresden (Hurvinek and Spejbl being incarcerated in a Gestapo filing cabinet), had a miraculous escape when the prison was burned down in 1945. Later he visited London and performed for several hundred English children and also for Czech refugees in this country. The Hurvinek and Spejbl Theatre in Prague is the best memorial to his work. Jiři Trnka, the great Czech maker of puppet films, was at one time a pupil of Skupa.

Slapstick. Specially constructed weapon used by 'low comedians' as well as by Punch, consisting of two flat sticks joined at one end, making considerable noise, but doing minimum of damage. Whence 'slapstick comedy' with its equivalent techniques for evoking laughter.

Sleeping Beauty (La Belle au Bois Dormant). Perrault's fairy tale of the princess who pricks her finger with a spindle provided by a wicked fairy and sleeps for a hundred years until a prince arrives to break the spell with a kiss. Story one of the most frequently adapted to the puppet stage. Theme also basis for puppet-cartoon film with music by Poulenc (Alexeieff, 1935) and designs by de la Rochefoucauld. In a new translation by Geoffrey Brereton (Penguin Classics: Perrault's *Fairy Tales*, 1957) at the climax the princess asks: ' Is it you, my Prince? You have been a long time coming.' Audience-reaction to *that* can be anticipated by any experienced performer.

Slider. Wire control in which to mount cut-out figure for use in Toy Theatre when pushed on stage from the wings; figures interchangeable.

Sliding-slot scenery. Simple mechanism for raising and lowering scenery in a hand or rod puppet booth (developed by the present author); vertical rail (plywood) $1\frac{1}{2}$-2 in. width, attached to top cross-rail and centre rail of front of framework, acts as runner for the 'slot'; latter consists of three pieces of plywood of about 4 in. width and 2 in. depth, placed one behind and one in front of rail – with narrow connecting pieces, the third piece also on the face side with narrow connecting pieces forming the slot in which a projecting 'foot' at the bottom of the scenery (tree, bed, etc.) is held. In the 'up' position a hole is drilled right through slot, foot and rail, to take a dowel-peg (attached to short string to avoid loss). When peg removed the scenery can be lowered, removed, further item inserted ready for raising. This gives front edge possibilities; a small shelf can be raised as by magic, carrying a pot or other object. (Illustrated leaflet available from Educational Puppetry Association, q.v.)

Smetana, Bedřich (1824-1884). Czech composer: wrote two humorous overtures for puppet-plays, *Doctor Faust* (1862) and Oldřich and Bozena (1863). The puppet-master Skupa's early repertoire included the opening chorus from the famous *Bartered Bride*, sung by marionettes in Czech national costume; also *The Kiss* (lullaby).

Smith, Barry. English puppeteer. See BARRY SMITH.

Smithsonian Institution, Washington, D.C. (United States Museum); endowed by £100,000 bequest (1826) of James Smithson (1765–1829), an Englishman; formally organised 1846; first building completed 1854; purpose: 'the increase and diffusion of knowledge among men'. Various funds added; library of over a million books; issues various publications on Science and Art, free to libraries, colleges and learned societies throughout the world; museum holdings include Javanese and Siamese shadow figures.

Snow box. Wooden frame or trough fixed above stage under a sack slit to allow finely-torn pieces of white paper to float downwards for snow effect. On marionette stage can also be blown or fanned from the wings.

Snow White. Folk tale best known by the Grimms' version (closely followed by the Disney film); one of the most popular items for puppet adaptation; ideal ingredients: the seven dwarfs, jealous step-mother theme, magic mirror, poisoned apple, hero-prince and beautiful heroine – with a happy ending. The DaSilva Marionettes production includes seven 'musical' dwarfs.

Societies. UNIMA (Union international de la marionnette) formed 1929, re-formed 1957, based on Prague and acting as link between puppeteers throughout the world; countries with 20 or more members may form National Sections which may be contacted through the national society or local guild (if any). British Section UNIMA Hon. Secretary: C. M. Macdonald, 9b Walpole Gardens, Strawberry Hill, Twickenham, Middlesex. BRITISH PUPPET AND MODEL THEATRE GUILD, formed 1925: Hon. Secretary, 90 The Minories, London, E.C.3. EDUCATIONAL PUPPETRY ASSOCIATION: Hon. Secretary, 23a Southampton Place, London, W.C.1. Also of interest: International Theatre Institute, International Federation for Theatre Research, Society for Theatre Research, q.v.

Society for Theatre Research. Founded 1948 following a successful public meeting held at the Old Vic Theatre, London. Aims: to bring together those interested in the history and technique of the British Theatre and to encourage further research into these subjects. It has international connections through its members all over the world and acts as a clearing house for historical and technical information. One of its chief aims is the preservation of source material either in its own collection or by distribution to other appropriate institutions. Library: books in University of London Library: MSS., play-bills, pictures, etc., at 77 Kinnerton Street, London, S.W.1. Society's *Bulletin* is included in *Theatre Notebook*, q.v., a quarterly journal published and distributed by Ifan Kyrle Fletcher, 22 Buckingham Gate, London, S.W.1. Occasional articles on puppetry, e.g. Vol. XX, No. 4, on CRAIG's theory of the actor-über-marionette. In 1962 collaborated with the British Puppet and Model Theatre Guild in the 'PUNCH TERCENTENARY' celebrations.

Sock puppet. (*a*) Sock (stocking) pulled over performer's hand bent from wrist to form head, thumb giving lower jaw movement, button eyes, wool hair, etc., added. (*b*) Self-stuffed head formed by knotting sock at ankle and bringing leg part over knot. (*c*) Top ends or toes can be converted into fisherman's cap with tassel added. Fraser *History of Toys* (Weidenfeld & Nicolson, 1966) mentions use for teaching deaf children to speak.

Somerville, Christopher Charles. English puppeteer and writer, colleague of Eric Bramall of the Harlequin Puppet Theatre, q.v., Rhos-on-Sea, Colwyn Bay, North Wales; Director of the 2nd International Puppet Festival, Colwyn Bay (1968); well known for Club 'floor show', q.v., act *Things on Strings* (under professional name of Tony Dexter); author of many articles for national magazines on all aspects of puppetry;

founder-distributor of *Harlequinade*, q.v., an open-forum and critical review for puppeteers; joint author with Eric Bramall of *Expert Puppet Techniques* (Faber, 1964).

Song of Roland (Le Chanson de Roland), by anonymous French poet (*c*. 1100); earliest extant example of the 'CHANSONS DE GESTE' or epic 'songs of deeds'. Theme: war between Emperor Charlemagne (742–814) and the Saracens – and mediaeval code of chivalry. In a later Italian version Roland becomes Orlando, one of the main characters in cycle of plays still performed by the SICILIAN MARIONETTES. Puppet plays on same theme also survive in Belgium and Northern France. English translation by Dorothy L. Sayers, available in Penguin Classics paperback (1957 and reprints to 1967).

Song of the Prairie. Czechoslovak puppet film (stop-motion, burlesquing the Hollywood 'western' – stage coach attacked by bandits, heroic cowboy, golden-haired heroine (who continues singing while hanging by hands on branch of tree); hero rides horse up precipice. Director, Jiři Trnka; story, Brdecka-Trnka; music by J. Rychlik.

Song of the Shirt, by Thomas Hood (1799–1845). 'With fingers weary and worn, With eyelids heavy and red, A woman sat, in unwomanly rags, Plying her needle and thread . . .' Dramatic poem which has had various puppet versions, e.g. Kate and Lucian Amaral, with Bunraku-type puppet, and Barry Smith (Theatre of Puppets) with rod type.

Sooty. Famous teddy-bear character of English puppeteer Harry Corbett; with companion 'Sweep' appeared in B.B.C. television series, without ever becoming a day older. Films can be hired, such as *Engineering Company, All-Star Variety, At the Organ, Bath Night, Pottery, Chemist's Shop, Garage.* (Gaumont-British Film Library, Perivale, Middlesex.)

Southwark Fair. Engraving by William Hogarth, plate dated 1733, print issued 1735, original painting of the scene in Duke of Newcastle Collection. Reproduced in *Wm. Hogarth, his original engravings and etchings*, Heinemann, 1913; also in Baird *Art of the Puppet* and (partially, and in reverse) in Speaight *History of the English Puppet Theatre*. The scene could be a composite one, but gives a good impression of a fairground – and shows three types of puppet show: (*a*) in the foreground, a bagpipe-player with marionettes à la planchette; (*b*) on a balcony, a simple hand puppet booth and two figures fighting with sticks, probably a piece of advertising for (*c*) an indoor performance of 'Punch's Opera', probably of the popular item *The Creation of the World* (a showcloth presents Adam and Eve on one half, and Punch pushing a wheelbarrow with his wife in and heading for Hell Fire).

Spain. Magnin, in his *Histoire des marionnettes en Europe* (1852), has brief chapters on Spain and Portugal mentioning the early use of statues with moving joints used in religious processions, and the travelling showmen of the type met in CERVANTES *Don Quixote* (which gives a good idea of the method of performance; but various illustrations probably suffer from artistic licence, e.g. that by Gustave Dorè, reproduced in Baird *Art of the Puppet*, 1965). Magnin says that at one time every important Spanish town had its permanent puppet theatre. McPharlin *Puppet Theatre in America* (1949) has an interesting chapter on the Spanish puppeteers who emigrated to Mexico, Peru and the Argentine (nineteenth century) and also mentions Cortés, the adventurer in search of gold, who had a private entourage which included a puppeteer (in 1524). The first

extensive documented history of Spanish puppetry was made by J. E.
Varey of the University of London, beginning as a doctoral thesis in 1950.
The UNESCO 'Courier' in a special puppetry issue (June, 1955) stated
that Spain had long depended on her Romance neighbours for puppeteers
and that some contemporary performers had been trained abroad.
'Dido' (Ezequiel Vigues, 1880–1960) used puppets of the three-finger
type due to his French apprenticeship with 'GUIGNOLS' – as distinct from
the CATALAN five-finger type – and was a notable performer, sometimes
giving as many as 16 shows a day. Daniel S. Keller, of the University of
California, did useful research on Spanish puppetry and contributed
article to the *Puppetry Journal* of the Puppeteers of America. Ada M. Coe,
in a small book issued by the Hispano Institute (New York, 1947),
Entertainments in the Little Theatres of Madrid, gives some notes on 'maquinas
de sombres' (shadow pictures) derived from France at end of the eighteenth century. Among the twentieth century puppeteers is the Englishman H. V. Tozer, q.v., who performed for many years in Barcelona with
marionettes. *The Geographical Magazine* (April, 1948) had an interesting
colour photograph of a Spanish street-booth, a simple screen, a small
audience, with a puppet bull dominating the stage. There is some historical material (in French) in *Quand les Marionnettes du Monde se donnent le
Main* . . . (collection of papers given at an international conference and
festival at Liége, 1958) dealing with the Catalan type, and another paper
on the educational aspects (in Spanish). Several small books have been
published in Spanish on the technical aspects.

Speaight, George. English puppeteer and puppet-historian. Vice-
President of the British Puppet and Model Theatre Guild; Member of
the UNIMA Praesidium, 1962–66; Chairman of the Society for Theatre
Research, 1959–63; Member of the Committee of the International
Federation for Theatre Research, 1964–67. Presented Toy Theatre
performances at Bumpus's Bookshop, Oxford Street, London, 1932–33–
34; worked with the Roel Puppets 1936; Manager of Benjamin Pollock
Ltd., 1946–50; presented the puppet show in Ben Jonson's *Bartholomew
Fair* with the Old Vic Company, Edinburgh Festival, 1950, and London.
1951; presented the Old Time Marionettes, in partnership with Gerald
Morice, Festival Pleasure Gardens, 1951; worked with Louise Hutton
glove puppets and the B.B.C. Television Puppet Theatre 1952–55.
Author of *Juvenile Drama: the History of the English Toy Theatre* (Macdonald,
1947) and *The History of the English Puppet Theatre* (Harrap, 1955).

Speech training. An understanding of the processes, physiological and
psychological, of 'voice production' is essential for actors and actresses
and is a subject studied in all schools of drama and to some extent in
general education. Breath control is the first requirement and then a
clear idea of how the speech organs function. The ability to 'project' the
voice in a hall so that this is audible to everyone in the audience must be
acquired; this may be influenced by the *type* of voice suited to a given
character. The study of 'character voices' demands an alert ear in every-
day life and the realisation that variations in voice quality, in enunciation,
are related to the 'shape' of the face, the use of the mouth, the position
of the jaw and teeth, air passing through the nose. Simple experiments:
hold the nose while talking in a normal way: listen: keep the teeth
together and talk: listen: project the lower jaw and talk: listen; twist
the jaw sideways and hold it in that position, continuing talking; place
the tongue against the back of the teeth, against the roof of the mouth,

in the side of the jaw. The enunciation of individual sounds (letters) leads to the realisation that some sounds 'carry' better, that some are difficult to hear at a distance. Peasants in fields know how to make the voice carry; their (unselfconscious) voice production is akin to singing. The actor-with-puppet has special problems, assuming he is providing the speech for his characters (performing against voices from a TAPE-RECORD-ING has different problems): these stem from the working positions necessary when holding a puppet above head or a marionette below – and to some extent the energy used in the handling – but also due to the construction of puppet stages; the hand or rod puppet operator is behind a curtain and may from time to time be turned *away* from the audience; the presence of a plywood or hardboard BACKSCREEN behind the puppets will help, acting as a soundboard; the marionette operator is not only leaning forward over the stage, he is also behind the top of the proscenium (unless using an 'open type' stage). So far as possible the voice must be directed down the hall, not sideways towards other performers; it is the audience that must hear and it is the puppets that must appear to be talking to each other. In a permanent theatre with a company there will normally be a producer, part of whose function is to check sound from the audience angle in various parts of the auditorium (including the balcony, if any).

Spejbl. Famous marionette character created by Czech puppeteer Professor Josef SKUPA, q.v., and carved by sculptor Karel Nosek (1920). Hurvinek, delightful show-stealing son of Spejbl, appeared in 1926. Skupa operated Spejbl but spoke for both characters, his wife handling Hurvinek. Their puppet theatre in Prague is named after these two characters. A number of records of their voices were made.

Spencer, Edmund (? 1552–99). English poet: *Faerie Queene*, etc. In his *Mother Hubberd's Tale* (a satire on Court favour, suppressed at the time) he said: 'Like as a Puppit placed in a play.'

Sports and Pastimes of the People of England: from the earliest period, including the rural and domestic Recreations, May Games, Mummeries, Pageants, Processions and Pompous Spectacles, illustrated by reproductions from ancient paintings in which are represented most of the popular diversions, by Joseph Strutt, Engraver (White, 1801, under the title *Gug-Gamena Angel-Deod*). 2nd edition added '*or the Sports and Pastimes . . .*'; a new edition published by Reeves appeared in 1830; a Tegg edition in 1833 and a further edition in 1838; Methuen, 1903, is 'much enlarged and corrected'. Although puppet shows are not mentioned specifically in the sub-title there is some interesting material, most of it quoted by later writers. There is a reference to Strutt in the chapter on English puppetry in Magnin *Histoire des marionnettes en Europe* (1852). Strutt, in 1801, is perhaps the first to complain that puppet shows are – or had become – an attraction for children only, and mentioned that shows were even then being given in Smithfield at Bartholomew-tide. He cites two early play-bills (in the Harleian MSS.), one for Bartholomew Fair, 'John Harris's Booth' – reproduced in Speaight *History of the English Puppet Theatre* and Baird *Art of the Puppet* – and the other for Crawley's show 'over against the Crown Tavern in Smithfield' to the effect that a 'little opera' would be presented, called the *Old Creation of the World*, with the addition of *Noah's Flood*. The subjects of the puppet dramas were formerly taken from well-known stories, with knights and giants added, says Strutt, and that the dialogue consisted of 'mere jumbles of absurdity and nonsense, intermixed with low immoral discourses passing between

Punch and the fiddler'. The latter, as seen in various early illustrations, stood in front of the stage and would like the modern 'bottlers' collect money from the onlookers. A section on the 'Modern' puppet showman includes a reference to a performance in 1751, the Tragedy of *Jane Shore*, given at Punch's Theatre in James Street in the Haymarket, London; also a reference to the Italian 'fantoccini' in the same place in 1770 (the premises were better known as Hickford's Rooms). It is interesting to note that Strutt uses the Elizabethan term 'motions' when referring to the showmen of his times carrying their theatres on their backs.

Springs. Ranging from tiny delicate coiled wire to heavy steel spirals of varying diameters and tensions; sometimes used in puppet construction when flexible joints required, e.g. neck of rod puppet, long spine of monster (marionette or rod). The *Spectator* (17th January, 1712) carried an account of a puppet made by the combined efforts of a milliner, watchmaker and Powell the puppetman, with 'several little springs to be wound up within it' and which could move all its limbs, but was sent to Paris to be 'taught' various 'leanings of the head, risings of the bosom, curtsey and recovery' as practised in France; possibly a trick puppet, possibly automaton. Two rod puppet boxers created for Jacques Chesnais by Fernand Leger had spiral arms and legs (illustrated in Beaumont *Puppets and Puppetry*: Studio, 1958).

Stag King, The (Il re Cervo). Fable-play by Count Carlo Gozzi (1720– 1806); various European productions including that of the Moscow Central State Puppet Theatre. Theme: Men transformed into animals or into other men; King Deramo confides secret of this sorcery to Minister, Truffaldini, and is transformed into a stag and then into an old man. Traitor usurps the throne and attempts to seduce the Queen. Plenty of stage tricks and transformations. Also popular with puppet theatres, by same author, *The Love of Three Oranges*, which see.

Stage (The) and Television Today. English theatrical newspaper (weekly); puppet contributions by Charles Trentham.

Stage Noises and Effects, by Michael Green (Jenkins, 1958). Useful item in the Practical Stage Handbooks series.

Stages. Design and construction are related to (*a*) type of puppet; (*b*) whether permanent structure or portable. Fundamental requirements: stability, maximum action scope, adequate backstage storage space. Dimensions: related to number of performers, size of puppets, but may be conditioned by space available. Construction materials: timber or metal (e.g. hollow scaffolding, Dexion angle sections); weight may be a factor with mobile stages, and type of transport available may influence assembly design. The different mobility problems during performance for above-stage and below-stage operators have an influence on design. Accommodation for lighting equipment, stage-props, is another consideration; light sources of small stages are often close to both performers and puppets. An inherited stage, unless it can be modified, imposes its own limits as to size of puppets, number of performers, and productions must be scaled to the stage dimensions and internal facilities. Most technical books on puppetry include adequate construction details, but the available craftsmanship is an important factor. Various attempts have been made to develop multi-purpose stages suitable for several or all types of puppets, but the flexibility usually involves some sacrifice of facility with each adaptation. The 'Universal Puppet Theatre', q.v., planned for Prague, the architectural plans for which were published by the Institute of Scenography (Vol. 77 of the Library of Theatre Space, 1966), will be the first independent building in Czechoslovakia specifically designed for puppets and which will 'serve all puppet theatre techniques without substantial compromise' confirms the fact that *some* loss of facility is unavoidable even where the maximum means are available.

Stageworthy. Puppet with good characterisation and so constructed as to be able to function effectively.

Standing scene. Term for a stage set which is left unchanged throughout the performance.

Stanislavsky, Constantin Sergeievich (Alexeyev) (1865–1938). Russian actor, director, teacher, outstanding theatre theorist, author. With Nemirovich Danchenko founded Moscow Arts Theatre. In the autobiographical *My Life in Art* (available in Penguin edition, 1967) tells how as a child he created a marionette stage with scenery, props, effects and pasteboard actors, this being erected on a table in a doorway, with drapes above and below. First choice of items for the repertoire were those of a catastrophic character, an act from *The Corsair* or Pushkin's *The Stone Guest*. More than one scene was burnt out. Obraztsov, the Soviet puppetmaster, early in his career performed several times before Stanislavsky, tells how the latter laughed as sincerely, as loud and merrily as could have been hoped from the best audience. His own autobiography *My Profession* (Moscow, N.D.) includes photographs of Stanislavsky watching the show.

Staples. (*a*) U-shaped galvanised wire type used by woodworkers, sometimes used for joints of wooden marionettes (two staples interlocked); (*b*) the wire-stitch variety used for clipping papers together can be used (with a stapling-gun) in creating of decor (paper, card, felt, etc.) and forming of cylindrical cardboard heads.

Star-Child, The, by Oscar Wilde (1856–1900). One of the fairy tales specially written for his children. Characters include a number of animals (wolf, rabbit, squirrels) and birds (linnets, turtledove, woodpecker, owl) – appropriate for puppet productions. Comic figure of Kasper was introduced by Edwin Arnet in version for the Zurich Marionette Theatre (illustrations in Gauchat *Marionettes* (Rentsch, 1944). Theme: woodcutter finds boy where star seen to fall, adopts him; boy grows into youth of great beauty, but arrogant; rejects beggarwoman who claims him as son, is in turn rejected by society. In search for mother meets magician, who sets him three tasks, is helped by animals he has aided. Gives gold, expected by magician, to leper – and mother and leper reappear as King and Queen, his true parents. (Penguin Books have an edition of Wilde's *Happy Prince and Other Stories*).

Statues. Liége (Belgium) erected a statue in 1936 of the favourite local puppet character Tchantches (held in arms of small girl); Collodi, the village (in Italy) which gave its name as the pen-name of the author of the *Pinocchio* story (Carlo Lorenzini), has its statue of that character; Koloděje nad Lužnici in Czechoslovakia has its Matěj Kopěcky Memorial (to a revered puppeteer) with a larger than life sculpture of the puppet Kašparek and a cracked comedian's drum (the original puppet is in the National Museum in Prague).

Stendhal (1783–1842). Pen-name of French novelist and critic Henri Beyle. In *Rome, Naples et Florence en* 1817, Delauney, Paris, 1817 (English translation by Richard N. Coe, Calder, 1959), describes marionette show given in a private theatre in Florence, everything beautifully to scale, with rapid set-changes, and adds 'I could conceive of nothing more enchanting.' The comedy was 'delicious, if somewhat indelicate' – an abridged version of Machiavelli's *Mandragola*. There was also an elegant ballet item. However, even more to be appreciated than the marionettes was the 'polished intelligence of the conversation' of the Florentine assembly. On another occasion records seeing puppets in Rome – apparently the only uncensored shows: as a security measure the inevitable police spy was intoxicated prior to the performances.

Stevenson, Robert Louis (1850–94). Scottish poet, novelist, essayist; retained boyhood interest in the Toy Theatre and wrote the much-quoted essay *Penny Plain, Twopence Coloured*, q.v., for the Magazine of Art, April, 1884. Besides being an annual event in the live theatre, his *Treasure Island* has had many puppet versions, including that of student group at Aberdeen College of Education, q.v., *Dr Jekyll and Mr Hyde*, his dual personality story has also been adapted – perhaps because of Gordon Craig's *Puppets and Poets (Chapbook* No. 20, 1921), in which he pointed out that puppets can change their heads, or even have three separate selves.

Stick puppet. Simple form of the Rod type – (*a*) the small figures used in the Polish 'szopka' – miniature church-like construction, operated through slots in floor; (*b*) types made by young children: vertical flat stick as main control (e.g. garden lath), to which are added cut-out card or cheese-box heads, costumes of paper or cloth, and operated from below stage; horizontal type operated from sides of stage, the figures being rigid and constructed from rolled newspaper; (*c*) Hans R. Purschke, in *The Puppet Theatre in Germany* (Neue Darmstädter Verlagsanstalt, 1957) uses the term for the Rhineland type operated by a thin iron rod encased in a thick wooden rod reaching to the floor, with a wire to control one arm.

Stock character. Any character who appears in a series of plays. Term usually associated with the Italian COMMEDIA DELL' ARTE performers of the sixteenth–seventeenth centuries, such as Arlecchino, Columbine, Pantaleon, Pierrot, Pulcinella, Dottore, who also moved into the French theatres and some surviving in the English pantomime. Each character had a recognisable costume and mask and played in the same way in every production. This establishing of a permanent role for the player had its advantages; he would not need to develop a fresh characterisation and he would be performing with other permanent characters. Many companies would each have their Arlecchino and individual actors would make a name as performer in a particular role. There is something of a parallel in television 'personality' puppets who serve as the main character in a series.

Stockholm. Marionettentheater, founded 1958; director Michael Meschke; stage adaptable for various production methods; extensive repertoire includes works by Aristophanes, Chekhov, Dürrenmatt, O'Casey, Pinter, Shakespeare and Shaw. In Jarry's *Ubu Roi* (seen at Edinburgh Festival, 1968) mixed human actors with large cut-out figures, some rod-controlled, some on wheels. Stravinksy made special arrangement of his *Histoire du Soldat* for Meschke.

Stok, Isidor. Soviet Russian playwright. His *Divine Comedy* is a satirical version of the biblical *Genesis*, produced at the Moscow Central Puppet Theatre, director Sergei Obraztsov. Live actors and puppets share same stage – God and the Archangels being human actors, Adam and Eve, the Serpent, the Seraphim and other characters being puppets.

Stop-motion puppets. Figures specially created for use in the production of 'animated' films, made by taking a series of single shots, the positions and postures (even the expressions on the faces) being changed *between* shots. A length of film consists of a number of 'frames', each of which shows one phase of movement (just as with cine-film); projected at the correct speed gives the illusion of movement on the screen. The puppets may be of wood or made of plastic moulded on wire shapes; limbs and heads may be changeable. For close-ups the figures need to be very highly finished. Problems are created by the heat from the lights. Only when the filming is finished can the results be checked and the necessity for any re-take realised. The process is unavoidably slow – and this is true also for the flat-figure (silhouette) films, with adjustment of positions and limbs, etc., made between shots (camera being above a glass-topped table, on which the scenery and figures rest). An early film, *The New Gulliver*, made by Ptushko in the U.S.S.R. (1935), employed a live actor in the title role; the crowd scenes involved multiplied the technical problems. The creator of stop-motion films needs to be a choreographer able to visualise every movement in advance (both of puppets and camera). Something of the work involved is disclosed in Jaroslav Boček's book on the Czech puppet-film master *Jiří Trnka* (Artia, 1965), profusely illustrated by scenes from his films, which include Shakespeare's *Midsummer Night's Dream*. A parallel technique is that of Lotte Reiniger with her silhouette films, requiring the same kind of vision, patience, skill. See also ANIMATED FILMS (with list of books on techniques).

Stopper. Block sometimes inserted in neck of hollow head of a hand puppet to prevent fingers entering too far; not necessary if the neck made the right width; for the maximum range of movement of the head, two fingers (index and middle) inserted as far as the knuckles give the necessary freedom and control.

Storia dei Burattini, La, by 'Yorick' (Bemporad e Figlio, Florence, 1902). A general history of puppets, largely based on Magnin *Histoire des marionnettes en Europe* (Levy Freres, 1852), but with interesting additional material on the Italian puppet theatre. Large section in English translation contained in Craig *The Mask*, q.v., Vols. 4 – 8, 1911–14. ('Yorick' pen-name of P. C. Ferrigni.)

Stowe, Harriet Beecher (1811–96). American author of best-selling novel of her period, *Uncle Tom's Cabin*, q.v., which has had puppet adaptations.

Straparola's Nights. Stories told, like the *Arabian Nights*, on succeeding nights; collection made by Italian novelist Straparola da Caravaggio (*c.* end of fifteenth – *c.* 1557). Stories were from many sources and were published in Venice 1550 and 1554, two series, with many subsequent editions, and provided storehouse from which Shakespeare, Molière and others obtained some of their plots.

Stravinksy, Igor Feodorovitch. Russian composer; co-operated with Diaghilev, q.v., founder of the *Ballets Russes*, for whom he composed *Firebird, Petrushka*, q.v., *Pulcinella*, etc. The Hungarian State Puppet Theatre, q.v., produced *Petrushka* as mime-ballet (seen at the Aldeburgh and Bath Festivals, 1968); Lotte Reiniger made a Silhouette Film *Dream Circus*, fantasy on the *Pulcinella* music (1939); the opera-oratorio *Oedipus Rex* (text by Cocteau after Sophocles) had an impressive production in the United States (presented by the League of Composers) with Stokowski conducting the Philadelphia Orchestra and massed singers (1931), puppets 10-ft. tall operated from a bridge 40-ft. above (additional operators at ground level); illustrations in Beaumont *Puppets and Puppetry* (Studio, 1958).

String-and-Rod puppets. (*a*) A type found in Southern India, figures approximately 4-ft. in height and weighing up to 40 lb. Control is by strong strings attached to a cloth-covered ring worn like a crown on the operator's head, running from the two sides of the puppet waist and (two sets) from the sides of the ears; the weight is thus taken, and the general movements controlled by the performer's head movements. The figures are legless, with long skirt-type costumes and are very effective in the dance movements typical of the region. The arm movements are controlled by two downwards rods attached to the wooden hands. (*b*) A type developed by TESCHNER for use with his 'FIGURENSPIEGEL', q.v. (now in the Austrian National Library collection), operated from below with rods and strings passing *through* rods (technical details in *Richard Teschner und sein Figurenspiegel*: Wancura, Vienna, 1956).

Stringing stand. Structure for supporting the marionette during the attaching of strings to figure and the control to ensure right lengths and tensions (related to working height of the bridge, if for use on normal stage, or to operating position if for floor show). Stand consists of upright post set into a slab base, with a top projection to which the control can be attached during stringing. The projection can be an adjustable piece to suit string-lengths for large or small stages, or the post can be made in two overlapping sections with a series of bolt holes for adjustment of height. The stand leaves both hands free for testing lengths and tieing off. The marionette will be in a normal standing position when the supporting strings are attached (to head or to shoulders), strings to movable parts being slightly slack.

Strings. Usually associated with the marionette type – the 'string puppet' – but sometimes used with rod type (operated from below-stage) and sometimes with shadow figures. Puppeteers differ among themselves as to whether the strings should be invisible or not; for television appearances the strings may be sprayed to minimise visibility. Some puppeteers tone the strings against the background; others maintain that the strings, in fact, 'vanish' if what the marionettes do is sufficiently interesting. The same theory holds for the visible manipulators of the Japanese 'three man' puppets (BUNRAKU). With the widespread adoption of the 'open type' stage, in which the marionette operator is visible, there is little point in trying to hide the fact that strings are the source of movement, are the life-givers. The creator of a marionette must have the strings in mind from the beginning; construction and control of movement are inseparables; strings can even *reduce* the range of movement, and some movements may require additional strings. Strings create other problems: there may be the risk of catching on projecting scenery, or of two marionettes becoming inextricably caught by arm strings. Strings create scenery-design problems: how is a marionette to enter or exit through a doorway at the rear-centre of the stage? or is the problem to be avoided by habitual use of the wings? The simple answer is that there are no problems (with *any* type of puppet) until the puppeteer creates them by wanting a certain type of action. A first consideration is *weight*; this means that the 'breaking strain' of the string (thread, fish-line, etc.) must be related to the weight of the marionette, with a good safety margin. Puppeteers vary in their practice of positioning the strings to take the weight; on a vertical figure the strings may be attached to the head (close to ears) or to the shoulders. The precise position governs the stance of the standing figure, e.g. on top or to the rear of the shoulders. Ideally each character is thought out technically *individually*; the way a figure stands, sits, moves about, is *part of* the characterisation. The Rajasthani marionettes with a single string looped from the back of the waist over the performer's hand and to the top of the head (and one string controlling the hands) are very agile; a dancer (legless, with long skirts) has a freedom which no legged figure has – but not all dancers will want to be legless or long-skirted. Chinese marionettes may have 20 to 40 strings, some giving individual finger movements; traditional BURMESE marionettes went up to 60 strings, involving harp-like fingering. In complex stringing some threads may be coloured to simplify selection. TESCHNER, in Austria, evolved a system with threads running *through* rods. The whole concept of string-controlled figures can be studied experimentally by *beginning with the strings*, attaching various objects in turn to a single length of thread and discovering the maximum range of movements possible. The experiment is then extended to two strings, and then to objects with moving parts, and then additional strings – and then the *need* for a control to which the top ends of the strings can be attached will be realised. The design of the control itself influences movement range, some movements being obtained by tilting the control rather than by handling of individual strings. The attaching of strings is usually done with the aid of a STRINGING STAND, an upright post set in a firm base, adjustable for different lengths of string, leaving both hands free for adjusting tension and knotting. If the first strings added are those to the shoulders the length will be adjusted to the standing figure – the length in the first place being determined by the working position above stage; longer or shorter strings have different range of movement. Strings may be attached to small screw-eyes (as used by model-makers), e.g. above the knee, if wooden, or may be sewn to a stuffed-cloth figure. Placement with hands may be in the palm, on the back of the hand, on the upper edge, or on the wrist. Leg strings may be to just above the knees, to the toes – or to both – with possible additional strings to the heels. A spine string is used for bend-from-the-waist movement. Eventually a number of simultaneous movements will need synchronising, following mastery of individual movements. The stringing of horizontal creatures, e.g. dragons, have similar problems – but usually involve use of a horizontal control approximately the length of the creature. Finally, there is the problem of preventing entanglement of strings between performances; the figure may be spun in the air, thus twisting the strings – and a tape tied around the twist. Some operators use slotted 'WINDERS'.

Strolling Players and Drama in the Provinces, 1660–1765, by Sybil Rosenfeld (Cambridge, 1939); mentions puppets in Norwich, Ipswich, Leeds, York, Bath, and Kent. Wandering Punch-men persisted right into early twentieth century. Walter Wilkinson, one of the pioneers in the 'revival', walked his show into various parts of England, Scotland, Wales – but had to rely on cars in the United States – and wrote a series of books on his experiences. 'Pantopuck' (A. R. Philpott) took his show around on a small hand-truck up to the commencement of World War II, for a time performing for the evacuated children in country districts.

Strutt, Joseph (1749–1802). English artist and antiquary; engraver. In 1801 published his last and favourite work *The Sports and Pastimes of the*

People in England, q.v., in which he has some scathing comments about puppets as he recalled seeing them in his youth. (Various reprints.)

Stuffed puppets. Head, torso, limbs of a marionette, may be made of stuffed cloth or felt (anathema to carvers). The parts are cut out with a margin for sewing, sewn on the wrong side, turned inside out and stuffed – sawdust, cotton-wool, granulated foamed plastic, etc. Knee and elbow joints are stitched across the sausage lengths, or upper and lower parts of limb made separately. Stretch materials are available which simplify shaping-by-stuffing – stockinette, towelling, 'Lurex', etc. At the Moscow Central State Puppet Theatre, noted for its experimental work, the designer Boris Tuzlukov has sculptured foamed plastic (from blocks) with scissors, covering the shapes with stretch-cloth, attaining a suppleness impossible with wood. A child can convert a woollen stocking into a hand-puppet head by tying a knot in the ankle and pulling the leg over the knot, i.e. a self-stuffed 'instant' head to which features (hair, eyes, mouth) can be sewn.

Stylisation. The stressing of the important and the eliminating of the unimportant characteristics and features – of puppet, costume, scenery – for increased theatrical effectiveness. If a 'realistic' or 'naturalistic' effect is required this will still need checking *from a distance* and will involve the principles of stage make-up, more especially with small puppets.

Styrene. Derivative of ethylene and benzine; soluble in alcohol and ether, insoluble in water. Used in manufacture of POLYSTYRENE (styrofoam); sometimes referred to as vinyl benzene. Some adhesives have a solvent property and should be tested before use with polystyrene.

Sutradhara. Sanskrit term meaning 'the holder of strings', the title for the principal actor in classical drama in India; regarded by some scholars as evidence of prior existence of puppet shows.

Suitcase Theatre, The, by C. W. Blanchard (Devereaux Publications, 1946). Small book on string-puppet stage which packs into suitcase. Brief sections on puppet history, making, manipulation, scenery, lighting, production; scripts for three plays: *The Three Bears, The Adventures of Mr Punch, Aladdin.* Illustrations by H. W. Whanslaw.

Supermarionation. Term for technique perfected by A. P. Films to give real life approximation to their television puppet characters (*Supercar, Fireball XL-5, Thunderbirds, Captain Scarlett*); eyes move sideways, and blink, lip movements being synchronised electronically by solenoid cells inside the heads (pre-recorded dialogue). Super-fine control wires (.005 in.) are sprayed with anti-glare for invisibility on screen; further development takes pupils from photographs of real eyes and transfers these to the puppets.

Surrealism. Word dates from *c.* 1917, applied to a burlesque play by Guillaume Apollinaire, *Les Mamelles de Tiresias.* The Surrealist 'Manifesto' of 1924 linked the concept with dreams, the unconscious and rebellion, and led to many experiments in the arts. Some Surrealists regard Alfred Jarry, q.v. (1873–1907), author of *Ubu Roi,* q.v., as their founder. In practice unusual combinations of objects may be used creatively; American puppeteer Bruce Inverarity, author of *Manual of Puppetry* (1936), co-operated on a play 'Z-739', in which figures constructed from household utensils took part. Most notable of the puppet surrealists was Fred Schneckenburger, q.v. (1922–67), Swiss. Other modern art trends are observable in some of the shows seen at international festivals.

Surrealist puppets. Because in the puppet theatre *everything*, including the characters, is created specially, the *style* is only limited by the technical ingenuity of the designers and makers. The puppet stage is itself a kind of dream world, a place where the normally incongruous elements of life can come together, a place where everything that happens is 'real' – as dreams are real while they last. Not only the events but even the anatomy of the characters, if they are puppets, can ignore the conventional forms. The musical instruments which form the bodies of characters in a Jugoslav puppet theatre version of Maeterlinck's *Blue Bird*, and which have arms in order to play on their own strings, would only be met in the world of the subconscious – or in the puppet theatre. The classic surrealist was SCHNECKENBURGER (1922–67), Swiss-born puppeteer, whose only concern when creating his figures was to materialise the hidden character of his victims; some of his figures are reproduced in Baird *Art of the Puppet* (Collier-Macmillan, 1965), and a number of others in Beaumont *Puppets and Puppetry* (Studio, 1958). These are rod puppets and the structural elements include lengths of bent metal tubing, the hand and forearm of a shop-window figure, a piece of gas-mask spiral tubing, and a whole range of symbols. An eye need not be on a face; it can be at the end of a stalk extended from the head; the mouth can be anywhere, any shape. The interesting thing is that he used the same puppets in shows for children as for the sophisticated cabaret audience. Children supplied with an assortment of scrap materials, nature-objects, 'found' objects, will produce creatures to equal those of any self-styled surrealist: and without requiring any label for their products. Many puppeteers have experimented with the use of the live hands as part of their puppet anatomy, and even using the live hands *as* puppets in themselves. A number of productions of JARRY's *Ubu Roi*, which so shocked the audience at the *Théâtre de l'Oeuvre* in Paris in 1896 – with its opening obscenity and a lavatory brush, and other ingredients – have been seen in recent years, either with human actors as at the Royal Court (with Max Wall in the title role), with sandwich-board type 'costumes' or inflated garments, or with the demi-puppets of Meschke's production from the Stockholm marionette theatre; the *original* theatre performance was based on Jarry's schoolboy puppet-satire on an unpopular teacher, presumably done with fairly conventional puppets. For an uninitiated audience the problem may be to distinguish between the truly surrealist and creations which burlesque the surrealist. The use of pots and pans and knives and forks and spoons as construction media may have quite the opposite effect than that intended.

Swazzle. Instrument used by Punch and Judy showman to obtain the typical Punch 'voice'; spelling varies, e.g. 'swozzle' and 'swatchel', and it is also known as a 'call' or a 'slim'. A letter published in *Notes and Queries*, q.v., about an article in the *Saturday Review* (June, 1900) which gave specimens of Punch performers' slang or 'bastard Romany', said the source of the information was a 'swatchel-cove', i.e. a Punchman. Literary references are sometimes to 'a squeaker'. The instrument is known throughout Europe and may be of very ancient origin. In France it is known as *sifflet-pratique*, or simply *pratique;* in Italy it is *pivetta*, in Spain *pito*. The Soviet puppetmaster Sergei Obraztsov in *Chinese Puppet Theatre* (Faber, 1961) comments on the use of a shrill 'whistle' by Chinese showmen having the same quality as that of the traditional Russian Petrushka player (Punchman); there was even a similarity between the onomatopoeic names given to the instrument by players in the Ukraine and China: 'Ru-tyu-tyu' and 'U-dyu-dyu' (with a resemblance, too, to the English 'Roo-ti-too-toot'). Mayhew, in *London Labour and London Poor* (1851), q.v., in one of his interviews with street entertainers, was told that the instruments were 'calls or unknown tongues' – without disclosing details of their construction. Payne Collier did not mention its use in the show recorded in *Punch and Judy* (Prowett, 1828) given by an old Italian performer. As far back as 1603, Dekker, in *The Wonderful Year*, has a reference to the 'quaile pipe voice' of the 'motion-man' (puppeteer). Burnet, in the satirical *Second Tale of a Tub* (1715), mentions 'wooden tubes' as the means whereby the showman Robert (Martin) Powell produced the 'squeak' – and the ' squeaks' are also mentioned in *The Spectator* (No. 14, 1711) in a comparison of the voices of Powell's puppets and those of some Italian singers (castrati). Swift (1728) in *Mad Mullinix and Timothy* (A Dialogue), q.v., mentions Punch's 'rusty voice'. In Rajasthan, India, the puppeteers use a related instrument which really does give a whistling or squeaking effect; this is made from thin pieces of bamboo with a 'reed' of thin leather or rubber in between. The swazzle construction is no longer a professional secret. Most professionals make their own and will usually have at least three to suit the varying acoustic conditions (out of doors, in a room, in a large hall, etc.). The instrument consists of two slightly curved pieces of silver, one above the other, the curves being outwards (convex); a reed is formed by stretching a piece of tape from side to side between the metal and binding the ends with thread. Mastering the use of it is a matter of considerable practice, preferably with some personal tuition. After a preliminary moistening with water (or beer) the swazzle is placed on the tongue and pressed up to the roof of the mouth; the Punch voice is produced *through* it, the other voices by-passing it. There is usually an initial apprehension of swallowing it; some performers never do achieve a *clear* Punch voice – which could be an additional reason for having a 'front man' (musician, collector) who will act as a stooge when Punch is talking, repeating the dialogue or 'interpreting', q.v., it. Note: *tin* should *not* be used, because of the danger of rust. Ivory has been used. Instructions and diagrams are given in Inverarity *Manual of Puppetry* (Binforts and Mort, 1936). However it is possible to *buy* swazzles from the commercial suppliers: Davenport's (the 'magic' shop) at 51 Great Russell Street, London, W.C.1 (facing the British Museum).

Swift, Jonathan (1667–1745). Irish born author of *Gulliver's Travels*, q.v., which has had many puppet productions. Among other references to puppets in his writings the Dialogue between *Mad Mullinix and Timothy* (1728), q.v., contains a lively account of a puppet show in which Punch dominates the scene, although in a period when the 'Punch and Judy' show had yet to develop. 'Observe the audience is in pain While Punch is hid behind the scene; But when they hear his rusty voice, With what impatience they rejoice!' That is unmistakable, the Punchman's 'swazzle', q.v., 'voice', 'call' used for Punch's speech. Later: 'There's not a puppet made of wood, But what would hang him, if they could.' The attempt of latter-day characters to hang him – including the hangman – failed. There is also a reference to 'motion', the old popular equivalent for 'puppet' and/or 'puppet play'. There are references to Punch in a poem *The Puppet Show*, included in Swift's *Works* (Faulkner, 1762), but the authorship of which has been questioned.

Szilagyi, Deszö. Hungarian puppeteer, Director of the State Puppet Theatre, Budapest; formerly a lawyer; authority on children's literature; his theatre has won international awards for productions of Bartok *The Wooden Prince* and Stravinsky *Petrushka,* seen at the Aldeburgh and Bath Festivals in Britain (1968); contributor of important chapter to the UNIMA book *Puppet Theatre of the Modern World* (1965), in which he discusses his approach to audiences – children and adults – the possibilities of moral and aesthetic education – 'stage metaphor' as the true means of expression: 'the puppet stage is far more a world of complete illusion', because of the homogeneity of puppet-stage and puppets – a homogeneity which is perhaps being destroyed by the contemporary trend to introduce live actors among (or *as*) the puppets.

Szopka (shopka). Diminutive of 'szopa': shed or hut; term for traditional Polish nativity performed by small puppets in a stage resembling architecture of a church. Performances originally given in monastery churches (as early as thirteenth century), moving into the streets and fairs and markets in the seventeenth century; characters derived from medieval Mystery Plays: angels, the devil, Death, mortals. The puppets are small figures controlled by single wire or thin stick operating in slots, the stage usually having two or three acting levels. Since 1937 annual competitions have been held for contemporary szopki; also television appearances. The form has also influenced live theatre productions. Small illustrated book, Polish text, English summary, *see next entry.* Outside Poland there are examples in The Horniman Museum, London, S.E., the Volkskunde Museum, Vienna, and the Ethnographic Museum, Budapest. *Also see* VERTIEP.

Szopki Krakowskie (The Cracow Szopkas), by Roman Reinfuss (Prasa, Cracow, 1958). Interesting small book illustrated by 16 black and white and 8 full-colour examples from Ethnographic and History Museums in Cracow, Poland. Polish text, summary in English on the history of the traditional form of Nativity and the development of the secular versions. Cracow is the place where the szopka has flourished most freely.

Sztaudynger, Dr Jan Izydor. Polish writer, puppet historiographer. One of the contributors to the profusely illustrated book *Od Szopki do Teatru Lalek,* on the traditional 'szopka', q.v., and developments in the puppet theatres of Poland. (Wydawnictwo Lodzke, 1961.)

T

Tabor. Inseparable from 'Pipe and . . .' (which see). Shallow type drum with single drumstick (other hand holding pipe). Origin uncertain. Old French 'tabur' and 'tabour' (latter also in English literature); 'tabourin' = small variant.

Tabs. Originally 'tableau' curtains, dividing in the middle and pulled upwards in a curve, forming festoons; today also used for type pulled to the sides (draw curtains); 'tab' also, sheet of canvas, framed or unframed, used to MASK off-stage areas.

Tabs. Journal published by the Strand Electric and Engineering Co. Ltd., 29 King Street, Covent Garden, London, W.C.2 (branches in Australia and Canada); of interest to all concerned with theatre lighting. Well-illustrated articles on new theatres and new lighting installations, on equipment and techniques. Details on application. Periodically there are lighting demonstrations in the Strand Electric Demonstration Theatre; admission is by ticket only, obtainable free on application (s.a.e. to 29 King Street).

Tale of a Tub, A. Comedy by Ben Jonson, written 1596–97, performed 1633 (Oxford edition 1927, edited Hereford and Simpson). As in Jonson's *Bartholomew Fayre*, q.v., there is a play within the play, this time a primitive type of shadow show, probably the first recorded in English (? European) puppet history. The apparatus is described: a large empty tub with oiled lantern-paper across its open end, and cut out silhouette figures which are moved by the heat from a candle (a technique reflected in modern 'Christmas Chimes' – table decoration with thin shapes of cherubs cut from brass, suspended on a revolving disc set in motion by heat rising from small candles). Also of interest is the specific use of the term 'MOTION' to this type of puppet and to the scenes, these being headed *First Motion, Second Motion* (up to five), with 12 to 18 lines per Motion, spoken by the 'INTERPRETER' out front (again as in the *Fayre*). This makes other references to 'motions' – and which give only titles of the items – confusing as to *type* of puppet, and may require re-consideration of the term's use in Shakespeare's plays. There is an illustration of a paper lamp used as a shadow show (from a Japanese print) in Whanslaw *Shadow Play*, but no details of operating.

Talking Hand. Improvised VENTRILOQUIAL figure consisting of the human fist, the thumb forming a moving jaw, eyes painted or mounted on wire held between fingers, optional wig. McPharlin mentions several old-time performers in his *Puppet Theatre in America*. Technique included in Houlden *Ventriloquism for Beginners* (Kaye & Ward, reprint 1968) with a variation using a knitted mitten.

Tandarica. 'Chip of Wood' – little boy marionette who comperes the variety shows of the Tandarica Theatre, q.v.

Tandarica Theatre. Leading State Puppet Theatre in Bucharest, Rumania, q.v. Director: Margareta Niculescu. Founded 1949 (and nine others, in Cluj, Craiova, etc.; now over 20 theatres). Has been centre of three international puppet festivals and has twice received principal award on these occasions. Repertoire for children includes items from Grimm, Andersen, Pushkin and Rumanian folk tales, and Verne's *Five Weeks in a Balloon*. Variety programme *Fun on Strings*. Award-winning adult item *The Hand with Five Fingers*, q.v.

Tatler, The (1709–11). Periodical which appeared three times each week, edited by Steele, q.v., with contributions from Addison, q.v., and which was later followed by *The Spectator*, q.v. Various references to the puppet show of Martin Powell, q.v., and issue No. 16 mentioned rivalry between the puppeteer and the strolling players, q.v.; the puppets attracted audiences by passing through the streets on horseback (Adam and Eve and 'several others who lived before the flood'), and during the show Punch and his wife were introduced, dancing in the Ark. The fashionables of Bath attended the show, the Mayor preferring puppets to the live actors; the Mayoress, too, thought it 'very proper for young people to see'. No. 44 has an interesting technical note about 'a thread in one of Punch's chops, giving him the appearance of enunciation', i.e. moving jaw and mouth. In the same issue, Steele (using the nom-de-plume Isaac Bickerstaff, Esq.) complained that 'a lewd Jester whom he calls Punch' had spoken during the Prologue to the dishonour of the said Bickerstaff, the dialogue being delivered by the puppeteer who stood behind and 'worked the wires'.

Tchantches. Traditional regional puppet character, 'the spirit of Liége' (Belgium) and one of the few puppets to have a statue erected in its honour (the others being Pinocchio and Kasparek, q.v.). Tchantches represents the type of the Walloon peasant and invariably wears a tall hat, is a buffoon, appears in every play along with Charlemagne and his knights (which are controlled from above by metal rod to the top of the head).

Teaching-aid. From the pupil's point of view = a 'learning' aid. Example: in Buenos Aires, Mane Bernardo uses puppets in lessons for the youngest children, and through the play *The Little Dwarf Writer*, q.v., the children learn to distinguish materials and their names. The same principle is used in teaching a second language by visio-verbal association (see LANGUAGE TEACHING). At the Shreyas school in Ahmedabad, India, the inter-relationship of lessons in the preparation of a puppet play 'A Day in the Life of an Eskimo', requiring study of the way of life, the costume, instruments, names, climate and so on. The puppet play provides the incentive for the necessary research. See also LAGO and LITERACY HOUSE *re* literacy campaigns.

Teatro dei Piccoli. Famous Italian puppet theatre founded 1913 in Rome by Dr Vittorio PODRECCA (1883–1959), its Director. Toured in 30 countries between 1912 and 1934, playing to over ten million spectators. Wide repertoire, variety turns and acrobats to opera – inspiring copyists everywhere, especially the eccentric pianist act (a burlesque of the Russian virtuoso Vladimir de Pachmann). The composer, Respighi, q.v., sometimes conducted the orchestra at the performances of his *La Bella Dormente nel Bosco* (*Sleeping Beauty*). The theatre was awarded a Diploma of Merit by the Italian Ministry of Fine Arts. Later productions showed the influence of 'musicals' and there were burlesques of Charlie Chaplin, Josephine Baker and the Marx Brothers. Beaumont *Puppets and Puppetry* (Studio, 1958) has illustrations.

Technik des Puppentheaters, by A. Fedotow (Hofmeister, 1956). This is only available in German or the original Russian, but is valuable for the technical illustrations; the 14 photos are from Russian sources; 175 text illustrations covering various types of hand and rod puppets, heads with moving mouths, moving eyes, technique for smoking a cigarette, etc., and on stage construction, scenery.

Technique of Film Animation, by John Halas and Roger Manvell (Focal Press, 1959). A standard work; part 4 is on Puppet and Object animation, the Puppet Film (production and processes); chapter on Silhouette Films as exemplified by Lotte Reiniger's work, and Flat-figure animation. Also see *Design in Motion* by same authors (Studio, 1962).

Telescopic puppets. George Cruikshank's illustrations to *Punch and Judy*, with J. Payne Collier text of the play include a composite drawing of a character (in an interlude) whose neck stretches (presumably with an internal rod) and who first raises his hat by one hand, to the left and right members of the audience – a trick which the old Italian showman PICCINI defied any other performer to imitate. In the U.S.A., REMO BUFANO created a 35-ft. tall telescopic-bodied Clown (marionette). A simple form of telescoping clown who is mostly costume and a plastic foam head has a hoop (e.g. embroidery ring) at the waist, supported by a short internal handle, a thin piece of curtain rod supports the head and after lifting head to maximum height descends and is concealed in the waist.

Television Films. Lotte Reiniger silhouette films: Fairy Tales: *Snow White and Rose Red*, *The Magic Horse*, *Aladdin* (Primrose Productions, London, 1953), *Sleeping Beauty*, *The Frog Prince*, *The Gallant Little Tailor*, *The Three Wishes*, *Caliph Stork*, *Cinderella*, *Grasshopper and the Ant* (PP, 1954), *Thumbelina*, *Hansel and Gretel* (PP, 1955); Music, Freddy Phillips. *Jack and the Beanstalk*, with coloured background, music Phillips (PP, 1955); *The Star of Bethlehem*, Nativity, silhouettes and colour, Christmas carols sung by Glyndebourne Chorus, Music Peter Gellhorn (PP, 1956); *Helen la Belle*, all colour, music Offenbach's Opera *La Belle Helene*, arranged by Ludo Phillips (Fantasia, London, 1957). *A Night in the Harem*, after Mozart's Opera *Il Seraglio*, music arranged Peter Gellhorn (Fantasia, 1957–58).

Television puppets. John Logie BAIRD (1888–1946), the Scottish inventor, used Bill a VENTRILOQUIAL dummy for his first screen model in the late 1920's. Puppets were 'in' from the earliest days of television and when equipment and technique were necessarily primitive and experimental. Two of the leading figures in the English puppetry revival, H. W. WHANSLAW and WALDO LANCHESTER, who had established their London Marionette Theatre, co-operated with Baird on the first broadcast from the Long Acre studios (1930), when, as Whanslaw put it (*Second Bench Book*), the screen was 'not much larger than a tram ticket'. Jan Bussell was the third operator; the marionettes were small, average height 10 ins. Whanslaw's puppet 'Soko' was a black-and-white character specially created for the screen appearance. The present author's puppets – also translated into black-and-white – took part in some of the late night programmes from the BBC Studio in the basement of Broadcasting House (1932), by which time the screen had grown somewhat, but results still resembled those of the early cinema films. In 1936 the B.B.C. began its public television service from Alexandra Palace, the first to present marionettes being JOHN CARR (The Jacquard Puppets), being followed by a long string of puppeteers associated with the BRITISH PUPPET AND MODEL THEATRE GUILD, including Bruce McLeod and other Punch and Judy showmen. All the early broadcasts were 'live' – after studio and camera rehearsals – and the facilities developed (cameras became mobile, could take close-ups; several stages could be pre-set and used in sequence). In 1937, H. W. Whanslaw and GERALD MORICE, just back from Germany, appeared on CECIL MADDEN's *Picture Page* programme, followed later by many others, such as LOTTE REINIGER. Up to the beginning of the War practically all the well-known puppeteers performed for screen-viewers: WALTER WILKINSON, ANN HOGARTH, WALDO LANCHESTER, OLIVE BLACKHAM, JOHN WRIGHT and many others. At the

R

resumption of the television service in 1946 came Muffin the Mule, with Annette Mills at the piano and Ann Hogarth and JAN BUSSELL at the strings; Muffin became world-famous. Children's T.V. began at Lime Grove in 1950 and some of the early favourites have survived several generations of young viewers without becoming a day older. Mr. Turnip, Andy Pandy, the Flowerpot Men, the Wooden Tops, Sooty, Pinky and Perky, and so on. From performing 'live' the puppets began to be pre-filmed, and some to be especially created for television, such as GORDON MURRAY's *Camberwick Green*. Adults were also catered for, and it is certain that millions of viewers have been introduced to puppets of an inter-national status that they would never have seen otherwise: the famous SALZBURG MARIONETTES, Professor SKUPA's troupe from Czechoslovakia and Podrecca's TEATRO DEI PICCOLI from Italy, the Moscow Central State Puppet Theatre directed by SERGEI OBRAZTSOV. Even the 'Goons', who had previously been just Radio Voices, handed over those voices for a puppet *Telegoons* series. Of more recent children's programmes *The Magic Roundabout* series, with 'Dougal' (by Serge Danot), has quite a few adult 'fans' and, like many of the earlier favourites, has also appeared in book form. In the Space Age it is not surprising that Sylvia and Gerry Anderson's T.V.–films have won a large export market for their *Supercar*, *Fireball XL5*, *Stingray*, *Thunderbirds* – and the last has moved on to the larger screen in the cinema. For such items the last word in 'SUPER-MARIONATION' technique puts the cost of a puppet in the £300 bracket; electronics are involved in synchronisation of lip movements with pre-recorded dialogue. Opinions are as divided relative to puppet programmes as to most other programmes; some adults adore children's items. With the coming of colour T.V. a vital element is being supplied which the live show has always had: *colour*. The whole subject of puppets and television provided the theme for discussion at an international puppetry Conference in Warsaw (1962), and it is possible that an entirely new concept of T.V.-puppetry possibilities may yet arise. One of the dis-advantages of television, with its vast audiences, is the high consumption rate of material, to which serials are only a partial answer (i.e. using the same characters in new episodes). Some 'favourite' characters have already become casualties. In the United States at least one troupe, the *Kuklapolitans* (Burr Tillstrom), seems to have found the recipe and have been playing to audiences of millions for some years, the recipe being that of the old showman, topicality; they play live and largely 'off the cuff' – instant theatre – and they have a colossal fan-mail. It remains to be seen whether, in addition to providing good entertainment of the more obvious kinds, puppeteers and technicians between them can evolve a television puppet-art form.

Tenniel, Sir John (1820–1914). English artist, work including cartoons for the periodical *Punch*. His illustrations for Lewis Carroll's *Alice in Wonderland* frequently used as basis for characters in puppet productions of the story.

Tennyson, Alfred Lord (1809–92). English poet. 'Falser than all fancy fathoms, falser than all songs have sung, Puppet to a father's threat, and servile to a shrewish tongue.' (*Locksley Hall*). 'We are puppets, man in his pride, and Beauty fair in her flower; Do we move ourselves or are we moved by an unseen hand . . .' (*Maud*: a Monodrama, I, iv).

Teschner, Professor Richard (1879–1948). UNIMA Member of Honour in Memoriam. Artist-puppeteer born in the Sudetenland (old

Bohemia); etcher, lithographer, woodcarver; creator of unique form of puppet-theatre (*Figurenspiegel*). First interested in lighting techniques and marionettes, seen in Prague, but decided that human speech and singing were out of place in the puppet theatre – whilst admitting that KASPER without speech was unthinkable. Decisive influence was from Javanese shadow and three-dimensional puppets acquired in Holland during his honeymoon (married daughter of Viennese master-carver); set up studio and theatre. First figures and plays derived immediately from the JAVANESE and INDONESIAN legends, but experiments led to development of original techniques, involving combination of rod and string control from *below* stage. To conceal the strings these were run through holes drilled through the rods (an engineering feat). Teschner relied a great deal upon special lighting for his effects, leaving the puppet heads almost unfinished, even eye-less, with atmospheric music scaled to the puppet theatre. His theatre, the *Figurenspiegel*, q.v., seen in London in April, 1934, at the National Austrian Exhibition (attended by the Queen), was also highly original in concept. After the earliest experiments he wrote his own plays and a number of these were filmed; from about 1925 he gave performances until the end of his life. His theatre and puppets are now in the theatrical collection of the Austrian National Library (there have been occasional demonstrations), and Dr Franz HADAMOWSKY, director of the collection, has contributed a valuable monograph on Teschner's life and work and technical developments in *Richard Teschner und sein Figurenspiegel* (Vienna, 1956). Beaumont *Puppets and Puppetry* (Studio, 1958) has six photographs which give a good idea of the quality of the productions, although lacking the colour.

Thackeray, William Makepeace (1811–63). English novelist; at one time on staff of the periodical *Punch*; his *The Rose and the Ring* (Fireside Pantomime for Great and Small Children) has had puppet theatre adaptations. In *Vanity Fair* (Chap. 56) mentions interest of the Todd family in West's famous Juvenile Drama characters for the 'pasteboard theatre'. *Vanity Fair* (Chap. 67), 'Come, children, let's shut up the box and the puppets, for our play is played out.'

Thailand (Siam). In an article in *Puppet Theatre Around the World* (New Delhi, 1960) dealing with the various forms of puppetry in Thailand there is, curiously, no mention of the shadow figures (The Nang) which Europeans associate with that country and which were exhibited a few years back, at the Victoria and Albert Museum, with a very wide screen and simulated firelight illuminating the figures. The characters are not articulated for individual action, but are part of a scene, elaborately incised, and supported by two rods, the operators performing a sort of dance during the narration of episodes concerning the Monkey King. Unlike the Javanese characters, always in profile, the Thai figures face the audience. Tramote, author of the article mentioned above, gives the word 'Hun' as the Thai for 'puppet' and meaning an effigy or likeness of a real object. The origins are as uncertain as in most countries, but there are Chinese influences in the case of the three-dimensional puppets (some also seen at the V. & A.) which have a main rod control (from below-stage) with strings passing downwards through eyelets and controlling limb movements. At different periods two sizes of these puppets were in use, the larger being known as the 'Big' or 'Royal', the smaller (about 12 ins. high) similar to the Chinese. The plays were taken from the popular dance-dramas. Later a type of puppet consisting only of a head,

R*

torso and arms, with highly stylised costume, was developed, with main supporting rod and smaller rods to the arms, a type still in use. Music is provided by drums, gongs and stringed instruments.

Theatre. *The Penguin Dictionary of the Theatre* (1966) does not define *theatre*, although there are entries for *theatre-in-the-round* and *theatre (total)*. Essentially a theatre is a place where dramatic productions are presented; it need not be a building with a roof, it can be an outdoor arena (as in classic Greece and Rome). This sense of *place* is included in such terms as 'theatre of war' or 'operating theatre' – but although the action in both cases may be highly dramatic it is not primarily for entertainment. In the realm of puppetry *theatre* may mean a mobile *stage*, to be erected in a building (theatre, hall, private room) or out of doors. In Europe the term may mean a company of performers – who may or may not have their own theatre-building, so that the question '*Where* is your theatre?' can be confusing, perhaps embarrassing. The concept of 'TOTAL THEATRE' probably derives from the experiments made at the BAUHAUS in Germany, concerned with inter-relationship of the arts. 'Theatre' is also used in the sense of 'theatrical entertainment' – in such phrases as (of a certain production): It is 'good theatre'.

Théâtre de la Foire. Theatre set up by provincial actors in Paris *c.* 1595 at the fairs at St Germain and St Laurent, where puppet shows were also established (for which LE SAGE, q.v., wrote over a hundred plays).

Théâtre des Amis (1847–89). Private theatre established at the chateau of George Sand, French novelist and playwright, at NOHANT, q.v., for the entertainment of her literary circle. Her son Maurice made the puppets, of the hand type (800 characters), George made the costumes, wrote plays; Maurice and painter friend Eugene Lambert also wrote plays. The theatre was burned down on one occasion, by an enthusiastic assistant. By 1872 the number of plays produced totalled 120. Delacroix, the painter, Chopin, Bizet, Liszt, were among the distinguished who saw performances. A two-page reproduction of a drawing by Maurice, showing the stage and audience, is contained in Baird *Art of the Puppet* (Collier-Macmillan, 1965).

Théâtre des Pupazzi. Opened in 1843 by Lemercier de Neuville, originally as a Gallery of caricatures, a little theatre of 'PANTINS' (flat jointed cut-outs of the 'jumping jack' type). Later used three-dimensional puppets at the suggestion of artist Gustave Doré; masterpiece was guitar-playing puppet pierrot.

Théâtres d'Ombres, Les, by Denis Bordat and Francis Boucrot (l'Arche, 1956). Well illustrated small book on the history and techniques of shadow theatre: Chinese, Javanese, Siamese, Turkish (with text for short scene); on the French silhouettes and 'pantins'; illustration of Geza BLATTNER *silhouettes à fils* (i.e. flat figure marionettes); human shadows (including illustration of MARCEAU, the great mime, in *Le Manteau*; illustrations of the figures used in the *theatre Seraphin;* the text for the famous 'BROKEN BRIDGE' item also seen in London (*Le Pont Cassé*), the origin of which was not known by the street showman interviewed by Mayhew (*London Labour and London Poor*); chapters on 'Le Chat Noir' and 'Le théâtre noir et blanc' of Paul Vieillard. Section on 'ombromane' or hand shadows (on wall or screen) with illustrations for a number of amusing creatures to make. Also on back-projection.

Théâtres d'ombres à Montmartre de 1887–1923, by Paul Jeanne (Les Presses Modernes, 1937). On the shadow puppet shows in Paris. Corrects some inaccuracies in Maindron *Histoire des marionnettes en Europe* (Levy Frères, 1852) *re* the famous *Chat Noir* theatre, cafe club with artist clientele.

Théâtre Érotique de la rue de la Santé. Established in Paris, 1862, closed after twelve months in spite of special 'attractions'; puppets by Lemercier de Neuville, also plays, and others by Tisserand, satirising popular public personalities such as Victor Hugo and Dumas fils.

Theatre Language, by Walter Parker Bowman and Robert Hamilton Ball (Theatre Arts Books, N.Y., 1961). A dictionary of terms in English, from medieval to modern times; first extensive dictionary on the special language of the theatre; defines over 3,000 terms and phrases (including some puppet items) and cross-references many more.

Theatre Notebook. Quarterly journal concerned with the history and technique of British theatre; includes the *Bulletin* of the Society for Theatre Research, q.v., and has occasional articles relative to puppetry, e.g. Vol. XX, No. 4, on Gordon CRAIG's theory of the actor-übermarionette. Published and distributed by Ifan Kyrle Fletcher, 22 Buckingham Gate, London, S.W.1; also supplied to members of S.T.R.

Theatre of Hands. Live hands, with or without white or coloured gloves, become puppets, with or without music, in lyrical, burlesque or items of high tragedy. Outstanding performer, French puppeteer Yves Joly. Live hands also used as though belonging to large rod type puppets. Live hands creating shadow characters on an illuminated screen. (See THÉÂTRES D'OMBRES.)

Theatre of the Bauhaus, by Oskar Schlemmer, Laszlo Moholy-Nagy, Farkas Molnar, with an Introduction by Walter Gropius; English translation by A. S. Wensinger (Wesleyan University Press, U.S.A., 1961). Gropius was the founder of the Bauhaus, q.v., which was concerned with the integration of the arts and crafts; Schlemmer contributes a section on Man and Art Figure; Moholy-Nagy on the Theatre, Circus, Variety; Molnar on the 'U-Theatre' – with further material by Schlemmer on Theatre. The concept of 'TOTAL' or 'organic' theatre carried over into the realm of puppets. Illustrations include some from *The Adventures of the Little Hunchback,* stylised marionettes. Experiments included live actors as puppets. (Experimental stages are now in the Munich Theatre Museum.)

Therapy. The old lady who goes to the cinema for 'a good cry' – to see a 'weepy' – and the spectator with the belly-laugh watching a 'funny', have both found an emotional outlet. The so-called 'cathartic' function of theatre, of entertainment in general, of hobbies, has been noted by psychologists down the ages. The small girl talking to her dolls or playing mothers-and-fathers with her small brother provides a clue to the possibilities of play-therapy in the Child Guidance Clinic, one function of which is to provide play facilities and to study the child engrossed in play – for diagnostic purposes. Children attending the Clinic are mainly those with social behaviour problems indicating emotional stresses or instability, insecurity, inability to cope with environment. Toys, dolls, sand, water, building and modelling materials, in the hands of a disturbed child are more effective and evokative than attempts at discussion, especially when the inability to express in words is a barrier. Puppets have been found to have exceptional advantages in this field. There are several possibilities: (*a*) the patient watches a show given by therapist or an assistant, reacts to it, discusses it afterwards, revealing an attitude to the symbolic characters, their relationships, the general action. It has been found that traditional folk tales are often of more value than a pyschologically slanted play concocted by the therapist. (*b*) The next step is for the patient to become performer, discovering the security and freedom of the stage, playing out those things it cannot or has not the power to discuss directly with the therapist. During such play it may begin itself to realise more clearly the origins of some of its problems. There may be an immediate release of emotional attention as well as provision of material for diagnosis. (*c*) The patient then moves on to making its own puppet characters; the very choice of characters will probably have significance as well as the situations these find themselves in during performance sessions. The physical activity and the after-play have therapeutic value. Among the first to experiment in this field was the famous Bellevue Hospital, New York, but other experiments were begun independently, e.g. in Switzerland. Work has been done with adults, including rehabilitation with soldiers in hospital during World War II. With adults the policy sometimes is to have patients in groups (Group therapy) performing to or with each other. This aspect, the various branches of therapy – which includes physiotherapy and occupational therapy – has been the theme for discussion at international level at various puppet conferences. The first comprehensive compilation of material on the therapeutic aspects is contained in a chapter in *The Puppet Book*, 3rd edition, edited by Wall, White and Philpott (Faber, 1965). The book also covers the practical aspects of puppet making with various age-groups, the making of stages, etc. Occasional articles appear in *Puppet Post*, official journal of the Educational Puppetry Association, and in medical and occupational therapy publications.

Thinners. Dilutents such as turpentine or 'turps substitute' (white spirits: petroleum distillate); used to reduce oil paint to required brushing or spraying consistency; also used for cleaning brushes. Some thinners also act as solvents.

Thixotropic. Substance of jelly consistency until stirred, becoming liquid; used in non-drip paints.

Thermoplastic. Material which softens when heated and hardens while cooling.

Thermosetting. Substance which becomes solid when heated.

Three-dimensional shadow puppets. Shadows themselves cannot be three-dimensional, but contemporary experiments have been made in the use of natural objects (vegetation: ferns, grasses, feathers, etc.), coloured balloons, pairs of scissors, wire-outline marionettes, and the deliberate use of 'depth' – as distinct from flat cut-out figures held close behind the illuminated screen. Other experiments combined with this include use of projected scenic effects. Some of the possibilities were demonstrated by students from the Berlin Hochschule für Bildende Kunst when visiting the Goldsmith's College in London in 1963.

Three Japanese Plays, edited and introduced by Earle Ernst (Oxford University Press, 1959). One play from each of the traditional forms of theatre, Noh, Kabuki and 'Doll' (Puppet), *The House of Sugawara*.

Through Wooden Eyes, by Jan Bussell (Faber, 1956), illustrated by drawings by Francis Gower; chapters on Some Curios from England, the Puppet Theatre of George Sand at Nohant, Naples, Marseilles, Tradition in

France, Switzerland, the Soviet puppetmaster Sergei Obraztsov, q.v., and South Africa; autobiographical travelogue, vivid account of tracking down puppets in many places.

Thunder sheet. Metal sheet suspended in a convenient position back-stage and shaken to obtain thunder effects, with or without a handle.

Tin-can characters. Sometimes appear in advertising films (animated objects), but also have possibilities as amusing bodies for hand puppets or marionettes: illustration in Batchelder and Comer *Puppets and Plays* (Faber, 1959) shows characters for an original melodrama and taking their names from the labels. No risks should be taken with sharp edges; these should be bound with strong, sticky tape.

Tin-snips. Tool for cutting thin sheet metal, short blades, scissors action; several sizes.

Tintookies, The. The title for the show of Australia's leading Marionette Company, director Peter Scriven. The name means 'the little people who live in the sandhills'. Repertoire includes *The Magic Pudding*, an adaptation of Norman Lindsay's famous children's classic. Characters have names such as Bunyip Bluegum, Uncle Wattleberry, Finglebury Flying Fox, and Sam Sawnoff. The Tintookies were selected for the inaugural nation-wide tour for the organisation formed in 1965 known as the Marionette Theatre of Australia.

Tissue paper. Can be used as a 'separator' over plasticine model when a direct cast is to be made; torn into pieces about 1 in. square, slightly damped and applied with slight overlap of pieces; next the layers of newspaper strips and paste, or muslin and plaster 'filler' are built up to required thickness, and cut in half when hard. Most of tissue is removed with the cast and plasticine is ready for re-use. Preferable to coating plasticine with vaseline. Colour: preferably white. Coloured varieties can be used for artificial-flower making or for tinting areas of perspex shadow figures or scenery.

Titeres. Spanish term for 'puppets', etymology uncertain. 'Puppeteer' = 'titerero'. Catalan variant: titelles. McPharlin (*Puppet Theatre in America*, 1949) discusses the 'speculative etymology' of José Galvez and of Covarrubias (*Treasury of the Castilian Language*) – seeing relationship with the sound 'ti ti' of a whistle at one time used in the show; alternatively, a Greek origin; but McPharlin suggests 'tyttos' ('small') or 'tityros' ('monkey', 'satirist', 'comedian') – which does not exhaust the subject.

Toby. The name of Punch's dog; origin uncertain. In the biblical story, *The Book of Tobit* (in the *Apocrypha*), Tobias' dog is thought by scholars to be the only example in Hebrew literature of a dog regarded as man's friend and fellow traveller; this may show the story to be of non-Hebrew origin. These biblical stories were popular in the Middle Ages and a number were played on the puppet stages (*The Creation of the World, Noah, Jonah and the Whale*, etc.); the story of Tobit was also a popular theme in art, e.g. sixteenth century painting by Martin de Vos *Tobit and his Dog* – which has a trimmed poodle! Performing dogs are sometimes seen in early illustrations of showmen with the MARIONNETTES À LA PLANCHETTE; French puppet shows introduced cats. Some Punchmen have used puppet dogs, such as the one illustrated by Cruikshank in the Payne Collier *Punch and Judy*; some of the present-day showmen, such as the famous Codman family, use live dogs, but some have neither puppet nor live animal. The R.S.P.C.A. may have had some influence. The main function of Toby is to bite Punch's nose – when given the cue. Traditionally, his 'costume' was a ruff around the neck. In Dickens' *Old Curiosity Shop* the owner of a performing-dogs act produces a little terrier from his pocket, and says to Short the Punchman: 'He was once a Toby of yours, wasn't he!' Dickens says the idea of using a dog was a modern innovation, and the showman interviewed in Mayhew's *London Labour and London Poor* stated that Pike (apprentice of PICCINI, who used a puppet dog) was the first to use a live dog called Toby. An earlier showman, Powell, had trained a Newfoundland. In the early issues of the periodical *Punch* there was a 'Diary of Toby' and the dog appeared on the cover. One thing is certain: it would be impossible to coin a more effective name for the animal. See also PIGS.

Tools. The puppeteer's workshop is usually equipped with the standard hand tools for woodwork – chisels, hammers, gimlets, screwdrivers, drills, planes, etc., and may even have power-tools today. Carvers have their own special tools. See the following for some useful additions: ABRAFILE, COPING SAW, HOLE SAW, RIFFLERS, TIN SNIPS.

Topo Gigio. 'That Italian mouse' and a top personality with T.V. viewers all over the Continent and in three or more weekly 15–minutes adventures on the English screen. Height, 10 ins. Type : hand puppet, but needing three to four operators and 'black theatre' setting. Creator: Signora Maria Perego, Milan.

Total theatre. The concept of a production technique which involves perfect relationship of performance, lighting, music, stage settings, costume; experiments which over-emphasise any of these elements at the expense of the script are *not* total. Some productions do not need music; some do not need lighting other than normal daylight; some can dispense with scenery; a strip-tease puppet show gradually dispenses with costume, and may even dispose of the puppets too: it is the content and the quality of the performance which are of prime importance in *all* productions. See *Theatre of the Bauhaus*.

Tottles, The. American puppet family whose adventures reflect family problems; weekly half-hour T.V. series for children four–ten years (Philadelphia). The puppets have their own miniature puppets.

Towelling, towel cloth. White variety, sold by the yard or in form of nappies (diapers); dyes easily; good texture and flexibility for some animal puppets.

Town Musicians of Bremen. Grimm's classic story of Donkey, Dog, Cat and Hen who leave their masters after being ill-used, join forces, surprise and scare away gang of robbers by a chorus of animal noises, and take over the feast. Many adaptations for the puppet stage, including delightful version by Ursula am Bühle for the Zurich Marionette Theatre (illustrations in Gauchat *Marionettes*).

Tozer, H. V. English puppeteer, born in Paraguay, domiciled in Spain since 1925; director of the Marionetas de Barcelona. First puppets made at age 10 years after seeing street Punch and Judy show in England. First carved heads while at school (age 15) for performances by brother Norman. Post in hydro-electricity public service company, Barcelona (1925) and became interested in the Catalan hand puppets. While convalescing in England (age 26) inspired by Walter WILKINSON's *Peep Show*; carved improved Punch heads, performances by brother Bernard. In 1934 contributed article to McPharlin's *Puppetry*: Year Book of the

265
Puppeteers of America, and then annually, bringing the unique CATALAN type to notice of outside world. In 1936 gave demonstrations to Spanish Civil War refugee children and made 18 marionettes for *Jack and the Beanstalk*, followed by 20 in. figures for *St George and the Dragon* and variety figures. After demonstrations for the Committee and members of the Formento de las Artes Decoratives, recruited assistants and performed in Spanish; first full-scale public show in 1946, in the Cupula del Coliseum, with rehearsal and storage space in basement of the British Institute; formed company of ten. 1949 transferred to French Lycée school. Change of Mayor in 1956 (and policy) resulted in loss of nearly completed permanent theatre – since when unable to have use of suitable premises. Troupe of over 90 marionettes (1967), some of which have never performed, with repertoire of plays, variety and circus turns sufficient for three different two-hour shows. During eleven years with company gave 141 full-scale shows. Over the years contributor of technical and other articles to the *Puppet Master*, journal of the British Puppet and Model Theatre Guild, q.v.

Transformation puppets. These come within the general category of 'trick figures' and involve special construction and stringing. *See* TRICK PUPPETS.

Translucent. Material which permits light to pass through but not sufficiently for seeing objects distinctly; shadow puppet screens are lit from the rear and only the figure held against the screen should be visible to the audience; there may be some shadows from the rod controls, depending on thickness and type of rod and the angle, position of light, degree of translucency of screen.

Transparent. Material which allows light to pass through sufficiently for seeing objects on other side (e.g. clear glass). For shadow-shows a TRANSLUCENT material is needed.

Trap. A removable section of a stage floor; used for dramatic entries and exits, or comic ones. The Goethe-haus at Weimar, Germany, has the remains of a *toy* theatre (possibly that given by Goethe to his son) which has traps.

Trick Marionettes, by Nicholas Nelson and J. J. Hayes, illustrated by Paul McPharlin (Puppetry Handbook VI: U.S.A., 1935). Mostly traditional types, some contemporary; details of construction and stringing. Transformations (e.g. lady into balloon), break-aways (dissecting skeleton), pole-tosser, weight-lifter, various balancers, stilt-walker, skaters, knife-thrower, trapeze artistes, man shot from cannon, dancers, etc. On principles shown almost any trick act can be worked out.

Trick puppets. In the basic sense, *all* puppets are 'trick' puppets, but in the special sense of characters designed and constructed for particular acts, these are the logical development from the straightforward constructions and probably evolved along with the dramatic types from the beginning of puppet history; examples have been found in India and China (still popular); the American Indian tribes used them in religious rituals (see McPharlin *Puppet Theatre in America*). There is a distinction between types which depend mainly on their construction and those which are essentially for special operational skill (e.g. Chinese hand puppet spinning a plate on end of stick). Some types, such as the 'transformations' must be re-assembled after each performance, but an item such as the 'dissecting skeleton' comes apart and re-assembles *during* performance, depending on double stringing of parts. Among the marionettes designed to perform particular feats are the stilt-walkers, pole-balancers, ball-jugglers, weight-lifters, acrobats and contortionists, tight-rope walkers; these sometimes enter the superhuman class, defying gravity. The 'transformations' include traditional types such as 'woman into balloon' (particularly popular in the days of balloon ascents), 'shepherdess into pot of flowers' – and then into a fountain. The 'Grand Turk' comes to pieces and forms a group of smaller figures. A hollow body character has a series of heads which emerge. A chest-opening type (also known to N. American Indians) reveals internal 'spirit' face. There are 'reversibles' such as the Rajasthani character with second head under skirt. Trick characters are also possible with the hand, rod, shadow types of puppets; transformations very popular feature in Chinese shadow-plays, one character being withdrawn from the screen and rapidly re-placed by another. Techniques: Stuart Robinson *Exploring Puppetry* has simple types that children can make: concertina-paper body shadow figure; shadow figure built from party blow-out toy; Jack-in-the-box operated by expanding scissor type control. Whanslaw and Hotchkiss *Specialised Puppetry* deals with traditional types and some developments. Nelson and Hayes *Trick Marionettes* mainly traditional, but techniques can be adapted for original acts. Inverarity *Manual of Puppetry*, suggestions for variety acts.

Trnka, Jiří (Yirshy). Czech puppet-master, distinguished puppet-film creator, brilliant illustrator of children's books; National Artist. First acquainted with puppets as a boy, both his mother and grandmother involved in toy and puppet making, father a plumber. First attempt to run a professional puppet theatre failed; influenced by SKUPA's show seen at holiday camps and eventually made puppets for him; became out-standing student at School of Applied Arts, pioneered in Cartoon and then Puppet Film production, and from 1946 onwards gained national and international awards in this field almost annually. The sequence of films show constant experiment with techniques. *The Story of the Double-Bass* is a visually humorous item based on a story by Chekhov; *The Devil's Mill* is dramatic, of Czech origin; *The Song of the Prairie* is a burlesque of the American 'Western'; *The Emperor's Nightingale*, after Andersen, is lyrical; Shakespeare without words, *A Midsummer Night's Dream*, was immediately controversial, although visually beautiful; *The Cybernetic Grandmother* was a satire on science fiction. A number of his illustrated books have had English editions, including *Bruin Furryball in the Circus* (Dakers, 1957), *Grimm's Fairy Tales* (Paul Hamlyn, 1961), *Hans Andersen's Fairy Tales* (Hamlyn, 1959), *Bruin Furryball in the Puppet Theatre* (Dakers, 1957), *La Fontaine's Fables* (Golden Pleasure Books, 1963). *A Midsummer Night's Dream*, adapted from the film, retold for children by Eduard Petiška, with photographs and drawings in colour (Artia, 1960). A biography and detailed study of his work, profusely illustrated, by Jaroslav Bocek *Jiří Trnka Artist and Puppet Master* (Artia: English edition, 1965) contains lists of books illustrated, films made, prizes and awards (up to 1963).

Trnka (Jiří): Artist and Puppet Master, by Jaroslav Boček (Artia, 1963; English edition, 1965). Biography of internationally renowned Czecho-slovak puppet-film maker, with many reproductions from films and drawings. Eighteen colour stills from *Midsummer Night's Dream*, showing some of unusual possibilities of wide screen. Puppets of the 'stop motion' types and films mainly for adults. List of awards impressive, almost annually since 1946, and given title of rare distinction in 1963, that of National Artist. Appendices: Books illustrated; Films.

Trois p'tits tours et puis s'en vent . . . , by Gaston Baty (Odette Lieutier, Paris, 1942). Scripts for classic string-puppet plays from MSS. of early puppeteers ('Les théâtres forains de marionnettes à fils et leur repertoire, 1800–90): *Temptation of St Anthony, The Prodigal Son, Victor or the Child of the Forest, John of Flanders, The Bleeding Nun.* Book title is from old French folk-song.

Tulukutu. Small puppets found in the Barotse Province in Africa, with unique method of operation. Two wooden figures about 9 ins. in height share one pair of arms about 4½ ins. long, attached to the shoulders by knotted string through small holes; head and body cut in one piece, with slight modelling and poker-work features; one-piece legs of same length as arms (all limbs of flat split cane). One male, one female figure, with lion fur loin-cloths. Operator sits on ground with legs flat and spread apart; looped thread from each puppet is controlled by the operator's big toes, giving similar action to the European MARIONETTES À LA PLANCHETTE; slapping the thighs induces movement in time to chanted music. Specimen in collection of present author sent by the 'Primary Puppets' Club at Chingola School in Zambia (1966); type had been demonstrated on the Educational Television Programme *Young Zambia Presents*, together with *Punch and Judy* and some Zambian folktales. A photograph of an African boy performing in the open appeared in *Child Education* (No. 13 of 'Children Round the World' series). Mr Gluckman, of the Department of Social Anthropology and Sociology, University of Manchester, observed similar puppets known as 'Totulika' among the Mbunda, Lubala, Chokwe and Luchazi tribes, and thinks the type could be of European origin rather than indigenous. The planchette type have a horizontal string running through the chests of the figures, attached to a short post at one end and looped around operator's knee. Early twentieth century English version made from clothes pegs had one string looped to chair leg and one held by operator.

Turnip control. Type of marionette control used with Venetian marionettes (eighteenth century); name derived from shape, made of wood with leather tabs for attaching ends of strings, and hook for hanging up.

Turps. Spirits of turpentine, distilled from pine-tree exudation (or spruce, etc.) and used in manufacture of paints, polishes, varnishes; also as thinner for tube-oil colours and brush cleaner. (Gk. terebinthos.)

Turps substitute. White spirit; petroleum by-product (inflammable), inexpensive and replacing pure turpentine in many paints. Also brush-cleaner.

Tussaud's, Madame. The most famous collection of Waxworks in the world (established by Marie Tussaud, 1761–1850), situated close to Baker Street Underground station, London, with Planetarium adjoining. During the Christmas season the well-known Punch and Judy showman PERCY PRESS performs regularly, making an extra attraction.

TV Programming for Children: For the Young Viewer, edited by Garry, Rainsberg and Winich (McGraw Hill, New York, 1962). Studies of programmes at local level; references to types of puppets that can be made by children age four, five, six to eight and nine to twelve; also for adolescents; simplest paper bag type to complex marionettes.

Types of puppet. See PUPPET (TYPES OF).

U

Übermarionette. 'Super-marionette.' Edward Gordon Craig's concept of the ideal actor, first expressed in an essay *The Actor and the Übermarionette* (in Volume I of his *The Mask*, 1908) and included in *On the Art of the Theatre* (1911); further references in *The Theatre Advancing* (1921), when he was still trying to correct the impression that the idea had had on the acting profession, viz. that human actors should be replaced by puppets. He explained the übermarionette as 'the actor plus fire, minus egoism'; and although he had said the marionette theatre was the 'true' theatre, he had also said that 'the puppet has become a reproach. All puppets are now but low comedians'. Craig's own experiments in puppet construction did not produce an übermarionette, but he made important contributions to the literature on the subject of puppets in *The Mask* and *The Marionnette*.

Ubu Roi. Satirical play by Alfred Jarry, attacking the bourgeoisie, the philistines, dictatorship, human imbecility, lust and gluttony. The first performance at the Théâtre de l'Oeuvre (1896) scandalised Parisian theatre-goers. The poet Yeats was among those present and recorded seeing actors 'supposed to be dolls, toys, marionettes' – and the unspeakable lavatory-brush-cum-sceptre. The play was, in fact, a re-worked version of a schooldays' puppet play satirising an unpopular physics master and who provided the name: Hébert, Hebe, Père Hebe, Père Ubu, Ubu Roi. Ubu is the dominant character in this and other plays and is 'an ignoble creature, which is why he is so like us all, seen from below'. He kills the King of 'Poland' (= 'Anywhere' or 'Nowhere'), becomes King in turn and proceeds to exterminate nobles, officials and peasants. The theatre was the trend-setter for anti-realist drama in France; the currently popular 'theatre of the absurd' and 'theatre of cruelty' were foreshadowed by *Ubu*. There have been revivals on both the live and puppet stage, but an audience 70 years later, with two world wars between and a daily diet of violence on television is not easily scandalised. Even the six-letter word with which the play opens falls flat in a period where such terms are commonplace in sound and print. A review in *Plays and Players* (September, 1966) following a live production at the Royal Court in London, gave 'two cheers' for management-courage and a third ('more heartfelt') for the designs of David Hockney. The real weakness was in the fact that the style was nearer to pantomime and simply a vehicle for comedian Max Wall. Rapid scene-changing was achieved (22 scenes) by 'flying' screens of appropriate suggestiveness (in both theatrical and vulgar senses), and, in spite of blown-up costumes and minor characters in sandwich-boards, the nearest thing to a puppet was the elongated horse (nearly stage-width) which divided in the middle to allow Max Wall to 'ride'. Opinions have also been divided as to the production of Michael Meschke's Marionette Theatre in Stockholm (included in an Edinburgh Festival programme) with puppets and sets designed by Polish-born artist Franciszka Themerson (who had illustrated the Gaberbocchus Press paperback edition of *Ubu*). This again used masked actors, life-size cardboard cut-out figures, based on Jarry's own drawings; the *Times Literary Supplement* (18th August, 1967) saw 'echoes of Klee and Thurber' – and of Picasso in the drop-curtain. However, this production gained the prize for Contemporary Artistic Expression at the 3rd International Puppet Festival at Bucharest in 1965. Hockney's working drawings were reproduced in *Art and Artists* (May, 1966) and were nearer the puppetic.

Umbrellas. French puppeteer Yves Joly has used umbrellas as puppet characters, each having its own style and mode of behaviour: City Gent, Lady's Man, Lady of Fashion, Flirt, and so on. Violet Philpott, in her hand puppet version of *The Three Pigs*, uses a child's umbrella as basis for prefabricated roof for the straw house. The ribs of umbrellas used by some shadow-puppet makers as rods, or extensions of rods, for the controls. Source: umbrella repair shops.

Uncle Remus. Collection of stories by JOHN CHANDLER HARRIS (1848–1908), originally in Negro dialect; a variety of editions, including children's illustrated items. The adventures of Brer Rabbit, Brer Fox and other characters, particularly suitable for hand puppet adaptation. See BRER RABBIT.

Uncle Tom's Cabin. Novel by Harriet Beecher Stowe, q.v., concerned to help abolish Negro slavery in southern states of America (1851) and had many melodramatic stage productions; also various adaptations for the puppet stage, including a French version *La case de l'oncle Tom* in the repertoire of the 'Cave Lilloise' (1885), listed in Gervais *Marionnettes et marionnettistes de France* (Bordas, 1947). Frequent re-issues, e.g. 'Everyman' Library, and Modern Readers' Service, N.Y.

Undercut. Problem arises when making casts in moulds of avoiding shapes which will prevent or impede removal of the cast, or risk damage to those parts, such as Mr Punch's nose and chin with their concave curves which will lock in a mould. Problem can be avoided by use of flexible type mould – and does not arise if head is carved direct from wood.

Underwater scenes. The 'floating' possibilities of marionettes suspended freely, without touching the stage floor, give a range of dramatic action outside the scope of the live theatre. Characters can include mermaids, King Neptune, fantastic fish and frogmen, an octopus, a sailor to be rescued. Scenery: remains of a sunken ship, all the colourful deep sea flora revealed by modern under-water cameras. It is just as essential to have control of movements of swimming creatures, the action of a sea-horse, as for the normal walking movements of marionettes. An interesting variation was the use of rod-type control (from below-stage) by group of student-puppeteers from Vincennes, France; groups of highly decorative fish were operated by thin wires fixed in wooden handles (horizontal), stage of the proscenium type with coloured gauzes and lighting effects, a back-cloth acting as a shadow-screen on which was depicted a realistic shipwreck. The shadow-screen also has its possibilities for under-water items, with various methods of control from above or the sides; the whole screen can represent the underwater setting, or the screen can be divided to give simultaneous above and below water action. Baird *The Art of the Puppet* (Collier-Macmillan, 1965) has a remarkable two-page full-colour reproduction from his own production *Davy Jones' Locker*.

UNESCO. United Nations Educational, Scientific and Cultural Organisation. Constitution adopted 16th November, 1945, London, by representatives of 44 governments. Aim: To contribute to peace and security

by promoting collaboration between nations through education, science
and culture ... without distinction of race, sex, language or religion,
by the Charter of the United Nations. The INTERNATIONAL THEATRE
INSTITUTE was founded in 1948 under the auspices of UNESCO; and
since 1960, on the strength of its work, UNIMA (Union internationale de
la marionnette) has been a regular member of the ITI and so affiliated
to UNESCO. In June, 1955, a special puppet issue of the UNESCO
'Courier' appeared. In 1963 UNESCO sponsored the 'Expedition
Alexandre' – a world tour in search of puppets – led by Philippe Genty,
a young French puppeteer, who made a colour-film record. The English
puppeteer Miles Lee was for a time UNESCO Theatre Expert at the
Asian Theatre Institute in New Delhi, conducting experimental puppetry
courses. Two special puppetry issues of *World Theatre*, the bi-monthly
review of the ITI (with assistance from UNESCO), appeared, No. 5 of
Volume XIV (1965) and No. 2 of Volume XV (1966). The UNESCO
'Courier', December, 1967, carried an article on the Shadow Puppets of
Cambodia.

UNIMA: Union internationale de la marionnette. International puppetry
organisation founded 1929, re-constituted 1957; headquarters in Prague;
members in more than 50 countries; countries with 20 or more members
may form National Sections. Praesidium consists of President, Vice-
Presidents, and other members elected at a Congress, and there are some
National Representatives. In the Preamble to the UNIMA Statute it is
stated that 'UNIMA unites the puppeteers of the whole world' and that
puppetry is one of the arts that can help to bring all countries together,
appealing both to children and adults. Since 1960 UNIMA has been a
regular member of the INTERNATIONAL THEATRE INSTITUTE and affiliated
to UNESCO. Every year there are international festivals in one or other
country, organised by the host country, usually with sponsorship of
UNIMA, and within the framework of these events, which attract many
hundreds of puppeteers from world sources, UNIMA holds its Congresses
and Conferences. A wide range of themes provide discussion material at
the Conferences, e.g. 'The puppet theatre in the system of theatre
creation' (Warsaw, 1962), 'Investigation of reactions of a child-spectator
at a puppet performance' (Karlovy Vary, 1964), 'The Puppet Theatre
in the life of a child' (Leningrad, 1964), 'The puppet theatre as an
expedient of ethics and aesthetic education (Bucharest, 1965)', 'The
actual situation and perspectives of the puppet theatre' (Cracow, 1965).
The audiences (usually in several theatres) at international festivals are
largely made up of puppeteers, whereas the national events – of which
there is an increasing number each year – have a higher percentage
of the general public. Performances range from the one-man item to those
by groups of 20 upwards in many different styles. There are usually
Exhibitions, sometimes Puppet Films. There have been two international
festivals in Britain, both in Colwyn Bay, North Wales (1963, 1968). One
of the outcomes of international co-operation has been the publication of
The Puppet Theatre of the Modern World in nine separate language editions
(from 1965) with material representing 36 countries and nearly 240
superb photo-illustrations; text (on various aspects) by notable puppeteers
from different countries. Various Bulletins have been issued (in the main
languages), e.g. No. 7, series 5: *Calendar* giving important anniversaries
and jubilees, living puppeteers, playwrights, musicians, etc.; No. 6,
series 4: *Bibliography*, part 1, commencing an international bibliography
of puppet literature. The National Section (if any) of a country can

usually be contacted through the national association or local guilds; otherwise direct contact can be made with the Secretary-General, Dr Jan Malik, Namesti M. Gorkeho 28, Prague 1, Czechoslovakia. The Hon. Secretary of the British Section is Mr C. M. Macdonald, 9b Walpole Gardens, Strawberry Hill, Twickenham, Middlesex.

UNIMA France. The journal of the French National Section of UNIMA, the international organisation; available to members. Subscription enquiries: UNIMA-France, 86, Rue Notre-Dame-des-Champs, Paris, 6e.

United States of America. In *Famous First Facts*, by Joseph Nathan Kane (Wilson, N.Y., 1933, 3rd edition, 1964), the entry for the first puppet show on record gives the honour to a Mr Holt; date, 12th February, 1738; place: a room 39-ft. long, 19-ft. wide and 9-ft. high, at Broad and Pearl Streets, New York City; admission charge 5/-; programme *The Adventures of Harlequin and Scaramouch*, or *The Spaniard Trick'd*. This was advertised in the New York Gazette. MCPHARLIN, in *The Puppet Theatre in America: A History: 1524 to Now* (Harper, N.Y., 1949), says that Holt was originally a dancing master from London – and comes to the conclusion that it is neither possible to prove that the show included puppets nor that it did not. McPharlin's history runs to over 500 pages and lists puppeteers from 1524–1948 and their repertoire; it is at the same time a partial history of the puppets of those countries from whence came the pioneers of the States. The puppeteer in the private retinue of Cortés when he went in search of gold in the Honduras (1524) left no details of his performance; McPharlin admits that only speculation is possible, and says that only scattered records of Spanish settlers have come to light. Moving on to eighteenth century English colonisation, because of a dearth of evidence, McPharlin provides a close study of puppetry in England. Once the nineteenth century is reached the process of documentation improves and McPharlin's powers of research are rewarded. English, French, German, Italian, Spanish puppeteers moved into America, and Latin America and Canada, once the transportation was possible, as earlier they had moved from one country to another in Europe. The early twentieth century saw the 'revival' – and the extension of puppetry into the fields of education, therapy and advertising; later into television. McPharlin himself was largely responsible for the coming into being of the PUPPETEERS OF AMERICA organisation (1937) and his *Puppetry Year-Book* became that Society's official organ; he also published a number of technical books and pamphlets. McPharlin died before his History appeared, and its final words are: 'If the art continues vital, if it is allowed to live, the puppeteer in America can look back upon this history as a mere opening chapter.' Among others who have already helped to develop it, his wife Marjorie BATCHELDER McPharlin has made her own valuable contributions to the literature on the subject and is a Vice-President of the international organisation, UNIMA. In 1965 appeared a magnificently illustrated book by BIL BAIRD, who has a puppet theatre in New York, who has created over 2,000 characters for his shows in theatres, night clubs, films and television, and toured in India, Russia, Afghanistan and elsewhere; the book is a readable general history of puppetry – and it also brings the American scene up to date. (*Art of the Puppet*: Collier-Macmillan, 1965.) He sees the *difference* between European and American developments as stemming from two factors: (1) the absence of any long single tradition; (2) television. Baird also sees the development of that essentially twentieth century style, the Floor

Show (puppetry without a stage), as due to the changed economy following 'the Crash and the Depression'. First in the field was Frank Paris. Puppetry was able to move into the night clubs with this simplified staging and sophisticated items. Walton and O'Rourke (who were responsible for the puppets in the *Lili* film based on Gallico's *Love of Seven Dolls*, opened in New York's Rainbow Room. In contrast to the many other forms of television puppetry, the 'KUKLAPOLITANS' (created by Burr Tillstrom) play 'live', the show being largely geared to topical events. It is watched by millions and has an amazing fan-mail intake. Baird sees nothing wrong in the use of puppets in advertising; the income can help to pay for 'a ballet or two'. There is also a special satisfaction in putting on a show (such as his own version of *Peter and the Wolf*) which had brought some of the best creative minds in the theatre together – and which was seen by 33 million people. The United States could be expected to produce some of the largest puppets – in line with Hollywood 'colossal' films – and REMO BUFANO came up with a 35-ft. telescoping clown on one show, some life-size figures of Don Quixote and Sancho Panza for de Falla's *El Retablo de Maese Pedro*, and some 10-ft. figures (controlled from above and below) for the Stravinksy oratorio *Oedipus Rex*, q.v.

Universal Plug. The 'Fittall' plug top, obtainable from electrical suppliers, can be adapted in seconds to fit the following outlets: 13-amp. flat pin; 15-amp. round 2-pin or 3-pin; 5-amp. round 2-pin or 3-pin. The pins are retractable and there is a selector lever; the pins screw-lock when in position. The plug is connected to main cable in ordinary way and contains a cartridge fuse, is made of high Polymer PVC and will not break if dropped. One plug instead of five.

Universal Puppet Theatre, published by the Institute of Scenography, Vol. 77 in Library of Stage Decor, 1966 (Prague). This is the architects' preview of the new central state puppet theatre planned for Prague, Czechoslovakia, with foreword by Dr Jan Malik, the Secretary-General for UNIMA, the international puppetry organisation, and Director of the existing Central Puppet Theatre. This will be the first building specifically designed for professional puppet theatre, adaptable for all styles of production with every type of puppet. Site will be parkland near city and main thoroughfares. Auditorium seating capacity 400–450, one floor only (balcony for technical purposes, lighting, film, sound projection). Height of seating will be able to be regulated for children or adults. Building will incorporate recording studio, studies, artists' studios, workshops, storage room, garage space, flats for some employees; library, reading room, documentation centre; independent section for international puppet museum, with special accent on Czech puppetry. This project will be the realisation of resolution passed at time of the Establishing Congress of UNIMA in Prague (1929), according to which that city was to be the centre of international puppetry documentation. Anticipated completion: 1970.

Unusual Concert. Internationally popular item in the repertoire of the Moscow Central State Puppet Theatre, director SERGEI OBRAZTSOV. This has been running for about 20 years and has been seen in Britain as well as the United States and many other countries. It consists of a number of individual items burlesquing bad performers, and is done with rod puppets. There is a particularly amusing compere, and the 'piano act' is a pleasant change from the hackneyed marionette versions.

Upstage. The acting area furthest from the audience. Term dates from period when auditorium floor was flat and stage floor sloped. See also 'down-stage' *re* hand puppet stage sight lines.

U.S.S.R. The only puppeteers in the old pre-Soviet Russia were the itinerant Petrushka-men performing at fairs, in courtyard in the towns, in the market places. In the seventeenth century the booth was an even simpler affair than that used until the early twentieth century and is shown in the earliest known picture (a drawing, *c.* 1636) reproduced in Baird *The Art of the Puppet* (Collier-Macmillan, 1965), which shows a sack-like affair suspended from a hoop above the head and belted at the waist – possibly related to the Chinese street puppet booth – with puppets performing at the top, the showman's feet sticking out from the bottom, obviously a 'walk-about' stage. Musicians are seen at one side, an old man with some sort of zither, a woman with a violin. The last of the PETRUSHKA men was ZAITSEV, mentioned in OBRAZTSOV's book *My Profession* (Moscow), 1950, and whose puppets are now in the museum of the Central State Puppet Theatre. Petrushka was of the same family as Punch, Polichinelle and Pulcinella, exact origin unknown. He dominated all the plays and had the typical big stick. After the Revolution and the beginning of cultural and educational developments, the first puppet experiments were concerned with children mainly. Pioneers in new forms of puppetry included the EFIMOVS, husband a sculptor, wife painter, who made the first developments with rod puppets and whose repertoire included items from Andersen's fairy tales, Krylov's fables, and Shakespear's *Macbeth*. Sergei Obraztsov, formerly an art teacher and actor, then a solo puppeteer, was offered the post of Director to the first State Puppet Theatre (1931), a mobile company which received an actual building of its own, with auditorium and stage, workshops and museum space in 1937. This developed until it has a personnel of over 200 – actors, musicians, sculptors and craftsmen, technicians, and so on. It has a very wide repertory – which has included *Aladdin* from the *Arabian Nights*, Perrault's *Cinderella*, *Mowgli* from Kipling's jungle tales, and Gozzi's *King Stag* – a universally popular *Unusual Concert* and an amusing satire on *Genesis* (the *Divine Comedy*). The policy is constant experiment in methods of production, changing with each item. Contemporary writers co-operate in evolving new material. Experiments include the use of live actors sharing the same stage with the puppets as in the *Divine Comedy* – with God and the Archangels being live actors, all the other characters, including Adam and Eve and the Serpent, puppets. The theatre has also become a training centre for puppeteers. There are over 100 theatres in the U.S.S.R., each Republic having at least one, as well as mobile units. Every age group is catered for. The Moscow Central theatre has two shows each day for children, evening shows for adults. The influence of Soviet developments, especially in the use of the rod type of puppet, as well as in production methods, is seen in the developments in many countries besides Poland, Rumania, Hungary, although the latter have allowed their national characteristics to take over. Moscow and Leningrad have been the centres of international festivals and conferences. Obraztsov, the puppet-master, still occasionally appears as solo artiste with hand puppets.

V

Variety turns. Short items, comic or spectacular, as interludes between main items of programme, or in floor-show presentations; traditionally of the MARIONETTE type, but there are some rich possibilities using the contemporary large-scale ROD PUPPETS; with HAND PUPPETS a slow-motion boxing match can be effective. Stock items include prima donnas with heaving (even bursting) bosoms, or taking the form of ostriches; birds or animals playing instruments; strip-tease items, long-haired pianists, trick cyclists and acrobats, mock bull-fights; sometimes burlesques of well-known performers of stage or screen, 'PERSONALITY' characters (e.g. Charlie Chaplin) – but burlesques need to be as funny as the originals; song-and-dance routines; any of the trick figure acts (transformations, come-aparts, etc.). For books on techniques of trick items, see TRICK PUPPETS.

Varnish. Protective coating applied over paint (with resin content). May affect colour. On puppets it may cause too much reflection of light, blurring facial details.

Vaseline. Petroleum jelly. Sometimes used as a 'separator' or parting-agent when casting a puppet head in a plaster mould. Can be used as a softener for plasticine which has become dry; break plasticine into small pieces and work in vaseline until right malleable consistency.

Vaughan, Robert Alfred (1823–57). A Congregational divine; in his *Hours with the Mystics* (1856) he refers to 'the countless marionette figures in the brain of the Theosophist'. (One of the concerns of Theosophy is the essential truth or truths underlying all religions and philosophies.)

Vecchi, Orazio (1550–1605). Italian madrigal composer who took Holy Orders. His *L'Amfiparnasso commedia harmonica*, q.v., was performed at Modena, 1594, published Venice, 1597, formed historical link between madrigal and opera and has relationship with the COMMEDIA DELL' ARTE. A marionette production by the LANCHESTER MARIONETTES had its first performance in 1946.

Vehicle. Term for the 'medium' or film-forming ingredient in paint.

Velcro. Trade name for 'touch and close' fastener consisting of two nylon strips, one with thousands of tiny loops and other with thousands of tiny hooks; pressed together, hooks grip loops to give tight, secure fastening; peel apart to open. Can be cut to required length and for some purposes has advantages over zip fasteners or press-studs – but not recommended for use on fine fabrics. Can be washed, pressed, pinked, notched, sewn by hand or machine. Has interesting possibilities for puppet costume, detachable wigs, etc. Available from drapery departments and suppliers of dressmaking accessories.

Venetian marionettes. Eighteenth century type, average height 30 ins., control by stiff wire to hook on head and thin wires to hands, sometimes feet. Used in plays by Goldoni, Molière, Shakespeare, opera and other musical items. Examples in the Civic Museum, Venice; the theatre and figures formerly in the Victoria and Albert Museum, London, have been transferred to the BETHNAL GREEN MUSEUM, East London.

Ventriloquism. Latin *Venter* = belly, *loqui* = I speak. The art of making the voice appear to come from someone, something, or somewhere else; as a form of entertainment which usually involves the use of a 'dummy' figure carried by the performer and having movable mouth and eyes – i.e. with marked visual elements – it has been surprisingly successful as Radio entertainment, probably because of the successful characterisation (through voice only) and because the puppet is given the superior position in its encounters with the ventriloquist. The ventriloquial doll is usually made specifically to a performer's concept of a character and, for the greatest performers at least, it becomes 'one of the family' with a very definite personality. Some performers will have a group of figures on the stage and use them in turn, even make one seem to talk before picked up (by the technique known as 'the distant voice'.) The initial training involves a study of voice production, the aim being to minimise lip movement (when the figure is supposed to be talking) and to develop voices of different pitch and timbre. As with conjuring tricks, part of the art of creating the illusion is to put the attention of the audience where the operator wants it – in this case, *away* from the speaker's own face on to the figure. See next entry for book on techniques.

Ventriloquism for Beginners, by Douglas Houlden (Kaye and Ward, reprint 1968). Complete set of lessons in the art of Voice Magic, with 30 drawings and photographs; chapter on making the figures and various novelty types such as the Talking Mitten and Talking Hand. Includes instruction on the Muffled Voice and Distant Voice – and how to build an act.

Ventriloquiste. Female ventriloquist.

Verne, Jules (1828–1905). French writer of scientific adventures which proved to be near-prophetic, and some of which have been produced in the puppet theatre, e.g. *Twenty-thousand Leagues under the Sea* (Teatro dei Piccoli, Rome), *Five Weeks in a Balloon* (Craiova, Rumania), *Around the World in 80 Days* (Theatre Joly, Lyons).

Vertiep. Russian equivalent, in the Ukraine, of the Polish 'szopka', q.v.; design of stage reflects the gold-domed churches; two-tier structure: upper for Nativity, lower for local, topical, satirical fantasies; two central exits; traditionally lit by candlelight.

Vesely, Professor Jindřich (1885–1939). Czech puppeteer, first President of UNIMA, the international organisation, and one of its Founders; took Ph.D. degree with a thesis on the Faustus element in Czechoslovak puppetry (1909); mounted a retrospective exhibition of puppetry at the Ethnographic Museum which attracted some 26,000 visitors; helped form a professional centre (Czech Union of Friends of the Puppet Theatre, 1911); editor of *The Czech Puppeteer* (Česky loutkař), two volumes, 1912–13, and later of *The Puppeteer* (Loutkař), which ran from 1917–39.

Vielgeliebtes Puppenspiel. Compiled and published by Dr Hans R. Purschke, Frankfurt, Germany; collection of 53 poems relating to puppets. English translation (*Well-loved Puppet Show*) in MSS. only, by Dorothy Parnum, with library copy of the Educational Puppetry Association. Poems vary in style and mood. In *My Daughter and Mr Punch* (Christian Anke), Punch comes to save the little girl, in her dreams, from the Devil's grandmother. Another, by Hans Arp, is very brief, ending 'Alas, alas, alas, our good Punch is dead!' Pierre Jean de Beranger's begins: 'The marionettes are loved by men of varying worth ... ' In *Punch and Judy Show,* Otto Boettger-Seni asks 'What would you and I not give for that which lights the children's eyes ... ' Johann Georg Geisselbrecht contributes *Jack*

Sausage's Farewell – to his gracious patrons in Frankfurt-on-Main at the Autumn Fair, 1802. There is a *Prologue to a Puppet Play* by Johann Wolfgang von Goethe. In *Ruins*, Anastasius Grün mentions some of the medieval religious plays – 'the water-dreading Noah upon the strings' and 'Judith with the head of Holofernes!' In Theodor Hell's *Puppeteer's Lament* a puppet cat comes to a sad end because someone ignored the notice forbidding live dogs to be admitted. Echoing other literary men with a fondness for puppets (Anatole France, G. B. Shaw), a Prologue by Hugo von Hofmannsthal begins "Twould please me more if this were played not by men but by large puppets.' There is one by Ludwig Schuster beginning and ending 'Scorn not the puppet show!' – because Goethe's *Faust* would not have been written if his parents had forbidden him to watch the puppets when young.

Vietnamese puppets. Two branches of puppet theatre co-exist dating from about the twelfth century: (*a*) rod and marionette types; (*b*) the unique 'water puppets', which perform on a raft on a lake. These could be related to an earlier form known in China, mentioned by Obraztsov in *Chinese Puppet Theatre*, but no extant details of the Chinese variety. Magic and acrobatics are main ingredients of performances. Puppeteers mainly non-professional. Present-day plays have themes relating to socialist aims and problems; there are aeroplanes as well as dragons, fireworks and music by gongs and cymbals. Two interesting accounts in English have appeared, with illustrations (1) *Puppet Theatre Around the World* (Bharatiya Natya Sangh, New Delhi, 1960), in an article by Lorraine Salmon; (2) *World Theatre* (International Theatre Institute), Vol. 14, No. 5, 1965, in an article by Leh Vinh Tuy.

Vinagels. New modelling and mouldings materials based on P.V.C. and supplied either in putty form or in semi-liquid consistency, in various grades, giving fairly flexible object or a more rigid quality. Advantages over other modelling materials: clean, non-odorous, good handling properties (will not adhere to hands); non-deteriorating in uncured state, partly finished model needs no protective covering; little shrinkage after curing; objects become permanent and practically indestructible. Curing is done in an electric or gas cooking oven at given temperatures. Available in several self-colours and can be painted with P.V.C. paints. Full details from: Tiranti, 72 Charlotte Street, London, W.1 (suppliers), publishers of H. M. Percy, *New Materials in Sculpture* (1962).

Vinamold. Trade term for Vinyl resin product used for making moulds flexible enough to allow considerable 'UNDERCUTTING' of chin, nose, ears. Technique: H. M. Percy, *New Materials in Sculpture* (Tiranti, 1961).

Vinegar. Added to Plaster of Paris mix, for making moulds for casting, slows the setting process. (Addition of salt speeds up the process.)

Viscosity. Resistance to flow; sticky or glutinous.

Vitez-Laszlo. Hungarian traditional folk-puppet hero, cousin of Punch.

Vitrina. Transparent glass-painting colours (supplied by Winsor and Newton); can be used for painting on projection slides.

Volatile. A substance which evaporates rapidly.

Voltaire (Francois-Marie Arouet, 1694–1778). French poet, historian, philosopher, dramatist; *Candide, L'Enfant prodigue, etc.* Edwin Arnet, in an introduction to Gauchat *Marionettes*, includes Voltaire with Goethe, Kleist, Haydn, Pocci and others, as lovers of puppets. The British Museum reading-room index devotes a large volume to his works, but no reference to puppet plays.

W

Wanderly Wagon. Horse-drawn Irish wagon presumably capable of transporting Eugene Lambert, his wife Mai, their ten children, Finnegan (ventriloquial puppet member of the family), puppet stage and countless Irish puppet characters. In Eire T.V. See LAMBERT.

Warm. Relative to colours of costumes, scenery, lighting: the range of reds, oranges, orange-yellows, in contrast to the cool blues. Values change according to quantitative relationships; try one spot of red with an otherwise all-blue setting or costume.

Water-colours. Paint pigment ground in water-soluble gum. Not washable.

Water Puppets. Type found only in Vietnam, but which were known in ancient China (mentioned by Obraztsov in *Chinese Puppet Theatre*). The stage consists of a raft on a lake, supporting a structure in the form of the traditional Vietnamese communal house; the puppets are large, 'the size of an eight-year-old boy', made of wood, operated by long bamboo poles or an intricate system of strings. The audience watches from the edge of the lake. Repertoire is partly traditional, dealing with the lives of the people, with plenty of magic and acrobatics, but today has modern themes concerned with socialist developments, puppet aeroplanes as well as boats, with traditional orchestral music. Illustrations of puppets in *World Affairs* (ITI: Vol. 14, No. 5, 1965), accompanying an article by Leh Vinh Tuy, and cover picture in colour of figures in water; a technical article with some illustrations in *Puppet Theatre Around the World* (New Delhi, 1960).

Wax puppets. In Oscar Wilde's fairy tale *Birthday of the Infanta*, q.v., there is a mention of 'Italian puppets made out of wood and wax' used in one of the birthday entertainments. Whanslaw, in his second *Bench Book*, q.v., quotes an old recipe for wax modelling (from the *Journal of Design*) and elsewhere refers to the specimens in the Will Day Collection at the Science Museum, South Kensington, London (small Chinese 'stick' figures made of coloured wax).

Wayang. This is a term used throughout Indonesia and has a general meaning of theatrical performance – although even the word 'theatrical' is somewhat suspect in view of the connection with religion, ancestor worship and so on. The precise nature of the performance is distinguished by a qualifying term – e.g. wayang purwa, wayang gedog, wayang kruchil (or klitik), wayang golek, wayang beber, wayang wong – the last being a performance by human actors; see individual entries. The qualifying term may indicate *type of puppet* or the *type of plays* (which have originated in different historical periods). It is interesting to compare the statements of various authorities as to the term 'wayang', its origin and meaning. Mellema, author of *Wayang Puppets* (Koninklijk Instituut voor de Tropen, Amsterdam, 1954), and Linguistic Advisor to the Royal Tropical Institute, insists that 'Wayang is not a shadow play' and that it is the puppet itself ('a materialised silhouette of a ghost of ... an ancestor') which is important; the male members of the audience see the

S

tangible puppet, the women see only the shadow. Certainly with the rounded forms of puppet the question of 'shadow' does not arise – but Mansor bin Othman in an article *Casting Shadows* (Shell Magazine, December, 1964) discusses various types of Wayang, includes the 'Kelantan shadow play', the 'Javanese shadow play' and the 'Siamese shadow play', with the accompanying illustrations being specifically shadow figures as seen by an audience facing an illuminated screen. Also, the description of a figure suddenly 'disappearing' (when withdrawn sharply from the screen) underlines the anomalous position: if an audience is divided on the two sides of the screen, the figure would *not* 'disappear' on the men's side. Again, in an article by Satyawati Suleiman, *Indonesian Puppetry* (in *Puppet Theatre Around the World*, New Delhi, 1960), the term 'shadow play' recurs with the suggestion that 'wayang or shadow' derives from 'yang' or *ancestor* – a theory which all three authors regard favourably, in fact. Mellema links 'wayang' with High Javanese 'ringgit', meaning flat *or* rounded puppet (non-shadow in function). Suleiman says 'wayang' is derived from 'bayang', which means shadow, that this may indicate an original form which *was* concerned with the 'shadow', but that this meaning was lost when the other types of puppet were developed and so has become the generic term.

Wayang beber. Form of entertainment at one time popular in Indonesia, but now no longer seen. A long cloth or paper scroll with painted scenes is unwound from one pole and re-wound on another during narration of a story. Repertoire connected with that of the wayang gedog (leather puppets now seldom presented) related to the history of Hindu period.

Wayang gedog. Type the repertoire of which deals with the history of late Hindu period in Java, using flat carved leather puppets (similar to Wayang kulit); Mellema (*Wayang Puppets*, q.v.) says traditionally regarded as of earlier origin than wayang purwa and attributed to a Moslem saint.

Wayang golek. In Indonesia generally, and particularly on the islands of Java and Bali, with a repertoire related to the period of Islamic influence, a rounded type of puppet controlled by rods; height approximately 20 ins. and made in three sections: head, body, with supporting rod (which can be rotated) in the neck; arms two-piece and loosely jointed, controlled by rods attached by cord; costume – of batik material. The stage is similar in type to that used for shadows – but without the screen. Baird, in *The Art of the Puppet* (Collier-Macmillan, 1965), suggests that this type of Wayang came from Bengal with the spread of Hinduism, and includes two interesting illustrations (one in colour).

Wayang kruchil. Also keruchil, klitik, kelitik. Indonesian flat wooden puppet cut from thin board and carved in low relief, finely painted both sides; leather arms with joints held by knotted cord, controlled by rods (manipulation similar to that of shadow figures). Repertoire derived from historical material. Now rarely performed.

Wayang kulit. Alternative name for the *Wayang purwa*, q.v. (which indicates the type of repertoire); *kulit* = leather, the material of which the flat figure puppets are made.

Wayang Kulit. 16 mm. colour film by the Malayan Film Unit, 1956. Interesting record of not only a performance of a traditional shadow-play but also of the preliminary ritual and of the audience arriving on foot or bicycle or by canoe. A leaflet available from the Commonwealth

Institute, Kensington High Street, London, W.8, in whose cinema the film has been presented (and from whom the film can be hired), says: 'After the final episode has been played, the puppet-master ceremonially bids farewell to the shadow-characters and in the name of Lord Siva expels all the powers of evil that may be lurking in the darkness to afflict the assembled people.'

Wayang puppets, by R. L. Mellema (Royal Tropical Institute, Amsterdam, 1954). Authoritative study of Javanese puppets, more particularly the Wayang Purwa, q.v.; on the techniques of carving, colouring, symbolism (English translation by Mantle Hood). Includes transcript from manual intended for younger generation cutters of the flat leather figures, with reproductions of the many and intricate design-motifs fixed by tradition, explanations of the significance of every detail of form, hair style, costume, face and other colouring (94 characters listed) used in the wayang purwa performances. Every detail is part of the characterisation, not of individuals but of *types*. For instance: 'Bima is always recognised by his large thumb-nail, a symbol of the greatest self-control and power of concentration.' There is also a description of a performance – which finished at six in the morning as the sun was rising.

Wayang purwa. Carved leather puppets also known as wayang 'kulit' (= leather) are used in a repertoire (cycle of) plays having their origin in the Hindu epics *Mahabharata*, q.v., and *Ramayama*, q.v.; the most popular type of 'wayang'. Performance is in front of a screen, the operator-narrator (dalang) sitting on the ground in front of this with a large array of characters placed right and left (good and the bad), responsible for the night-long performance, simultaneously controlling the orchestra (*gamelan*, mainly percussion instruments); the male section of the audience sits on the *same* side as puppets and operator; the women sit on the 'shadow' side of the screen (and right and left become reversed). The puppets have long split-rod controls, extended downwards to form handles for the operator, pointed ends being stuck into banana stems at the base of the screen during the performance. The themes of the plays have a religious concern with good and evil – and constitute more than simple entertainment. It is believed that the members of the audience are guarded against evil influences during the performance. The puppets are highly stylised, in profile, carved from leather – partly silhouette, a large amount of decorative filigree design in head-dress and costume, elongated shoulders and long, slim arms jointed at the elbows, thin rods attached to the hands. The characters are types rather than individuals and are recognised by their general form, the design of costume, quality of voices, and so on. The Javanese designer has strictly traditional motifs to be incorporated (the designer in Bali has some degree of individual freedom in his work). Techniques of carving, colouring, and symbolism are described in detail in Mellema *Wayang Puppets*, q.v., with diagrams and a list of facial colours (red rose, white, gold, black, etc.) for 94 characters.

Wayang suluh. Contemporary addition to the various forms of 'wayang' performance: 'educational wayang' – dealing with present-day life and topical problems.

Wayang Topeng. Indonesian dramatic performance in which masked actors take part; story narrated by a Dalang, as with the puppet shows.

Wayang Wong. A form of live acting developed from the puppet plays of Indonesia, actors with or without masks and speaking the dialogue.

Weber, Carl Maria von (1786–1826). German composer who, when young and 'in pecuniary difficulties' wrote a comic opera *Abu Hassan*, q.v., still popular in the live theatre and has had marionette productions, e.g. by the Zurich Marionette Theatre.

Welding rods. Thin copper rods, used by some shadow-puppet makers as controls. Available from any welding-supply firm in 7 lb. packets, or from British Oxygen Co., Worsley.

'Wendy House'. All-purpose Playhouse for young children; converts easily to Shop, Easel, Marionette Stage, Glove Puppet Theatre – designed to save space. Has no fourth wall; variations possible due to peg-and-slot construction. Suppliers: Caisenaire Co., Reading.

Whanslaw, Harry William (1883–1965). 'Whanny' to his friends and colleagues; the Grand Old Man of twentieth century British puppetry, whose book *Everybody's Theatre*, published in 1923, led directly to the formation of the British Model Theatre Guild in 1925 following a meeting of 'fans' who had found inspiration in the book, of whom the first was Gerald Morice, who became one of the co-founders. Some years later the name was changed to the British Puppet and Model Theatre Guild, reflecting the expansion of its horizon. 'Whanny' had been interested in model theatres in his boyhood and saw his first marionette show (Jewell's) at the Victorian Era Exhibition of 1897. During World War I, while serving with the R.A.M.C., he made a model stage and later wrote a series of articles on this branch of puppetry for *Chatterbox* (1923) under the title 'The Toy that Never Grows Old'; these articles, re-written and enlarged, were the basis for *Everybody's Theatre*. In 1927 he founded, with Waldo Lanchester, Jan Bussell and others, his first theatre, The London Marionette Theatre, in a Hammersmith mews, and which represented the Guild at the UNIMA Congress at Liége in 1930. By profession, Whanny was an artist and book-illustrator, talent which was deployed to the numerous books on puppetry he produced His hobbies included the collecting of old advertisements, booksellers' labels, stamps, toy soldiers. Following Lanchester's marriage and his move to Malvern, the original theatre was closed and Whanny set up his Studio Marionette Theatre at his home in Chiswick, and Waldo established his Malvern Theatre. Following early co-operation with Baird in the experimental days of Television, appearances were made in the pre-war BBC programmes at Alexandra Palace. For many years and until his death he was the well-loved President of the Guild. His contribution to the literature on puppetry is impressive, mainly published by Wells, Gardner and Darton, and several in a series of smaller items for the Religious Education Press. (Dates are not always given.) Following *Everybody's Theatre*, on making modern toy theatre with scope for shadow scenes and marionettes, he wrote the *Bankside Stage Book*, with directions for a model Elizabethan stage, *Animal Puppetry* (hand puppets and marionettes), *Everybody's Marionette Book*, for the professional puppeteer, full-size theatre and marionettes; jointly with Victor Hotchkiss, *Specialised Puppetry*, on the traditional trick marionettes – with some new ideas and techniques; *A Book of Marionette Plays*, ranging from burlesque melodrama to scenes from Shakespeare; *Shadow Play*; history and techniques, including the old English 'galanty'; two *Bench Books* (answers to all kinds of problems, arranged alphabetically, and a great deal of unusual information); *Bible Puppetry and Twelve* (Bible) *Puppet Plays*.

When Animals Talked, by E. Lucia Turnbull (Longmans Green, 1939, reprints). Stories involving animal characters, in dialogue form, some of which convert easily and effectively into puppet items. Hermit, Badger, Frogs, Crab, Jackal, Alligator, Wizard, Mouse, Lion, Bear, Monkey, Hare, Geese, Tortoise, Lizard, Toad, Porcupine, Ant and Cricket, Oyster, Elves and Woodcutters, a School for Crocodiles.

White shadows. The reverse of black silhouette cut-out shapes; shapes are cut away from black card, and light passing through gives effect of white figures or scenery (i.e. negative effect). Technique was used in Le Chat Noir (1887) shows in Paris ('ombres blanches').

Whittling. Simplest form of wood carving, craft dating from primitive times; requires few tools, principally a pocket-knife; blade shapes vary, usually a matter of individual preference based on experience; some whittlers work with small chisels and some make their own tools (e.g. leatherwork or other large needle fitted into wooden handle, the cutting edge being ground on an emery wheel and kept sharp by use of oiled carborundum stone, with final stropping on leather). Cutting is done by shallow slicing action. Characterisation of puppet heads is affected by wood finish; some makers leave knife-cuts visible, others file or sandpaper to a smooth finish and then paint. 'Soft' and 'hard' woods have different cutting qualities and durability; beginners should experiment with every kind available and acquire first-hand knowledge and preference for woods and tools. The Swiss surrealist puppeteer SCHNECKENBURGER made all his first puppets with a pocket knife.

Wilde, Oscar Fingall O'Flahertie Wills (1856–1900). Irish dilettante, wit, author of stories, plays, poems; puppet productions of some of his fairy stories, e.g. *Birthday of the Infanta*, *The Happy Prince*, *The Star*. (See separate entries.)

Wilkinson, Walter. English puppet-showman who pushed or pulled his handcart around many parts of England, into Scotland and Wales, and visited America, the various travels being recorded in a series of delightful books: *The Peep Show* (1927), *Vagabonds and Puppets* (1930), *Puppets into Yorkshire* (1937) and others. Present author crossed his trail many times in the mid-'thirties, and sometimes mistaken for him.

Winder. Accessory for marionette to prevent tangling of strings during transit or storage, consisting of piece of card, hardboard, plywood, slotted for string winding.

Wing nut. Steel nut for bolt (various diameters) can be turned with thumb and fingers. Variation is the 'thumbscrew' – bolt with own wings.

Winking ghost. Hand puppet illuminated from within by small hand torch; details in de Hempsey *How to do Punch and Judy*. (Max Andrews. N.D.)

Winnie the Pooh, by A. A. Milne, q.v.; children's classic; many adaptations for the puppet stage, including the Bil Baird Theatre, New York, with music and lyrics; most of the characters are 'naturals' for puppets: Piglet, Eeyore, Kanga, Rabbit, Tigger, Mice, Owl, etc., Moles, Spiders, Butterflies, Bees.

Wire. Armature principle used in clay modelling with basic wire shape to support clay can be adapted for marionette construction, sections being made from twisted wire – upper and lower parts of limbs – looped ends linked for joints, torso of wire rings and connections, profile and three-dimensional outline head. Finish can be application of paper pulp or paper layers, muslin and plaster-filler, or by padding and cloth. For large figures wire mesh of the rabbit hutch or chicken fence variety makes for time economy. Fantastic creatures can be left in the skeletal state. There are many types of wire useful in the puppet workshop: fine floral binding wire, galvanised or copper of various gauges, stiff birdcage variety, spring wire and actual springs, e.g. for neck joints of rod puppets. Special wire cutting tools may be needed for heavy grades; most pliers are equipped with cutters for up to medium gauge.

Wizard of Oz, by Lyman Frank Baum (1856–1919). Fantasy for children, which had tremendous success as a musical extravaganza and has had a number of puppet adaptations, including that of the Stockholm Marionette Theatre (seen at the Edinburgh Festival, 1967). Theme: A little girl, Dorothy Dale, and her cow Imogene (or her dog Toto) are carried away by a cyclone and deposited in Oz, a fairy garden, inhabited by creatures such as Cowardly Lion and Scarecrow, Witch and Wizard; is given a magic ring and two wishes, using first to bring the Scarecrow back to life – and then meets tin Woodman searching for his heart. In a motion-picture version the star was Judy Garland, the score including 'Over the rainbow.'

Wood scrap. Because puppets are 'purely theatrical' creatures they can be created from a very wide range of materials, the character of the materials being part of the characterisation; on a stylised head wood shavings can make effective 'hair'. Some interesting examples of puppets made from wood scrap – not only from the woodwork centre but also from the seashore or forest – are illustrated in Batchelder and Comer *Puppets and Plays* (Faber, 1959).

Wooden Prince, The. Ballet by Bela Bartok, q.v. (1881–1945). Fairy tale of a prince who, to win the love of a disinterested princess, carves a wooden prince to gain her admiration. She falls in love with the wooden one, he comes to life and dances off with her to the forest; but his life is brief and the hero comes to the rescue – ensuring a happy ending. The work had little success during the composer's lifetime – but it is now an award-winning item in the repertoire of the Hungarian State Puppet Theatre, Budapest, and in 1968 was included in the programmes presented by this theatre at the Aldeburgh and Bath Festivals.

Woodworker, The. Monthly periodical which includes technical articles, woodworkers' dictionary (in serial form), information on woods, tools, techniques; advertisements of timber suppliers. Published by Evan Bros., Montague House, Russell Square, London, W.C.1. Available at some bookstalls or to order.

Wordsworth, William (1770–1850). English romantic poet; in *The Excursion*, Book 5, 270, ' ... proficient in amusive feats of puppetry, that from the lap declare His expectations ... ' and, in *The Prelude*, 7, 713, 'Of modern Merlins, Wild Beasts, Puppet shows ... '

World of Toys, by Leslie Daiken (Lambarde Press, 1963). Guide to the principal public and private collections in Great Britain of Period Toys, Dolls and Dolls' Houses, Games, Puppets and Marionettes, Toy Soldiers, Musical Boxes and Automata; also Modern Toys, Toymakers and Toyshops, Puppet and Marionette Troupes, the British Toy Industry and Toy Trade Press; 49 plates. Gives names and addresses of 30 Punch and Judy showmen and nearly 40 other puppeteers. Half-a-dozen puppet-makers. Short articles on puppet theatres, toy theatres, and 'further reading'.

World Theatre. Bi-monthly magazine published by the International Theatre Institute, with assistance from UNESCO, distributed by Imprimerie Michel Brient et Cie, 64 rue de Saintonge, Paris, 3ᵉ. English distribution by H.M.S.O., 49 High Holborn, London, W.C.1. U.S.A. distribution by Theatre Arts Books, 333 Sixth Avenue, New York. Text is in English and French, surveying current theatre throughout the world. Occasional articles on puppet theatre, and two special puppet issues: (1) Vol. XIV, No. 5 (1965) with articles on *African Puppets* by Jacques Chesnais; *Puppet Theatre in Cairo*, by Leila F. Gad; *The Haps and Mishaps of the Brazilian Puppet*, by Olga Obry; *Puppets in Cuba*, by David Camps; *The Puppet Theatre in Mexico*, by Mireya Cueto; *Asian Travelogue*, by A. C. Scott; *The Bunraku Puppeteer and his Training*, by Shutaro Miyake; *The Shadow Theatre in Java and Bali*, by L. C. Damis; *Vietnam's Terrestrial and Aquatic Puppets*, by Leh Vinh Tuy. (2) Vol. XV, No. 2 (1966): *Through New Channels*, by Bil Baird; *Through New Functions* (education, therapy), by A. R. Philpott; *With New Materials*, by Emile Copfermann; *Sergei Obraztsov* (photos); *Towards a New Drama*, by Margareta Barbuta; and *The 3rd International Festival of Puppet-Theatres* (report). Both issues well illustrated by photographs.

World's Fair, The. English showmen's periodical, weekly, Saturdays; since 1938 has had regular column 'Punch and Puppetry Pars', by Gerald Morice, q.v., with up to the minute news and comments on events and the national and international scene, reviews of new books, etc.

Wortelmann, Fritz. German puppeteer, Founder Member of UNIMA (1929) and Hon. Member. Founder-editor of review *Der Puppenspieler* and *Das Puppentheater*, now incorporated in *Figuren Theater*; Founder-President of the Deutsches Institut für Puppenspiel; organiser of puppet festivals and competitions at Bochum (annually); responsible for publication of interesting series of illustrated booklets *Meister des Puppenspiels*, q.v.

Wright, Lyndie. Designer, scene painter, talented operator of glove, rod, shadow and string puppets with the Resident Company of the Little Angel Theatre, q.v., and wife of its Director, John Wright, q.v. Saw first puppet show while at school at the Pretoria Art Centre in South Africa: John Wright's Marionettes (of which there is a photo record in the Little Angel's archives (she was then Lynette Parker). Later became involved in the making of marionettes with Mrs Min Sack, and at 19 joined the John Wright company, touring the Rhodesias and Nyasaland (Malawi). Painted numerous landscapes; commissioned to design and paint six settings for 'The History of the Theatre', sponsored for the schools of Southern Rhodesia. When company temporarily disbanded travelled to England and studied at the London Central School of Art; met John Wright again and designed the puppets and settings for *The Wild Night of the Witches*; has since designed settings for 10 other plays and made a large number of puppets of all types. Has also produced a charming daughter, the family living happily in a cottage next to the theatre. Designed and constructed shadow puppets as part of *The Dragon* at the Royal Court Theatre (1967); designed puppets and settings for *A Trumpet for Nap* at the Little Angel (1968); designed and made set of spectacular figures (some of them 7-ft. tall) for a production of *The Soldier's Tale*, presented at the Queen Elizabeth Hall by the Festival Hall management (1968).

Wright, John. See JOHN WRIGHT and LITTLE ANGEL THEATRE.

Writers' and Artists' Year Book (1968: 61st year of issue). A Directory for writers, artists, playwrights, writers for films, radio, television; photographers and composers (A. & C. Black). Sections on Journalists, Publishers (international), Agencies and Societies (international); Press-cutting agencies; Societies and clubs of interest to authors, journalists, writers, musicians; classified list of photographers. Prizes and awards; markets for plays, broadcasting, sound and television. Reference section on Copyright Law (and U.S. Copyright). Classified index.

X

Xenophon (dates uncertain). Athenian author of about 40 books, mostly historical; pupil of Socrates. His *Symposium* (*c.* 421 B.C.) includes a description of a banquet for philosophers and an entertainment by young actors; a reference to 'my puppets' by the manager in conversation with Socrates could mean his actors *or* actual puppets shown on other occasions. This was one of the classical allusions cited by Father Mariantonio Lupi in his *Dissertazioni lettere ed altre operette* (*c.* 1720) – English translation in Inverarity *Manual of Puppetry* – and then by Magnin (*Histoire des marionnettes en Europe*, 1852) and others. Speaight (*History of the English Puppet Theatre*, 1955) says the sense has been distorted, but the allusion is still valid as evidence of existence of puppets.

X-ray film. The print can be cleaned off the negatives which can then be used for shadow-figure construction; materials such as coloured tissue paper, doileys, fern fronds, etc., can be sandwiched between two sheets to obtain stained glass or other effects.

Y

'Yorick.' Pseudonym used by Italian P. (Pietro) C. (Coccoluto) Ferrigni, writer, dramatic critic, author of *Storia dei Burattini* (History of Puppets), q.v.

Yoshida Bungoro (1869–1962). Japanese master-puppeteer renowned for his playing of female roles in the Bunraku-za, q.v., productions (with the three-man puppets); in 1949 made member of the Japanese Art Academy; in 1957 the title of Yoshida Naniwa no Joy the mark of supreme honour, was conferred upon him (Naniwa = Osaka); continued to perform when almost blind and into his nineties; contributed interesting essay on the early training of the Bunraku puppeteer in *Bunraku: Japanese Puppet Play*, q.v.

Yoshida Eiza (1872–1945). Leader of the Japanese Bunraku, q.v., puppeteers; first appeared as performer at age of 12; originally specialised in female roles, but became famous for his playing of male characters; he was succeeded by Yoshida Bungoro, q.v. Both masters contributed chapters to the beautifully illustrated *Bunraku: Japanese Puppet Play*, q.v.

Your Puppetry, by John Wright (Sylvan Press, 1951). First class small book on the carving and constructing of wooden marionettes by a master-carver, director of the Little Angel Marionette Theatre, London. It begins: 'This book is intended for those who propose to take their puppetry seriously . . . ' Illustrations include 135 precise diagrams and four full-page plates (from photographs). Chapters on designing, carving, joints, paint, costume and wigs, making the control and stringing, operating; also on stage construction, lighting, scenery, and production; appendix on bodies and heads (hollow) for large puppets. Bibliography.

Yugoslavia. Pavliha, another cousin of Punch, is not at all *like* Punch either in appearance or character, as is true of many human cousins. He is somewhat nearer to the German Kasper (Kasperle) in outlook and behaviour, comes in many plays as the main character, is perpetually young, cheerful, helpful, with a big smile like a country-boy, used to rescuing peasant girls or princesses. He is not mentioned by Magnin, the puppet-historian, but managed to get his photograph into Beaumont *Puppets and Puppetry* (Studio, 1958); nor did he appear in the UNIMA volume *Puppet Theatre of the Modern World*, which does, however, have illustrations from various Yugoslav puppet theatres: from *Ali Baba, Beauty and the Beast* and other productions. There are puppet theatres at Ljubljana, Zagreb, Split and elsewhere.

Z

Zagreb. In Yugoslavia. Has municipal puppet theatre founded 1948 (Gradsko Kazaliste Lutaka).

Zaitsev, Ivan Afinogenovich (1865–1930). Last of the itinerant pre-Soviet Petrushka-men in old Russia; Artist of Merit, U.S.S.R. In last

years privileged member of the State Central Puppet Theatre, Moscow.
Puppets, hand and marionette types, now in the Theatre's Museum.
An account in Obraztsov *My Profession*.

Zanni, Zany. Name for two of the characters in the Italian commedia
dell' arte, Harlequin and Brighella, thought to be descended from the
sannio of the earlier *Atellanae*; became synonymous with buffoon, clown,
droll, Scaramouche, Merry Andrew and the whole family of clowns.
Duchartre, in *The Italian Comedy* (Dover Publications, 1966), cites various
authors who see the origin in *Gianni* (John) or *Giovanni*, but as with many
other terms the current *meaning* (at any period) is more important than
the etymology. Instances of use as a proper name also (in Duchartre).

Zappelmann. German name for the 'jumping jack' figure with limbs
operated by single string, in Thuringia; elsewhere known as Hampelmann (sixteenth–eighteenth centuries). Specimens in National Museum
at Nürnberg.

Zeman, Karel. Czechoslovak puppet-film maker; created popular figure
of *Mr Prokouk* (stop-motion 'shorts'); *King Lavra*, full-length feature
Treasure of Bird's Island (combining techniques of cartoon and puppet);
Inspiration, bringing to life figures of glass with entire setting in glass;
A Journey into Primeval Times (live actors); *Mr Prokouk the Animal Lover*
(puppets).

Zinkeisen, Doris. English theatre designer; author of *Designing for the
Stage* (Studio, 1938); contributed designs for toy theatre play written by
J. B. Priestley, *The High Toby*.

Zoned scenes. With a wide puppet stage it is possible to set two or three
scenes side by side, the action moving from one zone to another with no
break in the continuity, the lighting being moved to the section in use.
In the traditional puppet shows of Ceylon the stage, consisting of some
screens and curtains and decorative panels, is divided into three parts,
the principle scenes taking place in the centre and the minor scenes at
the side areas. The technique has also been used in television studios,
where the cameras can swing from one pre-set scene to another. In the
live theatre, too, zoning may be done entirely by lighting different
ACTING AREAS in turn. Zones can also be at different ACTING LEVELS, as
in the traditional Polish SZOPKA and some modern hand puppet stages.

Zwyrtala the Musician. Puppet play adapted from a Kasimerz Tetmajor
legend, performed at the Lalka Theatre, Warsaw, Poland, Director Jan
Wilkowski, Art Director Adam Kilian. The mountaineer-musician
Zwyrtala dies and goes to heaven; his music and stories disturb the
harmonious working of the angels and, unmindful of St Cicely's baton,
they sing and dance the Zbojnicki (Mountain robbers' dance); even the
Archangel Gabriel hums mountaineer tunes. In the end, St Peter is
regretfully obliged to turn Zwyrtala out; from then on he wanders
aimlessly along mountain peaks and among the spruce trees playing
tunes on his fiddle; he is quite content, only the little angels are sad. The
production involves three acting levels of the stage, for the regions of
earth, mountain-tops and Heaven.